FOUL!

FOUL!

The Connie Hawkins Story

by David Wolf

Holt, Rinehart and Winston
New York   Chicago   San Francisco

Published simultaneously in Canada by
Holt, Rinehart and Winston of Canada, Limited.

ISBN: 0–03–086021–1
Library of Congress Catalog Card Number: 71–117279
Published, 1972; Second Printing, March 1972
Designer: Charlene Gridley
Printed in the United States of America

For Shawna, Keenan, Dawúd, and Laura

CONTENTS

PREFACE

This book is about one athlete. But it is also about American athletics, because there are few aspects of sport in this country that Connie Hawkins has not experienced firsthand. The hope and despair of the ghetto schoolyard, the pressure of high-level high school competition, the cutthroat college recruiting, the gambling scandals, the blacklists, the legal battles—Hawkins has been through all of them. He has played with the Harlem Globetrotters and in three professional leagues. He has been an outcast and a superstar—and he has emerged as a unique and perceptive man.

Hawkins is a testament to much that is good about basketball. On the court, the grace of this six-foot eight-inch giant is breathtaking. It has been said that, for the true fan, watching Connie for the first time is like discovering a lost Rembrandt in the attic. Hawk remains a legend in the black playgrounds, where his name is synonymous with the term "schoolyard ballplayer."

Connie has felt the joy of personal accomplishment and the camaraderie of team success. Sport has brought him recognition, freed him from poverty, and provided his first sense of self worth. It was Hawkins's pride and belief in his "game"—the distinctive style that is his alone—which sustained him through a tortured adolescence and then through years of unjust exile. Even now, his "game" is inseparable from his personality.

But Hawkins's life is also a chronicle of the corruption, racism, hypocrisy, and exploitation that are realities in modern, big-time athletics. Connie might have been the greatest basketball player who ever lived. But he never will be. Hawk spent eight years on the National Basketball Association's blacklist, wrongfully implicated in a gambling scandal. The mental pain and the absence of top-flight coaching, competition, and medical attention have left deep, irreparable wounds on Hawkins's psyche and on his game. Who is to blame? Surely the legal system in which a semiliterate black teenager could not find justice. But also the callous, high-handed administrators and entrepreneurs who run professional sports—men who have shown repeatedly that they believe ownership of a franchise places them above the law.

Connie was still an outlaw when I met him in January, 1969. Five months later I was able to write an article for *Life* magazine which helped clear his name. It was partly responsible for his acceptance by the NBA and the million-dollar settlement of his anti-trust suit against the league.

While I was working on the article, Connie and I became friends. It was our friendship that made this book possible. During my eighteen months of research and writing, we spent hundreds of hours together. I lived in Hawk's apartment for part of his first season with the Phoenix Suns and he spent eight weeks with me in New York City.

I'm sure no athlete has devoted as much time and thought to a book written by someone else. Yet this is not an "as told to." Connie had no control over the contents. I have interviewed more than a hundred other sources, and Hawk may not agree with every conclusion I have reached. Nevertheless, Connie was candid and honest—about everything.

Hawkins is a proud, sensitive, deeply emotional man. The candor—especially the self-depreciating revelations—did not come easily. But he was entirely open, because, "it might help if people have a better understanding of kids coming out of the same environment I did. And it might help a lot of young black kids to know the problems I've had —so, maybe, they can avoid some of them."

Connie is no longer the frightened, ignorant teenager who confessed to things he had not done. He is still uneducated and, in many ways, unsophisticated. But this is an intelligent man. His frank self-analysis, the open discussion of his painful childhood, and his willingness to be quoted as he speaks (his inconsistent grammar is not edited into "white man's English") are clues to the growth and strength of his personality.

I owe sincere thanks to many people. To my parents and to Susan, who didn't let me quit. To Wallace Exman, a helpful and patient editor. To Jeremy Larner for his serious reading and valuable advice. To Barry Stainback and Dave Maness at *Life,* who went out on a limb to get the original article published. To Vivian Reiff who typed and typed.

Thanks also to Eddie Simmons, Nancy Hawkins, Bob McCullough, Ernie Morris, Gene Smith, Sylvester Wells, Len Litman, Joe Gordon, Jim McCoy, Alex Medich, Jackie Jackson, Tex Harrison, Vinnie Brewer, Wilky Gilmore, Tom Washington, Art Heyman, Dorothy Hawkins, Howie Jones, Tony Bernhard, Fred Hawkins, Paul Silas, Billy Cunningham, Arthur Harris, Earl Hawkins, Scotty McDonald, Joe Proski, Nathan Mazer, and many people who prefer to go unmentioned.

Special thanks to Joe Gilmartin, Dave Hicks, Jim O'Brien, and George Kiseda for writing such quotable prose. To Jerry Colangelo, Al Stephan, and everyone connected with the Phoenix Suns for their complete cooperation. To certain nameless individuals at the New York County District Attorney's office for being honest cops.

To Joe Hacken for having the guts to tell the truth.

To Howard Specter, and to Roslyn and David Litman for opening their files and their hearts.

And, most of all, to Connie Hawkins for being himself—and for allowing me to write his story.

D.W.

New York City
September 1971

F O U L !

1

LONG TALL SALLY

"Of all the people I ever knew in New York, Connie was the poorest."
—*Billy Cunningham, Philadelphia 76ers*

Squad cars prowling streets heavy with the stench of uncollected garbage. Whores and winos crowding the sidewalks outside stark brick walkups. Apartments cramped and dilapidated, often without heat in winter or ventilation in summer, crawling with rats and roaches. Children running loose, hard-eyed youths with zip guns, ready to kill for a patch of turf, because the turf was all they had. This was the Bedford-Stuyvesant ghetto where Connie Hawkins grew up. For eighteen years it was his only frame of reference; it was where his horizons began and ended.

Cornelius Hawkins was born on July 17, 1942, the fifth of Dorothy Hawkins's six children. Bedford-Stuyvesant was a racially mixed working-class district then. But after the war, the whites began moving out, the buildings decayed, the Sanitation Department cleaned the streets less regularly, the crime rate soared, and Bed-Stuy became a slum.

He lived on Lexington Avenue—the armpit of the ghetto—beneath the tracks of an elevated train that poured soot into the street and rumbled overhead throughout the night. There were three small factory buildings jammed between the crumbling tenements. At the corner was a candy store where the Hawkins family got their phone calls, a grocery where Connie stacked cans at the age of nine, and a little shop where people bought ice for twenty-five cents because few had electric refrigerators. In the building next to Connie's, a husband and wife ran an all-night blackjack game. Across the street was a whorehouse.

The Hawkins family rented a four-room flat on the first floor of 86 Lexington Avenue. Garbage cans, filled to overflowing, stood outside the building. On hot summer nights women sat on the front stoop in pale cotton dresses fanning themselves until early morning. The "86" on the front door had been scrawled with an unsteady hand in dripping white paint. The glass in the door was usually broken, and the hall was lighted by a sin-

1

gle naked bulb. The plaster was cracked and peeling. Termites feasted on the wooden stairs.

In the Hawkins apartment, hot water was an occasional thing. The walls were bare except for two pictures of Christ: one a simple print, the other lit from behind with eyes that followed you across the tiny living room where his mother slept. There were two small bedrooms. His oldest brothers, Fred and Bobby, shared a single bed in one. Connie slept with two other brothers (Earl, older, and Randy, younger) on a cot in the second bedroom. When there was no heat his mother kept the stove on all night and the boys slept in their coats. Connie's sister Lena was thirteen when he was born. She slept in the living room with their parents and moved out before Hawk was old enough to remember much about her.

When Connie was ten his mother bought a secondhand bunk bed. Randy, who was two years younger than Connie, got the upper berth. Connie and Earl slept on the bottom and fought over the single coverlet, which Connie clutched when he had nightmares about being eaten by dragons.

Connie's parents had come up from the tobacco fields of rural North Carolina. There was Cherokee Indian in their background. Hawk thinks his father did some kind of work for the railroad. He recalls him as a "country-type man," who raised chickens in the small, dusty backyard and strangled them with his hands when he wanted chicken for dinner. He remembers that his parents often shouted at each other, especially when his father was drinking. But Isiah Hawkins was afraid to lay a hand on his wife. Fred and Bobby, who were eleven and six years older than Connie, were in gangs and could rumble. Their father knew they'd break him in half if he laid a hand on Dorothy Hawkins. And that's all Connie remembers about his father—except that one day when Hawk was about nine years old, his father went away and didn't come back.

Connie's mother was a large, simple, deeply religious woman who never quite adjusted to the pace and hostility of urban life. On Sunday mornings she was up early, cooking and singing as she listened to church music on the radio. She would dress her younger boys—Earl, Connie, and Randy—in their tattered Sunday best and put them on the Gates Avenue bus for the twenty-minute ride to Sunday school at the Cornerstone Baptist Church. Connie liked Sunday school, although he occasionally fell asleep in class. He was very afraid of God and sang enthusiastically in the school glee club. But, when he was ten, he declined an invitation to join the church choir; he was too nervous to sing in front of the entire congregation.

The boys would take the bus home, eat a large hot lunch—their biggest meal of the week—then return with their mother to spend the afternoon in church. Connie's Sundays were like this until he was fourteen years old. Then basketball replaced Sunday school.

When her husband left—and even after glaucoma brought her ever closer to eventual blindness—Mrs. Hawkins struggled to hold her family together. By the standards of Bedford-Stuyvesant, where children of broken homes roam the streets and crowd the Youth Houses, she was successful. None of her children had *serious* trouble with the law—until Connie.

Fred was a good amateur boxer. A local fight trainer named Reggie Nero wanted him to turn pro. Mrs. Hawkins wanted him to be a preacher. He compromised and wrote numbers in the local policy racket. Bobby didn't come close to finishing high school. Later he cut several records with a rock 'n' roll group.

When Hawk was 11 years old, Freddy got married and moved into an apartment around the corner on Clifton Place. But he often ate with the family and helped his mother discipline the younger boys. Mrs. Hawkins usually didn't need help. She was a terror with a belt or an ironing cord.

The family was very poor, even for Bedford-Stuyvesant. Connie recalls always playing with other children's toys. On Easter Sunday, when most neighborhood kids walked the streets displaying their new clothes, Connie stayed inside and peeked through the window, too ashamed of his one threadbare jacket and the khaki slacks which grew shorter each year.

"We ate," Earl recalls. "That's about all you can say." But they didn't eat well. Mrs. Hawkins, a cook in a local nursery school, could do wonders with collard greens or pork. But they had little beef, and sometimes there was very little of anything. Hawk's brothers still grew husky and strong, but Connie was tall, thin, and disquietingly weak.

"I guess I was always my mother's pet," he says now. "When she had time, she'd try to protect me. She called me 'sweetcakes,' and 'Nelius' (short for Cornelius). I was the goody goody of the family. And I worried a lot about her—the way she worked so hard. I felt guilty when she gave me things."

Their father never sent money, and despite his mother's job, the family was always on welfare. "We didn't have nothing," Earl remembers. "But me, and Bobby, and Randy, we'd say, 'Mommy, we want this, we want that!' Connie was different. He'd walk around with cardboard in his shoes and he wouldn't tell her when he needed something. He used to say, 'She ain't got no money, so what good it do to worry her?' "

His brothers often bullied or took advantage of him: "They were always usin me, makin fun of me. They would make me go to the store for them. When I was out playin ball, I'd come home and find they'd ate my dinner. They'd use me to show off in front of their girl friends, teasin me. When my mother started losin her sight we were all supposed to help out by cleanin one room in the house. I had the bathroom. But they cleaned so bad I'd end up doing the whole apartment, cause I was the only one that did it like my mother wanted. When I look back now, I see sometimes they weren't really tryin to hurt me, like when Bobby showed me card tricks. But if I couldn't figure out the tricks and people laughed, I'd think they was laughin cause they thought I was stupid."

Many youngsters emerge from the ghetto hard, strong, and self-confident. But for Connie, who might have been a troubled child in the best middle-class suburb, Bedford-Stuyvesant was overwhelming. He was slow, shy, and easily intimidated. The environment nurtured these characteristics, and they, in turn, made him less able to cope with the environment. He needed attention, sensitivity, even trained guidance. But everyone around him was too busy just trying to stay alive.

"Until I got good at basketball," Connie says, "there was nothin about me I liked, there wasn't a thing that I could be proud of. I was kind of quiet and insecure. It didn't seem like I had anything going for me. I was ashamed of the way I looked. We all wore hand-me-downs. But my brothers were short and wide and I was long and skinny, so nothin fit me right. I didn't feel sharp enough to talk to girls."

School was a frightening, depressing experience. Hawk started the first grade at P.S. 3, an old brick building on nearby Bedford Avenue. He was full of excitement. The older kids had always talked about school, and now he was going himself. Connie isn't sure what came first; the disinterest, the embarrassment, or the lack of success. But he vividly recollects not knowing what the teachers were talking about—and being too shy to ask. There was no *Sesame Street* on television in those days. He hadn't spent the first six years of his life humming the alphabet. "Instead of *learnin*," he recalls, "I tried to *memorize* everything and my head got all clogged up. I didn't have nobody to tell me different. Earl wasn't no better in school than me. Him and Bobby played hooky all the time. Everything confused me. And the things they taught—they weren't things *I* knew about. The readin book had these pictures of little blond kids running in the country with their dog. I came to hate school, hate doin so bad."

Each year he fell farther behind. P.S. 3 was a typical ghetto school; understaffed, underbudgeted, with outmoded facilities, overcrowded classrooms, and tired, beaten teachers, unable to relate to the sea of black faces before them. There was no time for special help—no time for a tall, skinny boy who didn't seem to catch on. Connie kept his fears inside and became convinced that he was a fool: "In class I was ashamed. I never knew what was goin on. I was afraid the teacher would ask me a question, cause I never knew the answer. I'd wish I was small so no one would notice me. Even when I knew the right answer, I wouldn't raise my hand cause I was afraid I'd be wrong and everybody would laugh."

Hawkins was always the tallest boy in his class. The other children found his physique uproariously funny. When he was ten years old he stood 5' 10" and weighed just 115 pounds. His hands and feet were enormous; his head—shaved almost to the scalp—seemed too tiny for his body. His classmates called him "Slim" and "Bones" and "Long Tall Sally."

"I'd try to hide my height by slouchin down," he says, "and I'd try to find a seat quick so I'd be inconspicuous. In class, the first day, the teachers always made a big joke out of me having to sit in the back row. They'd say, 'You, the tall one there! You better sit in the last row so the rest of the class can see the board! And all the kids would giggle and say, 'That Long Tall Sally get funnier-lookin every year. If he stand sideways you can't see him.' "

The easiest way to avoid the embarrassment of school was not to go. Soon Hawk was a constant truant. A family friend, Sylvester Wells, a church deacon who worked in the garment district, remembers many unsuccessful attempts to get Connie to class. Wells had a second job, on weekends, selling cakes and pies door-to-door in the local housing projects. He paid Connie, who was eleven, three dollars a day to help him. Once, when they were taking a lunch break, Wells said, "Connie, sometimes I come home in the middle of the day and I see you out in the street. I'm hearin rumors that you ain't goin to school all the time. That true?"

Connie nodded. Then his eyes filled with tears. "I don't like to go. Them little kids all make fun of me."

Hawk was also ashamed of his foot. Sometimes even Wells couldn't resist saying, "Connie, if your feet get any bigger, you'll need automobile tires instead of shoes." Hawk would cringe and try to laugh. But Wells stopped teasing him the afternoon he drove Connie and his mother to a cut-rate shoe-store. Connie was twelve and his feet had grown so much in the last year that his sneakers gave him blisters. Yet he resisted getting new ones. "At the store," Wells remembers, "Connie would ask the man to bring him sizes that were too small. Then he'd try to squeeze his foot in. Even the pair he finally got were too small. Outside, in the car, I could see there was a little water in his eyes."

"Connie," Wells told him, "you don't want to get your shoes too small."

"Yes I do," Connie said, sniffling. "People say my feet funny. But they don't stop growin."

"Look, you are a tall boy," said Wells. "You'd look silly if you had little feet, tall as you are."

"But I don't want to be tall neither," Connie sobbed.

When he wasn't embarrassed, he was afraid. The streets of Bed-Stuy throbbed with violence. This was the era of the gangs, and New York's toughest were in the Brooklyn ghetto. "You had to be a member of a gang to get from one side of the street to the other," Hawkins remembers. "It was like playin army. Each gang had its own territory, and a president and a treasurer and a warlord. If they caught somebody from another gang in their territory, they beat him up or stabbed him."

The gangs had names like "Quintos," "Stonekillers," and "Chaplains," and when they rumbled in the street, people died. But Connie was never in a gang. None wanted him. Fred and Bobby were members, as were a lot of Earl's friends. This was Hawk's protection. "A lot of times the gangs would chase me," he says. "Sometimes I got beat up. But mostly they'd recognize me and say, 'He Big Hawk's brother. He all right.' Freddie was Big Hawk and didn't nobody want to mess with him."

At school, however, Connie was constantly pushed around: "I just looked so weak anybody with a chip on his shoulder found me and kicked my ass." He rarely fought back. Instead, he ran home and Earl, who was only two years older than Connie, but husky and tough, would laugh at him.

"You a faggot, Connie," Earl would say. "You a chickenshit faggot. You let everybody run you off." Connie would say nothing.

In the ghetto you weren't supposed to let people beat you up or shake you down without fighting back. If a kid got his teeth kicked in protecting a quarter he was respected. But most of the time, Connie couldn't bring himself to fight. When he was nine years old he spent many afternoons at a community center, where boys who helped clean up the equipment each week got a pass to the Saturday matinee at the Regent movie house. Connie always volunteered. Apparently the news got around. One Friday, he was leaving the community center, the pass in his pocket, when he saw a teenager who lived a few houses down on Lexington Avenue, leaning against a car. As Connie approached, the older boy blocked his path.

"Hi," Connie said uneasily.

"You got that movie ticket?"

"Uh huh."

"Give it here 'for' I got to take it off you."

"But it's mine," Connie protested lamely.

"Boy, give it here!" the teenager repeated, cocking his fist. Connie handed him the pass, humiliated.

Each Friday thereafter, the older boy was waiting for him. Connie tried to fight back once, but he was thrown to the pavement. He never told anyone about the boy, he never asked for help—he just hoped no one would find out how easily he was intimidated. Finally he stopped cleaning up at the center and just sneaked into the movies.

When he was in the seventh grade at P.S. 3, an eighth-grader called "Dice" delighted in pushing him to the ground. If he spotted Dice a block away, Connie would turn and walk in the other direction. One Friday night, Earl took Connie to a party at a friend's apartment. Because of Hawk's height he was already spending much of his time with Earl's friends. They didn't pay much attention to him, but at least with them he wasn't so conspicuous. Hawk had never gone to their parties.

He stayed close to Earl most of the night. There was loud music from the radio, plenty of beer, and a funny-smelling smoke he later learned was marijuana. Connie had three beers. He was beginning to feel lightheaded enough to ask a girl to dance, when he heard a familiar voice.

"Look who's here! If it ain't Long Tall Sally! What you doin here?"

"Hi, Dice," Connie said uncertainly.

"Nice to see you here, Sally," Dice said, bringing his foot down hard on Connie's toe.

"Cut it out, Dice," Connie snapped, more harshly than he intended.

"You don't dig that, Sally? Well, how you dig this?" Dice clamped Connie in a headlock with one arm, reached inside his sports jacket, pulled out a zip gun, and placed it to Hawk's temple.

Many youngsters in Bed-Stuy, especially the gang members, carried zip guns. They made them at school, in the wood shop, with a piece of pipe and a rubber band. The guns could fire a real bullet, and there was a bullet in Dice's gun.

"Make a move," Dice warned, "and I'll shoot you."

For a moment, Connie couldn't focus on the gravity of the situation. The music, the crowd, the beer—all had left him fuzzy. He felt as though he were watching someone else in a movie.

"Get that gun away from my head," he heard himself say.

"Man," Dice repeated, "I ain't fuckin with you. I'm gonna blow your head off."

Connie's hand reached up and pushed the gun from his head. Then he heard Earl shouting at Dice.

"Cut it out man, leave my brother alone!"

Dice lowered the gun. As he did, it went off, firing the bullet into the rug. Connie's knees trembled as the realization of what had almost happened swept over him. He felt he was going to throw up.

"Earl," he whispered, "let's go home. Please."

They left the party. But the following Monday after school, Dice was waiting for Connie in front of P.S. 3. He punched Hawk hard on the side of the head. Connie broke free and ran. He could feel a large knot growing on his temple when he came through the door of the apartment. Earl, who had been playing hooky, was standing by the open icebox.

"Who did that?" he asked, munching on a piece of fruit. "Did somebody kick your ass again?"

"Dice."

"Where he at," Earl snapped, with a finality that convinced Connie his brother was going to fix Dice, once and for all.

"He at the playground by Three's."

"Let's go," Earl said.

Connie couldn't wait to see Earl fix Dice. But Earl had no intention of fighting. "O.K.," he said, staring at Dice through the wire fence that separated the schoolyard from Bedford Avenue, "beat him up, Connie."

Connie's eyes widened.

"I said beat up Dice," Earl repeated.

"I don't want to," Connie pleaded. "You do it, Earl. Come on, man."

"You beat him up," Earl warned, "or *I'm* gonna beat *you* up."

Connie was more afraid of Earl than he was of Dice. And it was this fear that carried him. Dice was so surprised to see Connie rushing at him that he didn't immediately react. This gave Hawk time to punch him in the face and drag him to the ground. They exchanged blows, but Connie was on top and his punches did more damage. He bloodied the other boy's nose, before Earl dragged them apart.

"That gave me a little confidence," Hawkins now reflects with a laugh. "I didn't back down as *much* after that. But I can't think of many more fights I won. Kids just kept knockin my hat off, pushin me on the ground and punchin me in the face if I tried to stop 'em. I was still the community punchin-bag."

There was something on the streets that scared Connie even more than the bullies and the gangs. The police. By the time he was in junior high school a gulf of hatred and distrust separated the blacks in Bedford-Stuyvesant and the police of the Eighty-eighth Precinct.

When Connie began playing basketball in the schoolyards, much of his time was spent on the asphalt courts at P.S. 45, four blocks from his home: "From where we played you could see the back of the Eighty-eighth Precinct station house. Almost every day, we'd watch them take black guys out there and beat 'em. They would hit people with their fists and with clubs, and with some hose-type things. And they'd kick 'em. Especially if they fell on the ground. We'd stop playin ball and stand there and watch. I guess they didn't care if we saw. What were *we* gonna do?"

Freddie, who was running numbers, never hid his hatred of the police. Connie heard him tell how cops would walk up to Freddie and a group of white men, and "always let the white cats go," Freddie would say. "Then they search *me*. If they don't find nothing, they curse me out. Them cops hate us cause we're colored."

One evening when he was walking home from school, a squad car swept around the corner on two wheels and screeched to a stop beside him. Connie froze. He had often seen blacks arrested on the street, but now all he could think was that the week before he'd watched a policeman pull his gun and shoot a dog that had been hit by a truck.

A stocky, red-faced officer bounded from the squad car. "Against the wall," he snapped, grabbing Connie by the arm, whirling him around, and pushing him against the side of a building. "Hands up. Get 'em on the wall. Fast."

A second policeman slapped his hands over Connie's sides and hips. "Turn around, you," he said coldly.

Connie was so frightened he still couldn't speak. "Don't tremble," he thought. "If I look scared, they'll think I done somethin." They ordered him to empty his pockets. He was carrying two dimes and a door key. The cops exchanged disgusted glances.

"O.K.," the first officer said, "get your ass outta here." He kicked Connie in the rear—hard. Hawk hurried down the street. He didn't look back. He never found out what they were looking for.

"That happened a couple of times while I was still in junior high school," he says. "I guess I looked older because I was tall. I was always scared of cops. I got uncomfortable if one just looked at me."

Connie went from P.S. 3 to J.H.S. 258 in the seventh grade. The building was new, the windows were wide and clean, and the desks weren't lumpy with the chiseled graffiti of four generations. But the shouts of "Long Tall Sally" followed him, for he stood 6' 1", weighed 125 pounds, and looked more than ever like a giant praying mantis.

By then his skills were so inadequate it was impossible for him to keep up in class: "Not doin well was a complete embarrassment to me. Worse than in grammar school. Teachers told me I was dumb, in front of the whole class. Once we had a quiz and the teacher collected the papers a few minutes before the class ended. He must have noticed I hardly wrote anything. He stood up and he said, 'I want you to know that Hawkins, back there, is the moron of the class.' And he waved my paper. Everybody laughed at me."

Hawk's consolation was that, among the friends he had made in the neighborhood, school was irrelevant. On Lexington Avenue there were few high school diplomas tacked to the wall: "We talked about sports. Later we also talked about girls. Mostly, we stood on the corner and had fantastic arguments about the Brooklyn Dodgers. We'd yell about who was better, Jackie Robinson or Duke Snider. Nobody ever said anything like, 'Hey man, what am I gonna do with my life?' We were just goin along from day to day."

Hawk's school attendance was fairly regular during the winter. It was a good place to stay out of the cold. "But when the weather was good," he says, "I'd usually go to the park and play softball, or sneak on the subway and go to the movies on Forty-second Street."

Connie was becoming aware that even among his neighborhood friends, he was the least affluent: "When you're little you don't know you're poor. It doesn't bother you so much. By the time I got to junior high, though, I knew we were pretty bad off. Even my friends had a few cents in their pockets most of the time. A lot of them had baseball gloves. And they had clothes: not a great deal, but they could change every two or three days. I had no baseball glove and my one old pair of dungarees and a couple of T-shirts were all my clothes—except my Sunday jacket and khakis."

About this time, Connie was getting interested in girls. The feeling, unfortunately, was not yet mutual. Timid, almost monosyllabic, he hardly cut a dashing figure.

Hawk worried a lot about his mother. Her sight was increasingly poor. She was still working at the school kitchen, but the money was not enough. He remembers getting up one morning and seeing her sitting quietly on her bed in the living room. Usually, she was busy preparing breakfast.

"Nelius," she said, "there's some fruit and cereal in the icebox. Fix that for yourself."

Connie opened the icebox. There was a small peach inside. That was all. The cereal box, on the table, was almost empty. He knew she hadn't eaten yet.

"Mom," he said, "I ain't hungry." Then Connie hurriedly pulled on his T-shirt and went out to the street.

"I felt she was the greatest woman in the world," he says. "I still feel that way. I loved her for her independence, for how she raised us by herself, how sweet she was, how innocent. She only had a third-grade education, but she was an honest, simple-type Southern lady. She was workin so hard, for us, and I loved her so much. But I didn't know how to help her."

Hawk had a few ways of getting money. He was one of the best penny pitchers in the neighborhood, concentrating on each toss as though he were pitching ten-dollar gold pieces. "It was like a job," Connie says. "I'd go around to people's apartments and ask 'em if they had empty bottles. I'd cash the bottles for two cents each and use the money to pitch. Me and this kid Theodous, who was about three years older than me, was the best. We'd walk around lookin for games. You could make a couple of dollars in an afternoon. But after a while nobody would play against me."

He also did some stealing. He took grapes from peddlers' wagons or grocers' stands. He stole comic books and candy bars. But his criminal career ended there: "I never got arrested, but I was always scared. People used to say if I wanted to be a mugger, I could be the greatest in the world cause my hands were so big. But I stayed out of crime cause of my back. It had a yellow streak down the middle."

Hawk had several jobs. In grade school, he delivered papers in the morning. The summer he turned nine he stacked cans and swept up at the grocery on the corner. When he was eleven he began working weekends for Mr. Wells, the family friend, helping him sell cakes. They would take the elevator to the top floor of a building in the Sands Street housing projects, then walk down the stairs, knocking at each door.

"We lived across the street and our families were close," Wells recalls. "He was a good, honest boy, but Connie could be a little mischievous."

If Wells was running late with the cakes, Connie would sell on one floor, while he handled another. Their agreement was that Hawk could keep one cake at the end of the day, plus any that were crushed accidentally while carried. When Connie sold by himself, he invariably came back with a crushed cake. "I didn't take any chances," he admits, "I stepped on the box."

Wells never mentioned it. Nor did he comment on a curious development that occurred almost every time Connie babysat for Wells's three young boys: the icebox seemed to empty itself.

As soon as Wells and his wife had left for the evening, Connie would call Freddie, six; Sylvester, four; and Harry, two, into the living room. "Let's play Cowboys and Indians," he would suggest. Then he pulled out a piece of rope and tied the three youngsters loosely together. "Try to get out," he'd say. And the boys would be free in minutes. "See, it's easy. Let's try it again." The children always agreed. But this time Hawk bound them tightly at the waist. Then he headed for the kitchen.

"They always had leftovers in the icebox," he grins. "Meats, cold chicken, and always lots of cake. I'd have a feast. The kids never knew what was goin on. They couldn't see me in the kitchen. I'd keep 'em tied till I thought they were gonna cry. Then I'd untie 'em. Mr. and Mrs. Wells didn't say anything about the empty icebox. I guess they knew I wasn't eatin much at home."

Possibly because of his inadequate diet, Connie slept an abnormal amount of time. He often fell out before dinner, could not be awakened when the meal was served, and slept through the night. The sleep was uncommonly deep. Even after ten or twelve hours it was hard to rouse him. For several minutes he always seemed incoherent.

Once when Connie was in high school, he slept through an entire weekend, rising only to go to the bathroom. Neighbors told his mother that he had "the sleeping sickness."

There was also about him a sense of total apathy. By the time Connie was thirteen years old he was unusually lethargic and had stopped caring intensely about anything. He played with his friends and had fun with them, but he often seemed oblivious to what was going on around him. There was a withdrawal into himself, yet without any accompanying introspection.

"Nothing seemed right in my life," he remembers. "People said I was stupid. They said I was ugly and weak, and I felt they was right. I was ashamed of myself and I was comin to see how things were with my mother and how poor our family really was. It didn't seem like things could be different. So I just tried not to think too much."

He showed talent in one area: sports and games. Not only was Hawk expert at pitching pennies, he won a marbles championship and excelled at stickball. More important, by the time he was fourteen, Connie had been putting his huge hands and long arms to good use as the basketball star of his school teams at P.S. 3 and J.H.S. 258.

But Connie Hawkins didn't like basketball.

"I played it all the time," he says, "but I didn't get much pleasure from it. I was good, but not enough for people to make a big deal. And when I played, I was always gettin pushed and bumped and hit. I got tired. It was hard to get me interested. I just drifted along, being depressed about myself."

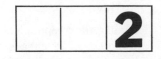

GHETTO BALL

"If you are looking for real ballplayers,
you start looking in a place like Bedford-Stuyvesant."
—*Al McGuire, Head Basketball Coach, Marquette University*

Basketball is New York City's game. It was the sport of the ghettos long before the ghettos were black. Even in the summer, when the pavement sizzles, New York kids are playing basketball. It requires no expensive equipment, no wide open spaces—just a hoop, a ball, and a boy.

Once it was the game of the Irish and Italian Catholics in Rockaway and the Jews on Fordham Road in the Bronx. It was recreation, status, and a way out. During the 30's and 40's the toughest tournaments outside of Madison Square Garden were played in their schoolyards, community centers, and YMCA's. The products of these games went on to St. John's, NYU, CCNY, and LIU to make New York City the mecca of college basketball. Those who weren't swallowed by the betting scandal of the early 50's continued into the pros, where they played a large role in turning the NBA into a recognized major league. The New York players were notorious for their savvy and ballhandling skill. They knew the game because they lived it. Today, graduates of the schoolyards are coaching everywhere. Al McGuire, Richie Guerin, Lou Carnesecca, Frank McGuire, Red Auerbach, Bob Cousy, Red Holzman, and Jack McMahon are just a few who grew up on New York asphalt.

The demography and economics of the city changed. The Jews and Catholics began the exodus to the suburbs and their children found cars and boats and summer camps. The city and its outlying areas still produced many good white ball players—but the best basketball was now played in the black ghettos. Children had no clarinet lessons or ballet classes. Their parents pushed them into community centers to keep them off the streets. In the summer, the schoolyard was the only place to play, and youngsters grew quickly with the pace of the competition. A kid could walk into a playground and find himself in pickup games with pros or All-Americans, defending their reputations against the challenge of neighborhood heroes.

Hundreds of independent teams were in action all year round. If a kid didn't like his high school coach, he could probably find the competition just as tough at a local church league or community center. There were enough summer tournaments for a top player to compete every day.

In Bedford-Stuyvesant, where basketball courts are crammed between tenements every few blocks, a tall kid with large hands and above-average coordination naturally gravitates toward the game. By the time Connie was ready for high school, he had played with college and NBA stars and with most of the good schoolboy players in the City. For all his lack of enthusiasm, he had more experience against top competition than any high school senior in Scarsdale, whose parents paid hundreds of dollars to send him to a basketball camp.

Like most kids in his neighborhood, Hawk began at a community center. Mrs. Hawkins worked at the nursery from eight in the morning until five at night. She didn't want Connie roaming the streets after school, but neither would she trust him with a key to the apartment. When he was eight years old she said, "Nelius, they open that gym at the school after your classes are over. They call it the community center. Play there till I get home."

Connie liked the center. There was shuffleboard, ping-pong, and pool—all of which he played well. And basketball—which he did not play well. At first, despite his height, he wasn't even good enough to play with boys his age. Hawk was at the other end of the court with the girls. "I still wasn't the best," he says. "I was learnin to dribble and shoot a layup. But this girl named Vickie had a hook shot and I couldn't guard her, so I was always on the losin team."

Connie's coordination improved during the next few years, even if his physique did not. Some of his friends, like James Mitchell—the only boy Connie knew who worked hard in school—and Henry Halliburton—a strong, wild-eyed kid who played hooky with Hawk—went to the Carlton YMCA near his home. When Connie was about eleven, he went with them. The Carlton was an all-black Y, famous for its basketball teams. Coach Gene Smith, a short, muscular black policeman, was a stickler for fundamentals. He had helped develop several players who later starred at Boys High, the Palace of Brooklyn high school basketball. It was from Smith that Connie began to learn the game.

There are Gene Smiths in every ghetto, especially in New York: anonymous men who spend their spare time in the schoolyards and community centers working with kids. To them, it's a second job, but a first love. They rarely have reputations as players—Smith was too small to make the team at Boys High—but they like the feel of a basketball in their hands and are happiest around the sport.

The first time Connie walked uncertainly onto the grainy wood court at the Carlton Y, his white shorts drooping over toothpick legs, Smith feinted a punch at Hawk's midsection. "I wanted to see how he'd react," the coach recalls. "Connie was so quick his hands were waiting for me. I thought, 'Hey, maybe this one'll be a ballhandler.' "

For some time, Connie wasn't much of anything. Yet as a substitute on the youngest of the three teams Smith coached, he got his first instruction in basketball fundamentals. Smith would place a row of chairs on the court and have the players dribble through them, like skiers taking slalom gates. He used blindfolds to force them to dribble with their heads up. The coach recalls that Connie was a quick learner. Typically, Connie recalls not learning quickly at all: "What I remember, what is still in my mind, is messin up the drills and bumpin into chairs."

Connie was seventh man on the team—when he showed up. "He missed a lot of games," Smith says, grinning. "We played Saturday mornings. Sometimes, if we were short of guys, I'd have to go over to his apartment and try to wake him. He was always sleeping."

Even when he managed to be there, Connie didn't stagger anyone with his performance. But there was a glimmer of something that caught Smith's eye. "He had those big hands," the coach recalls. "And he passed the ball very well for a kid his age. Most kids want to shoot every time, but Connie seemed to *prefer* passing. Really, he passed off more than he should have."

Connie's team finished in a tie for first place. There was a playoff against the Long Island City YMCA. Carlton lost. Connie overslept and missed the game.

The summer Hawk turned twelve, he began playing regularly in the schoolyards. There weren't many alternatives. The apartment was unbearably stuffy during the day. He didn't own a glove, so softball was a hassle. Older boys usually dominated the stickball game in the street.

That left basketball.

Connie played four blocks from his home, in the playground adjacent to P.S. 45, a school which was being torn down and would later be rebuilt as P.S. 270. The schoolyard swarmed with skinny kids in T-shirts and scuffed sneakers, bouncing worn basketballs from nine in the morning until it was too dark to see the hoop. As Connie played more often, it surprised him to find that he was better than most youngsters his age. He developed a soft two-handed set shot, could pass well, and discovered that if he pushed himself he could jump higher than many older boys. But he still tired easily, and on hot days he found sitting beside the wire fence more enjoyable than running up and down on the court.

One afternoon, as sometimes happened, Connie was in a game with older boys. The best player was a little backcourt man named Eddie Simmons. Connie had seen him many times strutting confidently at the Carlton Y, where Simmons was a star on the intermediate team. Hawk had heard that Simmons was going to be on the varsity at Boys High as a sophomore that winter.

Connie found himself guarding Simmons. The smaller boy drove, dug an elbow into Hawk's stomach, and as Connie stumbled backward, scored a layup. The next time Simmons's team got the ball, he repeated the maneuver, but his shot rolled out. "The man fouled me," Simmons shouted.

"What?" Hawk yelped. "You elbowin me."

"Hey motherfucker, don't give me no shit," Eddie said, grabbing the ball from one of Connie's teammates and preparing to toss in bounds.

"Wait," Connie protested halfheartedly, but Simmons had already passed the ball. He cut quickly by Connie, took a return pass, and scored. Hawk could only shake his head.

Moments later Simmons drove again. But, instead of going to the hoop, he stopped short and went up for a jump shot. Connie, off balance, lunged to block it. His hand slapped across Simmons's face. "Watch it, skinny cocksucker," Simmons shouted, shoving Connie in the chest.

"I didn't do it on purpose," Hawkins tried to exlain.

"You're a lying ass," Eddie snapped. "How you like it?" He slapped Connie's face. Hawk's cheek stung. Tears welled in his eyes. He took a wild swing at Simmons. The short, sinewy boy ducked, then hit Connie with a left to the face and a right in the stomach. Hawk fought back. He too threw a left and right. The second punch caught Eddie on the side of the head. Then the other players pulled them apart.

Simmons appeared to be grinning. Hawk looked at him quizzically, but said nothing. Play resumed, and Connie switched defensive assignments and he and Eddie collided no more.

When the game was over, Connie walked away from the group and sat by himself against the fence. "Even that little motherfucker push me around," he mumbled to himself.

"Hey man, shake."

He looked up to see Eddie standing over him, smiling. "Forget the scrap, man," Simmons said. "We blowed our cools. Ain't nothin to worry about." Eddie sat down beside him. And one of the most important friendships in Connie's life began.

"What I liked about Hawk, that first time we had the fight, was the way he threw a combination back at me after I did it to him," Eddie says now. "People would say he was dumb, but right from then, I knew it wasn't so. Soon as he threw the same kind of combination I did, I thought, 'Damn, this kid learns quick.' I watched him the rest of the game, seeing his hands and the way he jumped, and I got the feeling he was gonna be great one day. When I talked to him I could tell he was a nice kid. We took to each other. He listened to what I said, and he kind of came to idolize me and I admit I dug that."

Connie found Eddie Simmons the most impressive, commanding personality he had ever encountered. Simmons was everything Connie wished he could be: a tough, glib, self-confident extrovert; a hustler with an angle and a plan for every situation; and an athlete already known in the neighborhood and soon to be known throughout the city. If Eddie had grown up on Park Avenue instead of Lafayette Avenue, he probably would have been president of his class at a slick private school like Horace Mann and gone on to become a brilliant young business tycoon. But in Bed-Stuy there were two roads to status; the "bad" kids joined gangs, the "good" kids played ball.

"Eddie hardly thought about anything but basketball," says Gene Smith, who was also Simmons's first coach. "If the boys were talking about anything else, even another sport, he'd change the subject to basketball."

Simmons was in the process of becoming one of the finest guards ever to play in the New York schoolyards. Even today, years after Ed stopped playing, his name is spoken with reverence in Harlem and Bed-Stuy. A trim, steely-eyed youngster, who stood only 5' 9" and weighed 160 in his prime, Simmons was seriously classed with Bob Cousy and Lennie Wilkens as a ballhandler. Eddie's senior year, Boys was undefeated and won the city championship in Madison Square Garden. He was voted to the All-City team.

Eddie was an operator. He bluffed his way through Boys High, rarely attending class. While still in high school he was playing professionally on weekends, under an assumed name, in the Eastern League—the best pro competition below the NBA. He was one of the few kids who wasn't terrified of Mickey Fisher, the demanding little coach who built a basketball dynasty at Boys. "Ed was always the leader of everything," Hawkins recalls. "He could get guys to do what he wanted. One time he had this argument with Mickey Fisher and he said he was gonna quit the team. Mr. Fisher told him to go, but Ed said, 'If I go, the whole team's goin with me.' Mr. Fisher didn't think nothin of it, but the next day Ed comes in with *everybody* on the team and says, 'We ready to go.' So Mr. Fisher had to back down."

Virginia Union University gave Simmons a basketball scholarship. Instead of staying in the dorms, Eddie lived at the coach's home. While everyone else was going to class, Simmons, who was captain and star of the team, opened a dry-cleaning business at the school. He so dominated the campus he was nicknamed "The Czar."

Years later, when Connie and Ed were on the road together, Hawk would watch him charm hotel managers into tearing up checks, and doctor mileage meters in rented cars so they could travel for practically nothing.

"Ed took me under his wing for six years. I thought he knew everything," Connie says. "I depended on him for advice. He was like an older brother that really likes you." For a while, they met only at the schoolyards. Ed swung in too fast a league for Hawkins to hang out with him. But he always found time to discuss basketball. "You got a lot of potential," he would tell Hawk. "But you got to gain some weight. Man, you so skinny you ugly."

When Eddie had time, they practiced one-on-one. Simmons would dribble close to the basket, outmuscle Hawkins, sometimes even knock him down, and then throw in an easy shot. When Connie had the ball, he could occasionally shoot over the shorter boy. But more often Simmons's quick hands slapped away his dribble. "You got to get confidence," Ed would say. "You shouldn't let me push you around. And you ain't gonna get no better playin with little kids. Onliest way you improve is playin with guys older than you. They'll teach you something."

Late in the summer Eddie got Hawk into several "center court" games at the P.S. 45 schoolyard. Most of the players were on high school varsities. Each ghetto schoolyard has a social structure: certain courts are reserved for the best players; certain players don't have to wait in line for "winners." P.S. 45 had three courts marked in yellow paint on the asphalt. The one closest to the fence that separated it from Lafayette Avenue was for the younger kids. The best players used the center court, and on weekends the fence was lined with boys waiting for a chance.

But even before he was a high school sophomore, Eddie Simmons never had to wait. "No matter who was there first," Connie marvels, "Ed just walked in and took charge. When he wanted to get me into games, he just told them to pick me. I didn't play too good that first summer, but I was getting better, and I advanced much quicker than most kids, cause of the competition. When I went back to the Y and school, I was better than a lot of kids that used to be better than me. In the seventh grade I was the best player in the whole of P.S. 3."

The school had a regulation that only eighth-graders could play on the team. But when Connie was in the seventh grade he was six feet tall and could jump high enough to touch the rim. That didn't keep kids from beating him up or teachers from mocking his slowness, but it made the basketball coach fond of him—fond enough to ignore the rule.

"We had a good team," Hawk recalls. "We only lost one game all season. I was the best scorer. I still got pushed around easy, but I could outjump people. The next two years, they opened junior high schools in the city and I played at 258. I was really the best there. I could swing on the rim and palm the ball. That shook up a lot of kids."

He also continued to play for Gene Smith, first at the Carlton Y and then at the Bedford YMCA, when the Carlton was torn down. "He was coming on as a player," Smith says. "He was on our starting team, even though all the other starters at Bedford were in high school already. He was learning to use his hands to pass and dribble."

"Gene took us around the city playin other Y's," Connie remembers. "We'd go by subway to Harlem and Queens and all over Brooklyn. That was the first time I was really goin outside the ghetto. There was still a few white kids in my neighborhood then, and we got along O.K. They weren't poor as us, and I think I envied them, but I never felt they didn't like me. We were all just kids. We played. But when Gene took us travelin where white people lived, they had nicer gyms and schools and I got a different feeling. At this tournament in Greenpoint, a Jewish section, I was called nigger for the first time."

A group of white teenagers in duck tail haircuts and black leather motorcycle jackets, stood at courtside smoking. During the game, Connie noticed them pointing at the court and laughing. Then he heard one call, "Hey nigger. You, black nigger! You run funny, black nigger!" Hawk was confused. He stared at them the next time downcourt. "Look at the nigger," a boy shouted, "look at him and all his nigger friends!" The boys laughed. Connie didn't know what to do. He thought he was supposed to fight them, but he wasn't sure.

Gene Smith quickly arose and signaled for time out. He spoke to the Greenpoint coach while the black players glared at the taunting whites. The boys were eventually thrown out of the gym. But the incident troubled Connie. That night he told Fred about it. "Man," his big brother laughed, "that's the way it is. You'll learn, lot of white folks don't dig you cause you colored. Cops ain't the only ones gonna call you nigger."

Hawk's consolation was that the kids from Bed-Stuy usually gave white youngsters a thrashing on the court. "When we went to a place like Flushing or Greenpoint," Smith notes, "we were pretty sure we'd win. Those kids weren't as hungry or experienced. Our kids play all day, every day, in the summer. They got nothing else to do. You could see the difference when we played in Harlem. Every game there was a war! The Harlem kids were rougher than *our* boys."

At the Y, Connie got his first taste of New York City's most bitter basketball rivalry: Harlem versus Brooklyn. Kids from Harlem talked about Brooklyn as though it were in another state. Brooklyn ballplayers referred to playing against "guys from the city." Their playing styles differed. Harlem's was more physical, Brooklyn's more oriented toward outside shooting.

"Players in Harlem run more," Smith says. "They dribble and drive better, and they're tougher. But Brooklyn kids shoot better. That's because when you played halfcourt in Harlem you didn't have to take the other team's rebounds back over the foul line before you could shoot. You just put it back up. That makes for a lot of rebounding and shooting around the boards. In Brooklyn, you had to pass it back first, so there was more outside shooting and more passing. I think that's why kids from Brooklyn did better in college and pro ball. They had the outside shots to overcome the big centers."

But Smith adds, "More Brooklyn kids went to college in the first place. The Harlem schools were even worse than ours. Their kids dropped out faster, or they didn't adjust to their coach, so they played on outside teams. They didn't get noticed for scholarships. Many didn't even graduate. And the drug problem hit there first. A lot of the best players never left Harlem."

The toughest teenage games in Harlem were at the St. Phillips Church. The best known of the ghetto coaches, Holcombe Rucker (who organized the city's finest summer tournament, which now bears his name), always had a powerhouse. The baskets in the tiny gym were flush against brick walls, which also happened to be the only out-of-bounds markers. It was permissible to dribble off the wall, and Connie was shocked to see several St. Phillips players "hit the wall with their foot, then spring up and dunk."

The St. Phillips youngsters were not always ideal hosts. Before one game an opponent said matter-of-factly to Connie, "You win in here, man, and you lose your ass out in the street." During another trip to St. Phillips, Hawk was standing beside the court, watching a preliminary game, when he felt something poking against his side. He turned to see a boy, about fifteen years old, standing next to him—holding a gun. "Hand over them sneakers, or I'm gonna shoot you," the boy said.

There were few things that, at the age of thirteen, Connie Hawkins would have risked getting shot over. But he only had one pair of sneakers, he couldn't play in his socks, and the thought of another snickering shoe-salesman pushing sneakers over his enormous feet was intolerable. "Shoot me," Connie snapped, and walked away. The boy disappeared into the crowd.

Hawkins's game grew most rapidly outdoors, in the schoolyards, with Eddie Simmons. As Connie's play improved, Eddie let Hawk accompany him and his friend, 6′ 5″ Jackie Jackson, another varsity player at Boys High, when they traveled from playground to playground looking for action. "By the time I was in junior high school," Connie says, "I was playin against all the top guys at Boys High like Tommy Davis who plays big-league baseball, and Al Barden, who was All-City and played for NYU. They were the heroes of the neighborhood."

Outdoor pick-up games rarely have referees. An "honor system" is employed. If a man thinks he has been fouled, he calls it himself and takes the ball out of bounds. This results in a lot of arguing. No one argued better than Eddie Simmons. "Guys would take the ball off him clean as a whistle," Hawk laughs, "and Ed would holler, 'Foul!' He got away with it, cause he seemed so sure of himself."

The "honor system" also made the games more physical and forced the players to develop slick moves and off-balance shots, especially around the basket. These contortions are known as "schoolyard shots." They are an essential part of the ghetto game—and not simply because of their functional necessity. Ego is involved. Schoolyard ball is one-on-one, man against man, out in the open with everyone watching. In the top schoolyard games, if a player is burned by a spectacular shot or move, his teammates often yell, "Get back, get back," which means he must immediately redeem himself against his opponent—not just by scoring, but by performing an even more sensational maneuver.

For many young men in the slums, the schoolyard is the only place they can feel true pride in what they do, where they can move free of inhibitions (even from coaches), where people applaud their accomplishments, and where they can—by being spectacular—rise, for the moment, above the drabness and anonymity of their lives. Thus, when a player develops extraordinary "schoolyard" moves and shots, these become more than simple athletic skills. They are an inseparable part of his personality. The level of his "game" becomes his measure as a man. So it was—and still is—with Connie.

In those pre-high school years, Hawk learned much by observing the older players. "The schoolyard is where I picked up almost all my moves," he says. "All that twistin and bendin I do close to the basket, I learned that in the schoolyards. But it didn't come quick. I got the ball smashed in my face by older guys for years.

"The greatest schoolyard play I ever saw was by Jackie Jackson," Connie continues. "He was two years older than me, but me and him and Ed got along real good. Jackie always had pain in his knees, cause of these soft lumps on 'em. But when he was about seventeen the lumps hardened and he became the greatest leaper I've ever seen. People would put quarters on top of the backboard and Jackie would jump up and pick 'em off. He had this shot called 'The Double Dooberry with a Cherry on Top.' On a fastbreak, he'd take a pass at the foul line and jump toward the basket, holdin the ball in his two hands. While he was going forward and up, hanging in the air, he would lower the ball down to his waist, raise it over his head, lower down again, raise it back up, and *then* slam in a dunk. Nobody in the world can do that shot but him. People went crazy every time he did it."

The first player Hawk modeled himself after, however, was Jerry Powell, a 6′ 1″ guard who starred at Boys High and later at North Carolina A & T. Instead of a simple fake-left-drive-right maneuver, Powell would use three or four fakes before making his drive and sometimes changed direction several times while en route to the basket. When Connie was alone on the court, he tried to imitate the move. "Before that," he says, "I'd get the ball, bounce it once, and shoot. But after watchin Powell, I started gettin some moves of my own."

The summer Connie turned fifteen, Eddie often took him to Kingstone Park, the big league of Brooklyn schoolyard ball. There Hawk found himself on the court with Solly Walker, a former Boys High and St. John's star; 6′ 7″ Al Innis of St. Francis, the best college center in New York; Vinnie Cohen, an All-City player for Boys who was starring at Syracuse; Sihugo Green, who became an All-American at Duquesne after making All-City at Boys and was then playing for the St. Louis Hawks in the NBA; plus most of the good high school players in the borough. One day, a broad-shouldered teammate of Cohen's joined them. He also played football at Syracuse. His name was Jim Brown, and Hawk recalls that he was very rough.

"Connie was really in with the top people," Gene Smith says. "You weren't a ballplayer unless you played at Kingstone Park. That's where the action was. Every game, somebody had a reputation to defend, and things were always violent."

The notoriety of the players didn't dazzle Connie, however. In fact, he doesn't recall its really dawning on him. "I knew guys were famous," he says. "But sometimes I wasn't sure exactly *who* they were. I was just glad I could play there and get better."

Hawkins still wasn't crazy about basketball. "Until he realized he was gonna be great," Eddie Simmons says, "Hawk didn't like it too much. I'd have to keep goin over and wakin him up just to get him to play."

What Connie really enjoyed in the schoolyards was his proximity to the local heroes. "I'd sit and listen to them talk about sports and girls and I'd be proud I was in their company," he recalls. "I might have dreamed about being great as Eddie Simmons, but I never imagined it could happen."

When he was fourteen and fifteen years old, Hawkins preferred drinking cheap wine on the corner of Classon and Lexington, with his friends Joe Moore, Henry Halliburton, and Neville Smith. If they were broke the man at a nearby liquor store always slipped them a bottle free. "I like you boys," he would say. "You good boys. You ain't in no gangs, you ain't robbin and stealin like all them other kids round here." Night after night they stood on the corner saying crude things to girls and telling lies about their sexual exploits.

They also smoked marijuana. Theodous had introduced it to Connie when Hawk was thirteen years old. They had been pitching pennies against the wall of a factory down the block. Connie had cleaned Theodous out of fifty cents. The older boy reached into his pocket and pulled out what looked like a thin cigarette. "Hey man," he said, "you want to buy this for what you won off me?"

"No," Connie laughed, "I can get a whole pack of cigarettes for what I won."

Theodous shook his head. "You a dumb motherfucker. This ain't no cigarette! This weed, man."

"What's that?"

"It gets you high, baby. You go flyin with this here stuff. I give it to you for that fifty cents you won."

Standing on the sidewalk, Theodous showed Hawk how to draw in the smoke. At first, Connie had no reaction. "This ain't gettin me high," he said. Theodous giggled. "Yes it is man, you just can't tell." Suddenly Connie found himself laughing. "See," said Theodous, "you high."

"I still didn't think it was so great," Connie recalls. "But I tried it again with Theodous a couple of weeks later and I got a pretty good high. I went out in the street after I turned on. I knew I was high because the air smelt better. The whole place didn't seem so bad."

Later, Hawk often got high with his friend Henry Halliburton, who was a jazz buff. They played hooky from school, went to Halliburton's apartment—because Connie didn't have a record player until his senior year in high school—and rolled joints. Then they lay around all day listening to music, smoking, and drinking wine.

Like most NBA players who grew up in urban slums, Connie quickly took drugs for granted. "You could get anything you wanted in the neighborhood," he explains. "But it wasn't like it is today. They didn't have hundreds of junkies all over the street, noddin and stealin. They were already gettin 'em in Harlem, and some people around us was hooked—but very few you could *see*. In those days, the streets was filled with winos. *They* was all over. But few people used heroin. Mostly it was guys in gangs. One died of an overdose. That frightened me. I never messed with heroin."

He tried just about everything else, however. A friend gave him some opium at a community youth-group picnic. "We went behind some bushes and tried it," Hawkins says. "I didn't like it much. Another time he gave me some cocaine. I didn't like that at all. He gave me some hashish, though, and that was pretty nice."

But Connie stuck to grass: "It was easy to get. Plenty of grownups around there had drugs to sell. It wasn't junkies and real pushers then. Mostly just people who got ahold of hash or coke or pot and sold it to make a little extra money. It seemed like a natural thing to do."

Midway through the ninth grade, Hawkins still hadn't considered what high school he might attend. Since he was the best player at J.H.S. 258, many in the neighborhood suggested he go to Boys High and play for Mickey Fisher, whose team—led by senior Eddie Simmons—was on its way to another city championship.

"In Brooklyn," Hawk says, "the thing was to go to 'The High.' It had this great tradition. Ever since Solly Walker was there and went to St. John's, if you was black and a schoolyard ballplayer you wanted to play at The High. But I didn't give it much thought. It seemed like a lot of trouble and bother. I guess I planned to go to some vocational high school and learn a trade or something."

Eddie Simmons had other ideas. "Next year you are goin to The High," he told Connie that winter.

"I don't think I want to," Hawk said.

"You are *goin*," Eddie repeated. "It ain't hard. I hardly go to class. I'm taking you over to meet Mr. Fisher."

"O.K." Connie shrugged.

Mickey Fisher was to New York high school basketball what John Wooden has become to the college game. A spunky little gray-haired man, he had built a dynasty by harvesting the talent of the ghetto. Black youngsters flocked to him. He was a strict disciplinarian, but the kids knew he was a winner and that he worked to get college scholarships for his seniors.

Eddie and Connie found Fisher in Boys High's ancient, dilapidated gym. "Mick," said Eddie, "this here the boy I been tellin you about, Connie Hawkins."

Fisher scrutinized Connie, while Hawk fidgeted. Finally the coach frowned and said, "Simmons, he's very skinny."

"Yeah Mick," Ed said hurriedly, "but he can play."

"Can he touch the rim?"

"Sure. You want to see him?"

"Yes."

Hawk hesitated. "Go ahead," said Fisher. "Do it now, if you can." Connie trotted toward the basket. Instead of taking a running jump, he stopped under the hoop, *then* jumped and grabbed the rim with both hands. He swung there, looking down at Simmons and the coach.

"Get off of that rim before you break it!" Fisher yelled. Hawk dropped gently to the floor. "What did you say your name was?" Fisher asked, more interest in his voice.

"Connie Hawkins."

"Do you want to go to Boys High?"

Hawk didn't want to. But he heard himself answering, "Yes sir."

"All right," said Fisher, "we'll see what we can do."

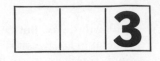

ALL-CITY

"The scouts and college coaches who infest schoolboy basketball
said Hawkins would be a superstar in the National Basketball
Association, that the only thing he couldn't do was
sign his name for autographs. It seemed unnecessarily cruel
at the time, but they were, of course, basically right."
—*Robert Lipsyte,* The New York Times

The level of New York high school basketball is the highest in the country.
But paranoia about racial violence has caused the Public Schools Athletic
League to move its championship playoff tournament out of Madison
Square Garden to isolated high school and college gyms—thereby shunting
into obscurity the black youngsters who dominate the event.

The situation was different in 1957 when Connie entered Boys High.
The names of schoolboy stars were familiar to even the casual reader of the
sports page. The PSAL tournament drew huge crowds at the Garden. The
greatest attraction, and the scourge of New York high school ball, were the
Kangaroos of Boys. Coach Fisher was noted for producing championship
teams and for requiring that *every* player on his squad—regardless of
height—jump well enough to dunk. The Boys High pregame warmup was
legendary. The sight of thirteen players, some as short as 5' 8", dunking the
ball in succession—from the side, down the middle, one-handed, two-
handed, backhanded—convinced most young opponents that Boys was in-
vincible.

Hawkins, an emaciated 6' 3", 140 pounds, played little as a sophomore.
The team had five veteran starters and was defending city champion. But
Hawk didn't regret Eddie's pushing him toward the school. Being even a
small part of something successful gave him a sense of self-worth he'd
never felt before. "The older players had this pride and it rubbed off on
me," he says. "Everyone in the neighborhood talked about our great team.
Just havin a uniform gave me a little recognition."

Still frightened by rough body contact, Hawk was hardly overwhelming when he did play. But he showed potential. The graceful moves were beginning to take shape. His jumping and ballhandling were excellent for his age.

"In the middle of the season," he recalls, "I got my name in the New York *Post*. It said, 'There's a skinny kid at Boys High named Connie Hawkins who's gonna be great some day.' I think Mr. Fisher told them to put it in. It made me feel fantastic. I kept starin at the paper, lookin at my name in print. I never dreamed that would happen."

Two of Connie's friends from the schoolyards, seniors Jackie Jackson and Neville Smith, were starters. The star was Billy Burwell, a 6′ 8″, 240-pound junior, already the best high school pivotman in the city.

Boys High won its division title and went to Madison Square Garden to defend its championship in March of 1958. "I'd gone to one or two Knick games," Connie says, "but I didn't have the money to go often. Just being on the bench in the Garden thrilled me. I wanted to play so bad."

He played several minutes in the first game of the tournament and scored two points. It was his only appearance. Boys was upset in the finals by DeWitt Clinton.

"After the game, we all cried," Connie recalls. "I thought to myself, 'Someday I'm gonna get real good and come back here and win the PSAL for Mr. Fisher.'"

At first, Hawk had been frightened by the stern, explosive coach: "He was tough. He'd stamp his feet and yell and grab you by the arm, for making mistakes." By the end of the season, however, Connie had seen through Fisher's drill-sergeant front and discovered that this was a man—a white man—who really cared about him. "I came to like him so much," says Hawk. "Mr. Fisher was a father-type person. He treated me like a human being, never made fun of me. He took time to talk about my problems in school—and I had a lot."

Boys High was a school in transition. The building, a grime-covered fortress surrounded by a black iron fence, had been erected in 1890. Once it was among the finest schools in New York, known as a breeding ground of doctors and lawyers. It was an "open school": students from any of the city's five boroughs could apply for admission. For years it was predominantly white. Then the Bedford-Stuyvesant neighborhood changed, fewer white youngsters would travel into the ghetto, and Boys became crowded with kids from Bed-Stuy. By the time Connie entered, the enrollment was more than 50 percent black. When he graduated, the percentage was closer to 70.

The staff was a remnant of bygone days. Most teachers were white, middle-aged, and unprepared to deal with the needs and problems of the new student body. Each year, the quality of the education at Boys High slipped further.

The New York school system offered two courses at its non-vocational high schools: a regular academic program leading toward college, and a "General" course, an effort to give supposedly less capable students a taste of education.

"The General course," says Nathan Mazer, then head of the Boys High English Department, "was a dismal failure. In most schools—including ours—standards were quickly reduced to attendance: 'Show up and don't punch anybody in the mouth and we'll give you a diploma.' There was no math, no real science, and no foreign language. And they just went through the motions of final examinations."

White students at Boys High invariably took the academic course. They dominated the student government and the school's various committees. The vast majority of whites graduated.

Almost by reflex action, black youngsters were channeled into the General course by guidance counselors who apparently took for granted that most black kids couldn't handle real academics. "The advisors didn't have time to give serious thought to each boy," says Mazer, now a professor at Cortland State University. "Seven out of eight black youngsters who graduated were getting that meaningless General diploma. Fifty percent weren't even graduating. We honestly tried to reach them, but our program didn't relate to their interests and backgrounds. Those dropouts are today's drug addicts."

A guidance counselor took one look at Connie Hawkins and plopped him into the General course. But even that was too much. Hawk could barely read.

There was no place to turn for help. In class, he was either mocked or ignored: "This teacher in Social Studies always called me an idiot. He'd give us a four-page booklet and you read about politics and places like Argentina, and you looked at maps. On the back of the book they had questions to answer—A,B,C,D—about what you read. I *never* passed one of those tests. After about a month, the teacher started sayin, 'Some people are doin pretty well. But if you intend to copy off someone, don't do it off Mr. Hawkins, cause he's an idiot.' Everyone would laugh. I felt ashamed, and I wanted to fight. But what could I do? I felt he was right."

Connie was usually too discouraged to do homework. But even when he tried, there was no desk or well-lighted empty table in the apartment. "I'd try to study in bed or in the kitchen," he recalls. "But my mother was usually in the kitchen. My brothers would have the TV set and the radio goin. There was no place I could concentrate."

His problems at Boys High weren't solely academic. For the first time, Hawk was encountering many youngsters from outside his neighborhood. Most of these were white and Jewish and—in comparison to Connie—very affluent. "I was jealous of them," he admits. "They took academic courses and they had neat clothes and money to buy lunch every day. I was ashamed of my clothes. Lots of times my mother didn't have fifty cents to give me for lunch. I'd have to bring mine in a paper bag. Sometimes, I wished I could be white and Jewish so I could have things like those kids."

There were days when Connie had neither money nor a sandwich from home. He'd tell his friends he wasn't hungry—but often he was. Occasionally he stole food from the cafeteria. One day during his sophomore year, he was caught: "I tried to slip by the cashier while another guy was payin. I got to a table. Then the cashier came over and grabbed me. A lot of guys saw. I was completely embarrassed and I started to cry."

He was taken to the principal's office. "This is disgraceful," the principal said. "Stealing can't be tolerated, Mr. Hawkins. Why did you do this?"

"I didn't have no money," Hawk blurted, bursting into tears again.

The principal's tone softened. "Stealing isn't necessary," he said. "I think you'd better see Mr. Fisher."

The last person Connie wanted to see was the coach. But Fisher never raised his voice. "Why did you have to steal?" he asked.

"I didn't have no money," Hawkins sniffled. "I was hungry for some lunch."

Fisher nodded. "Next time this happens, just come to me. I'll give you lunch money. You don't need to steal. Now here's fifty cents. Get yourself some lunch."

"Am I gonna be in trouble?"

"No," said Fisher. "I'll handle it. You eat. I'll see you at practice."

"Mr. Fisher was good to me, even before I was a star at basketball," says Connie. "But I felt funny hittin on him all the time." Consequently, when Hawk arrived without lunch money, he sometimes won it shooting dice. During his junior year he was caught in the men's room playing craps, and was threatened with expulsion. Fisher again interceded. By this time, he also had a selfish interest in Connie. Hawk was an All-City player.

"Why, Connie?" the coach asked when they were alone. "If you needed money, you knew I would have given it to you."

"But I wanted to win it on my own," said Hawk.

Fisher's concern for his players genuinely transcended his interest in them as athletes. But the famous coach had one glaring blind-spot: although he labored to secure college scholarships, he did little to ensure their readiness for college. He occasionally pressed Connie to do homework. As Hawk's truancy increased, Fisher halfheartedly threatened to throw him off the team. But Hawkins knew the coach wasn't serious.

In fact, Fisher used his considerable influence to pressure teachers into giving players passing grades, to keep them eligible for basketball. Most needed little convincing. The virtually all-black team had become Boys High's one source of pride. The teachers were fans.

"We covered up for kids like Connie," Mazer admits sadly. "I once coached basketball at Eastern District High, and I was sort of a father-confessor to the team. I suppose I was so fascinated by Connie's playing that I looked the other way when he didn't come to school or missed some classes. At Boys High, it took a hell of a lot of courage for any teacher to flunk Connie Hawkins. And few did."

A segment of the faculty, however, resented the prominence of Fisher and his team. They released their frustrations by taunting players in class. "They'd call me a fool," Hawk remembers, "and I believed them."

As a result, Connie played the clown. "The whole thing was a big joke to him," Mazer says. "He didn't care about school. He laughed his way down the halls."

Actually, school was anything but humorous for Connie. Every day was a constant reminder of his poverty and his inability to learn. "I acted like it was all a joke cause I didn't want people to know how bad I felt," he says. "I wouldn't even admit to myself how depressin everything was."

The summer after his sophomore year, Hawkins discovered there was at least one aspect of his life about which he need not be ashamed: basketball.

His game blossomed. The youthful awkwardness disappeared. He gained two inches and twenty-five pounds. Most important, he gained confidence in himself: "My moves weren't so lackadaisical any more. Everything I did became quicker and sharper. I found I was jumpin much higher and I could control what my body did in the air. I began hittin jump shots around the circle. I wanted the ball more, cause I felt I could put it in. All of a sudden, I realized I was really good. It was weird, but it felt great."

The summer months were an orgy of basketball. Every day Hawkins was in the schoolyards—most often, on the courts at P.S. 117, two blocks from his old haunt at P.S. 245. Bed-Stuy's best players were always there: Eddie Simmons, back from his first year at Virginia Union; Jackie Jackson, headed for Virginia Union that fall; Earl Wright, the star of Franklin K. Lane's powerful varsity; Connie's close friend Henry Halliburton, by then 6′ 2″, 210 pounds, and a starter at Eastern District; and Boys starters Neville Smith and Jerry Powell.

"We mostly played three-on-three," Hawk says. "When we wanted to play five-on-five, the guys from our schoolyard went down to Brownsville and played against Tony Jackson and LeRoy Ellis (All-City players at Jefferson High, who starred at St. John's), or uptown to play against Roger Brown (Wingate's sensational sophomore, already second-team All-City) and his buddies. We'd bet a case of beer and there would be some bloody games. But if Eddie couldn't find enough competition in Brooklyn, he'd call up Russ Cunningham and we'd go over to Harlem and play against his NYU boys, Satch Sanders and Cal Ramsey."

Ramsey, a stocky 6′ 4″, was an All-American at NYU. The 6′ 6″ Sanders —later a Boston Celtic star—was a junior at the same school. Cunningham, a flashy little guard, would be an NYU starter that fall. Their rivalry with Eddie, Jackie, and Hawk was to become a schoolyard legend. "The word would spread through the neighborhood that we were goin after them," Simmons recalls. "The park would start to crowd up. Games stopped on the other courts. People would stand around and cheer and argue and bet six packs. It was halfcourt, three-on-three—and people would talk about those games for days after."

Connie was just turning sixteen, but he played Sanders head-to-head. "At first," says Eddie, "Satch scared Connie. Then Hawk saw he could outjump him and get off his shot. Hawk already had that fantastic stride. He could make his fake in the corner, or at the foul line, and then boom— one long step and he's by his man and all the way to the hoop. You could tell Hawk was gonna be the better player."

That summer, Hawkins even played against Oscar Robertson, then an All-American at the University of Cincinnati. "He was comin through town and he had his sneakers, so he came out to the schoolyard," says Hawk. "Eddie asked me did I want to try guardin him. I tried, but he was too strong. He took me in the hole and crushed me. But it was amazin just bein on the same court with him, watchin him up close, and lookin at his moves."

"We'd also go over to Manhattan Beach, where a lot of white kids were," recalls Hawk's brother Earl, who often played with them. "One time we could see, on another court, this blond-haired kid and his father. The old man was makin the kid take a hundred layups with each hand. But the kid wasn't too good. We thought it was pretty funny—a big kid playin with his father. But that kid turned out to be Billy Cunningham."

"Me, Ed, and Jackie had become like the Three Musketeers," notes Connie. "We were together every day. But Ed ran things. If anybody knew where to find a party or had a scheme to get some money, he did. The last time I doubted him was when he said he could make girls go to bed with him by scarin 'em with his big Doberman dog."

One afternoon, Hawk found Simmons sitting at his kitchen table drinking beer with two girls. Connie was uncomfortable and wanted to leave. Ed wouldn't hear of it. "Have a beer," he said grandly. Simmons then grabbed a girl by the arm. "Come here, I want to show you something." They disappeared into the bedroom. Connie stared at the other girl—who yawned. A female scream came from the bedroom. Moments later, Ed emerged, wearing only his shorts. "Your friend want to see you," he told the girl at the table. When she entered the bedroom, Ed slammed the door. "Hold this while I get the dog," he ordered.

Hawk had reservations. "Grow up man," the Czar laughed, unleashing his huge Doberman. "Don't worry. This work every time." He opened the door, upon which the girls had been pounding. "See this here dog?" Simmons smiled. "He's a killer. He'll bite your ass off. You want me to sick him on you?"

"Those girls did just what Ed told them," Hawk recalls. "They were mad at him afterwards, but he didn't care."

Despite Eddie's novel ideas, basketball was the only solidifying factor in an otherwise aimless and unstructured existence for Connie and his friends. "I had no idea what was goin on outside Bed-Stuy," Hawk remembers. "I didn't have no goals, except to be a good player. I think some of the guys were already hopin basketball could take them out of the ghetto. But my thinkin hadn't even gone that far yet. I didn't like where I was, but I figured I was stuck. I felt I had no future, so I didn't give it no thought. I think the guys who kept feelin that way were the ones that wound up gettin hooked on drugs."

Boredom was a constant problem. When the courts became unbearably hot, the youngsters who played at P.S. 117 shot pool or retreated to Jack's candy store and listened to the Harptones and the Five Satins on the juke box. On Friday nights, they bought wine and beer, and partyed. Saturday morning, if any wine was left, they took it to the courts at Riis Beach and drank while they played. "One night," Hawk recalls, "we all got high and Neville Smith got the idea we should shave our heads. So we did it. Then we went to the beach and slept in the sand. Shavin seemed like a good idea at night, but when the other people started showin up to play ball the next morning, we were all pretty self-conscious."

Without money, there was little to do when they weren't playing ball. One evening, as they stood on the corner discussing the Dodgers' move to Los Angeles, Eddie said, "Hey, why don't we rob a bank?"

Apparently, no one could think of a reason. "We picked a bank down-town on Gates Avenue," Connie says. "Neville drew a map of the whole downtown area, just like they do in the movies. We made up a plan. Everybody agreed. When we went home that night, we were gonna go through with it. But, the next morning, I woke up and thought, 'Wow, what am I gettin myself into?' Turns out everybody thought the same thing. We just played ball in the schoolyard that day. Nobody talked about the bank."

In addition to the endless pickup games, Connie played in many school-yard tournaments that summer. Most teams had adult coaches who scram-bled to get the best players, occasionally supplied uniforms, and—as Hawk discovered two years later—weren't above paying a few dollars for super-stars. Connie was hardly at that level yet, but his reputation began to grow when he played in the Rucker Tournament in the playground at Seventh Avenue near 130th Street in Harlem. Holcombe Rucker, a junior high school teacher, initiated the tournament (which was actually a league) in 1946 to keep black youngsters off the street. Rucker gave substance to the schoolyard game by providing referees and trophies. There was action each weekend in four divisions: junior high, high school, college, and pro.

Hawkins played for Rucker's own team, the St. Phillips Seniors. Also with St. Phillips was Bob McCullough, who later led the nation's small-col-lege scorers while at Benedict and played briefly with the Cincinnati Royals. Today he is the Rucker Tournament's director.

"At first," says McCullough, "Connie was good, but nothing special. Then, during that summer, he started to come on. Each year Mr. Rucker took the division winners to Philly to play against the best kids in their age group. Our team won the high school division. And that's when Connie won me over. Philly's center was Wayne Hightower, who'd just graduated Overbrook. He was 6' 10" and a high school All-American. All the colleges were after him. Connie was just a 6' 5" sophomore then, but he played Hightower even—scored off him, outjumped him, blocked some of his shots. After that, everybody knew Hawk was gonna be great."

Connie was hardly oblivious to the respect he began to receive in the schoolyards. People he'd never met suddenly knew his name. Everyone wanted to be his teammate. He heard himself described as one of the best young players in the city. "I can't explain how wonderful that felt," he says. "I was finally good at *something*. So I started to really work at basket-ball—not just play it. I grew to love the game. For me, it became like a girl you can't live without."

That winter, Connie was not only a starter, but a star, on one of the most powerful teams in the city's history.

Boys High rolled to an unbeaten season, toying with every opponent and often winning by more than fifty points. The top seven players went on to college ball. The 6′ 8″ Burwell, voted the best schoolboy in New York that season, was heavily recruited and later had a successful career at the University of Illinois.

Connie averaged in the low double figures. His rebounding and ballhandling were exceptional. "Everybody on our team got along good because we had balanced scoring," he recalls. "Mr. Fisher wanted everybody to get his shots and be happy. That's where I learned to look for the open man before lookin to shoot."

Boys swept through the Garden field to take the city championship. In the final game, against Commerce, Connie scored 15 points and dominated the backboards. Boys won, 74-58. "The Garden didn't frighten me no more," he recalls. "I could hear kids callin my name. Winnin was great. The school even gave us new blazers. I wore that blazer every day."

The New York *Post* named Hawkins to the first All-City team. It wrote: "Skinny, bony, but 'cute' combination of height and backcourt moves (dribbling, passing, etc.) makes Connie a prime possibility for the pro game some day. Needs better outside shot, but inside, he'll do all you can ask of a schoolboy."

"From then on, in my neighborhood and even at school, I got treated like somebody real special," Hawk says. "The guy who ran the ice cream parlor, where we hung out, gave me free ice cream and sodas. Teachers talked to me in the halls. Lookin back, I can see it was all pretty phony. But then it was so important. I'd never had people be interested in me before."

Even as an All-City player, Connie had not been inundated with publicity. Burwell had overshadowed him at Boys. Roger Brown, Wingate's sleek 6′ 4″ forward, was the most publicized junior in town. But in the schoolyards, where a man's place in the pecking order was established and maintained by a continuous series of challenges and confrontations, Hawkins was soon acknowledged as the best teenage player in New York.

Brown was great. But Hawkins could do more things—and the summer before his senior year, he was doing them against pros, collegians, and the veteran schoolyard élite. His reputation mushroomed with each one-on-one success.

Hawk's skills had special appeal for blacks. Ghetto ball puts a premium on style, spring, moves, grace, and showmanship. Hawkins, even at age seventeen, had these in abundance. He was already stunning spectators with his hesitation hook. Connie would leap toward the basket, the ball raised above his head in one hand, then hang in the air—as though suspended by invisible wires—until, with a sudden windmill sweep, he slammed it through the hoop. The move had—and still has—a devastatingly intimidating effect.

Fisher didn't allow Hawk to throw many behind-the-back passes or dribble between his legs. But there were no restrictions on asphalt. It was a moment for uninhibited self-expression. Connie let himself go in a dance that was his alone.

"I could hardly keep track of the teams I was playin for," Hawkins recalls. "My friend Halliburton would say, 'This guy want you to play for him, they got big trophies,' so I'd play. Sometimes I was in three games in three different tournaments in the same day."

The best team Hawk played with was the New York Gems, run by Mike Tynberg, a parttime college recruiter. "They were like the Boston Celtics, famous for winnin," says Connie. "Tynberg had most of the top players in the city. That year I think we had Freddie Crawford, Roger Brown, Art Heyman, and me. We won almost every game we played."

Connie was closer than ever to Eddie and Jackie. But, that summer, his circle of acquaintances rapidly expanded. Hawk was a star. People wanted to be near him. One of his friends was white—Billy Cannon, a husky forward at Adelphi Academy. Their relationship was relaxed. Billy idolized Hawk. He was too preoccupied with basketball to get hung up on race.

Cannon's friend, Eddie Churan, had a car. They often drove Connie to the beach or to schoolyards around Brooklyn. Through them, Hawk played against most of the top white players in the borough, such as Billy Cunningham, Anton Muehlbauer, and Billy Galantai. Their games weren't as physical as those in Bed Stuy and Harlem. With the exception of Cunningham, the players weren't as good.

"I liked Cannon," says Connie. "We were friends for years. But I learned we couldn't ever be real close. He was white—and you never knew what his friends would do."

One afternoon, Connie was the only black on the courts at Ocean Avenue. After the game, the other players mingled with some white girls standing behind the basket. Connie found himself alone. He tried to be nonchalant, casually tossing hook shots at the hoop. Then he heard Cannon tell a tall, blond-haired girl: "I want you to meet a friend of mine, Connie Hawkins."

As Hawk approached, the girl stared at him and wrinkled her nose. "That's all right," she said to Cannon. "I don't want to meet him."

Hawkins turned and dribbled toward the opposite end of the court—

and slammed a savage dunk. Behind him he could hear Cannon cursing at the girl.

"Hawk, I'm sorry," Billy cried, trotting toward him. "If you want to go right now, it's O.K. with me."

"Forget it," Connie said coldly. "Just don't introduce me to nobody down here again."

Rucker's annual New York–Philadelphia matchup was an All-Star game that summer of 1959. Philadelphia had a seemingly unbeatable high school team, including future pros Wally Jones, Walt Hazzard, Jim Washington, and 6′ 9″ Tom Hoover, All-American center at Bishop John Carroll in Washington, D.C. But the day belonged to Connie Hawkins. "He was incredible," recalls Bob McCullough, who played in the game. "Hawk was sky-high because the New York *Post* had written that Bishop Carroll was the best team in the nation—not Boys High. Hawk took it out on Hoover. He blocked Hoover's first shot, then pointed a finger at him and hollered, 'Don't you shoot no more.' Hoover tried another shot. Hawk slammed it right in his face, wagged his finger again, and yelled, 'I told you, don't shoot no more!' There was a big crowd, and everybody went wild. Everything Hawk did was amazing. I kept waiting for him to jump over the backboard. We won the game, Hawk was MVP, and Hoover—the most publicized high school player in the East—practically got run off the court."

That winter, Connie and Boys were heavily favored to dominate the city. Their only real challenge would come from Wingate High and Roger Brown.

Connie and Roger had known each other for several years but had never gone head-to-head. Until the previous season, Roger had been the vastly superior player. He made second-team All-City, while Connie was still a substitute at Boys. Roger was not a skillful ballhandler, but he rebounded strongly and was a superb shooter.

Although Brown and Hawkins were the same age, Roger had always been more self-confident and mature. "A lot of people didn't like him cause he was pretty arrogant," Connie recalls. "But I liked his playin so much, I didn't mind his personality. We got sort of friendly the summer before our senior years. I dated a little, but I wasn't no cocksman like Roger. He was going steady with half the girls at Wingate. Sometimes he'd invite me to parties or fix me up. He introduced me to this girl named Lois, and we double-dated a few times. But we never got too close cause we knew we were gonna meet on the court."

With Burwell gone, Hawkins captained the Boys High team. Working at both high and low post, he still shot sparingly and—because Boys usually led by 30 at halftime—rarely played a full game. But he was so superior to even the other top schoolboy players in the city, he still averaged 25.2. In one game he scored 60 points.

Although Hawk had grown to 6′ 6″, 190 pounds, his body had not filled out. His diet was still inadequate and he lacked stamina. To compensate, Hawk often paced himself, going hard only when necessary. Some observers complained that he was lackadaisical. A sportswriter described him as "loping about the court like a sleepy gazelle."

Even before the season began, however, Connie was being hailed as the finest prospect ever to come out of New York. "He can do everything: run, shoot, rebound, and play defense," said Fisher. "He's got a sixth sense that allows him to see plays developing behind him. He can become a 6′ 6″ Bob Cousy."

Boys' third game, against powerful DeWitt Clinton, was televised. "I think everybody in the neighborhood was watchin," Hawk recalls. "People talked to me about it on the street for days before. I was kinda nervous." All he did was score 41 points, pass for 15 assists, and lead Boys to its twenty-first consecutive victory.

"After watching that game," said St. John's veteran coach Joe Lapchick, "I couldn't sleep all night."

The only tough division opponent was expected to be Brooklyn Tech, led by 6′ 4″ All-City forward Don Flatt. Tech matched Boys in height, and its coach Henry Goldman predicted an upset. "I hear they say Hawkins is saving himself for Tech," Goldman said. "Well, maybe Flatt is saving himself for Boys."

The teams met twice. Boys won, 85-66 and 92-42. Connie scored 33 and 34 points respectively. In the second meeting, he held Flatt to 0. College scouts were salivating. Said Lee Terrill, assistant coach at North Carolina, "I know Connie Hawkins is the best schoolboy in the country. I don't even have to see the others play to be sure of that."

Boys rambled into the PSAL playoff tournament at the Garden with a 17-0 record—but without Micky Fisher. The coach had left to direct the Israeli Olympic team. His spot was filled by his assistant, Howard Jones, an earnest young black man who had been Boys' captain in 1947.

"I felt bad when Mr. Fisher left," says Connie. "But Howie had been helping him since the fall. He didn't change anything Mr. Fisher did—except he didn't yell as much—so I figured we'd win anyway."

Riding a series of sensational performances by Hawkins, Boys rolled through the early tournament games and into semifinals. Roger Brown and Wingate were waiting for them. Both teams were unbeaten. The winner seemed assured of the championship.

It was probably the most memorable high school basketball confrontation in New York's history. But it was a game Connie would like to forget. He was nervous beforehand and couldn't get untracked. Howie Jones had assigned him to guard Brown. Connie liked the idea. But he picked up two quick fouls. "I told Howie I better switch off," he recalls, "but he said No. Roger had this fat kid named Feuerstein settin picks for him. I kept runnin into the pick. Roger would shoot these long jumpers just over my finger-tips. Once I touched it and it still went in. He couldn't miss. I got desperate and flustrated. I tried a couple of stupid drives and got two chargin fouls. I felt like everything was fuzzy and out of control."

As eighteen thousand fans looked on in disbelief, Hawk picked up another charge and fouled out just before the third quarter ended. "I was incoherent," he says. "I was sure we'd lose. Then Wylie Briggs, my teammate, stopped Roger in the last quarter, and we pulled it out." Boys won, 62-59. But Brown had outscored Hawkins, 39-18.

"In the dressing room," Connie says, "everybody was happy but me. I felt ashamed. All I wanted to do was redeem myself in the finals." He didn't get a chance. Boys won the title two days later, but Columbus High, hopelessly outmanned, stalled almost the entire game. Connie scored just two points. Boys won, 21-15. They were champions once more. Afterwards Connie joined the raucous shouting in the dressing room. He'd carried the team to the title and forty consecutive wins. But this victory had a bitter aftertaste.

"I got a lot of teasin cause Roger outplayed me," Hawk recalls. "It's funny, but I was so mad at myself cause I could see, even in *that* game, that I was really better than him. He couldn't do that much except shoot. I'd just let myself get too tense. I felt if we were both in real tough competition, I'd do better. But I thought I'd never get a chance to prove it."

The local coaches agreed with Hawk. Connie and Roger were both named All-City. But it was Hawkins who was voted New York's top schoolboy player. "With rare finesse for a lad his size," wrote the *Post*, "Connie passed off for almost as many points as he scored. His unselfish attitude impressed rival coaches and players and can't have been lost on the colleges coast to coast."

A few weeks later, Hawk was named to the first five on *Parade* magazine's high school All-American team. Brown was named to the third team.

That spring, Connie got a chance to justify the honors and soothe his bruised pride. He and Roger were invited to play in the All-American East-West game on June 29, 1960, at Jersey City's Roosevelt Stadium.

The game featured the greatest collection of high school athletes ever to play on the same court. The West team included current pro stars Joe Caldwell, Jeff Mullins, Paul Silas, and George Wilson, plus 6' 10" Bill Chmielewski, who led Dayton to an NIT title and played in the American Basketball League, and Cotton Nash, the Kentucky All-American who played pro baseball after a fling with the American Basketball Association. The East squad had Hawkins; Brown; Barry Kramer, an All-American at NYU who spent several years in the NBA; Archie Roberts, Columbia's famed football quarterback; 6' 10" Jay Buckley, who starred at Duke; and 6' 10" John Thompson, who spent a season with the Boston Celtics. The game was to be played outdoors, and twenty thousand tickets had been sold.

Connie almost didn't make it. When he got the invitation he was ecstatic. Then he realized that June 29 was his graduation night at Boys High. At dinner, he mentioned that he wasn't going to be at the ceremonies. His mother, who still ran the family with a strap, cut him off. "I waited too long for this night," she said. "You are gonna be there, so *I* can enjoy it."

Hawk was crushed. Roger snickered when Connie tried to explain why he couldn't play. The promoter Haskell Cohen, complained bitterly to Howie Jones. But Dorothy Hawkins didn't care how many tickets Haskell Cohen had sold, or how many people would be disappointed; she knew only that a lady on Lexington Avenue was going to see her son graduate before she went totally blind.

Hawk moped through the ceremonies. But afterward when, diploma in hand, he kissed his mother and saw tears in her near-sightless eyes, the Jersey game seemed very far away. Then he noticed Freddie waving at him from the back of the auditorium. "I got your playin stuff outside in a car," his brother yelled. "If we push it, we can get you to that game."

Hawk sprinted to the street. They were in Jersey City before you could say speeding ticket. Then Connie made an unpleasant discovery. His brother had packed a jock, white socks, a towel, and some soap—which was fine if he planned to play in his bare feet. "Fred," Hawk groaned, "you didn't bring no sneakers!"

At the Stadium he frantically searched for something that fit. The game had begun, and size 14 basketball shoes aren't generally lying around. Someone finally came up with a pair of size 12's. The fit was painful, but Hawk trotted to the bench and moments later was playing.

Connie took a pass, and George Wilson approached, waving a large hand in Hawk's face. Hawkins had heard a lot about Wilson. People in the Midwest believed the 6′ 8″ center from Chicago was the best frontcourt prospect in the country. Connie faked a drive, then swished a jumper from fifteen feet. Soon he repeated the maneuver for another basket. Then he drove around Wilson and slammed a twisting, backhanded dunk. Wilson tried to retaliate, but Connie blocked his shot.

Hawk could hear the crowd roaring. The pain in his feet was forgotten. His adrenalin was flowing, and he had something to prove. The game to showcase the talent of a nation instead had become his private stage.

"The outdoor court was slippery from moisture in the air," recalls Paul Silas. "Everybody was slipping—everybody but Connie. He didn't even seem to touch the ground. Once he showed up, we were beaten. He even went into his trick bag; dribbled behind his back, passed between his legs. Everything. I'll never forget it. I still can't believe a high school kid could have been that good."

When the game ended, Hawkins was exhausted. But within him was a calming sense of complete satisfaction. Players from both squads surrounded him. They shook his hand and slapped his back. The Wingate game no longer seemed so important.

Then he heard the public-address system blaring his name. He was the Most Valuable Player. His eyes caught Roger Brown's. Roger, who had been adequate but far from sensational, looked away glumly.

Connie walked to midcourt, the cheers washing over him. There he was presented the largest, shiniest gold trophy he had ever seen. Hawk tried to speak, but no words came from his throat. He stared at the trophy and gazed about the stadium. Twenty thousand people were on their feet applauding.

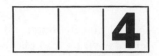

THE RECRUITERS

> "We were taken in. . . . It was like playing cards with
> a rigged deck. . . . I'm very against the whole thing now,
> recruitment, scholarships, letters-of-intent. It's organized for
> adult men to manipulate 18-year-olds to come to a university and
> provide it with a winning team, some money and fame."
> *Bill Bradley, Princeton, '65*

When Connie Hawkins was a high school senior his reading material consisted of comic books and the sports section—on those days someone told him his picture was in it. He had an elementary school reading-level and was so intimidated by the printed word it would be ten years before he got a driver's license, because he felt he couldn't handle the written test.

But 250 colleges wrote to Hawkins that winter. A dozen flew him to their campuses. More than 50 sent adults to tell him personally how much they wanted him as a student at their institutions of higher learning.

Recruiters took Hawkins to dinner and slipped him cash or basketball tickets. Coaches from every section of the country—who smugly assured their local Rotary Clubs they were building character—told Connie they would *pay* him to enroll. Some promised him free clothing, plane trips, and a salary. Prominent businessmen were eager to show the teenager from Bedford-Stuyvesant how to break rules with impunity. A professional basketball team even offered to put Hawkins on its payroll while he was in college.

At the time, Connie Hawkins's wardrobe consisted of two pairs of pants which ended above his ankles, a two-year-old blue serge suit he wore only on Sundays, and a blue blazer given him by Boys High for playing on a championship team. He wore the blazer to school every day. In winter, it was his overcoat.

The first letters had come while Hawkins was still a junior. He thinks one was from a service academy, but he isn't sure. When Coach Fisher showed him the letters, Hawk was befuddled: "Hey, I can't drop out of school now. I got to play next season."

Fisher laughed gently: "No, Connie. They want you *after* you graduate here. This shows how interested they are in you."

Hawkins was still painfully oblivious to what went on around him. Eddie Simmons had gotten a college scholarship. Bill Burwell was being heavily recruited. But it still hadn't occurred to Connie Hawkins a college would want him.

But the letters made him proud. He flashed them around the neighborhood. "See," he would say, "them cats interested in me." He was careful not to say too much, however. He didn't want anyone asking a lot of questions—like what a college *was*. Hawk had never gotten around to asking Eddie what he did when he went away to Virginia Union: "I thought college must be kind of a big Boys High, but with girls and a better basketball team."

The summer before his senior year, while Hawkins was playing at Kingstone Park, he was approached by a thin black man in his early forties, a cigar dangling in the corner of his mouth. The guys in the schoolyard called him "Spook."

Spook is the most notorious of the freelance recruiters. He prowls the schoolyards, community centers, and high school gyms, lining up players for whatever college will pay him the most. If a coach in the Southwest needs a backcourt man—and has money to spend—Spook can supply him. How long the kid stays in school is somebody else's problem.

"Spook," Connie says now, "would sell his mother to St. John's for room and board and a couple of those cigars he smoke."

That day Spook told Connie, "I can get you any school you want. Good price, too."

"Price?" Hawk said, frowning.

Fisher tried to protect Connie. All official inquiries had to come through him. This wasn't hard to enforce, since the Hawkinses still didn't have a telephone. Fisher also took Connie aside and warned; "Forget about taking a little bit of money here and there. It will pay off in the long run. You can earn plenty later, after you finish college."

Fisher was right, of course. "But," explains his assistant, Howie Jones, now athletic director at New York Community College, "it was *money*. Connie never had any. What he was going through was fantastic. He was wrong to take, but this kid didn't even have sheets on his bed."

So, when the recruiters gave him money, Connie simply didn't tell his coach. At first, the under-the-table handouts left Hawk surprised and confused. But he quickly caught on. Soon he came to expect them.

New York City is the most fertile recruiting ground in the country, and the recruiters were coming out of the woodwork by the start of Hawk's final season at Boys. He was a very desirable piece of merchandise.

Once the function of intercollegiate athletics was to provide students with extracurricular activities. Often, that isn't the function any more. Athletic departments must produce winning teams to raise money for the university through television contracts, gate receipts, and increased alumni donations. Nothing puts an unknown college on the map faster than having a nationally rated football or basketball squad. The schools make huge investments in their sports programs. They need winners to get a return. Coaches who don't win become insurance salesmen.

To succeed, coaches must have good athletes. So they offer inducements. Their inducements lead to bigger inducements, and soon the schools are buying athletes, often without regard to their qualifications as students. The process becomes most intense during the recruitment of a superb basketball player. A football star doesn't necessarily guarantee a winning team, because the game cannot be controlled by one man. But a single superstar can turn a losing basketball squad into the top team in the country. A Wilt Chamberlain, a Kareem Jabbar (Lew Alcindor), a Jerry Lucas, or a Connie Hawkins can do more for a school's athletic program, national prestige, and relationship with the state legislature, than any other athlete. They are recruited accordingly.

The phone in Fisher's office rang constantly throughout the winter of 1959–00. Someone in Denver or East Lansing or Chicago always wanted to speak with Connie Hawkins. The recruiters crowded the little gym, waiting for Fisher to introduce them to Connie after practice. They would smile and suggest dinner or the Garden. Some were alumni who recruited for their schools, but most were assistant coaches. Hawk recalls them as high-pressure types: young, well-dressed, smiling, and speaking so quickly he had to concentrate to catch what they were saying.

"When I think back on it," he says, "it was like they were all reciting a speech. Like they'd said every word over and over. They said they had a great school, the best coach in the country, and the dean was a nice guy. They talked about how they prepared you for the pros, or what a big fieldhouse they had. A lot of guys said how well they treated 'Negroes.' "

Hawkins has no recollection of a recruiter *ever* asking him what subject he wanted to major in or what he wanted to do with his life. Instead, most broadly hinted that if he wanted a car, clothes, or spending money, "We have some prominent alumni who might be able to work something out."

Soon, he could recite the last line of the conversations in his sleep: "Do you need a few dollars? Here, take this for carfare." They would hand him a ten-dollar bill. Sometimes there was money or basketball tickets under his napkin.

The entire process excited and awed Hawkins. He saved every letter and couldn't wait to tell Halliburton or Earl what the latest white guy from the Midwest had given him. "I liked the recruiters," he recalls. "They made me feel important, wanted, very valuable. I felt like I was a whole new person. My head was all swirled up. They told me how great I played, how I'd be great in college, how it was a cinch we'd win the NCAA. It was like Christmas and having the whole turkey to eat yourself."

There were a few uneasy moments. Eating out had always meant Nathan's hot dogs on Coney Island or Savola's Pizzeria. Suddenly Hawkins found himself in expensive Manhattan restaurants with black-tied waiters smiling and calling him "sir" in strange accents.

"I was very uncomfortable," he says. "I'd see three or four different forks on the table and I didn't know which one to use. I didn't know how to order. The menu had mostly things I didn't recognize. So, I'd just say, 'Oh, I'll take a steak.' The guy I was with might suggest something else and I'd say, 'O.K.,' real quick. After a while, I learned about steak: I could tell the difference between Porterhouse and New York cut and filet mignon. Then I tried lobster tails with butter sauce. I liked it. It was the first time I wasn't eatin just to keep from being hungry."

Even Fisher was overwhelmed. "I've never had a rush for a kid start this early," he told a reporter in December of 1959. "There are all kinds of pressures on me." The New York colleges were desperately trying to keep Hawkins in town. He would be a great attraction at Madison Square Garden. St. John's, a perennial national power, was the most persistent. Connie arrived at practice one day wearing a red satin St. John's uniform and a new pair of sneakers. During a preseason scrimmage, the St. John's freshman coach and chief recruiter, Lou Carnesecca, sat next to Fisher on the bench.

"Look, Mickey," said Carnesecca, who later coached the St. John's varsity and is now coach and general manager of the ABA New York Nets, "we want Hawkins badly. But I'm not going to bother you. You just collect the offers. When you get them all, pick out the best one and show it to me. Then we'll top it, no matter what it is."

Then there were the trips. Almost every weekend, the young man who once tried to steal lunch because he didn't have fifty cents, was flying to a town he had never heard of. Before he met the recruiters, Connie had left New York City only for basketball games in Philadelphia and Washington, D.C. He had never been in an airplane. Now Seattle, Indiana, Illinois, Northwestern, Iowa, Colorado, and Ohio State, were just some of the schools that made him their guest.

Flying terrified Hawk. He would fasten his seatbelt so tight it hurt. As the plane took off, he closed his eyes, pressed the back of his head against his shoulders, crossed his fingers, and waited to die. Once convinced he would live, he stared at the white paper bag in the seat pocket in front of him and waited to vomit.

Hawkins and his stomach always survived.

"The trips were fantastic," he remembers. "When I went to Ohio State, I met Jerry Lucas. They took me out to dinner and put me in a fancy hotel and really gave me the red carpet. I don't think I'd ever been in a hotel before.

"I was travelin fast, maybe too fast. I'd get home and buy things like more hot dogs, or wine for all the guys. I felt like I was in a fantasy. I had no money and no clothes and then suddenly people were givin me things. Every school bought me food and took me to night clubs and parties. They were offerin me money and tellin me to go downtown and pick out a few pairs of slacks. It was like the story of Cinderella and the pumpkin. My pumpkin turned into a Cadillac Eldorado."

Parties, fieldhouses, steak dinners—this was the picture painted by each school. There was no attempt to show him what life would be like if he actually enrolled. Hawk was never invited to sit in on a class. He never spoke with a grade advisor or guidance counselor. Instead, at Indiana, a recruiter told him: "You're a ballplayer. You want to get ready for the NBA. You'll get good experience here. The Big Ten is the toughest league in the country. You can't pick a better place if you want to play pro ball."

In New York, Spook continued to pursue Connie with new offers. Fisher wouldn't allow Spook in the Boys High gym, but one day he found Hawk and Roger Brown at the Nedick's hot-dog stand outside the old Madison Square Garden.

"You guys want to go to Notre Dame?" Spook asked. "I can work it out. I want to set up a package deal so you can play together. You want the Big Ten? I got a lot of connections out there. But the best one is Seattle. I can really get you money from them."

Actually, the last thing Connie wanted was to go to school with Roger. He liked him, but there was only one basketball in a game and Brown tended to have it. Connie and Roger did visit Seattle together, but Hawk turned down a car and salary (in addition to the National Collegiate Athletic Association-permitted room, board, books, tuition, and fifteen dollars per month) because he thought Roger would go there.

The most bizarre proposition wasn't really from a college. It came from the Boston Celtics of the National Basketball Association. At the time, the league had a territorial draft rule which allowed NBA clubs to draft out of turn in the first round to claim a player going to college in the pro team's immediate vicinity. The Cincinnati Royals, for instance, would later use the rule to claim Jerry Lucas of Ohio State. The New York Knicks sent their black star, Willie Naulls, to Boys High one afternoon in an effort to convince Connie to attend a New York college.

The Celtics went much further. Red Auerbach, the coach and general manager of the world champions, wanted Hawkins at Providence College in Rhode Island. Auerbach, who grew up in Brooklyn, visited Boys High himself. He met with Fisher, Connie, and a member of the teaching staff. The Celtics' offer was direct. If Hawk attended a school within their territorial draft range—preferably Providence—the NBA club would not only see that he got an attractive scholarship, but would pay him a small salary under the table.

Connie's head was spinning. He didn't want to stay in New York. An isolated, all-male Catholic school like Providence hardly appealed to him. He wasn't interested in an all-black college in the South. But there were dozens of other offers.

Hawkins was still lost in the classroom at Boys, but the shame was cushioned by the respect he now received from the other students. He was the best-known boy in the school. His name often appeared in the New York papers. And next year he would be going to college.

It never occurred to him that he might be unable to handle the classwork. Fisher warned, "You'll have to study hard there; college is different." But the recruiters spoke only of fun, travel, good money, and getting ready for the NBA. If they didn't worry about his grades, why should Connie?

When Fisher prepared to leave for Israel, he asked Nathan Mazer, the head of the English Department, to replace him as a liaison with the recruiters. As the "father confessor of the team," Mazer had spent three years enjoying Hawk's basketball. Now he was forced to see Connie from a different perspective.

"I realized," says Mazer, "that there was no way on earth this boy could be ready for college. His academic record was pitiful. These schools hadn't the slightest interest in him as a student. Most of them gave no thought to how he might fare in class. They wanted a ballplayer."

After the basketball season, Mazer invited Connie to his classroom. "You are really planning to go to college?" he asked when they were alone.

"Sure," Connie said.

"Do you know how hard it will be for you?"

Hawkins shook his head.

"Connie, they are fooling you," sighed the teacher. "The way things are now, you won't be able to succeed. What happened to you in the college board test?"

Hawk forced a grin. But the memory was disquieting, something he had tried to forget: "After I wrote my name and my class, everything was a total blank. I stared at the paper, and I filled in some multiple choices so people couldn't tell I didn't know what was goin on."

Mazer nodded. "If you are serious about college," he said, "you must have some credentials. First of all, you must know how to take a test. If you are willing, Connie, I'll help you after school. But you'll have to work. What do you say?"

Connie was surprised and a little worried. "O.K.," he said.

Mazer was a short, bald man who spoke a little like a Sholem Aleichem rabbi. Connie liked and trusted him. The first day they worked together, Mazer gave a reading test and an I.Q. test to the young man 250 colleges wanted as a student. Connie's reading level was seventh grade. His I.Q. was 65: low-grade moron.

Mazer had been teaching ghetto kids too long to put much stock in the actual scores. He knew the tests' "cultural bias"—the questions related only to a middle-class youngster's frame of reference. "I'd seen the intelligence Connie had on a basketball court," he recalls. "Not just instinct, but actual deductive thought. I knew he was much brighter than those scores indicated."

They began working. Mazer gave Connie another test, marked it immediately, and went over the answers with him. "I could see that on many of his wrong answers, he really knew the correct one," the teacher says. "But his mind wasn't conditioned to think in such a way that he would get it."

On one question, Hawk had marked the wrong synonym for "novice." "In the Golden Gloves, Connie, in what division do they put boys when they start out?" Mazer asked.

"Novice Division."

"Does that mean they're beginners?"

"Uh huh."

"Well here, one of the choices for the synonym of novice is beginner. Why didn't you choose it?"

"Oh," Connie said with surprise, "you mean *that kind* of novice."

Part of the problem, Mazer found, was that Hawkins did no reading. Words familiar to his ear, didn't register when he read them. He was confused by long sentences, intimidated and easily flustered by unfamiliar references, and even bothered by written questions themselves.

But Hawk worked with more dedication than he had devoted to anything away from the basketball court. They read together, practiced spelling and grammar, and went over I.Q. and reading tests. By graduation Hawk's I.Q. score had been raised to a very respectable 113—an increase of 48 points. His reading level was graded at the second month of the eleventh grade.

"I was so proud," Connie recalls. "The best part was that Mr. Mazer was happy with what I'd done. I felt I was ready for college then. I felt real confident."

The tragedy was that Hawk was now ready for *high school.* He could read a little and had some idea of how to take a test. But his improved scores hardly indicated an ability to deal with the world outside Bedford-Stuyvesant. If some college had sent him to prep school—or even to junior college—he *might* have had a chance. But Connie Hawkins was too valuable to be wasted or waited for. If a college sent him to prep school and he failed, the investment was lost. If he came directly to college and flunked out after a year or two, at least the school got some sellout crowds for its trouble.

"He hadn't the remotest idea of how to study; he didn't even know you had to get to class on time. But he actually thought he was prepared for college!" Mazer says. "The recruiters led him to believe he'd have no problems."

Mazer confronted one big-name coach. "How can you tell him he'll be able to succeed?" the teacher asked. "You've seen his college board scores."

"The boy will have the finest tutors," the coach replied impatiently. "He'll have all the help he needs."

"Tutors?" Mazer sneered. "The tutoring of Moses couldn't make up for a lifetime of lost education."

But they kept calling and visiting and promising—Iowa, Cincinnati, Loyola of Chicago, Niagara, Seattle—tugging him back and forth. Finally it came down to Colorado and Iowa. The offers were good, and he liked their recruiters.

Colorado got the inside track. Its recruiter, a New York businessman, suggested Connie *try* the school for the summer. "See how you like it," the man told Hawk. "You can take some courses. There's no obligation." A deal was arranged. Connie would spend part of the summer in Boulder, Colorado. He would take Math Skills, Speed Reading, and English in summer school. His brother Earl would come along, also at the school's expense. Connie would be given a job.

"I got good money," Hawk says. "My job was to keep seaweed out of the football stadium." That wasn't too difficult, since Boulder was more than one thousand miles from the nearest ocean.

If Connie had decided to stay, the job would have been his for four years. Other goodies were promised, too. The university rented Connie and Earl a private house off-campus. For the first time in his life, Hawk had a bedroom of his own.

"Everything was fine until classes started," Hawkins says. "Speed Reading was impossible. The first day, the teacher had a slide projector. She put a paragraph on the blackboard. You had thirty seconds to read it. When she pulled it out, I'd read about one line. You had to answer questions on what you read. I couldn't answer one. I peeked around and everybody else was markin their papers. I thought, 'Wow, Boys High again. I'm inferior.'"

Math was also a mystery. "I can get the numbers," Hawk told Earl one day, "but when they start puttin letters up there, forget it. How do you add an X and a Y?"

Connie was still mulling over the X's and Y's two weeks later, when Earl got into a fight with a white football player and threatened him with a gun he'd brought from Brooklyn. The Colorado basketball coach said Earl would have to go home. This made Connie's decision easier. They both went home.

Arlo Wilson was waiting for Hawkins. Wilson was a wealthy Manhattan businessman, president of the Iowa Touchdown Club, and a devoted University of Iowa alumnus. Connie was his pet project. Wilson had been after him since the fall. Iowa planned to become a national power in basketball. It had a bright young coach, Sharm Scheuerman; a talented sophomore forward, Don Nelson; and several capable guards. One more ingredient was needed: Connie Hawkins.

Gray-haired and conservatively dressed, Wilson reminded Hawk of "those British guys in the movies." He visited Connie's home, brought Mrs. Hawkins baskets of fruit and told her, "You have a lovely young man."

Wilson took Connie to lunch in the delegates' dining room at the United Nations. He bought him an expensive sports jacket so he wouldn't feel uncomfortable in the finer restaurants. During the winter, he had given Connie basketball tickets and a round-trip plane ticket to Iowa. The school also sent Connie a plane ticket. This one had a twenty-dollar bill in it. After a broad hint from Wilson, Hawk cashed one of the plane tickets and kept the money. Wilson later promised that if Connie enrolled at Iowa and wanted a visit from a Brooklyn girl, he would pay the fare.

"Mr. Wilson seemed different from the other recruiters," Connie says. "He didn't pressure me, even when I went to Colorado. He kept tellin me about how nice the people were in Iowa, about how happy I'd be there, and about how he'd make sure I was well taken care of."

When Hawk was in Colorado, Wilson continued to call Freddie—who had a telephone in his apartment—asking for news. He launched a new offensive when Connie returned. Hawk mentioned that Colorado had been a bit tougher than he'd expected. But Wilson brushed it off: "At Iowa, you'll have no trouble. Of course you'll need to study hard. But they have plenty of tutors to help. Remember how much you enjoyed your trip?"

Connie had visited Iowa in the spring, and it *had* been a good trip. He hadn't seen any classes, but "I liked how big and pretty the campus was, and how nice and genuine and countrylike the people seemed. Everybody was smilin at me. And they introduced me to this guy, Mr. Davies, who owned a feed store. The coaches told me if I ever needed anything while I was there at school, Mr. Davies would take care of it."

So, eventually, Connie picked Iowa. There were competing offers, even in midsummer, but Iowa's deal was the best. "They seemed like nice people," Connie says, "and they offered me the most money."

The Iowa arrangement was complicated by Hawkins's somewhat spotty academic credentials. The Big Ten had some minimum standards for athletic aid. Connie didn't come close to qualifying for a scholarship. But Iowa wasn't about to let a silly rule stand in the way of Hawkins's education.

The Athletic Department devised a complicated scheme for paying him under the table. He was admitted on probation as a regular student, supposedly paying his own way until he raised his grades enough to merit aid. He would be given a bogus job at a filling station. He wouldn't have to show up—except on payday. His salary would allow him to pay his tuition, plus room and board. Arlo Wilson would send money to Fred Hawkins, who'd take out a few dollars and send the rest to Connie. This would cover Hawk's other college expenses, plus his transportation, and still leave him with a nice piece of change. Wilson would also send money to Connie's mother, and give Hawk two hundred in front when he went off to school.

The money was hardly spectacular. Even including what Fred and his mother would receive, all the payments (after Hawk took care of tuition, transportation, and room and board) would total only about $150 a month. But to Connie Hawkins, who had lived eighteen years with nothing, $150 a month was beautiful.

"HAWKINS, I'M JACK MOLINAS"

"You callously used your prestige as a former All-American . . .
to corrupt college basketball players and to defraud the public. . . ."
—*Judge Joseph A. Sarafite sentencing Jack Molinas, February 17, 1963*

The summer of 1960 was the happiest—and most disastrous—of Connie's life. His Iowa decision wasn't made public until early September, so the recruiters continued their gifts and compliments. The men who ran the local amateur teams slipped him fives and tens for "expenses." The guys in the schoolyards treated him with respect and admiration reserved for the "Main Man." Neighborhood people told his mother she should be proud; her son was going to college—to make a success of himself—while a lot of kids in Bedford-Stuyvesant were going to prison.

And Connie met Jack Molinas.

"That summer I *really* felt good about myself," Connie says. "I even felt a little confident about the future. I decided I wanted to play pro ball. For a long time, I'd just said it cause I couldn't think of anything else. But that summer I really felt it could happen, like it wasn't a dumb dream."

There weren't enough afternoons and evenings for all the games people wanted Hawkins to play. But he was usually with the Gems, again the powerhouse of the City. There were tournaments everywhere—Rockville Center, Long Island; the Madison Square Boys Club; the Kennedy Community Center—and the Gems won them all. Roger Brown was on the team. So were Wylie Briggs and Walt Davis from Boys, Billy Cunningham, and a rugged white kid from Manhattan named Neil Johnson, who would one day be Connie's teammate with the Phoenix Suns.

Hawk was in such demand that every coach he played for gave him a few bills. He was more than worth the price. By the end of the summer, the roaches were scrambling over sixty-five glistening trophies in the dank little living room at 86 Lexington Avenue.

Hawk also played with Eddie and Jackie. It was fast action. The running feud with the NYU crowd—Sanders, Ramsey, and Russ Cunningham—continued throughout the city. Sanders was now an All-American, but Hawkins usually outplayed him on the courts of Riis Beach or Harlem. Cunningham was among the top backcourt men in the East. But Eddie ate him alive. Jackie, meanwhile, was soaring so high he had printed black-on-white business cards reading: "Jumpin Jackie Jackson. . . . Have Converse Will Jump." The cards had Jackie's phone number, and Hawk suspected every girl in the city had one.

But Connie was seeing less of Ed and Jackie. Instead, he was with Roger Brown. Circumstances seemed to push them together, just as their rivalry had linked them in the minds of the public. In the spring, Jack, Eddie, and James Mitchell had been away at college. When Hawk was invited to an All-Star game, tournament, or banquet, Roger was always there. The essence of their relationship was competition: two teenagers, convinced of their basketball abilities, constantly trying to outdo each other.

Because they were the best players in the city, a lot of people—coaches, recruiters, and promoters—were giving them money. For instance, a promoter in Schenectady paid Connie and Roger two hundred dollars each to appear in two games upstate. Their local "expenses" were usually ten dollars a game. But even this allowed Hawk to move around with cash in his pocket.

Hawkins and Brown had a curious friendship. For all the time spent together, they didn't talk much. Connie felt Roger was bitter because the recruiters rated Hawk a better prospect. "Our friendship was growing," he recalls, "but we really didn't know each other. We were *around* each other a lot, but we didn't say too much."

Vinnie Brewer, a star at Iowa State after making All-City at Bryant High in Brooklyn, saw them often in the schoolyards that summer. "They'd drive around together, but you didn't get the feeling Roger *respected* Connie. Hawk was still pretty naïve and out of it about a lot of things. Roger was a better-class Negro. Connie was Bed-Stuy. Roger lived in a little nicer neighborhood, went to a better school. Everybody thought he acted superior, and he was that way with Connie."

They often partied together, however. Brown got Connie dates. Later, Roger told Hawk he would have access to a car.

Early in the summer, Connie met the person whose car Roger was borrowing. Hawk was with Billy Cannon and Eddie Churan on the courts at Manhattan Beach, when a tall man with dark receding hair walked over and extended a hand that was almost as large as Connie's. "Hawkins," he said, "I'm Jack Molinas."

Molinas stood 6′ 6″ and was built like a ballplayer. He had been an All-American at Columbia and a star rookie in the NBA. But midway through the 1954 season he had been banned from the league for betting on games. Now he was a successful lawyer, player-coach of an Eastern League team, and at 28, still among the city's best schoolyard players.

Basketball had been in Molinas's blood since his youth in the Bronx. He thought nothing of screeching his shiny new Buick to a halt in front of some ghetto schoolyard, pulling a pair of sneakers from the glove compartment, and playing all afternoon with a bunch of black kids he'd never seen before.

But Molinas wasn't just a lawyer and an athlete. He was the key figure in a nationwide gambling operation that was in the process of bribing scores of college players to fix basketball games. Molinas used the schoolyards to meet young athletes and soften them up for eventual fixing propositions. Jack's greatness on the court had a Pied Piper effect on many youngsters. "The man had an incredible hook shot," Vinnie Brewer remembers. "Nobody could stop him. We all looked up to Jack."

Molinas came on warm and generous, like everybody's big brother. It seemed only natural for the dapper, affluent lawyer to take a few young players out to dinner after a tournament game or to drive them to the beach when everyone got tired and sweaty in the schoolyard.

Connie had never heard of Molinas. He had been twelve years old when Jack was booted out of the NBA, and Hawk knew nothing of the expulsion. As the detective who picked up Connie at Iowa eight months later was to learn, Hawkins didn't even know what a "point spread" was. "I'd never heard anybody talk about fixin games and spreadin points," Connie says. "In my neighborhood I knew about people playin the numbers—everybody did that—but I didn't know of people who bet with bookies on basketball games."

A few days later, Roger wheeled a big Buick in front of 86 Lexington Avenue. When Hawk saw the car he assumed Brown had decided to go to Seattle University, which had offered them both cars. "No man," Roger explained, "this is Jack Molinas's. Remember, I told you I can borrow it any time I want. And he says you can borrow it too."

"I ain't got no license."

"Well, I got one man, get in. I'm goin to see Pat. Lois is over at her house. You comin?"

They took the girls to Coney Island, spent all their loose change on rides, then strolled the boardwalk. Driving home, Roger turned his head to speak to Connie, sitting with Lois in the back seat. Brown's foot came off the brake and the car jumped forward, bumping the rear of a sedan. The woman driving the sedan pulled to the curb. Brown laughed and took off down Ocean Avenue.

(Months later, when Connie was at Iowa, he heard that Roger had been arrested in New York for leaving the scene of an accident. Brown's attorney was Jack Molinas.)

"I visited Molinas's law office a week or two after the Coney Island thing," Connie recalls. "Roger told me Jack wanted to talk to us about playing in a benefit game on Long Island." There were always people in the schoolyards who wanted to talk to Hawk about playing in games, and he had learned that a few dollars usually went along with such discussions.

Molinas rose from his desk and greeted them effusively. He was wearing an expensive suit, a little flashy for an attorney, but the kind that impressed a kid like Connie Hawkins. He told them about the benefit game that night; then he asked Hawk to step into another room. "There's a guy in here who'd enjoy meeting you," Molinas said.

They entered a small room, possibly a law library, off Molinas's office. Inside was a short, stocky man with heavy eyebrows, wearing a slightly rumpled sports jacket. "Connie," said Molinas, "this is Joey, he's a client of mine. Why don't you two talk for a while."

"Molinas and Roger were in the other room," Connie recalls. "Joey started talkin about basketball: who was better, Wilt or Russell? Then he asked, Did I know any good college players? I told him Wilky Gilmore of Colorado, Vinnie Brewer of Iowa State, and some others. Then he asked, Could I introduce him to them some time? I said, 'Sure.' I thought he was just another New York basketball nut. People were always askin me to introduce them to people."

Joey asked if Vinnie Brewer, or any other college players, might be interested in making some cash. If so, Connie could pick up a little money by providing introductions. Joey explained that he sometimes organized basketball teams, which he liked to coach. He said he was hoping to form a tough, all-black team for the following summer.

Joey *had* coached a little basketball. Just before the 1951 betting scandal broke, he had one of the best independent teams in the Bronx. But Joey wasn't your typical basketball kook. His name was Joe Hacken, and he was Molinas's partner in the gambling operation. He had nine bookmaking convictions on his record. Ten years before, when he was called "Joe Jalop," he had a college basketball player named Jack Molinas shaving points for him—and they'd gotten away with it.

Connie had never heard of Joe Hacken.

"The guy didn't say anything about bettin or gamblin," Hawk recalls. "He just wanted to meet some players. When I came out of the room, Molinas took Roger in for about ten minutes. Then he gave Roger twenty dollars and told him to give me half for expense money to the benefit game. I think he might have taken us to dinner afterwards at a Chinese place, but I'm not sure."

Hawkins didn't see Joe Hacken again until Christmas. But he saw Molinas. When Jack met Connie and Roger at the schoolyards he'd give them a lift home or loan them his car. Sometimes, after tournament games, he'd take them out for hamburgers and Cokes, or even a dinner. Once Molinas showed them stag films at a friend's apartment.

When Connie returned from Colorado, he occasionally bumped into Jack. Hawkins probably saw Molinas a dozen times that summer: "Jack seemed like a nice person. One time he told me he knew how hard it was for poor kids their first year at school. He said if I needed help or money, just let him know. He said he liked me."

Eddie Simmons and Jackie Jackson didn't like the entire situation. Primarily, they didn't like seeing Connie with Roger Brown. Eddie had disliked Roger for years and once punched him in a schoolyard fight. Simmons advised Connie to limit his contact with Brown. But Roger had a car—and they were always going to the same games anyway—so for the first time, Hawk disregarded Eddie's advice.

"I came back from school and saw Hawk hangin out with Brown, who was an arrogant cocksucker," Eddie says. "I saw Brown with Molinas, and I figured that was bad for Hawk. I knew Molinas was in some trouble in the past. Now Molinas was playin up to Roger. But I never thought Molinas was fixin games! I didn't even talk to Connie about Molinas. I just said, 'You ain't doin yourself no good hangin out with Roger and his fast friends.' Shit, if I knew what Molinas was up to, I wouldn't let him near Hawk."

Jackie's feelings were similar: "Hawk was kinda in another bag that summer, bein All-City and All-Everything. When me and Ed came back from school we wasn't as tight with Hawk—because of Roger Brown. But you never had no idea Molinas was settin 'em up. We thought maybe he wanted to use Hawk in tournaments, be his sponsor, and slip him money. Everybody did that. A kid in Bed-Stuy take it where he can get it. We all did. So you couldn't call Molinas a bad guy. But I had a feelin something was wrong. Why this guy gonna tag on Hawk all of a sudden? Then I thought, maybe he want to sell him to a school."

Molinas *was* setting Hawkins up. But not for sale to a college: he didn't care where Connie went, as long as there was a betting line on the games. His plan was to have Hawkins start shaving points at the start of his sophomore year. In the meantime, he told Connie nothing. Molinas never even asked Hawkins for introductions to college players. To Connie, Molinas was just one more white adult giving him small favors because he was a good basketball player.

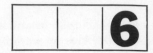

A LOAN FOR JOE COLLEGE

"Black students aren't given athletic scholarships for the purpose
of education. Blacks are brought in to perform. Any education
they get is incidental to their main job, which is playing sports.
In most cases, their college lives are educational blanks."
—*Professor Harry Edwards*

In September of 1961, Connie Hawkins packed his sneakers and his comic
books and went off to be Joe College. An apprehensive eighteen-year-old,
alone for the first time, he arrived in Iowa City to find an alien world, more
indifferent than hostile. He was another in the endless succession of black
athletes pulled from the urban core, plopped into a midwestern campus,
and told to make themselves at home. But Iowa wasn't anything like home.
Hawkins had nothing in common with the flaxen-haired farm boys who
populated his dorm. Once they finished discussing the basketball team and
the football team, there was nothing to talk about. Connie's classes—which
the recruiters had told him he could handle—were more overwhelming
and humiliating than his worst experiences at Boys High. Unfamiliar words
buzzed about his ears like angry mosquitoes, and reading assignments for a
month totaled more pages than he had read in his life. People were not unfriendly: they smiled and said how happy they were he had come to Iowa.
But Hawkins soon found life on the college campus dull, lonely, and sex-
ually frustrating.

The men who recruited him had painted an idyllic picture of what he
could look forward to. In exchange for playing basketball, Connie would
get good treatment, money, and a college education. They had neglected
to mention that his academic background did not qualify him to go to college, or that he would have almost no social life, or that the clothing store
where he was supposed to pick up a complete wardrobe at huge discounts
had nothing in his size but overalls.

The Athletic Department did keep some of its promises. The money from Arlo Wilson arrived, through Fred, every month. Connie didn't have to report to his job at Dean Jones's filling station, except on payday. Head coach Sharm Scheuerman took him again to see Mr. Davies, the feed-store owner Hawkins had met while being recruited. Davies told Connie, "I'm to look after you if you need anything." Occasionally he took Hawkins to dinner. At football games, where Connie *did* work selling programs, Davies always paid with a twenty-dollar bill and told Hawk to keep the change.

"It was nice to have a little money," Connie recalls. "But after I paid for tuition and books and my dorm fees and transportation and my phone calls home, it wasn't all that much. I'd spend it on movies and eatin. At least I wasn't short on food for once. I must have had hundreds of hamburgers. But I was awful lonely."

Hawkins's roommate, Frank Allen, was a black, twenty-two-year-old ex-GI and a sophomore on the varsity basketball team. Allen, from East Chicago, Indiana, was always pleasant. But their background and age difference precluded a real friendship.

Allen did, however, give Connie some valuable advice. The first night they were together in their room, Hawkins sprawled on his bed and announced, "Now baby, bring on them white girls!"

Allen stared hard at the freshman: "Man, you better cool it. Let me set you straight. Don't mess with no white pussy around here. Coaches don't stand for it. You're not in New York. People around here think Negroes ought to be screwin *Negroes* and that's it!"

Connie thought for a moment. "What they do to you, if they catch you?"

"Not too long ago there was this cat that played basketball," Allen said. "He was going everywhere on campus with this white broad. They threw him off the team and kicked him outta school."

But there were few black women on the Iowa campus and not many more in Iowa City. Those worth dating had long since been claimed by black upperclassmen. Skinny, reticent freshmen didn't stand much of a chance. So Connie's social life consisted primarily of going to the movies by himself, playing pool in the student union, and sitting in the cafeteria staring at white girls. Later in the semester, Hawk was so horny he called Arlo Wilson and reminded him of his promise to send a girl from Brooklyn. In a few days, a bus arrived with a young lady named Pattie. She spent a weekend, then went home. Connie was alone again.

Hawk would sit for hours at a table in the back of the union cafeteria, watching the white kids chatter with each other about their courses, fraternities, and hometowns. Occasionally he sensed white girls staring at him.

But he lowered his eyes, too uncertain to risk antagonizing the Athletic Department. He played a lot of pool, because it reminded him of Brooklyn. Sometimes he talked with the handful of other black athletes. Mostly he was by himself.

At the dorm, white freshmen knocked on his door to invite him to parties. He always declined: Why bother if the girls were out of bounds? The weekend of the Iowa–Ohio State game, Vinnie Brewer, his friend from the schoolyards, came from Iowa State to visit. Somehow, Brewer located a party. Connie remembers the weekend because it was one of the few times he went out while in college. "I didn't have no close friends there," he recalls. "People treated me nice, like I was important cause I was gonna be a basketball star, but I couldn't relate to them. And I was doin awful in class."

He had never been around so many white people before. It intimidated him: "I figured they must be smarter than me. Soon as I looked around in class and saw all the white kids, I *knew* I was gonna have trouble. The subjects were interestin at the start; at least they *seemed* interestin. I didn't know what the teachers was talkin about most of the time. I couldn't get my teeth into it. Boys High was bad, but this was a whole different thing."

The Athletic Department surrounded Hawkins with tutors and hoped for the best. Two sophomores were assigned to work with him fulltime. But, as Nathan Mazer at Boys High had warned, the tutoring of Moses couldn't have made up for Connie's lack of preparation. Hawk didn't know how to take lecture notes or outline a book or use the library. The tutors came to his room every night for at least an hour. They read aloud to him, tried to show him how to follow an assignment, helped him write papers, and finally wrote the papers for him. The Athletic Department's academic counselor, who selected courses for freshman athletes, hadn't exactly given Hawk pre-med. In fact, six of Connie's fourteen class hours were in Physical Education, where instructors knew what kind of grades to give prospective All-Americans. Hawkins got one hour of A and five hours of B.

But Connie passed *no* courses outside the Phys Ed Department. He finished the first semester with six hours of F (four in Freshman English) and two hours of Incomplete. The tutors had tried. Before exams they even accompanied Connie to basketball practice and went over material with him during breaks in the workouts. "But," Hawk remembers, "it didn't do no good. I couldn't keep up with the readin. That was the worst part. And I didn't understand a lot of the words the teachers were sayin. I guess I kind of felt like an idiot again. Everything was so flustratin. I hadn't expected college to be like that. So I gave up."

In his introductory math course, Hawk usually fell asleep at his desk. The instructor, an intense Japanese, stopped trying to awaken him, except once when he screamed in Connie's ear, "Mr. Hawkins, your snoring is disturbing my class!"

As always, basketball was his refuge: "I could see from how I was screwin up in class that I'd never be no brain, so I knew I'd have to play ball—NBA ball—if I was ever gonna have money and have people look up to me."

Hawkins was a sensation with the freshman team. More than ever, compliments and adulation were heaped upon him. The coaches made him feel appreciated. Dick Schultz, the freshman coach, would take him aside and ask how he was doing in class and if there was anything he needed. Hawk was too ashamed to admit his misery, but he liked the idea that the coach cared enough to ask.

A Big Ten rule, prohibiting intercollegiate competition for freshmen, confined Connie to intersquad scrimmages before the Iowa varsity's home appearances. Hawk's only real public test came in November, when the frosh played an annual game against the varsity. Connie, who by then stood 6' 8" and weighed about 195, left the fans bug-eyed.

The freshmen lost the game, 73-55, but Hawk was spectacular. He went one-on-one against the varsity's star, Don Nelson, a powerful junior forward who was to become an All-American and now plays with the Boston Celtics. Connie outscored Nelson, 24-13. He might have carried the frosh to victory had he not fouled out late in the third quarter.

Thereafter, his serious competition was limited to working against Nelson in practice. "He was better than me even then," recalls Nelson. "He was just eighteen years old, a lot of times he acted like a big kid, but he was a fantastic athlete. In the middle of practice, one time, he took off his sneakers and went over to where the track team was working out. He beat the school's best sprinters in the hundred-yard dash. And Connie was in his socks!"

Freshmen intersquad scrimmages usually offer all the excitement of a man fixing plumbing. But that winter Connie made them the most popular show in Iowa City. Ten thousand people were often in the arena when the freshmen came out to warm up, almost two hours before the varsity game. Hawk gave them an eyeful. Before the scrimmages, he and Andy Hankins, a freshman guard, put on exhibitions of fancy dribbling and passing. When the team took layups, Hawk would palm two basketballs and dunk them simultaneously. Visiting coaches cringed at the thought of facing Hawkins for the next three years. In Iowa City, people spoke of how Hawkins and Nelson would take Iowa to a national championship next season, and how Connie's impending clash with Ohio State's Jerry Lucas would be the greatest head-to-head confrontation in the country. It was taken for granted that Hawk would be an All-American. When Connie and the freshmen had finished playing, the crowd sometimes thinned considerably. A lot of people didn't bother to stay for the varsity game.

On campus, however, Connie still felt like a foreign student. He would laugh and joke to hide his discomfort, but he always felt out of place. He counted the days until Christmas vacation. When it finally arrived, Dean Jones, the man who owned the filling station where Connie was supposed to work, gave Hawk a large sum of money—an "advance" on his salary—with which Hawk was to pay his second-semester tuition and dormitory fees after vacation. Connie took the money with him to New York.

"When I got home," he remembers, "I wanted to impress everybody. I wanted them to think I was doin fine at college. I wasn't gonna show I was unhappy or I was messin up in class. I told 'em I was doin great in everything and I was makin a lot of money." To prove it, he started throwing cash around—the money Dean Jones had given him. Connie bought expensive Christmas gifts for his mother, made loans to several friends, and picked up tabs when he went out with the guys in the neighborhood.

One evening, he went to Madison Square Garden to watch the Holiday Festival Tournament. Many in the crowd recognized him. He shook hands, told people how well he was doing out west, and even signed some autographs. At halftime of the first game, Hawk was standing at a concession when he heard a familiar voice: "Connie, Connie Hawkins. How you been!" It was Jack Molinas.

Jack suggested they skip the second half and go out for a quick sandwich. They took a cab to a nearby restaurant. Molinas ordered, then excused himself to make a phone call. Fifteen minutes later, Joe Hacken walked in. Connie hadn't seen him since the summer meeting in Jack's office. Molinas and Hacken spoke together, then joined Hawk at the table. While Molinas puffed on a thick cigar, Joey casually asked Hawkins questions about basketball. Connie thinks most of the conversation concerned how Iowa's varsity would do that week in a West Coast tournament.

"Molinas got up to get another cigar," Hawkins remembers, "and then Hacken asked me how well I knew Vinnie Brewer. I said I knew him real good from the schoolyards. Hacken wanted to know if I knew Vinnie well enough to introduce him."

Since Hacken had told Connie during the summer that he was organizing an independent team, Hawk saw nothing unusual about Joey's request. But he didn't have Brewer's telephone number at Iowa State.

Hacken made a phone call and returned with a number. "I called from the phone booth in the restaurant," Connie says, "but they said Vinnie wasn't there. Hacken said, 'Never mind. Forget it.' We left, and Molinas gave me five dollars to take a cab back to the Garden. That's the last time in my life I ever saw or talked to Joe Hacken."

As Christmas vacation ended, Connie surveyed his funds and realized he was in trouble. "I'd squandered two hundred dollars," he says. "I was short two hundred dollars I had to pay for fees back at school. I felt I couldn't go back without the money. I was real desperate. I was too ashamed to ask Arlo Wilson, and I didn't want to let any of the people back at school know what I done. There was too many people out there that thought I was a fool already."

Connie tried to get the money from Fred, who was still writing numbers. But his older brother shook his head. "Man," he said, "not this time of year. I'm cleaned out, too. Christmas and everything busted me."

Then Connie thought of Jack Molinas: "I remembered what he told me about if I ever needed help. How he knew poor kids needed money their first year in school. He was the onliest person I knew who had that kind of money. I had his card in my wallet. I called him and asked for a loan."

Molinas drove to the Hawkins's apartment the day before Connie returned to Iowa. He handed Hawk an envelope containing three new bills: two fifties and a hundred. Connie tried to assure Molinas that the loan would be repaid, but Jack waved his hand. "Take your time," he said. "There's no rush."

Nevertheless, Connie told Fred about the loan and asked him to help repay it. Fred agreed. Hawk, his financial problems solved for the moment, returned to Iowa and his academic problems—which he was never able to solve.

That spring, the Iowa Athletic Department warned Connie—who had been admitted on academic probation—that he would have to do well enough in class to get off probation by the start of his sophomore year. They wanted to give him a regular athletic scholarship. The "paying his own way" scheme would be too risky once Connie stepped into the national spotlight. People would start wondering how a poor kid from Brooklyn managed to travel all the way to Iowa and pay his own tuition.

The problem of getting off probation—this required about a C − or D + average—had never been mentioned when Connie was recruited. But as Hawk found the second-semester courses even more mysterious, the coaches began to worry. "They kept tellin me to work harder," Connie says. "But it wasn't no use. I tried. In that second semester, there were times when I honestly *tried*. I didn't want to flunk out and have people laugh. I wanted to stay and play ball, so I'd be respected. But the readin was killin me."

Nevertheless, Hawkins was too valuable to lose just because of grades. With final exams a few weeks off, the feeling in the Iowa Athletic Department was that "something can be worked out." Then it all changed.

On Thursday, April 27, 1961, Connie was in his dormitory room studying with the tutors. There was a knock on the door. "Coach Scheuerman wants to see you," said a student, breathless from running. "He wants you at his office right away."

"What it about?"

"I don't know." The boy shrugged. "But he says come quick. It's important."

There was a thin, tight-lipped man in a dark suit sitting in Scheuerman's office when Connie arrived at the fieldhouse. The coach's young, boyish face looked drained and worried. "Have you done anything wrong?" he asked, pulling Connie to the side.

"No. What this about?"

"Connie," Scheuerman said, "this is Mr. Bernhard. He's a detective from New York City."

7

THE SCANDAL

"Don't be silly, I'll never do a day in jail.
I'll be with you forever."
—*Jack Molinas*

The basketball scandal was hardly unique. There had been one in 1945 and a massive exposure of corruption in 1951. But most of the fixes had gone undetected. The practice was ancient. Molinas's partner, Joe Hacken, bet on his first crooked basketball game when he was eighteen years old—in 1938.

The nature of college basketball has always made it an ideal target for fixers. It is played nationwide and attracts heavy gambling. Bookmakers use a point spread: a favorite must win by a certain number of points for the better to collect; a bet of an underdog can pay off, without the team actually winning, if the margin of victory is less than the bookie's spread. Kids can be induced to "shave" points even if they will not deliberately lose games. It's almost impossible to tell when a player isn't giving his best. Shots can miss by a fraction of an inch, an opponent can be given an extra step on defense—and no one knows but the fixers. Many times during the 1961 scandal, kids who shaved points were lauded by coaches for courageous play.

Of more importance than this, however, is the climate in which college basketball exists. Since one good player can make a championship team, recruiting is intense and often excessive. Kids are corrupted by coaches and enthusiastic alumni long before they meet the fixers. They come to recognize the fact that they have sold their basketball talents to the college for a price.

In 1951, when only the tip of the iceberg was uncovered, thirty-three players from seven colleges admitted fixing ninety games. Many of these young men wouldn't have been admitted to school if they couldn't play ball. Sherman White, of Long Island University, had recorded two C's, two D's, and an F during six months at Villanova. But he was joyously accepted at LIU, which gave him such trying courses as oil painting, rhythm and dance, and music seminar.

But almost every athlete caught in the 1951 scandal overcame the stigma of the fixes to lead an exemplary life. Today they are teachers, businessmen, social workers—even coaches. There is no evidence they were inherently corrupt young men. But they had been living in a corrupt environment. "Recruiting," said Ralph Beard of Kentucky. "That's the start of it. How they went out and got us to play. It got so big, we got so big. It was all too big."

A few men recognized this. "I was so absorbed in the victory grail I lost sight of the educational purposes of athletics," admitted Coach Clair Bee of LIU. Several schools deemphasized their programs. Most, however, blamed the kids and the gamblers and the permissiveness in society—and went right on commercializing an extra-curricular activity.

These paragons of higher learning couldn't comprehend the basic lesson of college sports: no matter how much money they slipped to a teenager, there was a guy in the street who could slip him more.

The 1961 scandal—which again only scratched the surface—listed forty-seven players and forty-three *known* games. This time twenty-seven schools were involved. As usual, there were some voices for change. Seton Hall's Honey Russell, who had retired in 1959 after decades of coaching, saw two youngsters he'd recruited swept into the scandal. "If it were up to me," he confessed, "I'd demolish the whole system of college athletics. And I'm a guy who has been around it all my life."

But, once more, the majority had other ideas. "We don't intend to do anything different than in the past," said LaSalle's president, Brother Daniel Bernian, "because we don't think we did anything wrong."

One of the fixers was named Ed Bowler. He was a twenty-three-year-old sophomore. He had attended high school at St. Peter's Prep in Jersey City, St. Peter's High on Staten Island, Lincoln High in Jersey City, and Dickinson Evening High. He'd gone to St. Peter's College on a basketball scholarship and left after one month. He'd gone to Virginia Tech on a basketball scholarship, played three varsity games, and dropped out. But LaSalle—Brother Bernian's school—took him with open arms, because Eddie Bowler was a fine basketball player.

It was at LaSalle that Bowler took money to shave points.

Jack Molinas grew up in the Bronx, around 188th Street and the Grand Concourse. Basketball was important there. So was gambling. In the late 40's, the neighborhood bookmaker was Joe Hacken. Kids like Molinas, Joe Green, and Aaron Wagman placed bets with him on the sidewalk outside a candy store near Creston Avenue. Everyone liked Hacken. He is a personable, intelligent man, well-read on many subjects, though predominantly self-taught. He picked up checks even when he couldn't afford to, and sponsored a basketball team called the Hacken AC. Molinas played on the team. Two weeks after City College had won the NCAA championship in 1950, the Hacken AC came within a point of beating them.

Molinas was an honor student at Stuyvesant High, and at 6' 5", one of the best players in the city. Jack's father was a Spanish Jew, who owned a successful business in Coney Island. His values were stringent, uncompromising, of the old world. He believed in hard plodding work and scorned frivolity. Friends recall the day Jack wasn't allowed to play in the championship game of a schoolyard tournament because his father thought he was wasting too much time on basketball.

"Jack got a great scholarship offer from Adolph Rupp at Kentucky," says a former close friend. "He could have gotten big money. But his father made him go to Columbia. After a while Jack rebelled. He tried to do everything the slick way. He knew he was intelligent and he believed he could outsmart anyone."

Molinas led Columbia to the Ivy League title in 1950–51. But the basketball scandals were in full swing, and Jack was shaving points. When the net dropped that spring, however, Molinas went undetected. He went on to become an All-American.

Another who escaped was Joe Hacken. His stepbrother Cornelius Kelleher was nailed for lining up Manhattan College co-captains Henry Poppe and Jack Byrne. But Joey slipped away.

By the time Molinas signed with the Fort Wayne Pistons of the NBA, at the start of the 1953–54 season, his personality was well established. A handsome, charming, guileful young man, he was totally amoral and absolutely convinced he could get away with anything.

Molinas quickly became one of the best rookies in the NBA. Few doubted he would be a superstar. But Molinas was thinking past stardom—to money. Jack had reached the conclusion that several of his Fort Wayne teammates were throwing games. He tried to join the clique, but was rebuffed.

"Don't do anything Jack. Just play ball this season," a pal from the Bronx advised him. "Soon as you're established, they'll have to come to you. It'll be tapouts for the next ten years."

"Sure," said Molinas. "You're right. I'll watch my step."

But Jack couldn't resist an opportunity to make a sharp move. He started betting on the Pistons to win the game *after* he thought his teammates had thrown one. He reasoned that they wouldn't fix two straight and, in fact, would play especially hard to make up for their previous performance.

Word spread through the Bronx that Jack was calling in bets to the candy store on East 188th Street. The Pistons' owner, Fred Zollner, and NBA Commissioner Maurice Podoloff were tipped by New York *Post* sports editor Ike Gellis. When Zollner first questioned Molinas, Jack said, "My mother should die if I'm associated with any gamblers." But the league hired a private investigator. Molinas's long-distance phone calls were checked. There were nine calls to the same number in the Bronx. Jack finally broke down and admitted he'd been betting—but only on the Pistons to win. That was enough for Podoloff. Molinas was suspended from the NBA for life.

Jack took his high I.Q. to Brooklyn Law School. His record there was excellent, and he was accepted by the Committee on Character and Fitness of the Bar Association. In his first year of practice, specializing in accident cases, Molinas earned over $25,000. But that was chickenfeed compared to what he was gambling. Jack had thousands riding every night.

By 1957, Molinas and Hacken were lining up fixed games. It was easy for Jack to meet college athletes, since he was a player-coach in the Eastern League and very active in schoolyard games throughout the city. He wooed youngsters with everything from prostitutes to new furniture to tips on horse races.

Sometimes, when he and Hacken needed additional capital, they "sold" fixed games to gamblers outside the city. These men paid them for the information and sometimes made bets for them. Their best customers were Dave Goldberg and Steve Lekometros of St. Louis.

Joe Green and Aaron Wagman, boyhood friends of Molinas, were also setting up players. But, since they had no money to finance their operations, they went to Molinas and Hacken, who introduced them to Goldberg and Lekometros. Hacken and Molinas got a percentage, plus the information on the fixed games.

Joey, cool and rational, cautioned Molinas to keep the operation small, tidy, and therefore inconspicuous. Jack nodded his head and did just the opposite. He started peddling games to backers in Chicago, Boston, and Pittsburgh. Wagman and Green were also selling games to other backers. The various groups had so many athletes that sometimes players on both sides of the same game were trying to dump.

The fixers were also involved in other sports. Several groups had pro football players doing occasional business. Molinas himself was locked into an AFL team in 1960. There was an eastern basketball referee in the fold, and a couple of whistle-blowers in Texas who were loosely connected to one of the betting groups.

Almost all the fixers had a college football player or two. The men in St. Louis had a southern fullback, who was so dedicated he fumbled four times in one game to keep the spread satisfactory. Molinas hinted broadly that he was working with some people in the NBA.

But the alliances among the fixers were loose and shifting—and it was impossible to know when Molinas was telling the truth. The fixers often tried to doublecross each other.

Jack wasn't content to sell only the fixes he actually had. He constantly touted games that weren't really fixed. He would tell a group of backers that a certain player was dumping. The player might never have seen Molinas, much less known anything about a fix. But Jack calmly demanded money from the gamblers for supplying the "information" and often pocketed additional cash that the backers believed they were sending to the supposedly corrupt athlete. If the game went as hoped, Molinas took credit. If things didn't work out, Jack always had a mouthful of glib excuses.

Molinas was also close to a veteran NFL lineman. They occasionally worked together, conning gamblers into believing that the lineman and some teammates were throwing games. On one occasion, Jack told the potential moneymen that—as proof the fix was in—the lineman would jump offside on the first play of the game prior to the game they planned to dump. There was almost a foulup. The other team jumped offside first. The quick-thinking lineman salvaged the situation, however, by openly punching an opponent on the next play. The backers were convinced. Molinas and the lineman cleaned up. Luckily for both of them, the lineman's team lost the following week, even though he wasn't really dumping.

Jack wasn't always so fortunate. One Sunday he touted a halfback he'd never met. The back proceeded to have the greatest afternoon of his career and trampled the point spread. Afterward Molinas spent several hours looking down a gun barrel—before he managed to talk his way out of trouble.

Jack led a charmed life. Once a Chicago mobster named Tony Dicci caught him touting a phony football fix and summoned him to Miami. "You go down there and they'll kill you," a friend warned.

"Don't worry," said Jack, "I'll talk to them and straighten everything out." They didn't kill him—they just broke his hand with a hammer.

On another occasion, some irate backers dangled Molinas by his legs out the window of a fifteenth-floor hotel-room until he promised to repay the money they'd lost on a game he guaranteed.

In the midst of all this, the unflappable Molinas decided that—as a respected member of the bar, who had lived an exemplary existence since his dismissal by the NBA—he deserved to be reinstated. When the NBA disagreed, Molinas filed a three-million-dollar anti-trust suit in 1960. The NBA, worried about the implications an anti-trust action might have on the reserve clause, offered a small out-of-court settlement. Molinas, ever the optimist, turned it down. He wanted the big money. But he didn't get it. A district judge threw the suit out of court.

Molinas sued the NBA because he needed a large bankroll. Despite the fixes, he was hardly getting rich. A compulsive gambler, Jack couldn't confine himself to betting on fixed games. And even the fixes didn't always work out. Some players got so wrapped up in the game, they forgot to shave points. Others failed to hold down the score even when they tried. One night Hacken and Molinas lost eighty thousand dollars on a game they thought they'd fixed.

Another evening, Hacken thought he had a tapout bet. Joey had three starters working for him. He bet everything he could get his hands on— and lost.

All five starters on the other team were dumping for someone else.

But the fixers made some fabulous killings, and by 1959 bookmakers were getting suspicious. The word went out: "Something's wrong with college basketball again." Law-enforcement agencies, however, came up with little until the fall of 1960. Then they got a break. Aaron Wagman tried to bribe a University of Florida fullback named Jon MacBeth. "Fumble the ball a couple of times," he said, counting out fifteen hundred-dollar bills in Gainesville, Florida. "Just make sure you don't beat Florida State by more than thirteen. There's plenty more where this came from."

"He mentioned other names and other schools," MacBeth said later. "He acted as if this was something they'd been doing right along. I guess there were some guys who took money."

MacBeth informed his coach, who called the cops. Wagman was arrested. A few days later, in Ann Arbor, Michigan, Dave Budin—a former Brooklyn College basketball captain who worked with Hacken and Molinas—was arrested for trying to bribe an Oregon halfback to throw a game to Michigan. Wagman and Budin were released on bail, but detectives of the New York County district attorney's office began to tail them.

For months, crack members of DA Frank Hogan's squad followed the conspirators throughout the country. With wiretaps, hidden cameras, and dogged legwork, they pieced together much of the operation. This information—some of which couldn't be used in court—was valuable in frightening players and fixers into case-breaking confessions.

It was an excellent piece of detective work. But some of the cops profited handsomely. When they learned from wiretaps that certain games were to be fixed, they used the information to place bets for themselves. A couple of times, however, the fixes didn't materialize, and a few detectives lost a bundle.

There was at least one crooked detective in the DA's office. Shortly before Hogan began bringing in players for questioning, this detective tipped off Hacken. Joey instructed Wagman and Green to call the players and tell them not to panic. He reasoned that nothing could be proved if no admissions were made. Every player involved in the fixes was called. No one called Connie Hawkins.

In March of 1961, Hacken and Wagman were arrested. The detectives flew across the country picking up athletes and transporting them to New York for questioning. Despite the advance notice, many youngsters were terrified. Most confessed quickly.

Some detectives who visited campuses were shocked at the reaction of coaches and athletic directors. Few, they recall, expressed sympathy for the players. The majority were angry and felt sold out. None gave any indication that they, as recruiters, might have set the stage for the scandal.

Then there was the southern football coach—notorious, though never exposed, for betting on his team's games—who rushed from the campus when he heard detectives were there. He thought they'd come to arrest him.

Eventually, the gamblers, as well as the players, made confessions. Only Hacken, who is noted for keeping his mouth shut, didn't talk. By the time Hogan closed the case, and a similar probe was concluded in North Carolina, twelve gamblers had been convicted of bribery and conspiracy. The careers of many promising athletes had been ruined.

Several of the best players had been only peripherally involved. Tony Jackson, an All-American at St. John's, was mentioned in an indictment because he failed to report a bribe offer he received over the phone. Jackson said he thought the offer was a joke. North Carolina's star forward Doug Moe was listed as having received seventy-five dollars' expense money from Wagman. Moe had turned down Wagman's offer to fix games, but hadn't reported the bribe attempt—because his best friend, Lou Brown, had set up the meeting. But the hopes of Moe and Jackson to play in the National Basketball Association were dashed.

It took until January of 1962 for the DA's office to arrest Molinas. Despite the other arrests and convictions, Jack thought he was safe. He often boasted—into his tapped office phone—that the "fools" in Hogan's office would never get him.

A New York State law prohibits convictions solely on the testimony of a co-conspirator. All the gamblers were co-conspirators. Thus, unless a player could testify against Molinas (or unless Jack made a confession), he was safe. In every instance but one, Molinas had been careful never to actually mention fixes to athletes; someone like Hacken, Budin, or Wagman always made the approach.

The player Molinas had bribed directly was Billy Reed of Bowling Green. Even this wasn't a clear-cut situation—and Jack was confident he could trust Reed. To ensure the player's silence, however, the cocky Molinas decided to act as Reed's attorney. Hacken urged him to stay away, to hire another lawyer. But Molinas, laughing, ignored him.

In Jack's law office, Molinas gave Reed graphic instructions on how to lie when questioned by the grand jury. This was his undoing. Reed had already agreed to cooperate with Hogan's office. He was carrying a concealed tape-recorder.

The tape was played in court. It opened the way for Aaron Wagman, a co-conspirator, to testify against Molinas. In February, 1963, Jack was convicted of conspiracy, bribery, and subornation of perjury. He spent four years in prison.

Even behind bars, however, Molinas remained the confident, conniving opportunist. He struck up a friendship with a stock swindler, who gave him several excellent tips. Jack passed messages to his broker, via guards and visitors, and wound up making a killing in the market. Today he's out of jail and has latched onto a seemingly appropriate occupation. He's living on the West Coast, producing pornographic movies.

How was Connie Hawkins dragged into the scandal? The DA's office got his name from Dave Budin, the former Brooklyn College player and public school teacher who worked with Molinas. When the detectives arrested Budin in early 1961, he panicked and admitted arranging fixed games. Then Budin tried to save his hide by implicating as many people as he could think of. One of the names he mentioned was Connie Hawkins.

The previous summer Budin had been along when Hacken bankrolled a whorehouse excursion for several players, including Roger Brown. Budin informed the DA that Hacken had told him, "Molinas has Brown and

Hawkins in the bag." That's all. There were no specifics. Budin had never met Hawkins. Hacken now denies mentioning Connie to Budin. But it was enough for the DA's office to dispatch detective Anthony Bernhard to Iowa.

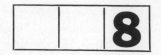

THE INTERMEDIARY

"The DA said Brown got $250 from Hacken for lining up
future prospects, and Hawkins got $210 for introducing a number of
players to Hacken. Iowa announced last week that Hawkins had
quit school 'because of academic and financial difficulties.' "
—*New York* Daily News, *May 25, 1961*

When Connie Hawkins walked into coach Sharm Scheuerman's office that
afternoon of April 27, 1961, he was unaware of the scandal breaking in
New York City. He still didn't know what a point spread was. His biggest
problem appeared to be his upcoming English final. But in the next two
weeks his life was to burst like a shattered eardrum. He would be dragged
down a gantlet of confusion, fear, and desperation. He would admit knowledge of the scandal and participation in the conspiracy, and drown himself
under such a torrent of incriminating statements that it would take eight
years to clear his name.

When Scheuerman told him that Anthony Bernhard was a detective,
Connie was frightened. Ever since he'd watched the men beaten behind
the Eighty-eighth Precinct, Hawkins had been afraid of the police. Now a
cop had come all the way from New York to talk to him. "I didn't know
what to think," he recalls. "But from that moment on, I was scared."

The detective took Connie into another room and closed the door. He
handed him pictures of Hacken and Molinas. "Do you know these men?"
he asked. Connie nodded. He told Bernhard that he knew Molinas from
the schoolyards and had been with him about a dozen times. But he could
identify Hacken's picture only as "Joey." Then Bernhard informed Connie
of the scandal.

Hawkins was confused. The detective, an intense, wiry man, began asking questions, probing for details of Connie's contact with the gamblers,
snapping the words from the corner of his mouth in a heavy New York accent. Hawkins told him about meeting Hacken at Molinas's office, the accident in Jack's car, the small tabs Molinas had picked up, Hacken's request

for introductions to college players, and Molinas's giving Connie and Roger Brown five dollars and ten dollars in "expense money" for playing in tournaments. Bernhard's official notes of that interview also read; "CH again said he never took money for doing anything wrong. Could not believe JM could be involved."

In fact, Connie didn't understand exactly *what* Molinas and Hacken were supposed to have done. "I thought the kid was trying to con me," Bernhard recalls now. "I thought, 'Nobody can be this dumb.' I had to try and explain what a point spread was. But he didn't seem to catch on." The detective's notes contain this shorthand remark in the margin: "Subj. slow to pick up ?'s." Later Bernhard wrote, "Told CH he was being used by JM and JH for intro. to other players for purpose of fix—CH appeared surprised—Asked how it could be done . . ."

The detective questioned Connie for about twenty minutes. Then he said, "I'd like you to come back to New York with me. We want you to help us by testifying about Hacken and Molinas in front of the grand jury." For a moment Connie was speechless. He didn't think Bernhard was saying that *he* had done anything wrong, but he wasn't absolutely sure— and he had no idea what a grand jury was.

"You better ask Coach," Connie said softly.

It was a Thursday, and Bernhard assured Scheuerman that Hawk would be back in school by Monday. The detective knew this was impossible, but he didn't want trouble from the coach. "I explained how Connie was having problems in class," Scheuerman recalls. "The detective told me not to worry, that Connie would only be gone over the weekend."

Hawkins was gone for two weeks. By the time he returned, his life was a shambles.

Bernhard tried to get plane reservations, but a storm had blanketed the Midwest and they were forced to stay in Iowa City for twenty four hours. "I got a hotel room for us and started questioning him hard," the detective says. "We kept going over his story. The kid seemed uncomfortable, but not all that scared yet. At dinner he hit me for two steaks."

Something else happened at dinner: Connie told Bernhard about the two hundred dollar loan from Molinas. "Hawkins volunteered the information," Bernhard remembers. "It didn't seem like he thought it was something he ought to hide." The notes read, "CH stated he borrowed $200 from JM. Said he told JM he needed money [would repay it] CH said he spent $200 given him at school to pay dorm fees when home during holidays Dec. 60."

Bernhard was experienced in sports investigations. Working as an undercover man, he had helped break up the Frankie Carbo boxing mob, had testified before the Kefauver Committee boxing hearings in 1960, and was later to be awarded a commendation for meritorious police work in the basketball probe. He couldn't believe the two hundred dollars was actually a loan. When Connie mentioned it at dinner, the detective slammed his hand on the table and yelled, "Come on, *I'm* not an idiot. Don't give me that shit!"

Connie jumped, startled. "It's true," he said. "It wasn't nothing but a loan."

Bernhard shrugged. There was plenty of time to get the story straight. "I wasn't sure if he was lying," he says now. "The loan business didn't sound right. But the kid seemed too stupid to lie." That night they shared a hotel room. The questioning resumed in the morning. Each time Bernhard went over Connie's relationship with Molinas, Hawk became more uneasy and disoriented. "I still didn't think I was in no trouble," he recalls, "but I didn't understand why he kept asking all those questions and why he wanted me to go back with him."

By the time they left for the airport, Hawkins was so mixed up he neglected to bring any clothing. He spent the next fourteen days in the clothes he wore that night.

During the flight, Connie read comic books and stared out the window. Occasionally Bernhard asked a question. Each time, Connie's story was unchanged. When they arrived in New York, Hawkins thought the detective was going to take him home. "No," Bernhard said casually. "We keep all the players at hotels. It's safer for them."

"I think I'd like to go home."

"Like I said," the detective repeated more forcefully, "we keep *all* the players at hotels."

As they walked from the terminal, Connie paused. "I'm gonna call my mother," he said, "let her know I'm here."

Bernhard shook his head once more. "You better wait till after you're questioned. We prefer you don't make calls."

They took a cab to the Tudor Hotel, an aging building on East Forty-second Street in midtown Manhattan. Bernhard officially placed Connie under protective custody. In the hotel elevator he asked, "Do you know Art Hicks and Hank Gunter?"

"Yeah," Hawk said. "They from Seton Hall. They tried to recruit me there."

"You'll be sharing a room with them upstairs."

"How come they upstairs?"

"They fixed games," said Bernhard.

The queasy sensation in Connie's stomach became more pronounced when he met Hicks and Gunter. The Seton Hall players had already been held for five weeks. They had admitted fixing numerous games and had begun cooperating with the DA. "You better tell everything you know," Hicks warned Connie, who was still trying to figure out what a point spread was. "Don't let them find out for themselves. They don't miss a trick. You better talk."

The DA's office was closed for the weekend. "I stayed in the room with Hicks and Gunter," Connie remembers. "We didn't talk too much. One time they asked me, 'How could a freshman fix games?' I didn't understand what they meant, and they laughed. There was always a detective in the room. He slept there. We couldn't make no phone calls. We watched TV and he took us across the street to eat in this little cafeteria. One night him and another detective took us to a movie on Forty-second Street. A couple of times Bernhard came to talk to me some more."

On Monday morning, April 1, they were awakened early. "Come on," said the detective who had slept in the room. "We go downtown today." Connie was apprehensive, but he assumed this would be the last of it. Some kind of jury wanted him to talk about Molinas. Then he could go back to school, as the detective had promised his coach.

An unmarked car took them to the DA's office in lower Manhattan. "We went up in an elevator and they took us into this large room," Connie says. "There were desks and chairs and a lot of detectives sittin around. Hicks and Gunter knew everybody. They were crackin jokes. I just stood there cause I didn't know what was goin on."

An attractive blonde in a tight skirt wiggled across the room. "Remember her?" Hicks asked Connie. Hawk shook his head. "You *sure* you don't remember her?" Hicks repeated, grinning. "Take another look."

"Man," Connie said, "I don't know who she is. I wouldn't forget something like that." Gunter and Hicks laughed and slapped palms. Later Connie learned that the woman was a prostitute Molinas provided for players who did business with him.

Hawkins was told to sit in a straight-backed chair against a wall. Hicks and Gunter disappeared. Soon other players started arriving with detectives. The room began to look like Riis Beach playground on a Saturday afternoon. Some of the players were tense and frightened; others seemed bewildered; a few were smiling. Then Bernhard arrived and ushered Connie into a small side room. The questioning began once more. But the detective's demeanor had changed. His thin face was grim. "Do you know what perjury is?" he asked Hawkins.

"No."

"Well, it's one to five years. You can lie to me now son, but if you lie when you go in the grand jury, that's perjury. You go to jail for one to five years," Bernhard explained coldly.

Connie didn't understand what Bernhard meant by grand jury or perjury, but he knew what jail was—and he knew the detective was talking about sending *him* there.

"That's when I really started feelin scared," Connie says. "When he said 'jail,' I started feelin shaky. He kept hittin me with questions and writin on this yellow pad. I told him about tryin to call Vinnie Brewer and about all the other stuff I'd told him before. But he kept askin the questions again and again, like he wanted another kind of answer."

Around noon, a detective stuck his head into the room, smiled, and asked what they wanted for lunch. Bernhard relaxed and chatted casually about sports. But when they had finished their sandwiches, the interrogation resumed. The detective was even more demanding, more skeptical. "We must have gone over that story about the loan for at least five hours," Bernhard recalls. "A couple of times I went out and cross-checked with guys who'd questioned Hacken and had taps on Molinas. But I couldn't get anything to contradict Hawkins. And I pressed him pretty hard."

At six o'clock, Bernhard dropped the yellow pad and flexed his shoulders. "That's it for today," he said.

"Now I can go back to school?" Connie asked.

Bernhard shook his head. "You'll have to stay awhile. Your story has to be checked out. Some other people want to talk to you and then you have to testify before the grand jury."

That night, Hawkins, Gunter, and Hicks were moved to another hotel, probably the Prince Edward. When they arrived, Roger Brown was waiting for them. "Hi ex-con," he said, laughing.

"This ain't nothing funny, man," Hawk said. "You wait till they get you downtown."

"What's gonna happen downtown?" Roger asked, his cockiness evaporating.

"You find out," Connie said.

"You damn right you gonna find out," Hicks chuckled.

Brown and Hawkins were placed in a room with a detective. Hicks and Gunter were in another room on the same floor. At 9:30 the next morning they were back at the DA's office. Sometimes Bernhard questioned Connie alone. Sometimes he was joined by other detectives. Their manner was gruff, impatient, disbelieving. They kept talking about perjury and sending people to jail if they lied in the grand jury. And Connie began to realize that they thought he was lying: "They would say, 'Lie and it's one to five years in jail.' I could tell they didn't believe what I was sayin."

The detectives openly challenged him. Soon they were dropping hints as to what they thought he might have overlooked. Hawkins remembers, "They would say things like, 'Didn't you get five hundred dollars for introductions?' or 'Don't give us that crap, that was no loan. Who did you introduce to get that two hundred dollars?' "

That afternoon, Connie saw Roger Brown emerge, weak-kneed and disheveled, from one of the side rooms. Moments later, Bernhard led Hawkins into the same room. Inside were two other detectives. A large man named Frank Marrone questioned him in a powerful, cutting voice. Again, Connie tried to explain that the two hundred dollars was a loan and that he had never introduced anyone to Molinas or Hacken. Marrone shook his head. "Listen, we have yet to prosecute a player who took money in this case. If you are smart, you will get on the bandwagon. Don't wait until it's too late, because one or two of you is going to fall."

Now Connie was terrified.

"You better understand about perjury, too," the detective continued. "I don't care if you lie now, but you lie to the grand jury, that is perjury and you're going to jail. You think it over. Hacken and Molinas used you. They are not your friends."

The detective's notes of this interrogation conclude, "CH tells writer everything I told you is truth—just want to go back to school and play ball."

Connie had been in the DA's custody for six days. Bernhard estimates that he had personally interrogated Hawkins at least twenty times. Hawkins's story was consistent. He had told the detectives about the expense money, the free meals, and the two hundred dollar loan from Molinas. He had mentioned the car he and Roger had borrowed, the unsuccessful phone call to Vinnie Brewer, and the meetings with Joey Hacken.

Bernhard says Hawkins also told him that Joe Hacken had asked if Vinnie Brewer or any other college ballplayers might be interested in making some money. Connie said he had been told he could pick up a few extra bucks by providing introductions. The detective says that Hawk also explained that Hacken said he was starting an all-black team that summer and needed recruits. "My notes were a summary of five hours of questioning that day," Bernhard says, "and I didn't include the stuff about the colored team. Maybe I didn't believe him. But later, Hacken told me that's exactly what he told Hawkins."

Thus, for six days, Connie had insisted that Molinas and Hacken never mentioned fixed games or gambling and that he hadn't introduced any ballplayers to them. Had Hawkins stuck to this story he might have returned to Iowa and gone on to become an All-American. But in the next eight days, his story changed and he buried himself in an avalanche of damaging statements, confessing knowledge of everything but the Great Train Robbery.

The statements Hawkins is alleged to have made in the DA's office between May 3, when his story changed, and May 10, when he testified before the New York County grand jury, are confused and contradictory. The DA actually had nothing to substantiate any of Connie's injurious admissions. There wasn't a single player who said Connie Hawkins introduced him to a gambler. With the exception of informant Dave Budin's vague "in-the-bag" reference, no one ever told the district attorney's office anything damaging to Hawkins—except Connie himself. But that was enough for the DA. Hawkins would be publicly labeled an "intermediary," who introduced gamblers to ballplayers for the purpose of setting up fixed games.

What is Connie supposed to have said? According to notes filed at the DA's office, Hawkins managed four different versions of the only player-gambler "introduction" he was ever to admit. He allegedly told Detective Kenneth Wheaton that he tried to get Colorado's star forward Wilky Gilmore to meet Molinas at a benefit game in Rockville Centre, Long Island, in the summer of 1960. Wheaton's notes read: "Gilmore didn't want to meet him . . ." Later Connie is supposed to have told Detective Joe San Pietro that Molinas asked for the introduction, but that before Connie could reach Gilmore, Jack had already introduced himself.

There is another set of notes on file. Inexplicably, they are unsigned, undated, and written in a handwriting none of the detectives now recognizes. There is reason to believe that two or three other players were being interrogated with Hawkins when these notes were made. But the DA attributes to Connie all the statements in the notes, which include two more versions of the Wilky Gilmore incident.

First they read, "JM asked me if I knew Gilmore. Then would he [Gilmore] be interested in making money? Yes, I introduced them . . ." Subsequently, these same notes contradict themselves, saying, "I told Gilmore do you want to meet Jack. He said 'no.' I told Gilmore JM wanted to talk to him about making money. I told Jack he [Gilmore] didn't want to meet him . . ."

Today, Maurice Wilkins Gilmore is a social worker in Stamford, Connecticut. He says the player who approached him in Rockville Centre was not Connie Hawkins. Gilmore adds that he told the detectives about the incident when he was brought into the DA's office—at the same time Connie was there. "I gave them the name of the guy who did it," Gilmore says. "He came over and asked if I would meet somebody who wanted to talk about shaving points. I told the detectives the player's name. I gave the name in the grand jury. I don't understand how they got the idea it was Connie."

The player named by Gilmore today admits the attempted introduction. He says that he admitted it to the detectives in the DA's office and repeated the admission before the grand jury in 1961. He adds that Connie Hawkins wasn't even at Rockville Centre that night.

Hawkins made other statements to the detectives. According to the DA's records, Connie said at least twice that Hacken told him he bet on games, wanted players to "work for me," and Connie himself could make "five hundred dollars if Vinnie Brewer cooperated." On May 10, the day he went before the grand jury, Connie allegedly informed Detective Joe Nardoza, "JH told me they would get one thousand dollars apiece per game if they would cooperate in shaving points . . ."

Joe Hacken spent 5 years in prison. It is hardly prudent for him to contradict Frank Hogan, the most powerful DA in the country. But Hacken is emphatic in stressing Hawkins's complete innocence. He says he never told Connie anything about his activities—not even that he gambled.

Hacken was trying to clear Hawkins even before Connie's lawyers filed suit against the NBA. In 1965, while a prisoner at Auburn State Prison (and therefore vulnerable to retaliation by the authorities), Hacken sent a message to a prominent New York columnist saying that Hawkins was innocent and that Hacken wanted to be quoted extensively to that effect. The columnist ignored him. A year later, at Wallkill Prison, Hacken signed an affidavit for Connie's lawyers, stating that ". . . I have no information which can in any way connect Cornelius Hawkins to the existence of any conspiracy. . . . As a matter of fact, I definitely know and can absolutely attest to the fact that Hawkins was not involved in any basketball fix conspiracies . . ."

Detective Anthony Bernhard, who honorably resigned from the police department in 1966, offers several reasons why Hacken should be believed. Bernhard has known Hacken since 1958, when the detective infiltrated Frankie Carbo's inner circle and found Joey a fringe character in the boxing mob. "Everybody around Carbo trusted me," Bernhard says. "Everybody talked to me. Everybody but Joey. He was the only guy in that deal who never said anything, because he didn't trust anyone. So when Carbo went under, Joey walked away. There's no way a guy like Hacken would have told a dumb kid like Hawkins anything. How did he know who Hawkins might tell? Of course he was setting him up for fixing later, but he didn't have to tell Hawkins anything then to do that.

"Another thing about Hacken. He won't lie about somebody. That's just

the way he is. If you ask about a kid who was involved, Joey won't bury him; he'll just change the subject. But he says this kid Hawkins really is clean, that he didn't know a thing. And Joey has nothing to gain by saying it. The last thing he needs is the spotlight."

Also in the unsigned, undated notes, Connie is recorded as saying, "I asked Brewer in Iowa at a party if he knew Jack [Molinas] and he said yes. I asked if he was fixing games for Molinas. He said yes . . ."

At the time Connie is supposed to have made this admission, even the DA's people don't appear to have believed it. If they thought there was even a slight chance Hawkins was telling the truth about Brewer, they certainly would have hustled him in from Iowa State for questioning. But they didn't. In fact, they never even contacted Vinnie Brewer. Today Brewer is an instructor with the New York City Youth Board. "We went to a party when I visited Iowa City for the Ohio State–Iowa football game," he says, "but Connie never mentioned Molinas, Hacken, money, or fixes. And that's the only time I saw him out in Iowa."

Then there is the matter of the two hundred dollar loan from Jack Molinas. Even when Connie was admitting everything but the Rape of Lucrece, he clung to his story about the loan as though this was his final link with the truth. On May 10, the day he appeared before the grand jury, Connie made all sorts of wild statements to detective Joe Nardoza. But about the loan, Nardoza's notes read, "I asked Jack could I borrow $200. JM said yes, when did I need it. I said, 'Before I go back to school.' Jack said, 'I'll bring it to your house.' The day I was going back to school JM came to my house. . . . He gave me $200 loan and I told him I would pay it back. He said, 'Don't worry about it, pay it back when you can.' "

Actually, the unsigned, undated notes are the only source for Connie's alleged admission that he received two hundred dollars as anything but a loan. These notes read, "JH gave me 5.00, 200 from JM in my house."

The detectives didn't believe Connie's stories of a loan. His explanations of how it would be repaid were always hazy. But there was a reason for this. Connie's brother Fred, who had promised to repay the loan, was writing numbers. Connie was afraid to tell the police about him.

Today, Fred says that by the time Hawk was picked up at Iowa the two hundred dollars had been repaid. Jack Molinas—on parole and in no position to antagonize the DA—says the same thing. "I never made any approach or gave Hawkins any reason to think games were being fixed or bets were being made," he says. "As far as that two hundred dollars is concerned, Connie called me in December [1960] and said he needed a loan or he couldn't go back to school. I never expected to see the money again.

Then one day, this guy walks into my office and puts two hundred dollars on the desk. He says he's Connie's brother. And that was well before the scandal broke."

Then why did Hawkins incriminate himself? "I was frightened," he says. "I thought they were goin to put me in jail if I didn't say what they wanted." It isn't surprising that Hawkins got this impression. Frank Hogan's detectives are the cream of the New York City police force. They are expert interrogators, who don't need rubber hoses to get teenagers to spill their guts. They created an atmosphere in which giving information against the gamblers—whether true or false—appeared to be the only alternative to prison.

"We didn't inform them of their rights," Bernhard concedes. "We didn't offer them counsel. Hawkins asked if he could call his mother from the hotel. I said I'd prefer he didn't. Actually, we weren't going to let anybody make phone calls until we were all finished questioning them."

Some detectives dispute this. "There was no policy against kids making calls," says one. "The kids I had made calls. I told several to get lawyers before I brought them in. Once kids started cooperating, I even let them out on their own, so they could get laid. Then I'd sit in the hotel room wondering what I'd tell the boss if they didn't come back."

But Connie was not considered "cooperative." Even when he brought his story in line with the detectives' suggestions, he didn't go as far as they wanted. So they helped him along. And Connie wasn't white. Some of the black players are convinced this made a difference, that white players received more sympathetic treatment. "A bunch of us tried to give information on this white player who introduced us all to Molinas," says a black. "He'd told us he fixed games. And he was a big star, man, real big. But the detectives didn't want to hear about it. Every time his name came up, it was like they stopped listening. His name never came out in public."

But many white players also broke. "They want more and more," a youngster was heard shrieking one afternoon, "I give them all I have and they want more!" Another player—a star backcourt man and honor student—became hysterical during an interrogation and had to be carried out. He was later found to be innocent.

The detectives pounded everyone because it was impossible to tell which players were lying. A number of sophisticated but culpable athletes simply refused to admit anything and walked away unscathed. One southerner—who eventually admitted numerous fixes—turned out to be such a compulsive cheat that, while he was still proclaiming his innocence of the dumping charges, he was caught dealing off the bottom of the deck in a card game with other players waiting to be questioned.

The detectives themselves were overworked, rushed, and pressured by their superiors. There wasn't time for extensive cross-checking of players' statements. Thus, at the moment Wilky Gilmore and the player who had tried to introduce him to Jack Molinas were both detailing the incident, Connie was being frightened into his contradictory confessions of the same introduction. "There was total confusion up there," says one detective. "There weren't enough guys to question all those kids properly. We were racing around the country bringing players in. Our guys were exhausted. A lot of them didn't know a damn thing about basketball. You'd be sent in to question a kid you'd never heard of. There wasn't time to do anything but skim the notes and start asking questions. And we were always getting pressed: 'Did you break him? Did you break him yet?' "

Bernhard has no apologies. "We were fighting an evil: organized fixing of college games," he says. "We did our job. We got the big people like Molinas. There were thirteen arrests and thirteen convictions, and we stopped the crooked games. The men I worked with are honorable. If our methods got a kid to make a false confession, I'm sorry, but we had a job to do. And remember, everything we did was legal at the time."

Wilky Gilmore has vivid memories of how the detectives worked. "They gave me the TV treatment," he says. "Once Andreoli [Assistant DA Peter D. Andreoli, who was in charge of the case] questioned me in his little room. There wasn't much light, and they had four or five detectives crowding around me, all smoking. It was a tense scene. Every five minutes this one little guy would say, 'All right, he's lying, let's lock him up as a material witness.' "

A white player recalls that detectives sometimes broke youngsters by pretending to befriend them: "They'd have a 'bad' detective and a 'good' one. The 'bad' guy would scream at you. The 'good' guy would say, 'Let's be patient, I think the boy is really all right.' He'd lull the kid into thinking he was looking out for the player's best interests and wanted to help him. Then he'd get the kid to say what they wanted—for the player's own good, of course."

Because they were frightened, or hoped for special favors, players who were involved in the scandal often exaggerated their stories. "I told them what they wanted to hear," says one. "In the grand jury I said anything that came into my head, things that could never have happened. Later I was told that if I went to see Hacken with a hidden microphone, they'd write a letter to my school exonerating me. I cooperated. But when I went to get the letter, Andreoli said they couldn't put it in writing. He told me to go out and rehabilitate myself!"

For Connie, it was an Orwellian nightmare from which there seemed no awakening. He didn't understand what was happening, why it was happening, or when it would end. Bernhard remembers that even before Hawkins changed his story, Connie was wandering about the DA's office, offering to say whatever was wanted, if they would let him return to school.

Itching and self-conscious in clothes that smelled worse each day, Hawkins became an emotional mashed potato. He has dim recollections of imploring detectives to call his coach, of overhearing a player wailing that he was going to jump out a window, and of waking up one night in the hotel room and thinking that he would never be free. "I could hear Roger and the detective snorin," he says. "And I heard the sounds from the street. I lay there and wondered if I'd ever walk alone down a street again."

Hawkins was the youngest player brought in for questioning. He was kept longer than anyone else who did not admit actually fixing games. His specific recollections are few. They merge in his mind as a whirlpool of fear—at the center a detective's face: disbelieving, threatening, barking the same questions over and over again. "They kept sayin I'd go to jail if I lied," he says. "Then they'd say they thought I was lyin. So I thought I'd go to jail if I didn't tell a different story. And I knew what they wanted me to say. They were always sayin, 'Didn't you get offered five hundred dollars for introducin players?' I decided I'd never get out if I kept tellin the truth."

The saddest aspect of Connie's "confession" is that he thought his whole incriminating story would never be made public. From the beginning, immunity from prosecution was explained to him. But he did not understand what it meant. "I thought it was that whatever you say won't be held against you and you will be cleared," he says. "I thought what I said to the detectives was a secret."

By the time Connie was to go into the grand jury, he was in such a state of panic he couldn't even remember how to ask for immunity. Bernhard recollects one officer, trying to prepare Hawkins, storming out of the room in exasperation, shouting, "How dumb can this kid possibly be? He can't even remember three words!"

Hawkins appeared before the grand jury on May 10, 1961. "I went into Andreoli's office and he read me the questions," Connie recalls. "I don't know if we went over answers, but I remember it was frightenin the way he yelled at me about perjury again. My head was swimmin. In the grand jury I remember being sworn in and all the people looking down at me. I couldn't see no faces. I don't have no idea what I said. I was so scared I could have admitted killing Cock Robin."

His testimony is privileged. But one detective speculates, "If what he told the grand jury is anything like what we have in our notes, the boy must really have buried himself."

On May 23, 1961, the grand jury indicted Joe Hacken. There was one count of conspiracy and seventeen counts of bribery. Fourteen players were mentioned in the indictment. Connie was named in four of the forty-one overt acts in the conspiracy count. Hacken was charged with giving him ten dollars in September, offering him five hundred dollars for introductions in September, meeting with him in December, and—surprisingly—giving him two hundred dollars in December. The two hundred dollars was not described as a loan, and there was no hint that the money had actually come from Molinas. Although no trial had yet been held, DA Frank Hogan told the press that Connie and Roger Brown were "intermediaries" in recruiting prospects for bribe offers.

Hawkins had been a tiny piece of evidence. One of the reasons he was grilled so intensely was that Assistant DA Andreoli had hoped to build such an overwhelming indictment against Hacken that Joey would testify against Molinas in exchange for a lighter sentence. Thus, everything was thrown into the Hacken indictment, even the two hundred dollars Molinas—not Hacken—had loaned to Connie.

But Hacken's reputation for keeping his mouth shut was justified. Joey pleaded guilty to two counts of bribery—neither involving Hawkins—and went to jail without implicating anyone. Hawkins was not among the twenty-two players cited when Molinas was indicted one year later. For Connie, though, the damage had long since been done.

When Hawkins emerged after testifying before the grand jury, an assistant DA handed him a plane ticket to Iowa City and told him he was free to go. "I felt like the whole world had come off my shoulders," Hawk recalls. "I'd survived. I didn't know people were gonna find out what I'd said. I thought my troubles were over."

Coach Sharm Scheuerman was waiting for him at the airport in Iowa City. Hawk assumed they would drive directly to his dorm. But Scheuerman turned his car onto a side road. "He started asking me about the DA's office. When I think back, I have a feeling he'd talked to somebody there," Connie says. "I told him what happened, and how I was glad I was back and everything was O.K. All of a sudden he's tellin me I'm too far behind in my work and there ain't no way I can catch up—and I have to leave school."

At first the coach's words didn't register on Connie. Then he began to beg and weep. "I told him I'd get extra tutors and work day and night to pass. But he said it was best that I drop out. I started to realize it wasn't just the grades, it was what happened in New York. He said droppin out was best for me—and best for the school. I think he mentioned something about havin 'a bad name.' I couldn't believe what was happenin."

Iowa wasted no time. Hawkins's letter of voluntary withdrawal is dated May 10, 1961—the same day he appeared before the grand jury.

9

IOWA POSTSCRIPT

"I have checked his work program thoroughly,
and I have found no irregularity or violations."
—*Forest Evashevski, Iowa Athletic Director*

Connie Hawkins got nothing more from Iowa. But Iowa still wanted something from Connie: complicity in maintaining its fiction of athletic purity.

That summer, while Hawk was moping around Bed-Stuy, wondering if his life was over, Jimmy Breslin, a freelance writer, interviewed him for a story on the basketball scandal. They talked in a bar for over an hour. Hawkins had a few beers, got loose-tongued, and told the journalist about his deal at Iowa. The story appeared the following fall in *Sport* magazine. It wasn't complete or entirely accurate, but it was basically true. The story caused a huge stir in the Midwest. Breslin quoted Connie as saying that the school paid him close to three hundred dollars per month and that "the coach had given me two hundred dollars to pay my dormitory fees." If Hawkins's statements had been substantiated, Iowa would have faced heavy punishment by the Big Ten and the NCAA. But it didn't work out that way.

Bill Reed, the Commissioner of the Big Ten, cleared Iowa on the spot: "We conducted our investigation long before *Sport* magazine came out. I have seen three different investigative reports on Hawkins dating back to early last fall, and all these contradicted the magazine article in regard to his financial support. On the strength of what we have, we do not think it necessary to pursue the article because of contradictory evidence."

Coach Sharm Scheuerman said, "We have not violated any regulations in our recruiting of Connie Hawkins." Iowa's Athletic Director, Forest Evashevski, snidely claimed that Hawkins "left a considerable debt which is being paid by his brother, who feels an obligation to take care of it."

The Iowa protestations were lies. But Connie didn't want more trouble. So he did what most athletes do when they wish they hadn't talked to a sportswriter: he said he'd been misquoted. But this did not close the case.

The NCAA investigated in the spring of 1963. They apparently came up with the real facts.

A formal letter to Iowa outlined the NCAA's charges against the school. "Friends and supporters" of the Athletic Department were accused of providing funds to underwrite Hawkins's education and of giving him money for trips to New York. The NCAA's letter named Arlo Wilson as the man in New York who had paid Connie. They even knew about the money coming through Fred Hawkins, and the two hundred dollar "advance" from Dean Jones.

The Iowa Athletic Department was in hot water up to its shoulder pads. If the NCAA allegations were proven, the school would probably have been put on probation for several years—barred from lucrative bowl-games, postseason tournaments, and television appearances.

So they pressured Connie Hawkins to lie for them in writing.

A handwritten letter, clearing the school of everything but responsibility for the Johnstown Flood, was sent to Connie. The coaches begged him to copy the letter, word for word, in his own handwriting and send it back to them. The letter read, in part:

> I'm sorry my coming to Iowa caused you so many problems, especially since everything was on the up and up. The magazine article probably caused a lot of it, and at that time I was so confused and discouraged I said yes to almost anything they asked. But they twisted a lot of things I said and made them come out different. As you probably know, I have done fairly well the last two years and have all my debts paid at Iowa. Again coach I am sorry for the trouble and hope everything came out O.K. for you.
>
> Yours one on one,
Connie

Apparently this was not enough. The school asked Connie to lie again—and this time to have it notarized. They sent him four pages of typed questions. Recalling his lack of success in the classroom, they also sent four pages of typed answers. All Hawk had to do was sign his name and find a notary public. He did it because they told him they were in trouble and needed his help—and Connie is that kind of person.

Some of the questions and answers went like this:

> Q. Did Coach Scheuerman or any other Iowa official or representative tell you they would provide you with aid even though you were not eligible for it?

A. No, I was told I would have to come on my own the first year, and if my grade point was good enough I would receive some the next year.

Q. When it was taking all the money you could earn and then some to pay your school and living expenses, how did you propose to repay Mr. Jones for this advance?

A. By working for him the following summer.

Q. Why did you drop out of Iowa?

A. I was working too many hours on my job and still couldn't make enough to pay my school and living expenses. This caused me many school problems and I fell quite a way behind plus going into debt.

Q. Have your debts been paid, and if so, by whom and how?

A. Yes, the debts have been paid. My brother sent so much a month, and I repaid him after I started playing professional basketball.

None of this was true. But it must have saved Iowa. The NCAA had caught the school with both hands in the cookie jar, yet Iowa got off with a comparative slap on the wrist. The school was placed on probation for one year, starting in January, 1964. This was a lesser punishment than Yale received six years later for not disciplining a student who followed his religious convictions and went to Israel to compete in the unsanctioned Maccabiah Games. The NCAA listed several reasons for Iowa's probation, but the only violation that related to Connie was Dean Jones's advancing Hawk the two hundred dollars—and this was something Iowa had publicly admitted. The school received no other punishment for its dealings with Hawkins.

A semiliterate eighteen-year-old had been brought to a college where he had no chance of legitimate academic survival. He had been paid to perform his basketball skills—until he found himself in trouble. Then the school's athletic officials suddenly had expressed dissatisfaction with his scholastic inability, about which they had always known. They had abandoned him—until they needed him again, this time to lie to save their necks.

The record isn't very pretty. It makes Coaches Dick Schultz and Sharm Scheuerman seem repugnant. That is one of the many sad ironies of big-time college athletics, for both men are decent, compassionate human beings. A strongly worded letter from Scheuerman, who is no longer coaching, opened the way for Hawkins's first job in pro basketball. Schultz—now Iowa's head coach—and Scheuerman went out of their way to help Connie's lawyers during his case against the NBA. They are not the sort of men who set out to exploit teenagers.

"I don't think Connie had the slightest idea what was going on with those gamblers," Schultz has said. "Here was a young fella, not worldly wise, and whatever his involvement may have been it was strictly unintentional. This was a very naïve eighteen-year-old. I'm positive he didn't know what point-shaving was. He is a real fine young man. I feel sincerely that he has been the victim of circumstances—if not the circumstance of the ghetto, then the circumstance of people who are looking for someone like him to take advantage of."

But Dick Schultz, although he didn't recognize it, was one of those people who took advantage of Connie Hawkins. The gamblers wanted Hawkins because he was in a position to help them. Hawkins was in that position because Arlo Wilson, Dick Schultz, Sharm Scheuerman, and everyone else involved in Iowa's unethical recruiting operation, put him there.

The Iowa coaches were not evil men. Hundreds of other coaches were also after Hawkins. The Iowa people were simply acting in the only manner it is possible to act—and still survive—in the big-time, profit-oriented college sports system. They had to win basketball games to keep their jobs, and to win they needed kids like Connie Hawkins. To get kids like Hawkins, they had to cheat.

10

A CONTRACT FOR THE LEPER

"If we allowed any of these boys to play,
we would be failing the youth of our country."
—*Maurice Podoloff, NBA President, May, 1961*

Connie returned to Brooklyn in the spring of 1961, the stigma of the scandal surrounding him. His name had been in all the newspapers. The *Daily News* even printed his picture in a row of mug shots that included three confessed fixers and Roger Brown. Everyone knew the story he thought would be kept secret, and few bothered to distinguish between intermediaries and dumpers. In Bedford-Stuyvesant, where he had been the neighborhood idol at Christmas, Hawkins was mocked and ostracized: the stupid kid who threw away everything for $210.

"His own people looked down on him; nobody would have anything to do with him," Jackie Jackson recalls bitterly. "They'd say, 'What you gonna do now? You fool, you can't play no more basketball. Why you done such a stupid thing?' "

For weeks, Connie rarely left the apartment. "I was embarrassed and ashamed," he says. "People thought I'd fixed games. I felt like an idiot for gettin into the whole mess. The only ones I tried to explain things to was Ed, Jackie, Fred, and my mother. They all believed me. I remember how my mother said, 'I believe what you say, son. Now don't worry. God will take care of everything.' I cried and cried."

He sat around the house like a zombie, trying not to think or feel, staring for hours at the figures moving on the TV screen, playing solitaire through the night, and avoiding mirrors because he wanted no reminders of his own existence.

For the first time, his sleep was fitful and light. He awakened sweating from a succession of nightmares. "I didn't think about suicide exactly," he says. "But I dreamed about hara-kiri."

One evening he pulled himself together, and called Arlo Wilson, the Iowa recruiter. The year before, Wilson would have done anything to please him. Now Hawkins was a leper. "I begged him to get me back in Iowa or in another school, any school. But he said nothing could be done, my name was blackballed or blacklisted and no school would take me. When I hung up the phone, I thought I was finished, washed up forever. I didn't think of pro ball, or gettin a job, or nothing."

His only escape was the schoolyards. Sometimes, during the day, when the kids were still in school, he took his ball to the deserted courts and shot by himself, drifting into a fantasy world where nothing had changed and he was back at Boys High or an All-American at Iowa. "That was the onliest thing I had goin for me," he says. "But when kids would show up, they'd recognize me and make fun of me. A couple of times I went over to Kingstone Park and people would yell, 'Here come the fixer, here come the crook.' I'd be mad inside, but I'd just walk away."

Connie assumed he was barred from professional basketball. When he heard the scandal discussed on radio and television, it was always mentioned that every player involved in the 1951 fixes had been banned for life by the NBA. Maurice Podoloff, the league president, was making it clear that his policy was unchanged. "I believe," he said of the fixers, "that if we take in any of these boys we'd be lowering the high standards we have set for our players."

Podoloff had been in close contact with the DA's office. On June 15, he met with a representative of DA Frank Hogan. On two other occasions, Detective Bernhard answered calls from Podoloff to Assistant DA Andreoli and wrote meeting dates on Andreoli's note pad.

There had been some question as to how the NBA would deal with players peripherally involved in the scandal: not the fixers, but those who took expense money, didn't report bribe offers—or were intermediaries. The league's position soon became clear. Any taint, no matter how small, doomed the athlete. No player mentioned in any indictment was allowed to sign for the 1961–62 season. Doug Moe, who had already signed with the NBA's Chicago franchise, was told his contract would not be honored, because he had accepted seventy-five dollars for expenses from Aaron Wagman.

There were newspaper reports that several teams had inquired about Connie. Under league rules, Hawkins was automatically ineligible until his class graduated at Iowa. But it was taken for granted in the press, and in basketball circles, that if everyone else whose name had been associated with the scandal was barred, Connie Hawkins was barred also.

Hawkins withdrew more deeply into himself, reluctant even to go to the schoolyards, unable to face anything or anyone. But Eddie Simmons and

Jackie Jackson stood by him. "The man was at the bottom," says Jackson, who now plays with the Harlem Globetrotters. "He didn't have no income, no job, no nothing. Me and Ed was working for the Parks Department that summer. We didn't have much, but we'd come around his house and slip him some bread and try to cheer him up. Hawk told us he didn't do nothing wrong, and we believed him."

Eventually, they convinced Connie to join them in the schoolyards. But there were painful incidents. Several times, just as a pickup game was to begin, someone warned a college player, "That's Connie Hawkins, you better not play with him. You could get in trouble, cause he been in the scandal."

"It was," says Connie, "like livin inside a nightmare."

Eddie Simmons, always the optimist, formed a team to compete in "money games" (both sides put up cash, winner-take-all) and local tournaments. He wanted Jackie, Connie, Bruce Spraggins (who had led the nation in scoring while a teammate of Simmons and Jackson at Virginia Union), and whatever fifth man they could scrounge up. Hawkins was apprehensive at first, but Eddie persuaded him to try. For several weeks they played money games in Brooklyn and Manhattan, and always won without incident. Connie's play was excellent. These were the moments when he could come alive: it wasn't Madison Square Garden, but at least he was playing, doing something.

One Saturday Ed heard some players at a Brooklyn housing project were looking for a high-stakes game. They piled into Spraggins's dilapidated car and drove to the project, where eight blacks were warming up on the outdoor court. As they approached, Ed offered a challenge which was immediately accepted. "Who you got?" asked one of their opponents.

"These my guys," Ed announced, waving his hand. "Where your money?"

The other man stared at Connie. "Ain't that Connie Hawkins?" he said finally.

"Yeah," Ed replied, anger already building in his voice.

"We ain't gonna play against him, man."

"What you talking 'bout?"

"He been in that gamblin fix. We don' want none of that."

"Man," Simmons shouted, "you a chickenshit motherfucker that scared to lose his money!"

"No man, we'll play you. But not with *him.*"

"Fuck you," said Eddie, walking back toward the car. The other players followed. Connie walked with his head bowed. "It ain't cause you was blackballed, Hawk," Simmons stressed. "The guy just don' want to lose his bread."

"Soon as he said, 'Ain't that Connie Hawkins?' I wanted to go back to the car and hide," Connie recalls. "I didn't want to hear the rest."

Soon after, Ed went to Connie's apartment and found him vacantly staring at the television. "Man," said Simmons, "I got us some good news."

"What?" Hawk asked without interest.

"We in the Ruckers baby, I got us in the Rucker Tournament. You, me, Jackie, Bruce . . ."

Hawk shook his head, "They ain't gonna let me play."

"It's all cleared, Hawk. I talked to Mr. Rucker. He say it's O.K. for you to play. We gonna call the team 'Brooklyn.'"

Connie rose and began pacing the room. "Them people all know me. If *they* walk off the court, if they don' wanna play with me, that's it man, I'm all finished."

"Fuck it, Hawk," Eddie said. "We goin. And we playin with you or we ain't playin."

Although Jackie Jackson still had college eligibility remaining, Simmons entered "Brooklyn" in the professional division of the Rucker Tournament. This was the toughest schoolyard competition in the country—and a major social event in the ghetto. Local playground heroes, and pros from the NBA, Eastern League, Globetrotters, and Harlem's numerous touring teams, put their reputations and ambitions on the line each summer weekend to the beat of bongo drums. Crowds of four thousand were not uncommon at the outdoor court on 129th Street. "Everyone was tryin to show up everyone else," Connie recalls. "They'd do their best tricks to make the people applaud. Sometimes the pole holdin up the basket was padded, sometimes it wasn't. Unknown guys was always lookin to rough up the stars, to make a name for themselves. But everybody played, cause it was for your pride."

Hawkins was sure the pros would leave when they saw him at "Brooklyn's" first game. The game, if there was to be one, was against a team of Cal Ramsey, Russ Cunningham, Tom Sanders, Wally Choice—and Wilt Chamberlain. "I was shook," Connie says. "The big fella! I'd idolized him since I was startin in high school. He was a pro. I was sure *he* wouldn't play against me."

But Wilt Chamberlain marches to a beat inaudible to other ears. Team owners, league officials, coaches—even teammates—rarely influence him. Whether its eating pie at halftime, ignoring practice sessions, never learning to shoot fouls, or supporting Richard Nixon, Wilt does as he pleases.

The media regard him as a brooding Goliath, a "loser" whose teams blow the big ones. But in the schoolyard, Chamberlain's size and strength, his scoring records, and his visible affluence (he drives a $27,000 Bentley) cloak him in a special mystique. Even in 1962, other players followed his lead.

"Dipper had no objections to Connie; he didn't say a word about it," recalls Bob McCullough, now director of the tournament. "Once Wilt played against Hawk, that was it. Everybody played. And Connie did real well against Wilt—for a while."

"I was gettin help from the whole team guardin Dipper," Connie says. "I was still too young and out of it to know to be afraid of him. So I was doin fine; scorin and reboundin. Maybe he wasn't really playin hard. Then I got a dumb idea."

During a time-out, with Brooklyn leading by several points, Hawk whispered in Jackie's ear, "Let's show 'em how great you jump. Next time Chamberlain shoot that fadeaway off the backboard, you jump up and trap it." The fadeaway jumper, released after turning toward the baseline, was Wilt's favorite shot in those days. He liked to bank it high off the backboard where it was impossible to reach—unless you happened to be "Jumpin Jackie" Jackson.

Connie overplayed Wilt on defense, giving him an opening toward the baseline. When Chamberlain got the ball, he whirled and lofted a fadeaway. Jackie took a running start at the foul line, went into orbit, and somehow reached the ball just as it hit near the top of the backboard. He pinned it with a loud smack, then came down waving the ball in his hand. The crowd was stunned, then began screaming.

"*I* didn't even know he could jump that great," Connie says. "The ref was so shook he didn't call goal-tending. Four thousand people were yellin and hollerin and dancin around. Then I looked at Dipper. He was just starin down at Jackie. I got a feelin maybe we made a mistake."

Spraggins shot for Brooklyn, and Wilt swatted it away like a man destroying an insect. Ramsey fed Wilt in the low post. Chamberlain turned, bumped Connie out of the way, and smashed in a dunk. The ball came through the hoop, hit the concrete, and almost bounced over the backboard. "I think he did that nine or ten times in a row," Hawkins chuckles. "He just went wild. When other guys on his team took a shot, he'd go up, catch it on the way, and dunk. Jackie kept sayin, '*You* and your motherfuckin ideas!' We must have lost by thirty points. I learned that day—and I'll never forget it, as long as I live—you *never* get Dipper riled."

But it was one of the few games Brooklyn lost that summer. They didn't win the Ruckers, but they came close. In a second meeting with Chamberlain, Connie did nothing specifically to antagonize the giant, but outscored him and hit the winning basket with a twenty-foot jumper at the buzzer. "Hawk was great in the tournament," Bob McCullough remembers. "He was playing against all the best pros, he was the youngest player in the pro division, but he was fabulous.

"At the end of the summer the pros from New York played the pros from Philly. They had Wilt, Hal Greer, Chink Scott, and Guy Rodgers— but Hawk blocked a lot of shots and scored from all over the place, and New York won. One time, Rodgers faked up and Hawk jumped too soon, so he grabbed the rim and hung there till Guy shot. Connie blocked it— while he was still swinging on the rim. It was goal tending, but the fans loved it."

People at the Ruckers were soon echoing a phrase heard repeatedly in the next few years: "One day, Connie Hawkins might be the greatest player who ever lived."

But no glittering future stretched before him. To most, Hawkins was still a leper. Even in many schoolyards, ballplayers feared he would contaminate them. He had no money, no marketable skill other than basketball, and no hope.

Sometimes Hawk, Ed, and Jackie made a few dollars when Simmons booked games for "Brooklyn" outside the city. Ed even arranged a week-long tour in Canada. But more often, they would sit in the Big Apple Bar in Harlem, sharing three drinks for a dollar and hoping a friend would walk in, because they hadn't enough between them to buy another round.

In July, Simmons was invited to bring a team to Kutsher's famed country club in the Catskill Mountains for a game against the club's team, coached by Boston's Red Auerbach. When they arrived, Connie was told he could not play. "Hawk talked us into stayin, cause we needed the money," Jackson recalls. "But it hurt Connie, and it happened all the time. One game in Jersey, the other team found out who he was and walked off at halftime. It ate him up inside. That was the time addicts was comin out heavy in the streets. Everybody in our neighborhood was gettin hooked on dope. Hawk was so depressed, all the people scornin him, it's a wonder *he* didn't become an addict."

It appeared Connie was destined to become part of the grim legion of schoolyard heroes who never escape the ghetto. Basketball stardom brings instant status and—for the fortunate—a college education or even a pro career. But the schoolyard can be a vicious mirage. Thousands spend their adolescence working to become basketball players, dreaming of the day when they will be Wilt Chamberlain or Oscar Robertson. But relatively few make it.

Many don't have the natural ability. Others lack the temperament and drive, the high school diploma, or the luck necessary to emerge from the schoolyards. Most colleges recruit a limited number of blacks. If a player can't make the starting team, he isn't likely to get a scholarship.

Among those who reach college, the dropout rate is appallingly high. Many, like Hawkins, are recruited under false pretenses to schools which offer them no social life or chance of academic success. They return to the ghetto, disillusioned.

The schoolyard player learns quickly that his basketball skills are meaningless when it comes to earning a living. Job questionnaires don't ask about hook shots. The glow of his playground reputation dims with the realization that the game will not lead to a better life.

The next step is often another form of escape: heroin. Many of New York City's greatest schoolyard players have died with needle marks in their arms or are rotting in jail for crimes committed to feed a habit.

But Connie's despair was not to reach such depths. Unknown to him, some curious things were happening in the peculiar little world of pro basketball. Abe Saperstein, the portly son of a London tailor and owner of the enormously lucrative touring black clowns, the Harlem Globetrotters, was in a snit. Abe, it seems, was convinced he'd been double-crossed by his buddies in the NBA. During the league's early days, Saperstein often made schedule shifts to bail out financially distressed franchise-holders. A few sellout crowds, induced by the Trotters' playing a preliminary game, were often the difference between survival and bankruptcy for some NBA teams in the 50's.

Saperstein thought that, as a show of gratitude, he'd been promised the league's first West Coast franchise in Los Angeles. But in 1960, the NBA apparently overlooked its commitment and moved the sagging Minneapolis Lakers to LA. In a fit of pique, Saperstein decided that if the NBA wouldn't let him play in its league, he'd start a league of his own. This temper tantrum wound up costing Saperstein several million dollars. But it was salvation for Connie Hawkins.

Saperstein issued eight franchises stretching from Washington, D.C., to Hawaii, and scheduled play to begin in October, 1961. The Pittsburgh franchise went to a prosperous local family named Litman. Family members owned beer distilleries, bars, and restaurants; there was even a fight promoter and a lawyer in the house.

Lenny Litman, the chunky president of the Pittsburgh Renaissance (known to their handful of fans as Rens) was a quick-dealing nightclub operator, who had booked twist contests and donkey basketball games, and still writes for *Variety*. "I also managed Hoot Gibson, the old movie cowboy, and Lee Powell, the first Lone Ranger," Litman said at the Rens' unveiling. "And I owned a thrill and rodeo show starring Gibson while I was a law student at the University of Pittsburgh. I was trying to produce the show at the same time I was preparing for my bar exams. I failed both." This undoubtedly qualified him for charter membership in the ABL.

One summer day, Alex Medich—chief scout, assistant coach, assistant trainer, equipment manager, and head laundry man in Litman's somewhat limited operation—was diligently keeping the team scrapbook out-of-date when he noticed an item in an old issue of the local paper stating that former Boys High phenom Connie Hawkins had left Iowa. Medich remembered Connie's name from a basketball magazine and tipped off Litman.

A letter was sent to Sharm Scheuerman. On August 16, the Iowa coach replied, "I am happy Hawkins is going to get a chance to show his great ability in pro basketball. He is not the type of boy many people think. He is well respected out here." In a second letter, Scheuerman eased Pittsburgh's fears that they might be tampering with a college player: "Feel free to make any arrangements with Hawkins you might," he wrote, "for there is no possibility of Connie returning to Iowa." The coach sent along a telephone number where Connie could be reached.

"By the end of the summer," Connie says, "I was really desperate. Jackie was goin back to school, Ed had a job and he was gonna play weekends in the Eastern League—and I didn't have nothing. Then, one night, Lenny Litman called and offered me a tryout with Pittsburgh. I was real excited. I wasn't sure I was good enough to play every day with pros, even the ABL, but when he sent me a plane ticket, I went."

Litman met Connie at the Pittsburgh airport and took him to the Webster Hall Hotel. "You've got a private tryout tomorrow morning at 10:00 A.M.," the owner said. "It's at the YMHA down the block. The coach will look you over and decide." Hawk was so nervous he couldn't sleep until well past midnight. This resulted in his sleeping until well past 10:00 A.M. He awakened at noon, convinced his pro career had come to a premature end.

Hawkins racked his brain for an excuse. Then, with some trepidation, he called Litman and said he had gotten lost on his way to the tryout. The owner wondered about this—the YMHA was only one block from Connie's hotel—but he agreed to give Hawkins another trial the next day. This time, Hawk showed up.

The Rens' coach, Neil Johnston, a thin, lantern-jawed, balding, economy-size version of Ichabod Crane, had brought his best forward, Jon Cincebox, from the club's regular preseason practice, to scrimmage against Hawkins. Cincebox, a rugged 6′ 7″, was the Rens' acknowledged "White

Hope." But Connie made him look hopeless. After five minutes, Johnston
—who had coached the Philadelphia Warriors and a fellow named Chamberlain the previous season—turned to Litman and said: "This kid could
be the greatest ever. Sign him."

Litman quickly dispensed with two major hurdles. First, he convinced
Saperstein and the other ABL owners to declare Hawkins a "hardship
case" because he was supporting his blind mother ("What else can he do,"
Litman argued, "drive a garbage truck?"). This permitted Litman to bypass the restriction on signing players whose college class had not graduated.

Then there was the matter of the scandal. Ed Boyle, Allegheny County
DA, called Hogan in New York. Boyle was told only that Hogan had not
arrested or indicted Connie and had no plans to do so in the future. Actually, this was irrelevant, since no players—even those who had admitted
fixing games—had been arrested or indicted. But the ABL needed ballplayers and Saperstein, on the basis of this relatively inconsequential information, gave Pittsburgh clearance to sign Hawkins.

The day after the tryout, Litman took Connie to New York. Hawk
wasn't old enough to sign his contract alone; they needed the signature of
an adult guardian. When their plane stopped in Philadelphia, Litman held
a hurried airport meeting with Kansas All-American Wayne Hightower,
who had dropped out of school. Litman thought Hightower was going to
sign with Pittsburgh. But Hightower had other plans. "The NBA beat you
out," he said.

Litman was stunned. He tried to convince Hightower to change his
mind, but the former Philadelphia high school star cut him short: "I don't
know what you're worried about. You don't need me. You got a whole
team over there." He pointed to where nineteen-year-old Connie Hawkins
was standing by himself, licking an ice cream cone.

"Is he really that good?" Litman asked.

"He's gonna be the greatest," said Hightower.

They left Hightower and flew to New York, then found a reluctant cab
driver to take them to Bedford-Stuyvesant. "His mother was practically
blind," Litman remembers, "so we went to this apartment above a saloon,
knocked on the door, and his brother Fred says, 'Come in.' The brother is
in bed with this wench. They're both naked. He turns over and Connie introduces us. Fred asks Connie if he wants him to sign the contract, and
Connie nods. So Fred signs in the bed without even reading it. We went
back to Connie's mother's apartment. There was no lock on the door, he
just pushed it open. There must have been a hundred trophies in the living

room and a hi-fi—and a bed. It was almost out of Dickens. Connie put the contract down to sign and a roach walked over it."

The contract was for the less-than-princely sum of $6,500. "But I was feelin great," says Hawkins. "I was gettin a chance to play ball. Now, I know it wasn't much money, but I didn't have nothing else goin for me, and shit, they were gonna pay me more than Iowa did."

That night Litman took Hawkins to the Park-Sheraton Hotel in Manhattan. As Litman was registering, he noticed Connie watching over his shoulder. Litman signed his name and then Connie, who had never registered in a hotel before, also signed "Lenny Litman."

They went out to celebrate, and returned at dawn, roaring drunk. Connie seems to have told Litman that he was a karate expert. Litman was understandably skeptical. Whereupon, Hawk's first day as a bona-fide professional athlete ended with him rolling around on the sidewalk in front of the hotel, playfully wrestling with the team president.

11

BOSS MAN IN A BUSH LEAGUE

"We bought jocks by the jock."
—Joe Gordon, General Manager, Pittsburgh Rens

"It's only a baby now, but we're going to nurse it until it grows to be a giant," Abe Saperstein boasted when the American Basketball League set sail in the fall of 1961. By midseason, however, basketball's version of the Ship of Fools was awash in a sea of red ink. Competition was overshadowed by internecine bickering among the owners, folding franchises, bouncing checks, absurd schedule-changes, last-minute cancellations, and microscopic attendance. Turnstiles rusted from inactivity unless Saperstein rushed in his Globetrotters for a preliminary game. Yet even this didn't guarantee interest. In Pittsburgh one night, 13,800 fans turned out. But after the Trotters had played the opening game, half the audience got up and went home.

The league seemed to go out of its way to keep people from taking it seriously. Saperstein, whose Globetrotters already conveyed the image of prearranged entertainment as opposed to legitimate competition, couldn't resist making himself commissioner—after all, it was his league. This created something of a conflict of interest, since Abe was also president of the Chicago franchise. Worse, news slowly leaked out that the ABL had numerous interlocking ownerships. Saperstein, for instance, owned a large chunk of several franchises, including Hawaii, where owner Art Kim was a longtime Saperstein associate.

The ABL was undercapitalized and mismanaged from its inception. Some owners were well-heeled—especially those with the foresight to have rich fathers—but none was willing to make the financial commitment necessary for the league to survive. Some were after a quick killing—Saperstein had enticed them with hints of a national TV contract, which never materialized—while others sought the ego-gratification and public attention that accompanies ownership. They spent with all the largesse of Ebenezer Scrooge.

To save money, traveling squads were cut to eight men (guaranteeing exhausted visiting teams), and clubs were prohibited from taking trainers on the road. Since none of the owners taped his ankles or needed medical attention during games, it didn't bother them that the home team's trainer had to care for both squads.

To juice up the product, referees were instructed to allow almost all body contact short of assault-and-battery. Pro football was the rage, and the owners assumed that if fans were turned on by brutality in shoulder pads, they'd be even more excited by brutality in underwear. Saperstein announced, "We're introducing liberal use of hands on defense, and we're going to make body contact legal in basketball."

This brainstorm resulted in games that bore a striking resemblance to the Battle of Bull Run. "We must have averaged a fight a night," Hawkins recalls. "Everybody played dirty."

Coaches took advantage of the official permissiveness and encouraged their players to rough up opposing stars. Connie, who still looked like an undernourished scarecrow, was a constant target: "They'd open the middle and let me drive. When I went up, two guys would hit me from either side. They tried to elbow you in the ribs or get you in the groin. They wanted to maim you a little and get you out for the night."

To make matters even more chaotic, ABL officials tended to be incompetent and biased. To cut travel costs, the league allowed the home team to select officials in its immediate area. Top referees, however, turned down ABL offers—fearing the loss of more consistent college work—and left Saperstein's league with the dregs. The referees who were available knew they worked solely at the discretion of the home team and bent over backward to make calls in favor of the hosts. Sometimes, when neighboring clubs like Pittsburgh and Cleveland met, there was one official from each team's vicinity. This led to the curious sight of referees working against each other.

ABL refs didn't command a great deal of respect—one had to be admonished for laughing as he walked up and down the court—and coaches spent entire games screaming invective at them. Saperstein never backed up the officials in a dispute. One owner escaped with a reprimand when he trudged into the officials' dressing room after a game and punched a referee in the mouth.

Certain ABL playing facilities made the Black Pit of Calcutta look like a vacation paradise. The Washington team used ancient Uline Arena, rumored to have been erected for James Madison's inauguration. Renovations consisted of renaming it the Washington Coliseum. Games degenerated into Keystone Kops routines when hockey ice, beneath the basketball floor, melted and seeped up through cracks in the wood. Players skidded about like grammar-schoolers at their first skating lesson. After an absurd 65-64 defeat in the opening game at Washington, Chicago protested to the commissioner. This multiplied the league's embarrassment. Commissioner Saperstein owned the Chicago franchise. He never quite ruled on the protest, and Washington never quite got all the water off its court.

When the capital's sports fans stayed away in droves, the franchise was moved to a place called Commack, Long Island. This was supposed to give the ABL a much-needed "showcase" in the media center of New York. But Commack was isolated sixty miles from the city and almost inaccessible without trained Indian guides. The team played in a converted cattle-pavilion called the Commack Arena, which boasted such features as no heat, broken bleachers, warped and cracking floor boards, and the lingering odor of its previous four-legged occupants.

The Los Angeles Jets—supposedly competing with the Lakers—were housed in the Olympic Auditorium. The place is still used for boxing and wrestling matches, but it was too small to hold a regulation basketball court. So the Jets didn't use the regulation court. Ventilation was so inadequate players risked black lung with every breath. The lighting was pre-campfire, the backboards pre-Mayflower, and the showers barely post-McKinley.

Compared to the rancid atmosphere in which games were often played, the quality of ABL competition was surprisingly high. The league offered two interesting innovations. The foul lanes were widened to 18 feet. This opened the middle and reduced the dominance of immobile behemoths. Three points were awarded on shots from more than 25 feet out, which encouraged long-range gunning and added an exciting "home run" to the spectacle. Not long after, the NBA widened its foul lanes from 12 to 16 feet, and years later the American Basketball Association adopted the three-point basket.

The NBA had only nine teams of ten players each in 1961, so there were plenty of capable athletes available. Twenty-one alumni of the ABL went on to play in—or returned to—the NBA. Fourteen others had previous NBA experience. ABL rosters included such names as Dick Barnett, Connie Dierking, Ben Warley, John Barnhill, and Larry Siegfried of Cleveland; Bill Bridges, Larry Staverman, Gene Tormohlen, and Win Wilfong of Kansas City; Ken Sears and Mike Farmer of San Francisco; George Yardley, Hal Lear, Larry Friend, and player-coach Bill Sharman of Los Angeles. The league also admitted several high-quality players who, like Connie, had been barred by the NBA for peripheral contact with a scandal. Tony Jackson, for instance, was with Washington.

But for all the capable professionals and nationally known players, Connie Hawkins, a gawky teenager with no college varsity experience, dominated the ABL. He was competing against adults, always double- or triple-teamed, beaten physically (hip, knee, eye, and elbow injuries, plus a broken finger), and forced to play more minutes than anyone in the league. He suffered from constant colds and flus, had a vitamin deficiency which caused his toes to become infected and his toenails to crack off, and became so fatigued his weight dropped from a skinny 195 to an emaciated 168. Yet Hawkins was the ABL's superstar. He was its leading scorer, top drawing-card, unanimous All-Star selection, and Most Valuable Player. He averaged 27.5 points per game, tied Kansas City's Bill Bridges for the rebounding title, and was fourth in shooting percentage.

In the league's best matchup, Hawkins constantly outplayed Bridges, an ex-University of Kansas All-American who went on to become an NBA All-Star.

One evening, after Connie had scored 49 points against Cleveland and forced three centers to foul out, Dick Barnett, who now stars with the Knicks, told him, "You shouldn't be allowed in this game. You're too good. You should be illegal."

Former St. Louis Hawks' coach Jack McMahon, who coached Kansas City and had a personal animosity for Hawkins, still said, "He's the best player ever to come out of New York City. He needs just a little more weight, but he can play inside, outside, shoot and block shots *à la* Russell."

Pittsburgh's own coach Neil Johnston, a former NBA All-Star center, maintained, "Hawkins would hit the NBA the way Oscar Robertson did. He'd be one of the top ten players right now."

Cleveland owner George Steinbrenner, the heir of a wealthy shipbuilding family, offered to trade his entire championship team for Connie. "Throw in one of your ships," Lenny Litman laughed, "and it's a deal."

The Litmans were the only ABL owners who were neither millionaires nor front men for Saperstein. But they ran the league's most legitimate and professional operation. The Rens played in a new $22,000,000 Civic Auditorium. The players—if not some of the creditors—were always paid on time. Schedules were met, and the team got good radio and television exposure.

Unlike his fellow owners, Lenny Litman was an irrepressible promoter. He went to any lengths to keep the team—and himself—in the newspapers. Before the season, he announced an attempt to sign Jan Kruminisch, who stood 7′ 2″ and had "slingshots for arms." Kruminisch happened to be the starting center for the Soviet Union's Olympic team. Litman said he was offering Kruminisch one thousand dollars a month to play for the Rens as part of a "cultural exchange program." Needless to say, culture took a beating, and Kruminisch never made it to Pittsburgh.

Litman tried to lure the fans with a multitude of extras, including halftime twist contests, indoor soccer matches, and preliminary games involving high schools, grammar schools, disc jockeys, and airline stewardesses.

Unfortunately, nothing could overcome the ABL's overall bush-league image. The Rens never caught on in Pittsburgh. The city's minor-league hockey team outdrew them. No one, however, was absolutely sure what the Rens' attendance was. Litman enthusiastically papered the house with free tickets and never gave out the corrected—and embarrassingly low—crowd figures. The announced attendance was derived by what might be called scoreboard computation. "In the second quarter," Litman recalls, "I'd look at the scoreboard, and if the score was 34-26, I'd tell the sports writers the attendance was 3,426."

With the team always in the red, Litman cut every corner imaginable. Only one gate was opened at the arena, so just one ticket-taker had to be hired. The team practiced at the local YMHA because there was no charge for electricity. Travel was done by car whenever possible. This led to horrendous rides through midwestern snowstorms and guaranteed that Connie never got over the flu. When flights were absolutely necessary, departures from Pittsburgh were made as late in the day as possible so the club wouldn't have to buy the players' lunches.

Joe Gordon—the team's administrative assistant, publicity director, and later general manager—was making all of $100 a week. The players didn't do much better—which explained why, despite all the loud noises, no NBA stars were convinced to jump leagues. Jim Palmer, an NBA jumper, was the Rens' highest-paid player at $10,000. Most of his teammates earned closer to $5,000.

Lenny Litman treated Connie warmly, but at $6,500, Hawk was probably the most underpaid superstar in sports history. With no agent or financial advisor, Hawk signed with Litman the following season for a whopping $7,500. A new car was also guaranteed in his contract. But the club presented it as a "gift" for winning the Most Valuable Player Award. When the ABL folded the next season, after Litman had sold out, Connie discovered that most of the payments had not been made. The car was repossessed.

Lenny left no stone unturned in his search for players. Unfortunately, many of those he came up with belonged under stones. By the time Connie arrived in Pittsburgh for the final phase of the Rens' training camp—at the University of Pittsburgh Pavilion, an obsolete, creaking court beneath a football stadium—Johnston had wrinkled his lengthy beak at over fifty players.

In pro sports, cutting the squad is a traditionally solemn act. Football players speak of "The Turk" knocking on their door. But, with the Rens, the Turk was a Serb and anything but solemn. During the final weeks of training camp, when many marginal players lived in fear of imminent unemployment, Alex Medich, the club's thirty-four-year-old Jack-of-all-trades, carried the message. Instead of calling a player to the side for the usual whispered conversation, Medich marched into the dressing room whistling taps. He walked behind the bench where the athletes were seated, and passed his hand over their heads—playfully pausing, then moving on—until he suddenly dropped his hand on the shoulder of the doomed player.

For variety, Alex placed an empty equipment-bag in the center of the locker room, unsnapped the unfortunate athlete's name tag from his warmup jacket, dropped it into the bag, silently handed him a plane ticket, and walked out, again whistling taps. The secure players thought this was hysterical. The borderline cases hated him.

Connie never feared being cut. But despite his success in the schoolyards, he was surprised to find he was the best player on the team. "Hawk was shy and withdrawn at first," recalls Jim McCoy, a black guard who roomed with Connie that season. "He didn't speak much to the other players. I don't even remember him dunking in the early practices. Then he started coming on. We'd see a great pass here and an impossible shot there, and we knew this guy was gonna be the star."

When Hawk got his professional baptism, during a six-game exhibition series with the Kansas City Steers, coach Jack McMahon decided to find out about Connie. McMahon ordered his boardmen, Bridges and 6' 10" Gene Tormohlen, the ABL's top hatchet man, to give Hawk a brutal going-over. Hawkins spent a week with other people's elbows in his mouth. His legs were bruised, his ribs swollen, and his head blurry.

While his players worked on Connie's body, McMahon did a job on his mind. "You can't play, Hawkins," the combustible Irishman screamed from the bench. "You can't play. *And you don't belong in this league anyway.*"

After several horrendous performances, Connie weathered the indoctrination. "I found I could move quicker than the guys that was beltin me," he says. "And I started hittin back a little. I started gettin my confidence again."

He broke loose for 31 points and several devastating dunks in Warrensburg, Missouri. In the final game of the series at Shawnee Mission, Kansas, Hawk had 18 points, including 4 dunks over Bridges. Then in the closing minutes, Tormohlen and Jim Palmer began trading punches. Players bounded from both benches, flailing at each other and belting a lot of air. Connie, back-pedaling before two Kansas City players, felt someone punch him in the spine. He turned to see Jack McMahon winding up to hit him again. The punch was never thrown. Hawkins landed a solid right hand on the bridge of McMahon's nose. The portly coach staggered backward. Hawk hasn't punched a coach since, but he still savors the moment: "I got him a good one, but the refs broke it up before I could get him again. I don't think he ever forgave me for that. He was cursin me from the bench the rest of the year."

The players who opened the season with the Rens were a peculiar combination of has-beens, maybe-laters, and never-wases. Phil Rollins, a starting guard, had flopped with half the teams in the NBA. His running mate, Bucky Bolyard, was a 5' 11" country boy from West Virginia, who reminded Hawkins of Will Stockdale in *No Time for Sergeants*. Bolyard subsisted on a diet of Clark bars and Cokes. He had an effective outside shot, which was miraculous since he also had a glass eye.

The forwards included rugged 6' 7" Jon Cincebox, who had starred at Syracuse, and George Patterson, who wasn't a very good player, but chased a lot of women. Patterson often stood outside arenas propositioning girls while his teammates were dressing. "He never actually missed a game or nothing," Hawk says, "but he come close a couple of times."

During the season, Pittsburgh picked up former St. John's star Allan Seiden from the Eastern League. The cocky little guard had suffered a damaged knee, and his sole ambition with the Rens was to avoid being cut until he made a trip to Hawaii. "He made it," laughs Connie. "Then he lay out on the beach every day and got so sunburned he could hardly play. As soon as we got back to New York, he quit."

The only other black players on the team were 6' 4" Walt Mangham, an honorable mention All-American at Marquette several years earlier, and 6' 1" Jim McCoy, his college teammate. Both were great leapers and aggressive players, with experience in the National Industrial League. They were five years older than Connie, flashy dressers, and very self-assured. Hawk thought they were good enough to be on the starting team, but neither was popular with Johnston, who complained that their play was undisciplined.

The eight ABL teams were scheduled to play eighty games. The season was split, with divisional winners meeting for a first-half championship. Then the first-half champion was supposed to meet the second-half champion for the ABL title. Cleveland and Kansas City were favored. But Connie led the otherwise undermanned Rens to an early lead in the East. Hawk scored 22 points against Cleveland in the opener, and followed with 27 in 27 minutes against Chicago.

But Connie's emergence as a superstar precipitated a sudden epidemic of righteousness among the league's coaches and owners. Several urged that he be banned because his class at Iowa had not graduated and because of the scandal. They weren't concerned that the ABL had already approved him on both counts or that his presence would aid the entire league by attracting fans. They just wanted him out before he cost their teams some victories.

The Pittsburgh owners were livid. "We're going to fight this," said Lenny's brother, David, the club's attorney. "We got clearance from the league owners and Saperstein before we even negotiated with him."

For Connie, who had been regaining a little self-respect, it was a bad dream revisited. "I was sure they were gonna kick me outta the league," he says. "It didn't seem this thing would ever end."

In the second week of the season, David Litman took Connie to Chicago for a private hearing with Saperstein and the league's attorney, Allan Bloch. "I was scared again," Connie recalls. "David kept tellin me not to worry; everything would be O.K. But I felt like I was goin back to the DA."

David Litman and his wife Roslyn were to become the most important people in Connie's life. It was their lawsuit that eventually cleared his name and forced the NBA to accept him. But at that time—in the fall of 1961—Litman's only interest was keeping Connie with the Rens. David didn't probe Hawk for details of the scandal: "Connie was just a frightened kid. I asked if he'd done anything wrong and he said No. I accepted it. When we met with Saperstein and Bloch, it turned out they weren't so concerned with the scandal or his eligibility as they were with stories that Molinas set up Connie with white women. *That* concerned Saperstein very much."

Saperstein and Bloch questioned Litman, then interrogated Connie. He apparently satisfied them that white womanhood had not been defiled by a black man. Litman was told Hawkins could continue in the league.

Hawkins returned to Pittsburgh to pace a 100-99 victory over Art Kim's Hawaii club. Kim was the owner who had pushed most openly for his ouster. Connie scored 11 of his 20 points in the final quarter as the Rens rallied. Kim sat on the bench cursing and raging at the referees. When Hawaii coach Red Rocha was hit with a technical foul, Kim went berserk. He kicked over seating markers on the floor, tried to dump the bench, and had to be restrained from going into the crowd to fight. "Who's the crazy little Jap?" Rollins asked in the huddle.

"The Hawaii owner," Johnston said disapprovingly.

"They'll kick him out of the league," Rollins predicted.

The prediction was wrong. Kim wasn't even fined, though Saperstein had to suggest that, in the future, he not attack fans.

As the season progressed, Connie's poise and confidence grew rapidly on the court, though he still had trouble with the more cagy veterans—like Chicago's thirty-eight-year-old Sweetwater Clifton, an ex-Knick and ex-Globetrotter—who used their experience to keep Hawk from getting effective position. LeRoy Wright, a 6′ 9″ center who played for Washington, often outsmarted Connie around the basket. "But," says Wright, "you couldn't fool him with the same trick twice. With his long arms and his spring, there wasn't much I could do after a while. Connie Dierking was an NBA center, but he didn't want no part of Hawkins either. Every time we were about to play Pittsburgh, Dierking got an upset stomach."

Despite the tacky surroundings, Connie enjoyed the ABL, especially during the first half of the season, when the Rens battled Cleveland for the championship. In Pittsburgh, people began to recognize him on the street. Kids chased him for autographs. Much to his teammates' dismay, Hawkins even liked the travel. Flying in airplanes and living in hotels was exciting for a nineteen-year-old. Simple luxuries like showers in his hotel room were a vast improvement over life in Bed-Stuy.

During the games, the older players treated him like a superstar. Hawk played center and dominated the Rens' offense. His teammates looked for him in the clutch. Off the court, however, he was treated like any uncertain, laconic teenager who read comic books and *Mad* magazine in the locker room. "Sometimes," Hawk recalls, "they wouldn't even let me go out with them after games on the road. In a lot of places I wasn't old enough to drink."

Mangham and McCoy, his black teammates, invited Hawk to share a small house they found in the Homewood section of Pittsburgh. They became his only close friends on the Rens. "Connie talked so rarely it took us a while to see what a nice kid he was," remembers McCoy, now a probation officer in Pittsburgh. "He didn't know how to act around grownup pros. But he became like a younger brother."

They saw that Hawkins still bore a large residue of pain and apprehension. Hawk was constantly aware that people knew—and discussed behind his back—that he had been "mixed up in the scandal." Around reporters, Connie was polite, but very close-mouthed and wary. There were still long periods when he seemed to lose interest in everything—even himself. "Hawk slept more than any person I ever knew," says McCoy. "We were roommates on the road, and I could never wake him up. It was like he was dead. I'd have to beat on his head. I'd end up packing his bag and plenty of times we still almost missed buses or planes.

"At home, it was like he didn't care about himself. He'd leave his clothes and shoes in the middle of the floor, where he took them off. And he wouldn't concentrate on things. He'd watch television and listen to the radio real loud at the same time. He'd sit up close to the television set and switch the channels every few minutes, never paying attention to what was on. I suppose he was a little hard to live with. But he was such a nice guy —so warm, not cocky or pushy—you overlooked it."

As months passed, Hawkins slowly emerged from his shell. His basketball success nurtured self-confidence in other areas. He became less hesitant to enter teammates' bull sessions. He joked back when players teased him about his funny build. There was even a little ham in him: while still in uniform, Hawk took part in several of the halftime twist exhibitions Lenny Litman staged.

Connie began to socialize more often with McCoy and Mangham—and found that Pittsburgh is an excellent town for a black athlete on the make. To his surprise, he also discovered that he was extremely attractive to women. Even now, Hawk could hardly be described as handsome. But the long, lean body, the enormous hands—and today, his cool, self-assured demeanor and bushy Edwardian sideburns—have a magnetic effect on female eyes.

There was at least one area in which the ABL wasn't bush-league. Its camp followers were as numerous and accessible as those in the NBA. These young ladies come in various shapes, sizes, and colors. The common denominator is that they all have a thing about very tall men, especially basketball players. Many phone the athletes in their rooms, hang around hotel lobbies and bars, or wait outside locker rooms in search of celebrity sex. Some don't have to search. Their names and telephone numbers circulate throughout the league. "If you can't find any action in Hawaii," Bill Bridges told Connie during the first ABL season, "go see the girl at the woodshop at the Hawaiian Village."

A surprising number of these women are almost as interested in basketball as they are in basketball players. A girl in San Francisco can give a thoroughly professional scouting report on every team in the NBA, throwing in such tidbits as personality problems affecting the clubs and a rundown of which players maintain their All-Star status in bed. Another girl in San Diego is so knowledgeable, the players nicknamed her "Coach."

Some women will go for anything in oversized sneakers. Others are more particular. "There was one in Kansas City that liked ballplayers with big asses," Connie recalls. "That left me out. There were some who'd watch games to see which guys had a lot of hair on their bodies, and they'd call 'em in their rooms. I didn't do too well with them either."

Most are loyal to a particular sport. A few, however, have what might be termed seasonal lust. In 1970, there was a good deal of tooth-gnashing among visiting basketball players in Phoenix when a certain young woman switched her interest to baseball during spring training.

Not all set out to be basketball groupies. Some just had a basketball player and discovered they wanted more. While Connie was with the Rens, he picked up a girl in the lobby of the team's LA hotel and took her to his room. An hour later, the young lady marveled for what seemed like the fiftieth time, "God you're so tall!" Then she added innocently, "Did you say there's a whole *team* of basketball players staying here?"

"Yeah," Connie joked, "you want me to get the room list and introduce you around?"

"Could you?" she sighed.

The best partying was still in Pittsburgh. But one evening, in the midst of the frivolity, Connie met a woman who later became his wife. It was not, however, love at first sight. A friend, Sterling Smith, told Connie and Jim McCoy to meet him at a night club. He wanted to introduce them to a pair of sexy sisters. When the players arrived, Sterling pointed to a striking woman with jet-black hair and high cheekbones, sitting at the bar. "That's one of 'em," he said.

Hawkins pondered the situation for about three seconds and announced, "*I'll* take her."

"Not so quick," McCoy cautioned. "Maybe the other one's a pig, and I won't want her. Let's wait."

A few minutes later, another tall, striking woman with black hair and high cheekbones walked in. "That," said Sterling, "is the other one."

"They *both* looked tough," Connie recalls, "but the new one was standin and you could see she was built good, so I told Jim I'd take her. He didn't care."

On the way to McCoy's car, Sterling introduced everyone. "This is Connie Hawkins," he told the girls. "He plays for the Rens."

"Oh, how nice," Connie's choice said sweetly, "you play hockey."

Hawk's ego was punctured. "The one I got is an idiot," he whispered to Jim, as they walked ahead for a moment. "I don't want her no more. Let's switch." Connie got into the back seat of the car. When the girls caught up, one of them slipped in beside him. The Foster sisters were three years apart, but so similar in appearance Hawk didn't realize he was sitting next to the girl he thought he'd discarded.

"Her name was Nancy Foster; her sister was Nadine," Connie says. "We took 'em dancin and out to eat. They ate like cows: pancakes, sausages, shrimps. It must have been two full meals. If Nancy hadn't been so good-lookin I woulda cut her loose. I wasn't makin enough to pay for dates like *that.*

"We kept seein 'em. But I still couldn't tell 'em apart. I'd kiss Nancy hello, and it'd turn out to be Nadine. Then one day I said to Nancy, 'I'm sure glad I got you instead of your dumb sister that thought I was a hockey player.' She laughed, but she didn't say nothing."

Months later, Nancy admitted she was the "dumb sister." By then, Hawk was willing to overlook it. He and Jim were spending a growing amount of time at the Fosters' home, where Nancy, the oldest, was supporting her retarded brother and five younger sisters by working as a cocktail waitress. Connie hardly closed the book on the rest of his social life, but he became increasingly attracted to Nancy.

He married her a year and a half later. "I was travelin with the Globetrotters then," he says. "I was lonely, and I missed her a lot. I thought she'd make a beautiful wife. So I married her. A few years later, McCoy married Nadine."

While they were still single, Hawkins, McCoy, and Mangham threw parties that were notorious throughout Pittsburgh. The night of a game, the women came in droves, sometimes in shifts. "We had some girls that came before the game, to get tickets," Connie explains. "After the game the real parties started. That's when the allnighters came. We had enough broads to invite the other team. Everybody in the ABL loved to play in Pittsburgh."

They immediately loosened things up by pouring grain alcohol—190 proof—into the punch. David Litman and his wife Roslyn were the only members of management who were always invited. "They had lots of beer and lots of ice and lots of punch and lots of girls," Roz remembers. "They ran out of ice, beer, and punch, but they never seemed to run out of girls."

Connie's friendship with Roslyn and David had been building since they accompanied the Rens on a road trip to Detroit, Los Angeles, Hawaii, and San Francisco—and watched Hawk's gallant attempt to carry Pittsburgh to the ABL's first-half championship.

The league's surrealistic schedule had buried the Rens. They were forced to play five games in five nights, then finish the first-half race with eight consecutive road games. Cleveland played seven of its last eight at home.

The Rens began the trip with a one-game lead and—because of Connie
—almost held on. Despite a heavy cold, a bruised hand, and an ankle injury that required cortisone shots and caused him to miss two games,
Hawkins had scoring nights of 47, 42, 35, 31, and 29. The Rens won five of
eight. But Cleveland won all seven home games and took the championship. "Connie tried so hard; it meant so much to him," Roslyn recalls. "On
that trip, we began to feel what a special kid this was."

Roslyn and David were in their thirties. They were younger than the
other Rens owners and mingled more easily with the athletes. They had
met as undergraduates at the University of Pittsburgh, were married while
attending Pittsburgh Law School, and started their own firm. They had already built a highly successful trial practice, specializing in personal-injury
cases.

Mrs. Litman, the product of a rather sheltered Brooklyn Jewish upbring-
ing, is a petite, high-strung, combative, but very feminine woman. In addition to being a top trial lawyer, she now teaches at the University of Pittsburgh Law School, is a gourmet cook, raises three children, works in the
PTA, and is chairman of the Pittsburgh Parking Authority.

Her slender, sandy-haired husband probably represents more liquor li-
censees than any attorney in the state of Pennsylvania. A dogged re-
searcher—which proved invaluable in Connie's suit against the NBA—and
skillful negotiator, David runs the Litmans' sizable law office. He is just as
aggressive and intense as his wife, but more low-keyed.

"We were friendly with a lot of the players," says David. "But that
western trip, I think we were both drawn to Connie. He was totally unsophisticated, but still gracious and considerate. He did little things like remembering to introduce us to his friends."

They were also struck by Hawk's reluctance to hurt others. While the
team was in Detroit a snowstorm hit the city. Connie had only a short rain-
coat. "The coat style in those days was just below the buttocks," David recalls. "My brother Eugene (also an owner) took Connie to a tall men's
store and bought him a heavy overcoat that came down below his knees.
Eugene selected it, and Connie didn't have the heart to tell him it was out
of style. So he kept saying, 'Thank you, thank you,' took it out of the store,
and proceeded never to wear it again."

A friendship was beginning, but its growth would be slow. "Connie was
still distant and withdrawn. He was almost on a different wavelength,"
says Roslyn. "He was so closed into himself, so afraid of being hurt. It was
a long time before he could really trust us."

The Rens did not play well in the second half of the season. They won
and lost in dreary fashion, stayed in contention because no one else in the

East did any better, and finally finished a lackluster third.

Spirit on the team was poor. Some Rens became disgruntled, others apathetic. Connie thinks much of the blame lies with coach Neil Johnston. "The man had absolutely no rapport with the players, even the white guys," Hawk maintains. "He never spoke to us off the court. In training camp, he didn't even bother to find out people's names. He'd just holler, 'Hey you!' "

Johnston was a fourtime All-Star center during his ten years in the NBA. Using a sweeping hook-shot, he led the league in scoring for three straight years while playing with the Warriors. But as Philadelphia's coach he had feuded with his successor, Wilt Chamberlain. "You can't coach a team when one player is given so many privileges," Johnston complained. Shortly thereafter, Johnston was given the privilege of not coaching the team. He quickly signed with Pittsburgh, which was looking for a "name" coach.

"Wilt is hard for anyone to handle, but you could see why it was an impossible job for Johnston," says a former Rens official. "Neil was a shallow, narrow-minded guy who hid his insecurities behind an authoritarian pose. A lot of coaches do that. But the Rens players saw through Johnston. They knew he wasn't a strong person. Toward the end of the season, the team lost all its drive."

The Rens found their coach annoyingly distant. He wasn't shy about berating officials. Sometimes he screamed at players, too, but more often, they got no vibrations from him at all. "At halftime, Johnston wouldn't give us no strategy or tactics," Connie recalls. "He'd come in and say somethin slick like, 'Well, we're thirteen points down. If we can outscore 'em by ten this quarter, we'll be in better shape going into the fourth quarter.' That really fired us up!"

Many players were surprised that Johnston, as an alltime NBA great, didn't attempt to impart more of his alltime greatness to them. "I don't think he tried to help me one bit as a player," Connie says. Hawkins once asked the coach to teach him his renowned hook-shot. Johnston stared at Connie for a moment, then said, "O.K. Watch this." He picked up a basketball and silently tossed in six left-handed hooks. Then, still without saying a word, Johnston walked to the other side of the basket and tossed in six right-handed hooks. "That's how you do it," he said, and walked away.

A super strait-lace, Johnston was devoutly religious and permitted no one around him to curse. When he said, "You freaking guys," the players knew he was furious. On Johnston's list of perils to a ballplayer's life and limb, women rated between bubonic plague and smallpox. "Girls and basketball don't mix," he often said piously. After a road game he invariably announced, "There's a one o'clock curfew and I don't want you guys frigging around with any girls."

Like many coaches (especially in high school and college), Johnston judged his athletes as much by their lifestyle as by their playing ability. His ideal athletes were Bolyard and Rollins: they wore white shirts and ties, didn't like booze, didn't chase women, made great displays of their hustle on the court, hung their heads in appropriate despair when the team lost, and generally fulfilled the role of clean-cut, All-American examples for the nation's youth.

Not surprisingly, Johnston found fault with his three black athletes. It annoyed him when they played their radios in the locker room, chattered after a defeat, or used the profanity which was an integral part of their vocabularies. "He was always lookin at you with his big nose wrinkled up like you'd just farted," Connie remembers. "We felt he was prejudiced."

The racial policies of most professional sports have generally been far more enlightened than those of other American industries. But even today, black players believe they are subjected to both overt and subconscious racism.

The Pittsburgh players felt Johnston restricted the number of blacks on the roster—and on the starting team—and that the coach worked to publicize whites instead of blacks. Johnston did praise Connie in the press, and even defended him against persistent rehashing of the scandal, but, says Jim McCoy, "He treated Hawk like he wasn't a star at all. Johnston had had one black superstar [Chamberlain] who gave him trouble, and he didn't want another one. So he hardly spoke to Connie. He didn't go out of his way to boost Hawk in the papers. White guys got most of the compliments at practice. Unless the team was in trouble, Johnston didn't even push for Connie to get the ball."

Hawk was still too awed by his surroundings to resent the absence of superstar status. But he did wonder why Johnston didn't give the other blacks—especially McCoy—more playing time. "Jim was much better than Rollins and Bolyard, but Johnston wouldn't start him," Connie maintains. "He wouldn't use his best players, cause it meant startin me and McCoy and Mangham. That was too many black guys. Anyway, what about what happened to Eddie Simmons?"

What happened to Simmons, Connie's close friend from Brooklyn, remains Hawk's most bitter memory of the ABL. When injuries reduced the Rens' roster to eight men early in the second half of the 1961–62 season, Hawkins invited Eddie to stay with him in Pittsburgh. Johnston said Simmons could work out with the team. Connie thought Ed was getting a tryout.

Simmons was clearly the best guard on the floor. After years of teaming in the schoolyards, he and Hawkins worked intricate two-man maneuvers like lifelong dance partners. Eddie filled the hoop with long set-shots. The Czar startled unsuspecting Rens with sleight-of-hand passes. Hawk was sure Simmons would be signed.

After the workout, however, Johnston said nothing about a contract. Finally, Hawkins asked the coach what he was waiting for. Johnston shifted uneasily, then mumbled, "This wasn't a tryout, Connie. We haven't got room for another guard. I thought your friend just wanted to practice with us."

Mangham and McCoy laughed when Connie, terribly distressed, told them of the conversation. "What you expect, man?" Mangham said. "You ought to grow up. They don't want any more Negroes on the team."

"They hurt Ed," Hawkins reflects bitterly. "He wanted to play pro ball so bad. But he couldn't get a chance. He'd got his hopes up, he'd proved himself, then they cut him down. I don't think he ever got over it. He started becomin a different person after that. They hurt him just because he was black."

Connie was encountering the quota system. It was widespread in professional sports in 1962, and was another reason why countless schoolyard stars, like Simmons, never escaped the ghetto.

The quota can be a formalized agreement between owner and coach or among the owners themselves. It can even be a specified league policy. More often, it is an unspoken understanding that "too many" black players are bad for business, hurt the team's image, and are "hard to coach." Sports entrepreneurs have always feared that white audiences will not "identify" with black players. In 1961, few pro basketball teams had more than three or four blacks.

"Of course there was a quota," admits a former ABL executive. "It was understood throughout the league. The Pittsburgh players may have thought Johnston was a racist—maybe he was—but he was just doing what every pro coach did. There was a limit—and there always will be, as long as most of the fans are white."

The quota was to become most obvious at the Rens' training camp the following season. Pittsburgh offered tryouts to almost a dozen qualified black players, including Connie's friend "Jumpin Jackie" Jackson. McCoy, Mangham, and Hawkins were still there. But it was soon evident that the team didn't want many blacks.

"They kept white guys that was below mediocre," Connie maintains. "It was ridiculous. Everybody knew it. Some black guys didn't wait to get cut; they quit and went home. Johnston kept people like Bob Weisnhahn, who was so lousy he could hardly shoot a layup without fallin on his ass. But he was real good at wind sprints, so Johnston liked him."

Jackie Jackson was impressive from the first day of camp. No forward could leap with him. "If he hadn't been black he would have made the starting team," says McCoy. As it was, Jackie didn't make the team at all. One afternoon he walked up to Hawkins in the locker room and told him he'd been cut.

"No man, not you Jack. That ain't possible!"

"I ain't shittin you, Hawk," Jackson rasped. "That motherfuckin Johnston cut me. I'm better than any white motherfucker on this team."

"I know," said Connie in confusion.

"You got to do something, Hawk," his friend pleaded. "You got to talk to somebody."

The Litmans had already sold the team. Connie was a superstar, but he knew he had no influence with the new management. "I can't do nothing, Jack," he sighed in shame. "I can't do nothing."

Black-athlete defiance had not reached the clenched-fist stage of Tommie Smith and John Carlos during the 1968 Olympics when Connie was with the Rens. The black players did "do something" to Neil Johnston during the first ABL season, but the moment will never be recalled in the history of the civil-rights struggle.

Mangham, McCoy, and Hawkins were driving to Cleveland in a rented car with Johnston and Bucky Bolyard. They stopped for lunch at a Howard Johnson's. The coach, who was driving, gave the black players a look of obvious displeasure when they topped their meal with second helpings of strawberry shortcake.

Back in the car, McCoy, sitting next to Johnston, flashed a devilish grin and loosed a loud fart. Johnston cast an annoyed glance from the corner of his eye. Then Mangham farted, even louder than McCoy. Johnston shook his head and grumbled, "You freakin guys."

Soon the odor was oppressive. Johnston rolled down his window—just as McCoy fired another booming salvo, followed almost immediately by a similar shot from Mangham. Connie, beside McCoy in the front seat, bit his lip to keep from cracking up. Bolyard, the clean-cut country boy, stared straight ahead, trying to act as though nothing had happened. Mangham farted again.

"Connie," Johnston snapped, "roll down your window." Hawk complied. McCoy farted. Mangham added three quick notes. The car smelled like an overworked outhouse. Johnston clenched his teeth, tightened his hands on the wheel, and glared at the road.

During the final hour of the drive, McCoy and Mangham continued to pepper the air with occasional blasts. And the coach kept mumbling under his breath, "You freakin guys, you freakin guys . . ."

Even then, Johnston got the last word. The Rens lost that night when McCoy missed a driving shot near the buzzer. In the locker room, Johnston trudged up to McCoy and barked, "Do you know why you missed that shot? Do you know why?" Jim shook his head. *"Strawberry shortcake,"* said the coach. "That's why."

While the Rens were sagging in the second half of the ABL's first season, the league itself was coming apart at the seams. The Los Angeles franchise folded. The Washington team evacuated the capital for the uncharted wilds of Commack. And, in Cleveland, there was a little matter of pay. The players weren't getting any.

The Cleveland organization was in disarray. Owner George Steinbrenner was acting out his fantasies by sitting on the bench, shouting at the players, and contradicting coach John McLendon. One evening the Pipers threatened to strike unless they were paid. Steinbrenner was indignant. He grudgingly doled out back wages. Then, in the best tradition of labor relations in professional sports, he proceeded to trade the "troublemakers" and "ringleaders." Coach McLendon objected. Charging front-office interference and sabotage, he resigned.

The ABL, meanwhile, had degenerated into a barnstorming venture, with games in Farrell, Pennsylvania, and Waukegan, Illinois. The schedule changed almost daily, often without the knowledge of the league office. Owners made unilateral decisions as the spirit moved them. Several proclaimed their teams would no longer take the floor if certain referees were assigned.

Not to be outdone, Steinbrenner decided that, since the Los Angeles team had folded, it was too expensive to travel to the West Coast. What about his scheduled games in San Francisco? Let them eat ticket stubs!

And how did San Francisco owner George McKeon respond? He ordered *his* team not to appear at a doubleheader in New Castle, Pennsylvania, sponsored by Cleveland.

Saperstein was unable to keep order. "Some of the things he did were inconceivable," recalls Joe Gordon of the Rens. "The man was a great promoter and a very generous person. But he had no leadership ability. If Lenny Litman talked to him one minute, he'd convince Saperstein to do what he wanted. Twenty minutes later another owner would convince Abe to do the exact opposite. If anybody lost their temper at a league meeting, they had him in their hip pocket."

Throughout the ABL, the ballplayers' most familiar refrain was, "Can we borrow your tape? We forgot ours." In San Francisco one night, Connie recalls, neither team could warm up properly. They had just three basketballs between them.

But Hawkins, still happy to be playing anywhere, ignored the holocaust around him and continued to excel. He was voted the league's Most Valuable Player. "I was amazed," he says. "I didn't feel like no big star. I still felt like a kid. But it gave me a great feeling to be Most Valuable."

He certainly felt better than the Cleveland Pipers did when they won the ABL playoffs, only to discover that the winner's share was identical to the loser's share—nothing.

One player, however, was paid. "I got seventeen dollars for the five games," recalls Dick Barnett. "But I never told anyone about it because I didn't want my teammates to feel bad."

That summer, it was Hawkins who felt bad. The ABL almost died.

At first, there was talk of a merger. Cleveland's Steinbrenner had pulled a minor coup. He somehow got Jerry Lucas, the nation's top college player, to sign with the ABL. In order to capture Lucas as an attraction, the NBA seemed willing to accept one or two ABL teams—possibly a combined franchise.

In the midst of those negotiations, Maurice Podoloff, the NBA commissioner confronted the matter of "tainted" players. Whatever ABL teams joined the NBA, he announced, they must leave their "undesirable" men behind. "We made the ruling before," said Podoloff, "and I see no reason to change it now."

Eugene Litman inquired specifically about Connie. He was told that Hawkins was "tainted" and therefore out of bounds.

Then, for some unexplained reason, Steinbrenner suddenly folded the Cleveland franchise. The entire ABL seemed destined to follow the Pipers into oblivion. "The papers kept sayin the league was gonna fold," Connie recalls. "I knew the NBA wouldn't have me. I worried every day."

But Saperstein managed to salvage the remnants of his once-jaunty dream—by throwing his own money into almost every franchise. Abe put ABL teams in Long Beach and Oakland, California. The Commack club moved to Philadelphia. Kansas City, Chicago, and Pittsburgh held their ground.

The Litmans, however, didn't hold for long. The family had lost close to

$100,000 on the Rens. They wanted out. The team went to training camp only after Saperstein promised to pay the bills. Three days later, Abe changed his mind. With no fresh capital forthcoming, Lenny Litman decided to fold the club.

The Rens were saved by a secret, last-minute deal. Paul Cohen, a wealthy businessman who already owned most of the Philadelphia franchise, became the new owner. Since it would have appeared a trifle awkward if people knew that one man owned two franchises in the same league—and he wasn't even commissioner—a boyish-looking ex-Ivy Leaguer named Bill Rosensohn was brought in as a front man.

Joe Gordon, the Rens' publicist, was named general manager at a whopping $150 a week. His first assignment, on orders from Cohen, was to renegotiate the contracts of every player on the team but Connie and Phil Rollins. The ABL had no minimum wage, and Gordon informed the players that everyone making $7,500 would be cut to $4,500 for the season. If they didn't like it, they could find other work.

That winter, while Connie again dominated the league, he drew closer to Roslyn and David Litman. Hawk, still shy and untrusting with whites, let down his defenses slowly. The Litmans—well-to-do, highly educated, and articulate—had no natural affinity for blacks. But they were relaxed and informal around Connie. He didn't feel they were pushing themselves on him because he was a basketball star.

When their family sold the Rens, Roz and David invited Hawk to their law offices. "They told me they wanted to stay friends," Connie remembers. "I got the feeling they liked me a lot. I think, from way back, I believed what they said.

"It was nice to have important people like them interested in me," he adds. "And I could really enjoy being with them. They never made me feel uncomfortable. They could joke and use profanity and have a lot of fun. They didn't seem shy about takin me to nice places. Later, I even took Roz up to Harlem to watch me play in the Ruckers and over to Brooklyn to meet my mother."

Says David, "Above all, I was struck by Connie's spontaneous kindness and sensitivity. I've never heard him say something truly vicious or intentionally unkind to anyone. He hurts people often—by *forgetting* to do something or by not acting when he should. But he would never *actively* hurt anyone."

They were moved by Hawk's concern for his family in Brooklyn and his halting efforts to send them money. "He wanted to be nice to everyone," Roslyn recalls. "When he came into our office he made a point of stopping at each desk. At the Arena, he knew all the guards and ushers and cleaning men—and he took time to talk with them."

Sometimes Connie invited the Litmans to the Luendi Club, an all-night bar and restaurant, long a meeting place of Pittsburgh's black élite. "When he was with the Rens, he was a big man there," says Roz. "He wasn't just socially acceptable, he was sought after. This pleased him so much. It wasn't being a star, as much as *not* being the dregs. He wasn't just a poor kid from the Bedford-Stuyvesant slums. He was welcome in a place where you were supposed to have class."

As Connie's trust in the Litmans increased, they began to handle his meager affairs: encouraging him to save a little money, putting it away for him, making sure his tax return was filed and his parking tickets paid. This would eventually lead to discussions—at first very casual and cautious— about the scandal and the NBA, and finally years later to the Litmans' decision to sue the league on his behalf.

Undoubtedly Roslyn and David liked their proximity to a star athlete. They enjoyed the evenings they spent with him in ghetto nightclubs. But the friendship—and the sacrifices they were to make for him—remained long after Hawk ceased to be an important name in Pittsburgh.

By December, 1962, Hawk was getting comfortable in his role as star of the Rens. He was again the best player in the ABL, and his social life reflected it. The league, however, was dying.

There had been disquieting rumors for weeks. Attendance had diminished to the point where ushers sometimes outnumbered spectators. In Philadelphia, where the average attendance was 450 for ten dates, three home games drew cozy little audiences of 96, 56, and 52. "Sometimes the players talked about it," Connie recalls, "but I tried to pay it no mind."

The Rens were playing their best ball of the season. On December 30, they defeated Kansas City for their fourth straight win. Connie scored 30 points. He was averaging 27.9 per game.

The following night, Hawk, McCoy, and Mangham were preparing to go out for New Year's Eve when a news bulletin put a damper on the celebration.

The ABL had folded. Saperstein had closed the cash box. Two million apparently was his limit, and he'd lost it. "I think," said Mangham, shaking his head, "we better start lookin for another job."

"I was petrified," Connie recalls. "I didn't know what to do."

The first thing to do was make sure they got their final pay checks. Early January 2, the next banking day, ten members of the elongated unemployed stampeded the Rens' office. "Even Johnston ran in and grabbed his check and raced to the bank to cash it," Gordon remembers. "All the checks were good, but nobody was taking any chances. Then everyone drifted back and just stood around talking. Nobody could believe it. An office girl was crying. The phones were ringing and the players milled about."

Some hoped for tryouts with Eastern League clubs. McCoy and Mangham discussed which NBA camp would be best for them. Rollins talked about a coaching job in Kentucky.

As he listened to the conversations, panic and depression swept over Connie. There was no place for him. "I walked out of there cryin," he says. "I went back to the house and went in my room and cried some more. I felt like my whole career was over. Everything I touched seemed to turn out bad. I didn't know what was gonna become of me."

This time, his depression was short-lived. A few days later, Lenny Litman got a call from Abe Saperstein.

Connie Hawkins became a Harlem Globetrotter.

12

TOMMING FOR ABE

Uncle Tomism: a policy of relationship between whites and
Negroes involving a benevolent but patronizing attitude
on the part of the whites and a willingly
submissive attitude on the part of the Negroes.
—The Random House Dictionary of the English Language

"The Harlem Globetrotters." Connie would whisper the words as the rickety bus rolled across the flat Kansas countryside. In dingy high school locker-rooms he would run his fingers over the blue satin jersey and feel a chill on the back of his neck. The Globetrotters weren't the NBA, but in February of 1963, when Connie joined them, they were—for him—an exciting, dignified alternative.

The Trotters were the best-known athletic team in the world. Since their inception in 1927, they had played in almost every American town large enough to have a basketball court. International tours, feature films, television appearances, command performances before royalty—all had made the Globetrotters a familiar name, even to people who'd never seen a real basketball game. The Trotters were known as the United States' unofficial ambassadors of sport and mirth. Old women in Bedford-Stuyvesant—who thought the Knickerbockers were a beer—recognized the Globetrotters as a black basketball team, the "Clown Princes" of the game.

"When I first got to the Trotters," Connie recalls, "I didn't think it was any kind of demoralization. Man, I thought they were the greatest. In the ABL, when they played the first game, I'd sit in the stands and watch and be amazed. They did things that were fantastic. I was so young and dumb I thought they could do 'em against real pros."

Hawkins spent most of the next four years with the Trotters, all but his first few months with the club's top unit. He made three international tours, visiting Asia, Africa, Europe, and South America. When he left the team in the fall of 1966, he had turned an important corner in the process of growing up. He was more polished, self-confident, and aware of the world around him. On the court, by playing the clowning game, he had acquired many of the colorful, distinctive traits—the one-handed rebounding, the sleight-of-hand drop-passes around the basket—that became his trademark. But Hawk also left with a bitter taste. He was convinced he had been exploited. He worried that his skills were eroding. And he harbored no more illusions about the dignity and glamour of life with the Globetrotters.

The Trotters, Connie found, were hardly aristocrats of the sports world. Shamefully underpaid, cramped into buses with jugglers and one-legged dancers who performed at halftime, bouncing along backroads to make a succession of one-night stands, often subsisting on luncheon meat and tuna fish, the Trotters lived something less than the high life their publicists proclaimed.

"On the road, in the States, we got no meal money," Connie recalls. "In Europe they gave us five dollars a day to eat. Most of the time, that wasn't enough. We'd wind up spending our own money to keep from goin hungry over there—and we were only making one hundred twenty-five dollars a week."

Almost as disappointing was Hawkins's discovery that the Trotters, with a few exceptions, were mediocre ballplayers. They looked great only because the referees and opponents were on owner Abe Saperstein's payroll, and cooperated accordingly.

But it wasn't until several years after Connie left the team that he fully recognized what he now feels is the most distasteful facet of the Globetrotter myth. "What we were doing out there," he says, "was actin like Uncle Toms. Grinnin and smilin and dancin around—that's the way they told us to act, and that's the way a lot of white people like to think we really are."

The Globetrotters' management had successfully depicted the team as a fountainhead of racial justice in sports. Traveling throughout the world, they supposedly symbolized America's commitment to equality and equal opportunity. Abe Saperstein, who founded the club on a shoestring and built it into a million-dollar operation, enjoyed being described as "The Jewish Abe Lincoln." He would have been shocked and heartbroken to hear anyone characterize him as a racist.

In 1927 Saperstein had been a daring liberal simply because he employed black athletes. But when Connie came to the Trotters, it was no longer 1927. Hawk found Saperstein a friend of the black man only in a paternalistic sense. "As long as you played the role of a grateful boy," Connie says, "Abe was good to you. We had a lot of fun together. He was nice to me. But you had to let him know you thought he was great, that he was always right. You had to go along with all his hangups and stereotypes. It was known on the team that the two things that could get you fired quickest was getting caught ownin a Cadillac or being seen with a white woman."

The worst aspect of the Trotters is that they affirm in the minds of whites—particularly youngsters—the stereotype of the black man as lazy, mischievous, and mentally inferior. On the court, the ideal Globetrotter exudes no pride or self-respect. He gallops about with high-stepping strides, loosing shrill jungle sounds, clapping his hands, waving his long arms, and grinning to show his teeth. He is the vaudeville blackface, Stepin Fetchit in jockstrap. He pulls sneaky tricks (like walking with the ball) on the white referee, shows off his athletic prowess, calls his friends by foolish names like "Meadowlark" and "Goose," and gives the impression that he is a devilish adolescent, full of "natural" talent, but in need of mature handling.

To start the show, the Trotters even exhibit their "natural rhythm" to the tune of "Sweet Georgia Brown," gyrating through their famed ballhandling exhibition at the center circle.

In the Globetrotters' successful movie, *Go Man Go*, the most memorable scene was a combination of every caricature of the slothful, stupid, but physically superior Negro. Marques Haynes, the great ballhandler, dribbled around the entire opposing team (white, of course), while his Trotter teammates dozed on the floor. Then Haynes passed the ball to the gangling Goose Tatum, the team's first great clown, who looked up superciliously from the comic book he was reading, picked the ball out of the air with one hand, and flipped it in the basket.

For a long time, however, Connie was proud and happy as a Trotter.

He began with an extra unit Saperstein set up when the ABL folded. The Trotters were so successful they always had two squads on the road. The top, or Eastern, unit played in most of the major cities, appeared in preliminaries to NBA games, was on TV, and—with some additions from the Western unit—made the international tours. The Eastern squad played in a lot of out-of-the-way places as well, but it didn't hit the rock-bottom whistlestops where the Western unit often pitched its tent.

Connie wasn't even on the Western unit. To give a few ABL players a chance to make some money—and seeing a chance to make a bundle himself—Saperstein formed a third Trotter squad that toured with the "ABL Stars," as the former ABL players were called. Connie was placed on this extra Globetrotter team.

Every Trotter performance is built around a chief clown, who usually plays the pivot and controls the ball. On this new squad the clown was J. C. Gipson, an eleven-year veteran. A huge, blubbery teddy-bear of a man, Gipson stood 6' 8", weighed about 260 pounds, and was not among basketball's deepest thinkers. Once, when he and Connie were interviewed on television, Gipson was asked what his initials stood for. He solemnly responded, "The J. stands for J., and the C. stands for C."

At first, Hawkins did little clowning. J. C. Gipson had told him: "Boy, you green. But don't worry. J. C. and Ermer [Ermer Robinson, another Trotter veteran] will take care of the reems [the team's word for gags]. You feel something funny, let it loose. Otherwise just stuff the ball and throw it behind your back."

Saperstein moved Connie to the Eastern unit—the Trotters' big league —in the fall of 1963. Most of the players were veterans, like superclown Meadowlark Lemon; the team's elder statesman, Tex Harrison; ex-Bradley All-American Bobby Joe Mason; and Hubert Ausbie, who had battled Oscar Robertson and Elgin Baylor for the collegiate scoring title when he played at Philander Smith. As a group, they were less sophisticated, affluent, and educated than the men Hawkins would later meet in the NBA. "They were soulful," Hawk fondly recalls. "Just average black people. The ones who'd been to college mostly didn't graduate. Many of 'em hadn't gone to college at all. They didn't try—like some guys in pro ball— to be something they weren't. They were from the ghetto. They'd go to nightclubs and hang out with street people."

Hawkins may have been a superstar in the ABL, but his records and reputation carried no weight with the Trotters' road-hardened veterans. To them, he was still a naïve rookie. Before Hawk became part of the group, they made him the butt of persistent hazing. Harrison and Lemon ordered Connie to carry their suitcases. Veterans sent him out for sandwiches at midnight and constantly took advantage of his still-gullible nature.

As the youngest player on the team, Connie was responsible for the three trick basketballs the Trotters used in their act (one was deflated, another was weighted to bounce crazily like a jumping bean, the third was attached to a string). Early in the tour, Harrison said to Hawk, "You better be careful with the basketballs, ol' dude. People always tryin to steal 'em at night. Then the club'll be in your pocket for one hundred dollars. Take my advice, take 'em to bed with you. Everybody who cares for the balls does that. Keep 'em right in your bed."

Two weeks later Parnell Woods, the team's road manager, noticed Connie sitting bleary-eyed in the locker room. "Hawk," he said, "you look awful tired. You been playin around too much at night?"

"No," Connie said, "it's the balls."

"What are you talkin about?"

"The basketballs. Man, if you move around too much they fall on the floor."

When the older Trotters weren't hazing Connie, they ignored him. On the bus, while the others shouted loudly over high-stake games of Whist and Tonk, Hawk stared out the window. On the court, while his playing skills made him an immediate starter, Hawkins didn't participate in any of the gags or comedy routines. When the other four starters went into a figure-eight passing and cutting maneuver, Connie stood in a corner until the gag was over.

One day, however, Harrison said to him: "Ol' dude, you want to make some extra cash? Get real good at some reems and get in the circle before the game. The guys in the circle get twenty-five dollars extra a night."

As usual, Harrison was kidding. And, as usual, Connie fell for it. He was being paid so little that an additional twenty-five dollars a night sounded like a piece of King Solomon's Mines. He also hoped that his being in the circle might hasten the veterans' acceptance of him—or at least get them to stop treating him like an assistant porter.

In his hotel room at night, Hawk practiced tricks in front of the mirror. For a while, he wasn't very successful. There were complaints from neighboring rooms about basketballs bouncing on the floor at three in the morning.

Weeks later, Hawk announced he was ready. More likely, he just needed twenty-five dollars. Parnell Woods reluctantly gave him a chance.

When the Trotters ran onto the court before a packed house, yelling and clapping their hands, Connie's mouth was so dry that no sounds came out. Lemon rolled the ball down his back, flipped it between his legs, then tossed it to Hawk. Connie froze. For what seemed like minutes he stood motionless, just holding the ball. He could feel thousands of eyes staring at him.

"I was so scared I forgot what I was goin to do," Hawkins recalls. "Meadowlark finally yelled, 'Give it here,' and I passed it to him. All the guys were crackin up, laughin at me all through the warmups. While I was standin in the circle, hearin them laugh, I saw a nail on the floor. I wished it was me, so I could go right through that floor and get away."

"Let's wait awhile before you try *that* again," Woods said sympathetically after the game.

"You're right," Connie conceded. "But at least I get the twenty-five dollars."

"What twenty-five dollars?" Woods asked.

Hawk realized he'd been taken again. "Nothing," he said. "Forget it."

That night, Harrison found him sitting forlornly in the hotel lobby. "You don't have to feel embarrassed, ol' dude," Tex said. "You can practice in the dressing room for a solid year, but everybody freezes the first time they get in the circle."

Connie shook his head. "I made a fool of myself."

"I told you," said Harrison, "*everybody* does it. I'll tell ya, *I* did. Oh yeah, I most certainly did."

Connie looked up, surprised. "You mean it?"

"Sure. And now you got to forget about it. Why don't we find us some broads?"

"In *this* little town?" Connie asked. "Where you gonna find any broads at midnight in this place?"

"Jus' you stick with Ol' Choker Red," Tex laughed. "If there're any broads around here, Ol' Choker'll find 'em."

Tex found them.

From then on, "Choker Red" Harrison took Connie under his wing. Acceptance by the other players followed quickly. Hawk soon felt part of the team.

Several weeks later, after a game in the South, Connie stood alone in front of the Trotters' motel, on the outskirts of town, trying to muster nerve to look for a place to eat dinner. The town was clearly Cracker country. Hawk had never been in the South before. He was afraid he wouldn't be able to tell, until it was too late, which restaurants served blacks and which shot them. Harrison, as always the best-dressed Trotter, slapped Connie on the shoulder. "You gonna stand here all night, ol' dude?"

"I don' know," Hawkins shrugged.

"Come on," Tex laughed. "I'll show you where the service don't include cattle prods." He led Connie to a small diner not far from the motel. While they were eating, Tex smoothed his thick mustache and looked around the near-empty room. "*Somewhere,*" he said, "we got to dig us up some young ladies."

Connie shook his head. "Man, there ain't a broad around here. We ain't got no car. We got no place else to go anyway. What you gonna do, hustle the waitress?"

"Never leave a stone unturned."

"Choker Red! That got to be the fattest, ugliest colored woman I ever seen. What you want with her?"

"Be cool," Harrison said. "When you been on the road long as I have, *then* you give me advice, Hawk."

When the waitress—folds of flab pressing against the neck of her perspiration-drenched uniform—waddled over, Tex began a conversation. Soon, Harrison rose and followed the woman into the kitchen. Connie was too embarrassed to look. But Tex returned, smiling.

"Choker," Connie said. "I'm 'shameda you."

Harrison fixed Hawk with a scornful stare. "We'll see how 'shamed you are, dude. That girl got a couple of friends back there. Thin an' young an' fine. They got a car and nothin to do the rest of the night. All the fat one want to do is watch!"

In most towns, Harrison didn't have to hunt for women. He'd been there before—and they came to him. But for all his nocturnal prowess, Tex was by far the most sophisticated and mature man on the team. One of the few Trotters with a degree, he had graduated from North Carolina College in 1953 and joined the team the same year. At school, Tex had been a roommate of Sam Jones, who later starred with the Boston Celtics. Many thought Harrison's skills once compared favorably to Jones's. Even ten years later, Tex was among the best serious players on the Trotters.

Harrison was also a great clown. But, unlike most of his teammates, he never seemed to lose his dignity, no matter how involved he became with the act.

"Tex had more class than anybody in the organization," Connie says. "He knew *everything* about the Globetrotters: the players, Abe, the secretaries, everyone. And he could tell you everything you needed to know about livin on the road."

"I took a little extra care and interest with Connie," Harrison says today. "Here was this great potential. You could see it all over him. He was so young he didn't fully realize how good he could be on a basketball floor."

While they sat on the bus, Tex would advise Connie, "People will shake your hand every place we go. But be careful. What they like is what they think you *got*. When you get paid, take out some, then send the rest home."

Harrison's advice was always sound. Hawk's execution, however, occasionally left something to be desired. During the next three-and-a-half years, the Litmans received postcards from all over the world with the word "broke" scribbled at the bottom.

"Connie was just an easy-goin kid," says Inman Jackson, an oldtime Trotter star who sometimes traveled with the team as nominal coach. "He didn't take real good care of his money."

One morning in Seattle, Connie reported that someone had stolen three hundred dollars from his room. "Wasn't there two guys in your room yesterday?" Jackson asked.

"They were friends of mine," Hawk said.

"Where you know them from?"

"Oh, right here. I met 'em yesterday."

"How you know they was your friends?"

"They seemed like nice guys."

"And you wonder what happened to your money!" Jackson groaned.

Harrison also warned Connie that stealing was not unheard-of among the Trotters themselves. Again, Hawk found out the hard way. With an amazing run of luck, he won one thousand dollars in a card game. He put the money in his traveling bag on the team bus. Later that day, when Connie checked the bag, the money was gone.

Neither did four years with the Trotters make Connie any more punctual. "Wake up, Hawk," his roommate Hubert Ausbie would yell almost every morning. "The bus about to leave!" He'd drag Connie into a sitting position, pry up one eyelid, and holler again: "Hawk, they say they're gonna leave you this time, man!"

Connie would nod, lie down, and go back to sleep.

Hawkins missed more buses than he did layups. But Harrison couldn't criticize him on that score. Tex and Connie were often out so late the bus had left before they returned to the hotel in the morning. "No problem," Tex would say. "We just rent a car."

Harrison was nevertheless devoted to the Trotters, and deadly serious about his position as team captain and assistant coach. Smooth, articulate, and a consummate diplomat, he labored to minimize the personal friction that inevitably resulted from the fatigue and tedium of the grueling schedule. Primarily, this meant soothing his roommate, Meadowlark Lemon, the best-paid Trotter and the high-strung clown prince of Saperstein's road show.

Lemon was a great comic on the court. He had large hands, long arms, quick reflexes, and no inhibitions. He would do anything to make people laugh. "Lemon gets involved one hundred percent," says Harrison. "He doesn't care if there are five thousand or fifty thousand in the stands. He *believes* he can be great at anything, and he'll do whatever he must to convince you."

Offstage, Lemon—like many top comedians—was not an especially humorous man. In fact, he was often sullen, suspicious, and easily upset. "Lem could be an extrovert," says Harrison. "You could joke with him, but only so far. He had his hangups. He'd lose his temper real fast. He'd forget it the next day, but when Lem got mad, he'd go wild. The time not to bug him was when he was already upset. I tried to teach the young players, Connie in particular, how to get along with him. But Connie had a lot of kid in him. He didn't know how to be diplomatic."

Harrison would warn Hawk, "On the court Meadowlark has to control everything. Look, he *is* the show. You can't do things on your own."

Connie found Lemon edgy and insecure, desperately jealous of the spotlight. "When anybody else got a big laugh," Hawkins says, "Meadowlark would get mad. Right away, he'd try to do something to top it."

One night the Trotters were playing in a small rural high school where a bell rang through the gym every forty-five minutes. "Next time the bell go off," Hubert Ausbie whispered to Connie, "I'm gonna punch you. Fall down." When the bell rang, Ausbie broke into an exaggerated "Ali Shuffle" and loosed a flurry of jabs. Hawk sprawled on the floor. The crowd's laughter increased when Ausbie placed his foot on Connie's chest and yelled, "I'm the greatest!"

They repeated the stunt the following evening, using the timer's horn instead of a bell. The noise had hardly subsided when Lemon rushed over. "Tomorrow," he snapped, "*I* do that reem." Then he glared at Hawk. "And I'm gettin somebody else to fall!"

Lemon was wary of Ausbie. Some Trotters believed Connie's roommate was a superior clown. "Meadowlark had to *work* to be funny." Connie says. "Ausbie was a naturally humorous man. He was lovable and lackadaisical and he always had a smile."

When Lemon was ill, Ausbie took the chief clown role. "The show was great," Hawk says. "Everybody got into the act. Meadowlark was supposed to be out a week. But he came back after three days and played so sick he could hardly stand. He was afraid things were goin too well without him."

Lemon was also sensitive about his playing ability—apparently with good reason. "As a player," says Inman Jackson, "Lemon ain't worth five cents."

Connie, who had thought the Trotters were great athletes, was shocked. "He was quick," Hawk recalls, "but he was a bad ballplayer. A couple of times in New York Lemon tried to get into schoolyard games. They ran him out. He couldn't play serious ball. He'd try the things he did when he was clownin against the Washington Generals. But the guys in the schoolyard weren't paid to make him look good. Lemon would dribble high, exaggerate his fakes, wave his arms and head around, and end up lookin like a fool."

It is probably a measure of the importance Connie places on the level of his own game, the pride he derives from it, and the degree to which it is central to his entire personality, that Hawk finds it difficult to separate his feelings about a man as a basketball player and as a human being. If he believes that an athlete—like Jerry Chambers, later a teammate at Phoenix—is gutless on the court, Connie can't have any regard for him, even outside a basketball context. If Hawk doesn't like "the way a man plays," he usually doesn't like the man.

This is not, however, a matter of looking down on the less skilled. In fact, possibly because Connie struggles to generate such qualities within himself, Hawkins gets rhapsodical when discussing someone—like Dick Van Arsdale or Don Nelson—who compensates for a lack of size or great natural talent by hustle and aggressiveness.

But if Connie thinks a player, particularly a teammate, has an inflated self-image (reflected by overshooting, hogging the ball, or even the manner in which the man carries himself), Hawk tends to dislike him more than might seem justified. Such was the case with Lemon.

Meadowlark, Connie, and Tex sometimes partied together. Usually Hawkins followed Harrison's advice and watched his step. But once Hawk felt secure among his teammates, there were times when he couldn't resist needling, or talking back to, the great clown.

The Trotters were always teasing each other. Lemon was usually immune. One afternoon, however, while they were playing cards, Connie initiated a mocking critique of Meadowlark's playing ability. "You know," he said, "you ain't worth a shit as a ballplayer. You just can't play, man. You got no shot, you can't. . . ."

"Hawkins," Lemon snapped, "you got a big fuckin mouth."

Connie continued his analysis. "You can't jump, I don't think I ever seen you dunk, Lem. . . ."

Lemon sprang to his feet. "We'll see about that," he shouted. "I'm challenging you. One-on-one, man. One-on-one. We'll see what happens!"

Challenging Connie Hawkins one-on-one was like drawing on Marshal Dillon. They went to the gym early and, with mercifully few people watching, played halfcourt for twenty minutes. Hawk won without breaking a sweat.

"That night," Connie chuckles, "Lemon got back by makin me look bad—throwin the ball off my knees, timin his passes so they bounced off my hands. He was a prima donna. He thought everyone should go around tellin him how great he was."

On occasion, Lemon became so angry he went after Connie with blood in his eye. Hawk never shied away. Meadowlark turned out to be one of the few people not confined to a wheelchair that Connie could lick.

In Czechoslovakia, Hawk was having an especially good afternoon. Lemon, playing badly, was in a sour mood. Late in the game, Meadowlark went to the foul line. He had learned several humorous Czech expressions and intended to shout them when the crowd hushed just before his shot.

But as the stadium fell silent, Connie—who was on the bench and didn't know what Lemon planned—ran to the scorers' table and grabbed the scorebook. Hawk held the book over his head, out of reach of the tiny scorer, who stretched ludicrously trying to retrieve it. The spectators howled.

Lemon glared at Hawkins, who was too intent on his own clowning to notice. "Tell him to cut that out when I'm doin my reem," Meadowlark told Harrison.

But Lemon returned to the foul line before Harrison could speak to Connie. Hawk repeated his act with the scorer. Again Lemon's routine was ruined.

Soon after, the Globetrotters walked jauntily to the locker room. Despite Lemon's poor showing, they'd performed well. But Meadowlark was boiling. He looked out at his happy teammates and hissed, "Some of you guys fucked up. We wasn't no good."

Anger rose within Hawkins. "I notice I got more laughs than you Lem," he said with a forced grin.

"Shit Hawkins," shouted Lemon, "you was fuckin up my reems."

Connie still didn't know he'd spoiled Lemon's gag. "Only time we fucked up," he said, "was when you was out there."

Lemon grabbed a metal water-bucket and waved it menacingly: "Say that again and I'm gonna belt you with this fuckin thing."

Hawkins tried to act cool. He ignored Lemon, bent over, and began unlacing his basketball shoes. "Like I said, Lem, we fucked up when *you* was out there."

Lemon rushed at him. Connie looked up just in time to see the bucket heading for his face. He raised his hand, blocked the blow, then wrestled Lemon to the ground. They rolled on the floor, exchanging punches—with Connie doing most of the damage—until teammates dragged them apart.

They fought again in London. Connie had stolen the show by doing pushups on the court, then walking into the stands, finding a seat, and reading the program. But, in the locker room, Lemon berated Hawkins for upstaging him.

"You know something?" Connie finally responded. "You're crazy."

Lemon, standing fifteen feet away, threw a Coke bottle at him. It shattered against a wall, inches from Hawk's head. Then Meadowlark charged. He pinned Hawkins against a row of lockers—not an especially smart move. While Lemon held Hawk around the waist, Connie punched downward, bouncing a succession of blows off Meadowlark's skull.

Lemon was still raging when they were dragged apart. "You gonna get it," he screamed. "I'm gonna get a gun and blow your head off."

"Be careful, boy," Inman Jackson warned later, "Meadowlark crazy enough to do it."

Tex was less concerned. "It'll blow over," he said correctly. "Meadow always forgets real quick. Anyway Hawk, you're in good company. Lem always wanted to fight Chamberlain, when Wilt was travelin with us. One time Lem dove at Wilt's throat. Dipper just caught him in the air. He lifted Meadowlark over his head and held him there till he calmed down."

Despite the sometimes unnecessary altercations with Lemon, Connie Hawkins was growing up. The Litmans could see the changes during his periodic returns to Pittsburgh. "He was much more confident," says Roslyn. "He wasn't as uncomfortable in strange situations. Each time he returned from Europe, he'd picked up some phrases he wasn't afraid to use. In a hotel in New York, the chambermaid spoke to me in what was clearly a European accent. As we were leaving, Connie turned to her and said, 'Good afternoon, it's been nice seeing you,' in Czech. The woman almost fell over. You could see how proud it made him. He would speak a few words to the waiters when we took him to foreign restaurants. He could order food in four or five languages. And his English vocabulary was growing, too."

Connie still spoke slowly, had awful syntax, never read books, thought little about race and politics, and had no aspirations beyond the basketball court. But his horizons had widened. He was building an inner self-assurance that would be vital to him in the years ahead.

In Europe, the team bused from town to town during the day and played in the evenings. There was little time for sightseeing. Most players absorbed nothing more cultural than the local whorehouse. "I don't think they realized what they were being exposed to in Europe," Tex Harrison says. "I'd had a little more schooling, and I knew this was an opportunity most people don't get. I bought some cameras and a couple of dictionaries, and I even got Connie to buy a camera. Then I'd say to Hawk, 'Look here ol' dude, let's look around. It'll be good for you.'"

Connie's international experiences are not to be confused with a year at the Sorbonne, and he wasn't exactly rushing from one museum to another. But just seeing the Colosseum in Rome, finding out that the Leaning Tower really leans, and discovering that Italians' favorite food isn't pizza, took him a long way from Bed-Stuy.

Hawk liked England best of the European countries. *Sometimes* he could even understand what the people were saying—although he refused to believe it was *English*. In Germany, he fell in love with the food. In France, he decided that "French is the sexiest language in the world." One summer, he sent Nancy—who was by then his wife—a picture postcard of

Botticelli's "Birth of Venus" and wrote on the back, "See why I want you to grow your hair long?"

In Europe, for the first time, Hawk didn't feel inhibited by the color of his skin. Sitting with Tex at a sidewalk café in Paris, watching the girls walk past, he tried to explain: "As soon as I got off the plane, man, I felt like this pressure came off me. People treat you different here. Man, they smile at you. Back home I always felt like people were down on me cause I'm colored."

He told Tex about a day in Brooklyn when Billy Cannon had taken him to a pool hall called Spinelli's. Hawk had been the only black man in the room. "Everyone looked up. I could hear them whisperin," Connie said. "I could tell they was talkin about me."

"Ol' dude," Tex chuckled, sipping his cognac, "enjoy it over here. On this side of the ocean—maybe cause we're Trotters—we're kings. Back home, we're still nothing."

Typical of Connie's pleasant memories of life with the Globetrotters is the charity game in Los Angeles against a group of baseball stars when everyone in the locker room was shocked to discover Bo Belinsky didn't wear underpants and even more shocked when he shot the ball like a girl; the morning in London when J. C. Gipson called on the hotel phone and announced: "Wake up Hawk, wake up. We got to go see the Queen at Birmingham Palace"; and later the same day, during very formal introductions, when J. C. grinned at the Duke of Edinburgh and said, "Howdy, Dukie-Dukie."

Then there was the afternoon the meek almost inherited the earth by accident—and very much against their own wishes. The Trotters' publicity flacks billed their traveling opponents as tough pro teams. Actually, the Washington Generals, Atlantic City Seagulls, New York Nationals, or whatever the team called itself that season, were composed of third-rate ex-collegians, headed by little "Red" Klotz, who'd lost his hair sometime in the late 40's when he was a veteran guard with the Baltimore Bullets. The PR copy claimed the opposition had "but one order from the Globetrotters: 'Beat us if you *can!*' " In truth, the order was: "Beat us if you don't feel like working any more."

Occasionally, the straight-men found losing a problem. "Whenever we played near an NBA city," Connie recalls, "the players on Klotz's team tried much harder to be impressive. They were always hoping an NBA team would pick 'em up. The Globetrotters tried harder too. Especially Meadowlark. One game he was takin all kinds of crazy shots, tryin to prove what a great player he was—and missin everything. Meanwhile, the Generals were playin damn good. We were supposed to do five reems in the first quarter and five in the second quarter, but the game was so close we hardly had time for any in the whole first half."

The third quarter was more of the same. The fans, who had come for laughs, not competition, were getting restless. The Trotters began to pull gags, but many wound up with the ball going over to the Generals.

Late in the fourth quarter, the Trotters still trailing by 2, Lemon hurried a pass. It sailed over Hawkins's head, out of bounds. Red Klotz came back with a two-handed set as he crossed midcourt. It was a give-away shot. He never intended it to go in. But it did. Lemon threw the ball away again. Klotz shot from midcourt once more. To his amazement, this too went in. Suddenly the Trotters were in danger of losing, something they hadn't done in over a year.

"You all better start missin," Lemon screamed at Klotz. "You fuckin up the whole show!"

The Generals' players, always the Trotters' punching-bags, relished Lemon's distress. When Meadowlark saw them snickering at him, his rage grew. "You beat us man, and Abe's gonna fire all your motherfuckin asses. You guys better stop fuckin around!"

Klotz, aware that Lemon was telling the truth, took matters into his own hands. The next three times the Generals had the ball, he hurriedly heaved it out of bounds—fifteen feet from his nearest teammate. The Trotters fed Connie, who scored a succession of quick dunks—and another glorious victory was added to the Globetrotters' streak.

Walking off the court, Lemon was still angry: "You fucked everything up, Red."

"What was I supposed to do?" yelled Klotz.

"You was supposed to lose, motherfucker!" Lemon shrieked.

"Shit," snapped Klotz, "if you'd play worth a damn it wouldn't be so hard."

Tex Harrison was primarily responsible for whatever improvements were made in Connie's game during Hawk's years with the Globetrotters. But the first man to help Hawkins when he joined the team was Sweetwater Clifton. Old Sweets had returned to the Trotters when the ABL folded. At Hawk's first Trotter training camp, in Chicago in the fall of 1963, Clifton pulled Connie to the side. He urged Hawkins to handle the basketball almost exclusively with one hand. Previously Connie had palmed the ball on dunks and thrown some flashy one-handed passes. Now Clifton wanted Hawk to carry his physical advantage (eleven inches from pinky to thumb, ten inches from heel of palm to tip of middle finger) as far as it would take him.

"With hands like you got," Sweets said, "you don't have to waste both of 'em holdin the ball. You can control it, pass it, and make your drive all with the one hand. Then you got the other one free to protect yourself. Skinny as you are, you better learn how to keep people offa you."

Today, one-handed ball control is Hawkins's calling card.

Harrison, meanwhile, insisted that some Globetrotter maneuvers could be used effectively in serious competition. "You can catch people by surprise," Tex would say. "They ain't lookin for you to do a reem or take it behind your back or between your legs."

Connie was skeptical. Then he began to find out for himself. He grabbed a rebound against the Generals and dribbled into the forecourt, easily breaking past the last defender. At the foul line he decided to clown. Instead of going straight for the layup, Hawk stopped, threw the ball against the backboard, grabbed the rebound one-handed, and stuffed. Soon, it occurred to him that his hands were large enough and strong enough to take many rebounds one-handed—freeing his other hand to help him maintain position against more meaty opponents.

During a game against real opposition—a group of former college stars—Hawk saw that Tex's "surprise" theory was sometimes workable. Connie and Harrison were playing pattycake, tossing the ball back and forth in the forecourt. Suddenly Hawk faked a one-handed pass toward Tex. His arm followed through but didn't release the ball. The defender lunged toward Harrison and couldn't recover. His legs became tangled as he tried to shift back toward Hawk. Connie dribbled in for an unmolested layup.

"See," Tex laughed as they trotted down court, "that dude was no flunky and the reem worked just fine."

Harrison also tutored Connie in the nuances of getting along with Abe Saperstein. The owner's ego needed constant flattering and reassurance. Tex, the diplomat, knew just what to say.

Intelligent and articulate, Harrison was the closest Trotter to Abe. When the boss went on a private fishing trip, he sometimes took Choker Red along. "Abe was a little fella," Harrison recalls. "I think that's why he got such a kick out of people thinking he was important. The trick was to go along with it." When the Trotters were in Moscow, before Connie joined the team, they were invited to a reception at the Kremlin. Several players arrived before Saperstein. Premier Khrushchev greeted them warmly. Then Abe bustled in and vigorously pumped the premier's hand. "When we got home," Tex says with a smile, "Abe would tell people *he* was the first one to shake Khrushchev's hand. Abe would say, 'Tex, tell 'em who Khrushchev recognized right away. Tell 'em who he wanted to shake hands with first.' And I'd always say, 'You Skip (Abe liked the players to call him Skip). It was you,' and he'd be all smiles.

"We went fishing one time," Harrison continues, "and someone caught a big fish the first day. When we got back to Chicago, Abe told everybody that *he'd* caught the fish. I think he really believed it. I just agreed with him."

A certain shuffling subservience was required of all Trotters. Saperstein, years before, had chosen to put "Harlem" in the Globetrotters' name because he wanted no doubt that the team was black. The fact that the club was based in Chicago, and didn't play a game in Harlem during Abe's lifetime, was irrelevant. Saperstein was selling vaudeville basketball. The team's act was created at a time when Stepin Fetchit and Lightning were "Yes-ma'aming" Shirley Temple. Years later, Abe saw no reason to change it. The athletes understood their role—on and off the court.

Saperstein had a genuine affection for many players. They were his children, his boys. If they behaved, he responded with effusive paternalism (except when it came to paying them). He found jobs for many faithful Trotters when their playing days were over. He was quick to reward a good performance with a few bills.

Connie got his first glimpse of all this at training camp when Saperstein decided to "show you Oscars some basketball." Abe rolled up his sleeves and trudged to the foul line. Ernie Jones, a 6' 10" center, was ordered to guard him. "Watch," Saperstein said, "I'm gonna show you how to protect the ball. Inman, throw it over here."

Jackson's toss hit Saperstein's hands and bounced off his stomach. A rookie snickered. The veterans, straight-faced and silent, glared at the newcomer. Jackson hurriedly retrieved the ball. He walked to Saperstein and handed it to him.

"O.K.," said Abe, dropping into a semicrouch and holding the ball at arm's length in front of him. "This is how you protect it in the pivot. Ernie, try and take it away from me."

Jones towered more than a foot and a half above Saperstein. He could easily have leaned over and batted the ball from his boss's pudgy fingers. Instead, Jones leaned backward from the waist, as though attempting to Limbo. When his shoulders were as far from Abe as he could get without falling down, Jones reached forward tentatively. Once assured he couldn't reach the ball, he pawed awkwardly and cried, "I can't touch it Skip. I can't touch it!"

"See!" said Saperstein.

When the team was in France, Abe cornered Connie in a hotel lobby and stretched to slap him on the back. "I hear you like ice cream," he said.

"Sure Skip."

"Well, you haven't tasted ice cream till you've tried *real French* ice cream. I'm gonna show you what it's like."

He led Connie to a small store. Inside, Abe whispered, "I'll order in French. That way we're sure to get the best."

For several minutes, Abe addressed a portly woman behind the counter. While Saperstein gestured wildly, the woman stared at him with a blank expression. Occasionally she said, *"Qu'est-ce que c'est?"*

"Damn Frenchmen," Abe grumbled to Connie. "They don't even know how to speak *French!*"

Finally Saperstein shouted, "Vanilla ice cream, please!" The woman smiled and handed Abe two vanilla cones.

"Isn't that the finest you ever tasted?" the boss asked.

As far as Connie was concerned, it tasted like the Borden's he ate in Brooklyn. But he nodded his head with vigor and said, "Sure Skip. This stuff is great. I never tasted better." Abe laughed heartily and slapped him on the back again.

Saperstein continuously reminded the Trotters of his prowess as a cardsharp. Tonk and Whist were considered "colored games," but Abe was convinced he could beat any "Oscars" in his employ. "One time, in France," Connie recalls, "me and J. C. Gipson gave Abe and Tex an awful beatin at Whist, while we were riding on the bus. We were laughin and teasin and harassin him.

"That night we played a real good game, by Globetrotter standards. The crowd was very responsive. But Abe came into the locker room steamin.

" 'You stunk up the court,' Saperstein shouted. 'You were the worst. One more bad game and I'm gonna send all you dumb Oscars home. I'll have a whole new team sent over here!' "

The players were shaken. Connie turned helplessly to Tex: "Would he really do that?"

Harrison shook his head. "Not if you wise up. It's your fault, beatin him like that on the bus. You shouldn't have beaten him and you damn sure shouldn't have rubbed it in. Tomorrow you got to let him win big. Then everything will be all right."

The next morning, Abe was in the front seat glowering. The players said "Morning Skip," as they climbed aboard. Abe said nothing. He waved disgustedly when Connie and J. C. suggested another game of Whist. Tex saved them. "Come on Skip," he said, "let's show those two something. We'll really teach 'em a lesson."

Saperstein thought for a moment, then cried, "Get the cards." J. C. and Hawk made sure Abe was a big winner. "Skip," Harrison marveled, "You sure know this game." Saperstein beamed.

The Trotters' play that night was so horrendous they feared Abe might really ship them back to the States. Instead, Saperstein walked into the locker room grinning. "You played a hell of a game," he announced. "I got one hundred bucks here for each of you. Go out and enjoy yourselves."

The Trotters, Connie discovered, had several unwritten rules. "Guys been kicked off this club for gettin caught with white meat," a veteran warned. "Abe don't care what you do with colored, but don't let him catch you with no white broads. A lot of guys got 'em. But don't get caught. And don't let him see you with a Cadillac. He don't stand for that either."

It was also understood among the players that Saperstein had a strong preference for athletes with very dark skin and very ugly faces. "The blacker you are," Tex told Connie, "the better your chances with Abe. *I* may just be the last of the light-skins. He's pretty partial to the ones who are far from ravin beauties too. He likes 'em to look the part. That's show business."

Veteran players told of the day the team was traveling through a Southern town and Saperstein spied a man with glistening black skin, wide eyes, and huge lips, walking down the street. "Stop the bus," he yelled at the driver. Abe hopped out and approached the man. "Can you play basketball?" he asked.

The answer was No, which didn't faze Saperstein. "Just get on the bus," he said. "We'll get you a uniform and *teach* you how to play." The man stayed with the team for several weeks before Abe reluctantly concluded he was too uncoordinated to learn the game.

The players didn't seem offended by the required subservience. "The guys on the team were proud to be Trotters," Connie says. "They thought of themselves as entertainers as well as ballplayers. A lot of them were really dedicated. I saw J. C. get out of a sickbed to play. Abe treated Tex kind of like a son. But Tex had to kiss his ass. And Abe didn't treat anybody else with real respect. But it didn't bother 'em."

At the time it didn't bother Connie either. He was a long way from developing the race pride he has today.

What did concern Hawk, and the other Trotters, was money. They weren't getting very much of it. Saperstein was notorious for publicizing the huge salaries his players were supposed to receive. In truth, the paternalism ended on payday. When Connie joined the club, Lemon was the only man making over twenty thousand dollars for the full year of work—and Meadowlark wasn't making much over twenty thousand dollars.

Hawk's bitterness toward the Trotters began after he married Nancy

Foster. Connie was soon supporting a wife and daughter—Shawna Lynn—plus the seemingly countless members of Nancy's family (actually five sisters and her retarded brother) who had made his home their home.

He was also helping his mother and his brother Randy in Brooklyn. Mrs. Hawkins was now totally blind. Unable to work, she relied on her meager social-security and welfare checks—and whatever Connie and Fred could spare. Hawk always sent money. But he was often hard-pressed to come up with it. For the next few years, finances were to be a constant concern.

Hardly frugal to begin with, Connie was unprepared to manage the little he had. Until the summer of 1969, he didn't even have a savings or checking account. If he and Nancy had some cash, they hid it around the house.

Sometimes he could barely make ends meet. The Litmans began quietly loaning him enough to keep his head above water. His Trotter salary was pitiful, but not untypical (Harrison's top wage was $16,000 after *thirteen years* of service).

In 1963, when Connie didn't go to Europe with the team, he earned $4,466.92. The following year, when he toured in the States from October to April and spent the entire summer overseas, he earned $7,077.98. Since Hawk played close to two hundred games, his pay worked about $35 per game (less than the weekend players in the Eastern League).

When Connie finally left the team, his total earnings while a Globetrotter (from February, 1963, to September, 1966) were $27,811.62—about what Wilt Chamberlain was getting per month.

"I never had much money in my pocket, unless I did good in cards," Hawk recalls. "I didn't make much and I didn't know how to care for what I got. I wear size fourteen shoes. You can't buy those in a regular store. I had to pay thirty-five to forty dollars. Plenty of times I needed shoes and I didn't have the money for them. But you have to keep up a front. Everybody thinks the Trotters live real good."

The Globetrotters' organization has gone out of its way to create this impression. When Bill Russell graduated from the University of San Francisco in 1956 as the top college player in the country, the Trotters announced they were offering him a $50,000 contract. Russell says the offer was really $15,000. He signed with the Boston Celtics instead.

The Trotters of Connie's era still were better off than those who played before the NBA integrated in 1950. Then Saperstein had a virtual monopoly on black basketball talent. While Connie was with the Globetrotters, several veterans told him that Saperstein once threatened to boycott any NBA team that broke the color line and tried to sign blacks. Most NBA clubs were then nickel-and-dime operations. To survive, they needed the large crowds attracted by Trotters' preliminary games.

Bill Russell, in his book *Go Up for Glory,* writes, "Saperstein threatened Walter Brown—the late owner of the Celtics and the key founder of the league—when Brown was getting ready to sign Chuck Cooper as the first Negro on the Celtics. . . . Saperstein thought he had a lock on all Negro players. He came at Brown hammer and tongs and told Walter that if the Celtics signed Cooper then the Globetrotters would boycott Boston Garden."

Brown wasn't intimidated, however, and the league did integrate. But with so many talented black players looking for work—and the NBA's quota system restricting blacks to about four per team until the mid-60's—Saperstein could still maintain a coolie wage scale.

Until years after Connie left the Trotters, he never spoke badly of them. He was afraid he'd have to go back someday. Now, however, he admits that for a long time he even hated the clowning.

Being fancy was one thing; he dug it—it's still a large part of his game. But people laughing *at him* was something else. His reasons, at the time, had nothing to do with race. It was a matter of personal dignity.

"I'd felt like a fool so much in my life, I didn't want to make more situations where people laughed at me," Hawk remembers. "The first year the guys tried to get me into the reems, but after that screwup in the circle—when I did it for money—I tried to stay away from that stuff. They'd pass me the ball in the middle of a reem, and I'd just pass it back."

Lemon and Harrison had a routine in which they danced with each other, while the defense feigned shock. The sight of two grown black men, arm in arm, always seemed to give the crowd a charge. Lemon once tried to dance with Connie. But Hawk planted his heels on the court. Finally, to avoid an incident, he walked in a circle while Lemon swung on his arm.

Gradually, however, his resolve and inhibitions broke down. He'd been making fancy passes and shots all along. After a while, he found it wasn't so hard to act the fool when everyone around him was doing it. By his second year, Hawk took part in group reems. He would lift Lemon on his shoulders so Meadowlark could dunk. He'd participate in the figure-eight maneuvers, and eventually even in the pregame circle.

Some of his teammates, possibly to annoy Lemon, pressed Connie to work in the pivot. Hawk held back. "I could be in on the gags as one of five," he says. "But I didn't want the spotlight on me. I didn't want to be the chief idiot."

Finally he agreed to try the pivot. But, at first, he couldn't bring himself to clown: "I thought, 'you got to grin and holler and wave your arms,' but I couldn't do it. I threw regular passes, a couple behind the back. It was dull."

"Then one night, maybe I gave up inside. I don't know. But all of a sudden I said to myself, 'I'll try it.' I did a couple of leg-kicks, I yelled a few times. Next thing I knew, I was really involved: tossin the ball between my legs and over my shoulder, dancin all around."

He threw himself into the clowning for a long time thereafter. He would bounce the ball off people's heads, swing from the rim, yell and show his teeth. He was resigned to being a Globetrotter. Everything else seemed hopeless.

Podoloff's firm statements about barring everyone involved in the scandal, and the NBA's rejection of him during talks with the ABL, left Hawk no doubt that he was blacklisted. Confirmation came in the spring of 1964. His class graduated at Iowa. He was eligible for the NBA draft. But no team took him. Connie stopped hoping.

Since November of 1963, David Litman had been writing the NBA's new commissioner, J. Walter Kennedy—a former Globetrotter PR man—and the individual NBA clubs, informing them of Connie's availability and desire to play. By 1965 Roz and David had begun to talk seriously about suing. Still, Connie withheld his emotions. He didn't dare hope again: "Sometimes, sittin on the bus, lookin out the window at the farms and houses and the highway, I'd think about playin in the NBA, about the years goin by. But I tried not to think about all the money I was losin, about how people outside the schoolyards didn't even know who I was. A couple of times I fell asleep and I dreamed about playin against Wilt and Oscar. But I'd always end up the dream with me on the side of the court watchin. I was sure I'd never play in the NBA. When I was with the Trotters, the Litmans hadn't even started the lawsuit yet. I had no hope, no pride, nothing—I was just a Globetrotter."

Connie Hawkins playing the clown in some gym in Des Moines was like Dame Margot Fonteyn dancing in a go-go cage, or Sir Laurence Olivier playing Howdy Doody. "You could see he was never happy," Harrison says. "His aspirations were higher. Sometimes he just didn't have any interest on the court. He wouldn't dunk in the warmups. Some nights he wouldn't even run. I had to keep talkin to him to keep him up. Then he'd get into a good thing for a while. But he'd always slip back."

The Trotters' occasional serious All-Star games against such top players as Cazzie Russell, Dave Bing, and Dave DeBusschere, may have shown Connie that he could use Trotter moves against top competition. But they also frightened him. His statistics were good. The men he played against raved about his ability. Yet Hawk felt he was losing something. "It got harder and harder to be really competitive," he says. "It took a half to get going at all. Then my shot and my moves would come back, but I couldn't drive myself to play defense or get on the floor and fight for every loose ball.

"There was times against the Generals that I wanted to play competitive ball. I might make a move, a good move, and the *feelin* would come over me. But it would be time for a gag and I'd have to turn everything off. Then maybe I'd try a move in a real game against the College All-Stars— and I couldn't make my body do just what I wanted. Sometimes, I was afraid I'd never get it back."

During the summers, between trips with the Trotters, Hawk went to the Rucker Tournament to see how far he had slipped. The fans still cheered his every move. Stylish plays and new Trotter tricks increased the adulation. But Connie worried: "Nobody else noticed, but I couldn't make certain moves as quick as before. I didn't rebound as tough cause I wasn't used to rough contact. A lot of times, there was no spark inside me. It was depressin. Sometimes it got so bad I didn't want to play."

Hawkins played in an All-Star game in East Harlem in 1965. Holcombe Rucker had died that winter. The game was a benefit for his widow. Many NBA players participated. But Connie was the Most Valuable Player. "I felt real good," he says, "till I went back to the bus."

Hawk could usually hide his feelings behind a happy-go-lucky front. His Globetrotter teammates acknowledged his playing ability. He remained a virtual demigod in the schoolyard. And there was always the consolation of traveling with Tex Harrison.

Then, he wasn't traveling with Harrison any more.

On November 20, 1965, Tex was arrested carrying hashish into the country from Mexico. The Trotters rarely had to bother with Customs when they traveled as a group. But Tex, who had gone to Mexico with a Trotter unit, stayed a few extra days and came across the border alone.

For several weeks no one on the team knew if Harrison would rejoin them. Connie was shaken. "The club ought to be doin something for him," he told other players. "Tex was everything to this team. He did everything for them. They *owe* it to him. If he don't come back, I don't know if I want to play here any more."

Harrison came back in mid-December. He had received a suspended sentence. He was a first offender, and he'd been carrying a very small quantity of hash. Everything seemed forgotten.

But in January, several minutes before the Trotters took the court at the University of Illinois' new gym in Champaign, road manager Parnell Woods got a call from Chicago. Harrison thinks it was from the Trotters' attorney Allan Bloch. Woods was instructed to withhold Tex from the game. Apparently the Globetrotter organization thought the college kids would become junkies by just looking at him.

Three days later, while the team was in Louisville, there was another call from Chicago. Saperstein wanted to talk to Harrison. It appeared the Trotters would pull Tex off the tour. "Parnell told me they were going to pay me for the rest of the season," Harrison says now. "They just wanted me to sit out a few months till the thing blew over. Then, I was *supposed* to come back."

Tex was packing when Connie and two other young Trotters burst into his room. Hawk was so angry his hands trembled. "After all you done for them, Choker!" he cried. "After all those years, how can they do it?"

Harrison shook his head silently. "Choker," Hawk shouted, "you want us to back you? You say the word, man. I'll walk right down the hall and tell Parnell to tell Abe if you don't play, *I* don't play either!"

Connie Hawkins was no longer the scared kid who slept with three basketballs. He was never again to be frightened or intimidated by an owner or coach. Hawk had learned the essential lesson of big-time athletics: management—pro or amateur—treats athletes as it does lightbulbs; when they burn out, or are no longer useful, it throws them away. "Fuck it Choker. I don't give a shit about this club if you ain't here!"

"No Hawk," Harrison said. "I don't want you jeopardizing yourselves. Not because of me. I'm grateful, man. But I'm gonna be all right."

"Connie will never know," Tex says now, "how warm that made me feel. I knew then that this kid—this great kid—really cared about me. And after all *he'd* been through. It was really something."

What happened when Harrison returned to Chicago was really something also. "I met Abe at the Globetrotters' offices," Tex recalls. "He said I should take a short vacation. He said he would pay me, that it was nothing to worry about. Then I met with the lawyer, Allan Bloch.

"Bloch wanted to muddy a whole lot of things. I tried to explain that I'd done everything I could to keep the club out of the papers. And I had. There was almost no publicity. I hadn't even called them for legal help. But Bloch didn't seem interested. I said to him, 'I don't have a deplorable character. You know my record, what I've done for the Trotters.' He said I should talk to Abe again. When I went back the next day, Abe's attitude had changed completely. He wasn't even talking about paying me, he just said, 'Good luck.' "

Today, Harrison lives comfortably in Houston. The man the Globetrotters would not touch is employed by the Federal Government in an Office of Economic Opportunity youth program. He also sells life insurance and runs a nursery school with his wife. Surprisingly, Tex harbors little bitterness. "I had many good years with the Globetrotters," he says. "Sure they exploited us. None of us were paid what we deserved. But I still feel kindly toward Abe. I think that lawyer turned his head. Anyway, I think Abe was gonna take me back the next season, I'd already had feelers. But he died."

Saperstein died on March 15, 1966. With Harrison gone, Connie's affection for the Trotters was already dead. "Tex may say he isn't bitter," Hawk says now. "But, he *ought* to be bitter. Those people fucked him good—and he'd gave them the best part of his life. I'll never forget that."

Hawkins went overseas with the Trotters that summer. Without Tex, it wasn't the same. He returned to find his career with the team about to end. His reaction was numbness—he didn't care any more.

David Litman had met in May, 1966, with NBA Commissioner J. Walter Kennedy. The meeting had gone badly. "I'm convinced," David told Hawk, "that the league isn't interested in finding out the truth." The time had come for a lawsuit.

But, Litman explained to Connie, it was vital to the case that Hawk be available to join the NBA if the league did decide to take him—otherwise it would be hard to claim he was being blacklisted. The Trotters had created a problem. While Saperstein was alive, Connie had not been asked to sign a formal agreement. Now Allan Bloch, the lawyer, with an eye toward the sale of the team, was demanding that every player sign a contract.

David asked several times for an immediate escape clause, pleading its importance to Connie's case. The Trotters' response was an attempt to sign Hawkins without Litman's knowledge. They offered him $1,250 per month for five months. They neglected to mention, however, that the small print in the contract would have bound him indefinitely to the club. The Trotters would also have had the right to "assign [or] transfer the contract or to loan player's services to another team."

Despite pressure from Bloch and Saperstein's former secretary, Marie Lenihan, Connie refused to sign.

When Litman learned the Trotters were attempting to deal with Hawk behind his back, he wrote an angry letter of protest. But Litman reiterated that Connie was willing to play—if the club gave him an escape clause. Mrs. Lenihan's reply was terse: ". . . as a result, our plans for the forthcoming season will not include player Connie Hawkins."

Connie was no longer a Globetrotter. That didn't bother him very much. But he was twenty-four years old. He had a wife, a daughter, a son on the way, a blind mother, and a lot of relatives living in his house. He was unemployed. And basketball was the only thing he knew.

13

OLD HURTS AND A NEW LEAGUE

"Connie Hawkins plays against us in the summer.
We all know he'd be a superstar in the NBA."
—Willis Reed, New York Knicks

A six-million-dollar treble-damage anti-trust suit was filed against the National Basketball Association on November 3, 1966. The NBA reacted with a hearty ho-hum. When a marshal served a subpoena on J. Walter Kennedy, the league commissioner smiled coolly and said, "I've been expecting this." There was little precedent for such a lawsuit in pro sports, and there probably wasn't a legal expert in the country who thought the Litmans would win.

But Roz and David had done extensive research and felt they had a chance. Connie had placed what was left of his career in their hands. There was little he could do but wait. "That was the most depressin year of my life," he says. "I didn't have no job. I didn't do nothing. I figured the suit was my only chance, but I didn't want to think about it. It looked like I was finished."

Connie, Nancy, and their three-year-old daughter Shawna; Nancy's sisters Bernita, Dorothy Jean, Franceen, and Nadine; and her retarded brother, Nathaniel—all lived in a small, rundown three-story frame house on Charles Street, in the heart of Pittsburgh's North Side ghetto. It was nicer than Lexington Avenue—which was about all one could say for Charles Street. Inside, the house was clean, but the furnishings were cheap and worn and seemed about to fall apart.

Connie had money problems. The few dollars the Litmans had been able to bank for him while he was with the Globetrotters were soon gone. Hawk had to borrow from them so his family could eat.

One evening, as Hawk sat with Nancy in their tiny living room, her eyes lit up. "Connie," she cried, "why don't you go back to teaching English?" Hawk stared at her incredulously. Then he remembered. When they had been dating, in an effort to impress her, he'd made up a story about being a substitute English teacher in the New York City school system.

A sad smile crossed his long, mustached face: "Honey, what I done told you then was a bold-faced lie. I ain't never taught nothing in no school. I never been no teacher."

Nancy laughed. Then she became serious. "Well, what else can you do Connie? What else can you do besides basketball?"

"Nothing," he said softly. "You *know* that. Nothing."

He had time on his hands—lots of it. During the week he would rise about noon, put on his sneakers, and go to the schoolyard or YMCA. For hours he would shoot by himself—a lonely figure gliding silently across the court, twisting, driving, throwing up long jump-shots—the stillness in the gym broken only by the uneven heartbeat of the ball on the floor and the crackle of the net as it sliced through. "I would try to be creative, try to work on moves and things," he says, "but I'd wonder, was I ever gonna be usin 'em again in a real game?"

He spent more time in bars that winter than ever in his life. At the Florentine Lounge—where Nancy was once a waitress—and the Aurora, a loud, bustling after-hours joint, he drank and talked "about anything but the NBA." Connie didn't feel that people on the North Side looked down on him. But neither did he sense the respect and admiration he'd received when he was with the Rens and the Globetrotters.

Several evenings a week, Connie Hawkins could be seen for an admission price of fifty cents, playing in a YMHA league in the middle-class Oakland section. His team was called the Porky Chedwicks, and his teammates included Walt Mangham and Jim McCoy, old friends from the Rens. They now had jobs in Pittsburgh and were playing weekends in the Eastern League.

The opposition at the YMHA was out-of-shape and under-skilled. Connie never played very hard. He often arrived in the middle of games. On the court, he took rebounds flatfooted, played defense with hands on hips, leisurely dribbled between his legs, and sometimes paused in the midst of a foul shot to wave at the Litmans' eight-year-old son Harry. "Not that I'm pretending to be superior, but this isn't work," Connie tried to explain to Pittsburgh Press columnist Roy McHugh, who came to see him play. "In a pro game I'd be rough, I'd be exerting myself. This kind of basketball hurts me. It's been hurting me the last four years. I went with the Globetrotters, and the brand of ball they play—well, it just isn't conducive to NBA ball."

Some in the sparse crowd at the Y were annoyed by his play. They felt

Hawk was lazy and that he tried to embarrass and humiliate his opponents. Sometimes he did: he would dangle the ball in their faces, throw passes between their legs, leave them an opening to the basket, then block their shots at the last second—and even laugh at their ineptness. His heart wasn't in the games. They were a reminder of what he had become. Inside, there was anger and hurt, and he took this out on those against whom he played.

"The games at the Y was so depressin," he remembers. "There was no competition. Fifty or a hundred people would pack the place. I'm not kidding; in those days a hundred people comin to see me play was a pleasant surprise."

His only income came on weekends when he played for one hundred dollars a game with the Harlem Wizards, a poor man's imitation of the Globetrotters. Eddie Simmons, who was then directing a Bed-Stuy poverty program, called from Brooklyn to tell Hawk about the team. It made Hawk feel good that Simmons still cared enough to help him out. Ed, who was married and gaining weight at a disquieting pace, occasionally played with the Wizards, as did Tony Jackson and LeRoy Wright, the 6' 9" center who'd given Connie trouble in the ABL. But the Wizards were a ragtag operation, performing before small crowds in high school gyms throughout upstate New York.

"It was the same idea as the Globetrotters, but less professional," Connie recalls. "I was feelin low all the time. But I had to play for the money. I hated the clownin worse than ever—and I wouldn't do it."

One evening, Bobby Hunter—the team's ace clown and now a Globetrotter—said to Hawk, "Come on man, get in on this gag." Connie shook his head with such vigor it was obvious to everyone in the tiny gym. Hunter, a natural showman, promptly incorporated it in the act. He began a lengthy pantomime, pretending to remonstrate with Connie for his lack of participation.

The crowd howled as Hunter waved his bony finger in Connie's face. "He treated me like I was a naughty boy and everybody laughed," says Hawkins. "I was embarrassed, but I just smiled. I couldn't get mad at Bobby. He's a nice dude and he was just doin his job, but I hated the whole thing."

Connie wanted to play in the Eastern League, which still had the best pro competition below the NBA. The league had always had an extremely liberal policy regarding players involved in the fixes. Sherman White, Ed Roman, and others who had admitted dumping games in 1951 had been allowed to play. Roman even became a coach, as did Jack Molinas. Connie was sure they would take him.

Jim McCoy, Walt Mangham, and McCoy's brother, Julius, played with

Sunbury, Pennsylvania. Julius was the league's Most Valuable Player. Connie asked Jim to help him join the team.

"I'll speak to Julius about it," Jim said. "There shouldn't be any trouble." But there was. The Eastern League, which operated as a minor league for the NBA, had a new rule: no players involved in gambling scandals were welcome.

"Julius talked to the owner," Jim told Connie several days later. "I can't figure it man, but he says you can't play in the league."

"Why? They even had Sherman White, they had guys who done games. I ain't done no games!"

McCoy shook his head. "I don't understand it, man. What can I tellya." Connie turned and walked away. He wanted to scream or cry, or punch someone. "When the Eastern League turned me down, I felt completely rejected," he says. "They were doin me wrong. I knew it. I wanted David to sue 'em. But he said the NBA was trouble enough."

The ostracism and inactivity, the shame of being out of work, were made more painful by the fuller realization of his own greatness. Despite fears that his skills were wasting, Hawk had come to recognize, within himself, that he was among the best players in the world. By 1966 he had been on the same court with almost every top NBA player and had outplayed most of them.

For years there had been an almost cosmic quality to the level of his game. No one played basketball like Connie Hawkins. The feathery grace, the flair for showmanship, the one-handed ball control, the lithe 6′ 8″ body that moved like a backcourt man's, the dazzling stuff shots that only Chamberlain could match—when all these elements came together, Connie had something that was his alone.

"In Harlem," says Rucker Tournament director Bob McCullough, "Connie Hawkins was a magic name. Any game he played in the schoolyards drew a big crowd. One year, Hawk missed every game in the tournament, but the coaches still voted him to the All-Star game. Then he went out and won the MVP award over a lot of guys from the NBA.

"I remember one summer we were having an exhibition game before the tournament started. Hawk was just sitting in the stands watching. He was still with the Trotters and he was leaving for Europe in a few days. But everybody in the crowd wanted him to play. They kept chanting his name. It put me in a funny position because Willis Reed and Henry Aken of the Knicks were in the game. I had to ask them if they minded playing with Connie. Aken said, 'Mind? It would be an honor.' So Hawk walked onto the court in clamdiggers and a T-shirt—and scored twenty-six points in the first half. Then he left."

In the spring of 1966, Hawk, McCoy, and Mangham had played for a team called the Hot Dog Shoppe in the East Liverpool Basketball Classic, a pro tournament. In the finals they defeated Johnson Pontiac of Wellsville, Pennsylvania, led by Cazzie Russell and Dave Bing, the best college seniors in the nation. Despite Bing and Russell, Connie was named Most Valuable Player. He received one hundred dollars. A few weeks later, Bing and Russell, the first men picked in the NBA draft, signed multi-year contracts for over one hundred thousand dollars.

The following year, in the same tournament, the Hot Dog Shoppe lost in the finals to a team headed by Gus Johnson and Ray Scott of the Baltimore Bullets. Johnson may be the best forward in the NBA. He and Connie went one-on-one at both ends of the court for the full forty-eight minutes. When it was over, Johnson had 23 points, Connie had 34, and Johnson said, "He is a tremendous athlete. I've never seen a man his height move so well."

Later Johnson added, "He could do everything: shoot, jump, handle the ball. His all-round game is greater than any big man—Hayes, Russell, Wilt. Most of the guys who play in the East know how great Connie is. We talk about him a lot. It's too bad what happened to him. He'd be a natural All-Star in the NBA."

Instead, when the NBA played its 1967 All-Star game in San Francisco, Connie was sitting in front of a television set in the living room on Charles Street. He saw Willis Reed, Hal Greer, Wilt, Oscar, and the others he had played with so often—and he tried to enjoy the game. But he couldn't. "I look at all those guys, the NBA All-Stars, and I knew I was better than so many of 'em. I couldn't stand to watch it."

At halftime, he clicked off the TV and walked toward the stairs. "Honey, what's the matter?" Nancy called after him. "Are you all right? I thought you wanted to see the game."

"I'm tired," he snapped, "I'm tired, that's all."

He went up to their bedroom, turned out the light, and buried his face in the pillow. He had become a trivia question. It was an "in" thing to know who Connie Hawkins was. It had been four years since he played in a competitive league. Now he wasn't even a Globetrotter. "I tried not to lose hope," he says, "but I was sure I'd never play in the NBA. I was so worried. I had responsibilities; my wife, my little girl, my son comin, my mother—everything was so fucked up. I didn't know what to do. I was ready to shove it all and clown again for the Trotters." He fell asleep and didn't awaken until late the next afternoon.

But rich men were once more at play, and a new pro basketball league was in its prenatal stages. The climate had profoundly changed since Saperstein launched his abortive venture. The American Football League had become a moneymaker by using television to force a merger with the established National Football League.

Even the NBA was on much stronger fiscal footing. Its attendance was far above 1961 figures and—despite financial trouble still plaguing many NBA clubs—the price of a franchise had risen from $200,000 in 1961 to $1,750,000. There were plenty of buyers. Ownership, even of a team that wasn't making money, offered potentially huge tax write-offs, great publicity, and public relations advantages for an owner's other ventures. In addition, owning a sports franchise—and the vicarious vitality that went with it—had become a new fad among the wealthy.

The American Basketball Association was the brainchild of a Madison Avenue type named Constantine Seredin. His main interest was the marketing aspect of sports. He wanted a league in which the member clubs were franchised by *his* PR firm: Professional Sports Management. The firm would centrally handle "merchandising, endorsements, promotion, and public relations" for the clubs at a modest fee of only $230,000 per season.

"We will employ concepts concurrent with modern business practices and a marketing and merchandising approach," Seredin said at the time. Then he and several cohorts set out to locate some wealthy men, anxious to make a large investment in a rather speculative venture. Seredin was confident he'd find them. "The meaning of the word 'owner' has changed," he explained. "In the old days you were a socialite or a saint, now you're an owner. People feel they must have that title and all that goes with it. This is a lousy investment right now, if you're anxious for instant profits. But you become an owner and you're knighted. The sword touches your shoulder and you go out searching for the Holy Grail."

Seredin correctly envisioned the ABA as a long-range proposition with heavy initial losses before anyone could expect a return. "We can't have weak sisters," he emphasized. "If you can't handle the financial burden over the long haul, get out."

Eventually, he rounded up a dozen rich investors and presented them at a press conference. Then he convinced attorney George Mikan to become commissioner. Mikan, a 6′ 10″ behemoth who led the Minneapolis Lakers to four championships in the early years of the NBA, had been voted the top player of basketball's first half-century. He later flopped as coach of the Lakers and lost as a Republican candidate for Congress. But Mikan was a big name, and his appointment made the ABA a reality.

Seredin made one mistake. He apparently trusted the wealthy men with whom he was dealing. Once the franchise owners were together, they examined the "financial burden" Seredin had spoken of—and decided Seredin was part of that burden. They didn't really need his PR firm, not at $230,000 a year. So they threw him out.

The league, however, was established with franchises in Denver, Dallas, Houston, Anaheim, New Orleans, Minneapolis, Louisville, Indianapolis, Oakland, Pittsburgh, and—probably in memory of the ABL—Teaneck, New Jersey.

"I was happy when I first read the articles about the league," Connie says, "but I thought they was bullshittin. I thought, after the ABL, nobody'd be that crazy."

But Hawkins was soon contacted by Ermer Robinson, the old Globetrotter, who wanted him to sign with the ABA's Oakland team. Hopeful, yet afraid he might again be barred, Connie met David Litman at his office. "We were both pleased," David recalls. "Connie desperately needed money and he badly wanted to play. I saw it as an aid to our lawsuit. I didn't think his ability had been sufficiently established during his period in the ABL. I wanted to be able to prove in court that he was a great player. I explained this and he understood."

David was not pleased, however, by the prospect of Connie playing in Oakland. The first major issue of the lawsuit was a battle over venue. The NBA wanted the trial moved from Pittsburgh to New York. The Litmans wanted it to remain in the more friendly Pennsylvania surroundings. Their argument would be strengthened if they could show that Pittsburgh was Connie's place of current employment, as well as his residence.

David called the Oakland club and was informed that an ABA meeting was in progress there. Moments later he was speaking with Gabe Rubin, who owned the Pittsburgh franchise. Rubin informed him that the Pittsburgh Pipers now had rights to negotiate with Connie and that he would meet with David upon his return.

Litman was also concerned about Connie's eligibility. He didn't want to initiate negotiations and then have the ABA bar Hawkins. Rubin assured him Connie was eligible and would have no problems.

"Our investigation," Commissioner Mikan would later announce, "told us that these boys [Connie, Roger Brown, Tony Jackson, and Doug Moe] should be allowed to play." Actually, there had been no "investigation." Mikan's assistant, Thurlo McCrady, had met with officials from DA Hogan's office and received the same irrelevant information the ABL got in 1961. But, like the ABL, the new league needed players. Rather than investigate and possibly discover something they didn't want to know, the ABA struck a posture of condescending forgiveness. The league assumed that the players *had* done whatever Hogan accused them of, but decided that—since they had never been arrested, had never fixed games, and hadn't committed any serious rapes or assaults during the intervening years—they were "rehabilitated" and "model citizens." Thus the ABA permitted them to play. This was jolly for the league, but did nothing to lift the onus of suspicion from the players. Nevertheless, it was the best Litman could hope for.

Gabe Rubin, a portly, dapper little man, was known as the "Sonny Werblin of Pittsburgh." He was thought to be the town's most astute promoter. By introducing foreign films and bringing the city such hits as *Hello, Dolly* and *The Sound of Music,* Rubin had amassed a small fortune. That, however, was the problem: he only had a *small* fortune. Despite Seredin's warnings, Rubin, like many of the original ABA owners, really wasn't financially equipped for a long-haul struggle against the NBA. He was hoping for a quick merger, which would drastically increase the worth of his investment.

In the meantime, he talked an opulent game and operated on half a shoestring. His PR man, Charles "Brute" Kramer, couldn't afford to take sports writers to lunch. No Piper employee had a credit card. Rubin's favorite tactic was getting people to work parttime *before* he hired them. Hal Blitman, the coach at Cheyney (Pa.) State College, was considered for the general manager's spot. He later turned it down, but not before making all of Rubin's draft choices. Don DeJardin, now general manager of the Philadelphia 76ers, worked in Rubin's office for weeks, then left. Jim O'Brien, who now writes for the New York *Post,* was editing a snappy little paper called Pittsburgh *Weekly Sports* when Rubin prevailed upon him to write numerous press releases. "I put in a lot of work for him," O'Brien recalls. "Then he'd phone me and pick my brain for hours. But when I mentioned money, Gabe always said, 'We'll discuss it later.' Finally, after I'd bugged him for months, he paid me two hundred dollars. It came out to about two dollars an hour."

Originally, Rubin wasn't interested in Connie. He wasn't sure Hawk's feats with the Rens were legitimate, and didn't understand why a supposedly great player would be in a YMHA league. At one point he asked Jim O'Brien, "Are you sure he's so good? I don't think he can make my team."

"Gabe," answered the stocky O'Brien, "*I* could make your team."

Rubin's opinion of Connie changed considerably after he mingled with basketball people at the ABA meeting in Oakland. He returned very anxious to sign Hawkins—but not at all anxious to spend money doing it.

This played into David Litman's hands. "The ABA was only a hiatus and a tool that we were using to get into the NBA," he explains. "My major concern wasn't money, it was getting a clause in the contract that would permit Connie to go to the NBA in the event the case was settled."

At the time, Litman had done minimal legal work in the sports field and wasn't fully aware of the radical nature of his proposal. Pro basketball did not have a reserve clause like baseball's (which binds a player to a single team for the duration of his career—or until he is traded, sold, or dead). But both basketball leagues then kept their athletes in non-negotiable straitjackets by means of an option clause. Each year, the player signed a contract which granted the team an option to his services for the succeeding season. Unless the team violated the terms of the contract (which happened in the case of many players who have recently jumped leagues), the athlete could free himself only by refusing to sign a contract and not playing for one season.

Litman knew that once the suit came to trial—in about two years—they stood little chance of winning or settling if they could not show that Hawkins was free *immediately* to join the NBA. So, in a precedent-setting move, he knocked the option clause from Connie's contract. He also added a phrase which effectively prevented Hawk from being traded. Rubin was so busy trying to get Hawkins cheap, he either didn't realize the import of what he was agreeing to—or didn't care.

"Gabe and his lawyer, Skip Kaufman, offered us a contract for fifteen thousand dollars," says Litman. "I didn't want to bargain too much and antagonize them. I did ask for a five thousand dollar bonus in front, because I thought the odds were at least even the ABA would never have a center jump, and Connie needed the money so badly. They responded by asking us to add a second year to the contract at twenty-five thousand dollars. I agreed, but I explained that I wanted to make sure Connie would be free to leave—a free agent—at the end of the second season."

The option clause was deleted, and the words, "after such renewal this contract shall not include any further option to the Club to renew the contract," were typed in. It is unlikely such words had ever been typed on a modern pro-basketball contract.

Litman protected him against a trade by inserting a phrase which gave the "Pittsburgh Basketball Club" the sole right to renew the option for the second year of the contract. Thus, Connie could have been traded during the first ABA season, but he would have become a free agent at its end, since the Pittsburgh Basketball Club no longer owned his contract and therefore couldn't claim right of renewal.

Why did Rubin agree to such a contract? Why did Commissioner Mikan—who turned out to be almost as ineffective as he was bellicose— approve it? The league and the Pipers never dreamed that Connie could win his lawsuit. They were humoring Litman. They assumed that, in two years when Hawk became a free agent, he would still be able to deal only with ABA clubs. And, as far as the ABA was concerned—free agent or not —he belonged to Pittsburgh.

Pro sports lives by its own rules. The athlete is a chattel. Football players, who are technically permitted to play out their options, have discovered it's one thing to become a free agent, and quite another to get other clubs to negotiate. The ABA planned to operate the same way with Hawkins. But they had outsmarted themselves—and supplied Litman with, what was to be, a crucial lever in his dealings with the NBA.

$$\boxed{14}$$

WEIRD WINNERS

> "I've played with the best ballplayers in the world and
> I've seen the best ballplayers. Connie Hawkins is the greatest
> and I'm not just saying that. He would give you his heart."
> —*Arthur Bruce Heyman during 1968 ABA playoffs*

The American Basketball Association forced the NBA into serious merger-discussions as soon as it began practicing what it preached: spend money. When it signed college stars for huge bonuses and drove the NBA into the economic stratosphere to secure others, talks began. But this didn't happen for three years. The original ABA owners were supposedly prepared—and able—to endure huge initial losses, go first class, and eventually push the established league to the bargaining table. "Our owners," trumpeted Commissioner Mikan, "could buy the NBA lock, stock, and ballboy." For several seasons, however, most of the owners either didn't have, or weren't willing to spend, enough money to buy the ballboy.

The Kentucky Colonels, owned by the multimillionaire Gregory family, lost their first coaching choice by refusing to put money for his three-year contract in escrow. They signed a high school coach instead. The Houston Cougars didn't get around to hiring a public relations man until just before the season started, and the Anaheim Amigos turned their PR man into a player when the team was shorthanded.

Mikan made loud predictions about the All-Americans his league would sign. But the ABA bungled negotiations with Elvin Hayes, Wes Unseld, and Kareem Jabbar, and became notorious for making astronomical offers through the media—*after* the player had decided to sign with the NBA.

The ABA was still a far cut above the old ABL. Schedules were met, players were paid, and nobody traveled by station wagon. Salaries were generally reasonable. Indiana, Denver, and Kentucky had strong franchises from the start. But, in its infancy, the ABA had plenty of bush-league features. Anaheim's trainer didn't go on road trips because flying made his nose bleed, one club picked its draft selections from a six-month-old basketball magazine, and an owner threatened to kill a referee with "one ka-rate chop." A game between Pittsburgh and New Orleans in Memphis was delayed thirty minutes during the second quarter when a power switch failed and the arena was plunged into darkness. The players were told "a possum got caught in the wiring." When the lights went on, they discovered that most of the crowd of four hundred had gone home.

The New Jersey Americans played their first exhibition game in practice sweats, with numbers scribbled on the back in crayon, because their general manager forgot to order uniforms. They were housed at a converted drill-shed in Teaneck. When covered with bunting, it looked like a freshly opened supermarket. At the home opener, fans could buy a fifty-cent program that didn't include the players' numbers and listen to a gaggle of chubby preteen cheerleaders chanting, "Block that ball." New Jersey was eliminated from the league's first postseason playoffs by forfeit when the circus forced them out of Teaneck. They rescheduled the game at the Commack Arena, where the basketball floor—unused since ABL days—had so many warps and potholes it was declared a health hazard. "You step on one side," noted a player, "and the other side comes up."

Then there was Mikan, lumbering along with his foot in his mouth. He proclaimed the league had a "healthy and substantial" network television proposal. No ABA team was seen on network TV for the next three years. One night he told an audience, "It's always nice to come back to Oklahoma." He was in Oakland at the time.

By the ABA's fourth year there had been thirteen franchise shifts, nine changes of ownership, and one new commissioner.

The Pittsburgh franchise was among the league's least stable. There was a constant turnover in Rubin's front office. The slightest expenditure had to be cleared by the owner. Accurate attendance was rarely announced, and *announced* attendance dipped as low as 670.

For Connie Hawkins, however, the ABA's first floundering season remains the most enjoyable and exciting of his career. He scraped the cobwebs from his reputation and reestablished himself as a superstar. The ABA had some talented players, but Connie dominated the league even more than in the ABL. He won the scoring title (26.8), was second in rebounding and shooting percentage, and stood fourth in assists. He was voted the ABA's Most Valuable Player and was the only man unanimously chosen for the All-Star team. More important, he carried a bizarre collection of outcasts and rejects to the ABA championship.

The Pipers were a legion of the lost. By the end of the season, the starting five was composed of two men barred by the NBA for alleged involvement in gambling scandals, a rookie who did W. C. Fields imitations during games, a backcourt man with a drinking problem, and a forward whose personality was so singular that—after his retirement—when sportswriters in the ABA and NBA gave unofficial awards for the flakiest player in their respective leagues, *both* awards were named after him.

Connie was just twenty-five years old. Yet had been a professional longer than any of his teammates. He was the Pipers' captain and, for the first time, was forced to become a leader. He led quietly, sometimes with a few pointed words of advice or reprimand, more often just by example. The other Pipers came to view him with awe on the court and with respect off it. He was no longer afraid to speak his mind. When four of them participated in a local TV commercial that took a seemingly endless six hours to shoot, Connie bitched and got everyone an extra one hundred dollars.

But first there was a long, agonizing period of adjustment. No matter how often he worked out during the summer or how many games he played at the Ruckers Tournament, Hawk had been away from serious competition for four years. There were problems from the moment he reported to training camp. His sinuses, which go berserk each fall, left him weakened by flu. His weight dropped below 190. His chronic toe-infections reappeared—as they had at each training camp since 1961—and a nail had to be removed. By the time he joined the workouts, he was far behind. In his first one-on-one drill, he tried to be "overly impressive," got his feet tangled and fell on his face. Tom Washington, a strong 6′ 7″ rookie from Cheyney State, ate him alive.

Slowly, Hawk got his game together. But, although it was clear he would be the Pipers' star, he was far from his peak when the season opened. Pittsburgh was expected to battle the Indiana Pacers (who had signed Roger Brown) and the Minnesota Muskies (who had the ABA's top rookie, 6′ 9″ All-American Mel Daniels) for the Eastern Division title. Rubin had gathered a strong starting team, by ABA standards. Chico Vaughn, a five-year NBA veteran, and Charlie Williams, a 6′ rookie from Seattle University, gave the Pipers a solid backcourt. Both had quick hands, excelled on defense, and could shoot from outside. Center Ira Harge had been dropped by the Philadelphia 76ers, but had once been an All-American at New Mexico and was still a very strong rebounder. Tom Washington, though a poor shot, was aggressive and agile, a ferocious competitor, strong under the boards, and one of the best defensive forwards in the ABA.

The bench was less imposing. Guards Barry Liebowitz, Steve Vacendak, and Jim Jarvis could handle the ball and play some defense. Craig Dill, 6′ 10″, was frail, but had a good hook shot, and 6′ 8″ forward Richie Parks could add some muscle underneath. But Connie was the player Rubin depended upon to attract fans and win games.

The Pipers got off to a disjointed start. With little teamwork or cohesion, they lost as often as they won. Connie showed flashes of brilliance. But, much of the time, he seemed in a daze—listless, almost aloof. His defense was weak, his rebounding inconsistent, and he passed off so much there were games when he took less than ten shots. Hawk scored under 20 points in eleven of the Pipers' first twenty-three contests.

In a game against Denver, Connie could manage just 2 points in the first half. "I can't get going," he told coach Vince Cazzetta in the locker room. "I feel lost out there." Trainer Alex Medich, who had been with the Rens, handed him a green, heart-shaped pill. "Take this," he said. "It'll pep you up."

The pill was a three-milligram Dexamyl, an amphetamine widely used by players in the ABA and NBA. It was the first pep pill Connie had taken, and it did the job. He felt more alert, a bit stronger, scored 27 points in the second half, and led the Pipers to a victory.

But even pep pills couldn't ignite Hawkins during many early-season games. When Washington broke his wrist falling under the basket and was lost for a month, attendance waned, and the Pipers floundered, Connie became the target of constant criticism. The most scathing was in Jim O'Brien's Pittsburgh *Weekly Sports*: "Quite often Connie is conning the fans. . . . What really bugs a guy about Hawkins is that here's an athlete endowed with all the physical assets necessary to make it big . . . and all he does is go around believing he's the greatest and that the world owes him a living. . . . Hawkins doesn't work hard . . . doesn't seem to care enough. . . . Cazzetta ought to kick him in the pants instead of pampering him."

Added New Jersey's coach Max Zaslofski: "He plays just when he feels like it, and everybody in town thinks he's the greatest."

Hawkins pretended not to hear the criticism. But it hurt him deeply. Some, however, was justified. He still had trouble sustaining intense involvement. The motivation was there. He knew—perhaps too well—the importance of excelling that season. He craved the recognition and self-satisfaction superb play would bring. But some evenings his competitive juices simply refused to flow. Hawk found it difficult, after four years, to psyche himself up night after night.

Underweight and easily fatigued, he must pace himself even today. But Connie is something of a hypochondriac. He overreacts to small hurts. In some of those early ABA games he was still pacing himself at the final buzzer.

Nevertheless Hawkins didn't dog it as much as his critics believed. He often appears to be loafing when he is not. His expression rarely changes during a game. With his placid demeanor and graceful loping stride, he makes things look so easy, some wonder if he's trying.

His defensive play was poor. But this was due less to lack of effort than to lack of training. Hawk hadn't had any real coaching since high school, and Mickey Fisher used a zone defense at Boys. The Globetrotters didn't even play defense, and schoolyard ball had emphasized blocking shots and stealing passes. Hawk was forever losing his man when he turned his head to watch the ball.

He was also overpassing—shooting less and setting up his teammates more. Gabe Rubin, who wanted a high scorer to attract fans, was angry. He and Commissioner George Mikan nagged Connie to shoot. One evening in Pittsburgh they took him to a private club for dinner and Mikan boomed, "I used to take thirty-five or forty shots a game. I didn't bother passin the ball around. Nobody looks at your assists! They don't care how many shots you take. All people want to know is what you score. Get those points! This league needs you havin those sixty and seventy-point games."

Connie wasn't impressed: "Mikan seemed like a big galoot, a Jolly White Giant. He was real masculine, but I expected a commissioner to be slicker, to have class. Anyway, he wanted me to change my game. I don't do *that* for nobody."

Since his days at the Carlton Y, Hawk instinctively looked for the open man. His game is basic one-on-one, but it works best when his teammates are hip to what he's doing. He likes to isolate himself against a defender, face the basket, hold the ball in one hand, then shoot or make his move off a series of fakes. He drives to the hoop, with the option of pulling up for the jump shot, going all the way or—if double-teamed—dropping the ball off to the free man. The Pipers' opponents constantly double-teamed him, so his first reaction was to pass.

"I wanted him to shoot more," recalls coach Vince Cazzetta, "but he's a naturally unselfish player. He attracted a crowd, and Tom Washington was always open. Washington's a weak shooter, but he had the best percentage in the league because Connie got him so many easy shots."

Hawkins didn't always have the ball anyway. Vaughn and Williams, intrigued by the three points the ABA awarded on field goals of twenty-five feet, fired continuously from outside.

In early November, Hawk began to open up. His play became more aggressive; he rebounded better and shot a little more. "I still wasn't myself," he recalls, "I wasn't real comfortable yet. But it was startin to come back."

Hawkins's scoring picked up, and the Pipers won five straight. Then they stumbled once more. In Louisville, with Pittsburgh down 103-102 and ten seconds remaining, Charlie Williams ignored coach Cazzetta's instructions to pass to Connie (who had 38 points). Williams missed a wild jump-shot, which sealed the defeat. In the locker room, Hawkins said angrily, "He had plenty of time. All he had to do was pass it to me and I would have won it."

Pittsburgh began another tailspin. There was bickering and more sloppy play. "Everybody was blamin everybody else," Connie says. "Nobody could take criticism. Whatever you said was taken as a personal thing."

Coach Vince Cazzetta, a tall, even-tempered forty-one-year-old, who had an excellent college record at Seattle and Rhode Island, somehow kept his composure during the rocky start. Occasionally he blew up at the team. More often, he tried—through quiet persuasion and individual discussions—to get them to play together.

Cazzetta's controlled demeanor belied the tension within. He had lost twenty-six pounds since the season started and was sleeping three hours a night. On November 24, the Pipers broke a three-game losing streak by slaughtering Houston at the Civic Arena. But Cazzetta suffered dizzy spells in the locker room and was taken to the hospital. He didn't accompany the team on a four-game road trip. Pittsburgh lost all four.

The Pipers' lack of cohesion—and Cazzetta's stay in the hospital—were partly due to the discordant personalities that populated the team. Charlie Williams was cold, distant, and humorless, his small features fixed in a sullen frown. He was then on the NBA blacklist. While captain of Seattle University's team, in 1965, Williams had failed to report a teammate who told him about being offered a bribe. When the prospective bribers were arrested and the story broke, Williams was expelled from school. He was not charged in the case, and was later readmitted, and graduated from the university. The NBA's new Seattle franchise tried to sign him. But Commissioner J. Walter Kennedy would not approve the contract. It seems the NBA, in typical heavyhanded fashion, had a rule which states, "No player who has been suspended by an academic institution for other than scholastic reasons shall be eligible to play in the league." Williams signed with Pittsburgh and became one of the ABA's better guards.

But Charlie went for his points first, *then* worried about the team. Hawkins didn't like him. "He was a very arrogant-type person," Connie maintains. "Wasn't nobody on the team real friendly with him. Charlie took a lot of shots to get recognition. It's in plenty of ballplayers' minds that scorers get all the money. I would try to get him to coincide with the team more, but mostly he didn't listen."

Tom Washington, Connie's roommate and closest friend on the Pipers, was the antithesis of Williams. Large, outgoing, and usually uninhibited, Wash was the Pipers' comic; his full, booming laugh resounded through the locker room, his wide mouth curled in an almost perpetual smile.

Washington even smiled on the court, where he entertained the men he guarded with non-stop monologues—passable imitations of Tom's idol, W. C. Fields. Against Denver's burly Tom Hoover, Washington would bark from the side of his mouth, "Smooth move Hoove. Smooth move by the Hoove. Good smooth move Hoove. Sensational smooth move by the Hoove." Hoover would laugh so hard he couldn't concentrate on the game.

The Pipers nicknamed Washington "Swoop," because he swept young ladies off their feet. He thought nothing of jumping on stages to dance with go-go girls. In the locker room he stomped about in his lime-colored silk underwear trading jokes with Connie and shouting in his best W. C. voice: "Drat, Shadrach and Abednego. I've been hoodwinked!"

But Washington was also an intense, deeply emotional twenty-three-year-old. But beneath the laughter, he was the Pipers' hardest loser. He often brooded, was easily hurt by criticism, and sometimes wept after a defeat.

Chico Vaughn had a taste for Scotch. He also had a taste for rum and a taste for Catawba wine and most other alcoholic beverages. For three seasons Chico (a black man from Ohio, not a Latin) had been among the best defensive guards in the NBA. Then he floated downhill. The St. Louis Hawks traded him to Detroit in 1965. The Pistons placed him in the expansion pool and he'd been claimed by San Diego. But Vaughn jumped to the ABA, and San Diego didn't jump to get him back.

Chico, however, had a great season for Pittsburgh. His hands were still surprisingly quick, and the three-point field goal breathed new life into his outside shot. Vaughn became so dedicated he didn't miss a single game because of drunkenness or hangovers (although he rarely played without first downing at least two amphetamines). The same cannot be said of practices. "I'm gettin too ol' to practice," the twenty-seven-year-old Vaughn explained to Connie. "The Chic got to save his strength for the games."

"He'd come in like he was on a three-day bender," recalls trainer Medich. "I'd tell the writers he couldn't work out cause he had the flu." Sometimes Chico didn't make it to practice at all. He seems to have been plagued by an extraordinary number of deaths in his family and was habitually in mourning. "That was his big excuse," says Alex, "Chic lost four aunts, ten brothers, and five sisters that season—and his father died about five times."

Early in the year, after Chico missed two straight workouts and his phone at the Carlton House Hotel did not answer, Medich called Gabe Rubin, who also stayed at the Carlton. "Something might be wrong, Mr. Rubin," Alex said. "Maybe you better knock on Chico's door."

Rubin called back half an hour later. His voice was solemn. "Chico's feeling very bad," he said. "His father died. The poor guy is really distraught." The club sent a wreath of flowers to his father's home in St. Louis. His father sent back a note thanking them for the flowers.

Charlie Williams and Chico had a close relationship, based almost entirely on mutual dislike. They were often together, but Connie recalls that their conversations were limited to exchanging insults and arguing about who was a better player. When Chico was chosen over Charlie for the All-Star game, he took great pains to make sure Williams didn't miss any details. "Look at this here ring, this here *beautiful* star-sapphire ring," Chico would drawl. "Ain't it beautiful Charlie? I got it at the All-Star game. Got me a color TV too, and a hair dryer and records and . . ."

"Look," Charlie would reply, "I don't care what you got."

"Yes you do," Chico would announce, eyes widening. "You wish *you* was The Chic!"

In hotel bars, while the Pipers were on the road, or when the players congregated at Pittsburgh's Aurora and Luendi clubs, Chico would strut about, waving his glass of spirits, proclaiming, "I'm The Chic from Puerto Ric and all the girls wants my body!"

"Man," Hawkins would say, "get out of my face."

"A lot of the guys didn't like him," Connie recalls, "cause he'd get drunk and curse everybody out. But mostly he just cursed out Charlie. He'd call him a 'little yellow motherfucker,' cause Charlie had light skin. Then he'd say, 'You can't play good as The Chic. You ain't got as many girls as The Chic.' Charlie would just tell him he was crazy and he was a drunk and they'd curse each other out some more."

Toward the end of the evening Chico usually became depressed and dragged Connie into a corner to discuss his troubles. "He'd tell me how bad he felt that his wife left him, and how it was his fault and he wanted her back," Hawk remembers sadly. "I listened to him to pacify him, that's all he wanted. He wasn't an *evil* dude.

"Then he'd start tellin me about his money problems. See, he had these kids in cities around the NBA. I think there was one in St. Louis, or maybe two in St. Louis. I don't know if Chico knew. And there was one in California and maybe a couple in other places. Chic spread his love around pretty good. But he had to make these payments and he was always short. I'd end up goin to Mr. Rubin and helping Chic get an advance."

Adding to the raucous atmosphere was Alex Medich, the brawny, wavy-haired former minor-league pitcher, who served as trainer, traveling secretary, and self-styled "assistant to the coach in everything but coaching." As with the Rens, Medich set the tone at training camp by mincing about whistling taps while he informed players they had been cut. "There was some guys that laughed," Connie says. "Some guys wanted to kick his ass."

Later, the forty-year-old ice-cream-truck-owner spiced the Pipers' printed itineraries with witty little poems like:

> And you call yourselves a bunch of pros!
> You think you have it made, that everything goes!
> But if you do not have discipline on your squad
> Everyone, everywhere, is sure to think . . . Very Odd.

Alex was overwhelmed by Connie's skills and pampered him openly. He was everything from Hawk's chauffeur and errand boy, to cheerleader and publicist. This infuriated many of the other players and led the volatile Medich (who topped the ABA's trainers in technical fouls) to shout: "You'll be treated like The Hawk when you plays like The Hawk!"

Then there was 6′ 8″ Dexter Westbrook, one of the quickest, most graceful big men to come out of the Harlem schoolyards. Westbrook had gone to Providence College. He played well, but flunked out and returned to the ghetto. The ABA seemed to offer him a second chance. Pittsburgh acquired Westbrook via a trade with New Jersey two weeks after the season started. He appeared infrequently and was not impressive, but Rubin felt he had great potential.

One evening, while the Pipers were in the midst of the disastrous road trip without the coach, Hawkins got a call in his Denver hotel room. It was Westbrook's roommate Richie Parks. "Something's wrong with Dexter," Parks said frantically, "he's passed out in the bathtub and there's blood in there."

"Did he hit his head?" Hawk asked.

"No."

"I'll be right over."

Hawkins sprinted down the hall to Medich's room and roused the trainer. They found Westbrook on his back, eyes closed. There were drops of blood on the rim of the tub. Alex cautiously reached into the soap compartment and picked up a small box. Inside they found a needle and a piece of rubber hose. "I don't believe it," Alex whispered, "a junkie playin' ball. We'd better hide this before somebody finds out."

They put the box in Parks's gym bag, then called the desk for an ambulance. Westbrook was taken out on a stretcher. A call was placed to Rubin in Pittsburgh. He ordered them to say nothing to the other players or the press. There was a terse announcement that Westbrook had become ill. Several days later he was cut from the squad. Rubin sent some money to Westbrook's wife in New York.

Cazzetta emerged from the hospital reading a book entitled *How to Handle the Problem Athlete,* written by two psychiatrists. When he spoke with Rubin, the coach knew he had the right book. Into the Pipers' already steaming bouillabaisse, the owner was about to plop one Arthur Bruce Heyman, pro basketball's superflake.

Even at Duke, where Heyman was an All-American and the nation's leading collegiate player, he was known as "Crazy Artie." Sputtering on an ever-shortening fuse, Heyman was in so many fights he almost turned the fieldhouse riot into a varsity sport.

Art was the Knicks' top draft choice in 1963. He signed for a bonus and hit New York like a storm. New York hit back and things spiraled from there. Heyman stood 6' 5" and weighed 215. He was a thunderous driver and had an adequate outside shot, but he wasn't quick enough to play guard in the NBA. The league was going through an infatuation with towering forwards. So, after averaging 15 points per game his rookie year, Heyman found himself on the bench. He couldn't hack it. Familiar only with success and stardom since his days at Oceanside High on Long Island, Heyman reacted to adversity with a succession of memorable tantrums. Meanwhile, his nervous, non-stop chattering, and compulsive repetition of questions (to find out how people *really* felt) had driven most veteran Knicks into the darkest corners of the locker room.

Heyman's departure was hastened by a little tête-à-tête with Knicks' coach Harry Gallatin. Artie was playing cards on a plane with several teammates when Gallatin asked to join the game. "You don't let me play in your game," Heyman said smartly, "so I won't let you play in mine." While the coach was digesting that, Artie added: "No, I'll change my mind. You can play for two minutes. That's how long you let me play." Brief interludes with San Francisco, Cincinnati, and Boston followed.

Then it was the scoring championship of the Eastern League, a short-lived friendship with Joe Namath, a restaurant on New York's swinging East Side, and in 1967 an ABA contract with the Jersey Americans. Heyman's stay in Teaneck was highlighted by technical fouls ("I warned him not to come any closer to me," explained one official) and heated disagreements with coach Max Zaslofski. Cazzetta got a preview of Heyman when Artie dove for a loose ball near the Pipers' bench, looked up at Cazzetta, and asked: "Coach, do you think this game will have any effect on the war?"

Gabe Rubin was desperate for drawing-cards. The team was losing, all the starters were black, and the people of Pittsburgh were turning a cold shoulder. After Heyman had concluded a game at the Civic Arena by fighting under the stands with one of his Jersey teammates, Gabe asked Connie if he thought Arthur might help the Pipers. Hawk had known Heyman since they played together for the New York Gems. "Yeah," he said emphatically, "he's one of the strongest drivers in basketball. No way in the world he can't help us."

"Do you think the other players will dislike him?"

"A lot of guys dislike a lot of guys around here," Connie answered. "Anyway, Arthur's flakiness ain't like criminal-type flakiness."

So the deal was made—Larry Liebowitz for Heyman. The reaction of the Pittsburgh players ranged from violent disapproval to stark terror.

The night Heyman arrived at the Arena the Pipers had lost 7 of their last 8, and 4 in a row. They had an 11-12 record, a beehive of personality problems, and a coach just leaving the hospital. Art burst through the locker-room door, a vision of modness in turtleneck sweater and bushy sideburns. He dashed to Connie's locker, embracing Hawkins as though he were Stanley finding Livingston. "Hawk, baby, Hawk, it's great to see you baby. What's it like here?"

"It ain't . . ."

"Remember the Gems, Hawk?"

"Yeah, that was . . ."

"What was it like with the Globetrotters?"

"I didn't . . ."

"I'll talk to you in a minute. I better say hello to the coach," Heyman spouted, rushing off.

Connie may not have gotten a word in edgewise, but he had only good words for Heyman when the evening was over. Artie was still an effective player, when properly deployed. Working at both guard and forward, he captured the fans immediately with punishing drives, aggressive rebounding, and alert passing. His enthusiasm was contagious. Washington (recovered from his broken wrist), Hawk, and Harge out-rebounded Indiana. Connie, getting the ball more often, threw in 29 points. Pittsburgh won, 103-100.

Denver, Oakland, and Kentucky soon fell. With Heyman the catalyst, the Pipers put their separate skills together. When the dust settled, they had won fifteen in a row and were back in the Eastern Division race.

"Everybody forgot they didn't like each other," Connie recalls. "We stopped doing things individually. When you start winning, something catches onto a team. You stop being so selfish and sensitive. Chico and Charlie even worked together on defense. We all helped each other out.

"Same with offense. Wash knew he wasn't gonna shoot much. He was the garbage man. He'd set picks for me or lay close to the basket. I'd hit him when I got double-teamed. Chico and Charlie still chucked a lot, but they passed more and Artie fired everybody up. We had confidence in ourselves."

Heyman led the charge, scoring 314 points during the streak. Fans raged at the way he trudged about the court, muttering to himself, shouting at everyone, and pausing periodically to push his thinning locks back in place. In the South and Midwest they yelled about his sideburns and the fact that he was Jewish. He was punched several times on his way to the locker room. In Kentucky someone emptied a can of beer over his head. But Art reveled in the attention, occasionally rousing the crowd by blowing kisses or waving a one-fingered peace-sign. "There was," says Cazzetta, "never a dull moment around Arthur."

Victory made everyone more tolerant and less sensitive. "Guys accepted constructive advice without gettin mad," Connie says. "There was a closeness with blacks and whites. Sometimes we even partied together. I'd invited 'em to join us down to the Aurora after a game, and they'd come."

Connie got along well with the rambunctious Heyman. When Art called him a "Nigger," Hawk laughingly dubbed Heyman a "Honky Jewboy." He saw past Arthur's blustering exterior, recognizing his desire for friendship and his determination to win. "We kept each other loose," Connie recalls. "Arthur is a good guy and he played great for us. When he went off his rocker, I could usually tone him down."

Hawk's teammates were less devoted to Heyman. In fact, the Pipers were united on the court by Artie's driving play and unified off it by a mutual desire to wring his neck.

Connie wasn't annoyed by Heyman's racial jokes, but they drove some black players up the walls. Art called them "Spades" and "Buddarinis" and dubbed Charlie "Half-and-Half."

Arthur never learned to avoid Washington after a defeat. One night he spied Wash, head in hands, before his locker. "That's all right Buddarini," Heyman cried, apparently trying to console him. Washington glared.

"What we doin tonight?" Heyman persisted.

"Leave me alone man."

"What's the matter Wash? Aren't we friends?"

"Yeah," Washington grumbled, "we're friends."

"Well, what's the matter?" Art implored, suddenly contrite. "I was only kiddin, Wash. We're friends aren't we?"

"I *tol'* you, we're friends."

Heyman smiled. "Great, Buddarini. You're my man."

When Arthur had bounded off to console someone else, Washington turned to Connie: "One more minute and I was gonna bust him in the mouth."

"Easy Wash, he's just kiddin."

"I know man, but he pulls that Nigger and Buddarini shit with me much more and I'm gonna bust his ass."

Washington never went after Heyman. But Alex Medich did. At half-time of each game Art would take two or three slugs from a Coke bottle, then pour the rest on the floor. When Medich complained, Heyman said, "Just clean it up. That's your job." One evening he called Alex a "fat honky" and they rolled around the locker room, punching each other. As they were dragged apart, Arthur shouted: "Go ahead, hit me. Hit me on my million-dollar chin!"

Dill—whom Artie dubbed "Pickle"—and Jarvis shared an apartment with Heyman. He drove them cockeyed by his inane questioning ("Do you think we'll win tonight? What do you think the crowd will be?") and con-stant tension. They got tired just watching him pace the floor.

Jarvis was always bleary-eyed on the road, because Heyman, his room-mate, kept him awake. "He'd wake up Jimmy like at four in the morning," recalls Hawk, "and he'd say, 'Tomorrow I'm gonna have a good game.' Then Art would go back to sleep and Jimmy would be layin there tryin to figure out what happened."

Adds Jarvis, "It wasn't enough to just keep your eyes closed and talk to him. He'd come over and pry them open."

Chico kept telling Connie that Art was crazy. Art would tell Hawk that Chico was crazy. Connie told each of them they were right.

An ordinary coach, hung up on the traditional coaching values of author-ity, discipline, and conformity, would have blown his mind—and the championship—trying to cope with the Pipers. Instead, Cazzetta, a father of six, was greatly responsible for their victory.

The players weren't impressed with Cazzetta's knowledge of the game. "He didn't have no real strategy," Connie says. "He wasn't an expert." But the Pipers were an experienced team by ABA standards. They required less teaching and tactics than younger clubs. What Pittsburgh needed was a leader.

Cazzetta believed his job was winning basketball games. He knew he couldn't stop Chico from drinking, make Hawkins punctual, or eliminate Artie's eccentricities. He just wanted them to play as a cohesive unit on the court. By earning their respect and affection, Cazzetta got what he wanted.

"A lot of coaches," says Cazzetta, "say they don't want to win popularity contests. But if your players like you, I think they respond better."

Charlie Williams agrees: "Vince was always in your corner and easy to get along with. He has a knack of getting players to play for him. He'd take you aside and tell you what you're doing wrong. He'd never jump on you in front of your teammates."

Looking back, Connie isn't even sure the coach really liked them: "He had this plagiarized smile, like you wasn't sure he meant it. But that didn't matter, cause Vince gave us all the *feeling* he liked us."

Cazzetta had his hangups. He was preoccupied with getting the largest suite in every hotel and was upset all season by Rubin's refusal to give him a credit card. But these weren't the sort of things which alienated players. "The man was so nice," Connie says, "you wanted to play good for him. He understood people's problems; like Wash being sensitive about missin layups. So he never talked about it in public. He knew when Chico was too drunk to practice, but long as Chico was ready for games he didn't bug him. We didn't have much bitchin on the team cause he listened to everybody's suggestions."

When the press derided the Pipers, Cazzetta told the writers to "criticize me, not the players." He attacked league officials for leaving Williams off the All-Star team. When Connie was roughed up—which seemed to happen every few games—Vince blasted the officials publicly. After one game, in which a Kentucky player blatantly punched Hawk in the face and wasn't even assessed a foul, Cazzetta threatened, "The next time we play them, if the officials don't make calls for deliberate roughing, I'm taking my team off the floor." He was forever complimenting the athletes in the media and by midseason was calling the Pipers "an NBA club—minus a center."

"We knew," says Williams, "he was always in our corner."

The players also knew Cazzetta could be tough. He sent them through exhausting drills during training camp. In Indiana, after sympathizing with Connie's minor physical ailments for several days, he barked, "Darn it, Connie. I need you in there and you're going to play. You won't die!" Cazzetta benched both Chico and Charlie several times for shooting too much. "But," says Connie, "he didn't have a Caesar complex like many coaches. He didn't feel inferior and have to show how tough he was by making a lot of rules."

When the Pipers wanted a record player in the locker room for soul music, Cazzetta agreed. "If it relaxes them," he explained, "why not? I don't believe in discipline for discipline's sake. With a coach and a player a lot of ego is involved. Why create a situation where you must hurt the player's to assert your own?"

He dealt with each athlete as an individual. Some needed pushing, others needed pampering, and Arthur Heyman required both.

The day after Art arrived, Cazzetta held a practice to acquaint him with the offense. During the workout, the coach tossed up an awkward, girlish shot. "Coach," inquired Heyman, a mischievous gleam in his eye, "did you ever play basketball?"

Cazzetta, who played at Bridgeport University, ignored him. "No really," Art persisted, "where did you play?" An embarrassing silence fell over the other players.

"Arthur," replied Cazzetta, smiling coldly, "how would *you* like to play in Anaheim?"

"I got angry and had to jump on Art sometimes," says Cazzetta. "He would get carried away and annoy people, or he'd sulk and I'd ask him if he wanted a stick of candy. But when he got down—which was often—I had to pat him on the back, let him know I thought he was a fine ballplayer."

Cazzetta delighted Heyman by dubbing him "King Arthur." Art responded, "Vince motivates me, and it's about time I've been motivated in the pros."

Sometimes his response was excessive. Heyman felt compelled to give Cazzetta a detailed account of his daily life. "Arthur," Vince would say, "I'm not your warden, I'm your coach."

One evening, before an open date, Cazzetta told the Pipers to go out and enjoy themselves. But Arthur announced piously that *he* was going home to sleep.

Cazzetta bumped into him and a young lady in a restaurant around midnight. "I'm sorry coach," Artie said frantically. "It's that girl's fault. I didn't want to stay out, but *she* made me."

The coach worked overtime protecting King Arthur from his teammates. Before one game he called a meeting and, while Heyman sat in a corner snickering, announced, "I know a lot of you guys want a piece of Arthur. But hold off till we win the playoffs. After the last game I'll pass out boxing gloves and you guys can line up and take turns." When the laughter died down, the grinning Cazzetta added, "Just let me have him first."

Cazzetta was also effective with Connie. In the beginning of the season, when everyone was jumping on Hawk for not shooting enough, the coach remained calm. "Connie is a very sensitive person," says Cazzetta. "I don't believe anyone will get anything out of him by hollering at him or pushing him around. He has too much pride for that. But Connie does respond to quiet, logical talk."

Cazzetta could have initiated a struggle of wills over Hawk's chronic tardiness. Instead, he took Connie into his office and discussed it. "We've got a rule and you're putting me on the spot. I don't want your money. But you're the captain, the guy I'm supposed to turn to, and you're setting a bad example coming here half an hour late. If I don't fine you, aren't we gonna have worse trouble with the other guys?"

"Yeah," Connie nodded, "you're right."

"What's the problem?"

"Man, we start so early! I ain't even awake at nine thirty. Then I ain't got no car. I got to wait for a ride. And sometimes my wife forgets to wake me up."

"Would it help if we switched the workouts to noon?"

"What?"

"Noon. We could practice at noon. There's nothing sacred about nine thirty."

Cazzetta not only pushed back the workouts, he ordered Alex Medich to call Connie an hour before practice and—when necessary—drive him to the gym. Eventually Alex chauffeured half the team to practice—which consequently started on time.

"We kept after Connie," says Cazzetta. "I knew it was a real problem for him. He sleeps so soundly. On the road, I'd have Alex call his room half an hour before team meetings. I could have made an issue of his being exactly on time. But it's silly to provoke an issue. Then the coach has to do something—mete out a punishment—and he creates resentment and loses cohesiveness."

The fifteen-game winning streak was broken in early January. But the Pipers kept rolling. For two months they battled the Minnesota Muskies for first place. Every night someone emerged to lead them. Most often it was Connie. His defense still didn't win any awards, but he was holding his own and putting many more on the scoreboard than he gave away. Thirty-point and forty-point nights became his norm. No ABA defender could contain him.

When Rubin traded Ira Harge to Oakland—against Cazzetta's wishes—for an obscure forward named Willie Porter, who arrived with an ankle injury and rarely played, Hawkins moved almost exclusively into the pivot. He wasn't happy playing with his back to the basket. The physical pounding increased. But Cazzetta needed him there, and Hawk did as the coach asked.

His body was soon covered with welts and bruises. Several nights he awoke screaming with cramps in his legs. He was kicked in the thigh, suffered a blood clot, and missed seven straight games. (Pittsburgh lost four.) But two days after he returned, he started the Pipers on a twelve-game winning streak. Once he overslept and missed a flight to Minnesota, caught the next plane, arrived shortly before the game, and still scored thirty-three points in a crucial victory.

"Everybody on the team was playin great," Connie recalls. "Chico and Charlie were fantastic. When we got down, Arthur picked us up. And Wash, nobody worked harder than him. He'd drive himself till he cried. He out-rebounded guys much bigger. We just kept winnin."

During a game against Minnesota, Hawk hit 10 of 13 shots over Rookie-of-the-Year Mel Daniels. Several were twisting schoolyard drives that had his teammates leaping off the bench shouting, "Fly Hawk fly!" Twice he hit sweeping dunks. "What are you going to do when a guy goes eight feet off the ground and throws the ball *down* through the hoop?" asked a dejected Daniels after Pittsburgh's victory. "I couldn't believe how high he went and how long he stayed up there. I just said, 'The hell with it.'"

Throughout the league, there was no longer any question of Connie's stature. He was billed everywhere as the answer to the NBA. Said Cazzetta, "I coached Elgin Baylor in college. But Connie is the finest *professional* basketball player in the country." The praise made Hawk's adrenalin flow. NBA fans and writers—as opposed to players—still questioned his feats. But he was no longer a candidate for *Who's Who in Obscurity*.

Hawkins was again a recognized figure on the streets of Pittsburgh. The Pipers' home attendance, however, remained depressing. The players were dismayed by the city's lack of support. Connie felt this most of all. The sea of empty red seats at the Arena was a reminder that he still wasn't in the big time.

Hawk also felt sorry for Gabe Rubin. The owner was hurting himself by constant feuds with the local press, but Connie liked him. "Right from the beginning Gabe struck me as a genuine guy," he recalls. "He was always available to talk to us. He'd take players out to dinner and treat 'em nice."

Hawk convinced several of his teammates to volunteer for personal appearances. "Gabe was real shook up and grateful that we would help for free," he says. "Me and Arthur went to a Jewish father-and-son banquet. I visited a couple of schools. But didn't nothing really help. The fans just wasn't interested in us."

Despite the empty seats, the Pipers continued to win. Late in the season, with Pittsburgh holding a slight lead, Connie suggested to Cazzetta that they sign 6' 9" LeRoy Wright, the man who had given him so much trouble in the ABL. Wright was working for Technical Tape in New York and playing weekend ball in Connecticut. "LeRoy was knowledgeable," says Hawk. "They signed him and he really helped. He never scored much, but he could handle the big centers like Mel Daniels."

Wright was a mature twenty-nine-year-old pipe-smoker who dressed conservatively and kept to himself. His presence, even in the locker room, had soothing effect on the younger players. Under the backboards, he took pressure off Connie.

Hawkins no longer had to push himself to get involved. During the final weeks of the regular season, he was even calling the wire services for late scores when Minnesota played on the West Coast. "I really wanted to win," he says. "That season was the most fun I'd ever had. I was eatin well and livin at home. The team was good, I knew I was doin good. I didn't feel too much pressure. I'd come to have confidence in myself."

His confidence was well-placed. With the regular season title on the line, Hawk had another run of great performances. He scored 40 against Kentucky, 36 against New Jersey, 33 against Minnesota—and finally it was over. With three games remaining, Indiana defeated Minnesota, clinching first place for Pittsburgh. "I felt so proud to finally be on a team that was first in something," Connie recalls. "It's a beautiful feeling."

"Going into the playoffs," Hawk says, "I wasn't worried about the team. I knew we would win. I guess, deep inside, I felt no matter how bad things got, I could always handle it myself."

Hawkins's awareness of his own ability had reached a new level. The visible rust of the Globetrotter years had been scraped away. He now believed that every time he stepped on a basketball court he could—provided he drove himself hard enough—accomplish whatever he wanted.

Before the first game against Indiana, Hawk was so charged up, he shouted at Roger Brown, "We gonna kill you."

"Oh yeah," Roger sneered, "I bet."

Roger would have lost his bet. Hawkins had 38 points and 19 rebounds, as Pittsburgh rolled, 146-127. "We'll sweep in three," Hawk predicted after the game. He was right again. Heyman bombed Indiana for 32 points in the second game and threw kisses to the irate fans. The sweep was completed two nights later when Hawk scored 29.

The powerful Muskies should have been more trouble, but LeRoy Wright neutralized Mel Daniels, Hawkins had a field day, and the Pipers won four games to one.

In the final series, against Western champion New Orleans—and the Bucs' strong front line of 6' 4" Doug Moe, 6' 8" Red Robbins, and 6' 7" Jackie Moreland—Hawkins (whose weight had dropped to 180) reached his peak when it counted most. He sat out eleven minutes of the opener with foul trouble, but still flew over Moe for 39 points. Charlie and Art had 26 each. The Pipers won, 120-112. In the locker room they laughed and pounded each other on the back as though they'd already captured the title.

But they played the next two games as though they thought they really had. Heyman, hobbling on a fallen arch, was useless. Washington, the most unnoticed but most courageous Piper, had aggravated the wrist he broke earlier in the season and was also playing on a swollen knee. Charlie and Chico, apparently convinced it was time to play "I can score more than you," froze Hawkins out.

The Bucs won the second game 109-100 in Pittsburgh and won again, 109-101, before a screaming, sellout crowd at the steamy Loyola Fieldhouse in New Orleans. "Connie never saw the ball," Cazzetta recalls. "Our guards had a tendency to go one-on-one and forget about him when they got overconfident." (The situation was hardly novel. During the regular season, Charlie took 350 more shots than Hawkins and Chico took 125 more.)

"In the locker room, I was tellin myself to keep cool," Hawk recalls. "Chico and Charlie been pullin that shit all season. I had to count on Vince gettin them out of it." His thoughts were interrupted by a commotion outside. Then armed policemen were pushing their way into the locker room.

"One of your boys punched a fan," drawled a cop. "Knocked him down and hit his head. The boy's on the way to the hospital. May have a serious concussion."

Cazzetta stepped forward. "Is this a joke?"

"No sah, no joke. Boy was fifteen years old. Wanted to shake hands and one of your players punched him." The Pipers stared at the cops in disbelief.

Then, from the hall, a voice yelled: "It was Art Heyman."

"All right," cried the cop in the dressing room, "we're here for Art Heyman. Which one of you is Art Heyman?"

"I'm Arthur Heyman."

Connie thought, "If you don't be cool Arthur, you ain't gonna be Arthur Heyman for long." But Art was angry.

"We're taking you in," said the cop.

"Where?"

"Jail."

"You aren't taking *me* to jail," Heyman shouted, his voice panicky. "Alex, Alex, get Mr. Rubin." Medich raced from the room and returned moments later with the owner and George Mikan. They conferred in a corner with the police, while Art paced about, hands outstretched, pleading, "What's wrong? What's wrong? I didn't do anything!"

Finally Mikan approached Heyman, a worried look on his face: "Art, you can go back to the hotel. But you can't leave town till we see what happened to this kid."

"But I didn't do *anything* to any kid!"

"You still can't leave town Art, try to calm down."

In a cab back to the hotel, Connie said to Wash, "This really gonna fuck the team up. Charlie and Chico go crazy, now Art hits a kid. He'll still be down here when we come back *next* year."

By morning, the situation had changed. The police version turned out to be slightly inaccurate. The fifteen-year-old with a serious concussion was actually a twenty-three-year-old with a cut and a bruise. When Hawkins saw Art in the hotel lobby, Heyman was smiling again: "It was all a big mistake. The guy has some kind of rare disease. He has these blackouts. When we were going through the crowd to the locker room, he tripped and fell against me. I must have thought he hit me, so I pushed him and he fell. They're dropping the charges. You didn't think I'd really push a little kid, did ya Hawk?"

"No man."

"You really didn't think so, did ya?"

"No Arthur, you ain't the type."

That night Cazzetta was grim as he spoke to the team: "Too many people in here think they can win it by themselves. Well, it isn't working out that way. Tonight we've got to get the ball inside—to Connie. Is that understood?"

Hawkins could feel the excitement building in his stomach as the Pipers came out to warm up. The small, muggy arena was again overflowing. Connie dunked a layup. "Nice shot, nigger," yelled a red-faced man standing under the basket. Hawk's head snapped around, seeking the voice. "Hey nigger, way to go nigger," the man yelled again.

"Yeah, nigger," called a man next to him, "nice shot."

Hawk, already keyed-up, started toward them. LeRoy Wright grabbed his shoulders. "Come on man, take it easy."

"Fuck it LeRoy, them guys called me a nigger. I'm gonna kick ass right now!"

"That won't do no good," Wright said soothingly. "You know the people down here is crazy. Forget it Hawk, you got a game to play."

Connie spun and returned to the layup line. "Whatsamatta boy," hollered one of his antagonists, "can't you take a little joke?"

Hawkins took out his anger on the Bucs. Neither Moe nor Moreland could handle him. His only problem in the first half was Chico and Charlie. And Cazzetta handled that. "I told you to get it to Connie," the coach raged in the huddle. "Now both of you sit down! Vacendak and Jarvis, get it to Connie or you're coming out too." They got it to Connie, and Hawk hit 17 of 34 shots for 47 points. Tom Washington took down 25 rebounds and smothered Red Robbins. Connie led a frantic fourth-quarter rally and Pittsburgh won in overtime, 106-105.

But Hawkins shared none of his teammates' exhilaration as they pushed through the crowd to the locker room. Pain had been building in his right knee throughout the second half. Had the game lasted much longer, he could not have continued.

It was a torn ligament.

He watched the fifth game in Pittsburgh sitting on the bench in street clothes. The Pipers lost, 111-108. They were one defeat away from elimination.

Dr. Fred Burkey, the team physician, had told Hawk the injury would not be permanent and would not require an operation. But he didn't know if Connie could play the sixth game, four days away. "I can't believe it could end like this," Hawkins told Wash late that night. "The whole fuckin season come down to two games, we got to win 'em, and my leg is fucked up."

"You be all right Hawk," Washington said, his voice trailing off. "You got to be . . ."

The day before the sixth game, the Pipers worked out in Pittsburgh. Connie's knee was still rigid and painful. He couldn't run. That night, while he ate with Nancy and the children, the stiffness increased. He rose and limped to the phone. "Coach, this is Connie Hawkins."

There was a long pause on the other end. "Yes Connie?"

"You remember, you told me once, I should let you know in advance if I didn't think I could play a game?"

"It's worse?"

"It feels bad. Real stiff."

"O.K.," Cazzetta said, inhaling deeply. "The decision is up to you. Just take care of it tonight. I'll see you on the plane."

"I couldn't sleep," Connie recalls. "All night I was tossin and turnin and worryin and feelin sad. The pain kept wakin me up."

He managed a few fitful hours, but it felt no better in the morning. He was the last player to board the plane. His teammates stared dejectedly as he hobbled down the aisle and slid into a seat beside Washington. "It's bad man," Connie said, stretching out the leg. "I don't know what I'm gonna do."

At their hotel in New Orleans, Alex wrapped the knee in hot towels. The heat soothed the pain, but the throbbing returned when the towels were removed. Connie was beginning to panic as he and Alex took a cab to the fieldhouse several hours before the game. In the locker room he put on his uniform and lay on the rubbing table. Alex massaged the knee with analgesic balm. The heat was intense. At first, it felt good. Then he screamed, "Stop, stop man! It's burnin me!" Alex quickly whipped off the cream. The trainer then bound the knee in a thick ace bandage.

"Fuck it," Connie said, "I'm gonna shoot around." He grabbed a basketball and hobbled onto the empty court.

Hawk could hear the pounding of his feet ricochet through the building. He ran as much to let out his frustration and disappointment as to loosen the knee. The stiffness did not decrease. He couldn't make lateral movements without excruciating pain. After ten minutes he was ready to give up, return to the locker room, and change.

Then he felt the knee beginning to loosen.

Hawk drove himself harder: "I was excited, I couldn't believe it. The more I moved on it the more it got loose. It still hurt, I was still draggin it, but I felt maybe I could play."

He went back and ordered Alex to apply more balm. "But it burned you," the trainer said.

"Damn, man, I got to play. Put it on."

An hour later a doleful Vince Cazzetta walked in. "How is it?"

"I don' know, but I'm gonna try it," Connie said.

The leg was tightly wrapped. Connie couldn't straighten it. The best he could do was limp. But even half-crippled, he was effective. By halftime Hawk had 17 points. But his teammates, on the brink of defeat, were choking. The Pipers trailed by 13.

Moe raised the margin to 15 with a jump shot to open the second half. Then Connie took charge. Still limping, he drove, leaped and twisted through the New Orleans defense, hitting dunks, followups, jumpers, and several impossible schoolyard specials. Washington owned the backboards. Chico and Charlie pressed the New Orleans guards and began stealing the ball. This time they got it to Connie. Seconds before the quarter ended, Hawk hit a resounding stuff to tie the game, 93-93. In the huddle, his teammates stared at him open-mouthed. Pain still gripped his knee in the fourth quarter, but Hawk kept scoring and Pittsburgh pulled ahead. He had 11 points in the final period, including 5 of 6 free throws in the last minute.

With thirty-five seconds left, New Orleans still had a chance. Pittsburgh led, 115-112. Jess Branson drove, hoping for a three point play. Hawk's arm swung like a giant windmill. His hand smashed the shot to the court.

The final score was 118-112. Connie had 41 points. They were going back to Pittsburgh for the final game.

Hawk lay exhausted on the rubbing table, eyes closed, while Alex massaged his knee. His teammates were shouting and cheering around him. Connie felt too peaceful, contented, and tired to yell. But Art Heyman, who had scored 20 points, was almost beside himself. "Hawk," he shouted, "Hawk is the greatest ballplayer in the world!"

Outside at the press table, Bill Sharman, who had coached the San Francisco Warriors that season and was moving to the ABA, was dumfounded. "He had his leg taped up like a race horse after a knee injury. He was moving on sheer desire," Sharman marveled. "I've never seen a performance like that. He made some moves I've never seen before. Hawkins belongs in the same class with Jerry West, Elgin Baylor, and John Havlicek."

Pittsburgh's basketball fans, who had ignored the Pipers all year, turned out 11,457 strong for the seventh game. They saw the team put everything together. Heyman, so keyed-up, vomited four times in the locker room, waved his fists at the cheering crowd after every basket, and scored on a succession of solo drives. Chico and Charlie forced the New Orleans backcourt into errors. Chico fired home three 3 pointers, and Charlie hit from all over the court, scoring 21 points in the first half.

Hawkins and Washington controlled the backboards, and Hawk went into his Trotter routine; waving the ball over his head, passing it behind his back, between his legs and over his shoulder, piling up assists. The Pipers' fastbreak made an expressway of the middle lane in the third quarter, as their lead rose to 20 points. New Orleans rallied, but it was not enough. Pittsburgh won the ABA title, 122-113. All the Piper starters scored in double figures. Hawkins had 20 points, 16 rebounds, 9 assists. When the buzzer sounded, he was dribbling; gawky, limping, fatigued, but proud figure, running out the clock while the Bucs tried hopelessly to steal the ball. The fans swarmed over the court.

Connie found Tom Washington in the hall outside their locker room. Standing in a sea of shorter men that swirled beneath them, they embraced. Washington, who had taken down 27 rebounds, sobbed uncontrollably: "I tried, I tried. I did the best I could."

"You were beautiful Wash," Connie said softly. Then he was crying too, the tears wetting his mustache and dripping off his chin. Then Arthur Heyman had his arms around both of them, burying his sweaty hair in Wash's chest. All three men were weeping.

Moments later they were dousing each other with champagne and throwing Rubin and Cazzetta into the showers. Finally, Hawk slumped in front of his locker. Alex, a glass of champagne in his hand, unwrapped the knee. It hurt, but Connie was feeling no pain. One by one, each of his teammates gripped his hand and thanked him. In the center of the room,

Arthur was making an enormous racket, toasting everyone but Harry Gallatin. Hawk heard him yell, "I'm twenty-five and I'm a winner." Connie smiled. This wasn't the NBA, where the Celtics were still kings. But for this night, at least, he could forget about where he wasn't, and enjoy where he was. He would soon be twenty-six, and he too was a winner of sorts.

15

SUPER COACH

"My word is law."
—Jim Harding, Minnesota Pipers training camp, 1968

That summer, the ABA's Most Valuable Player remained in the North Side ghetto, running a series of basketball clinics for the Mayor of Pittsburgh. It wasn't very lucrative, but it was work he enjoyed. "A lot of those kids reminded me of me," Connie says. "Especially the shy, quiet ones. I tried real hard to make sure they wasn't left out."

Those who watched him teach marveled at his patience and sensitivity. "You remember that one drill we had today," Hawkins told writer Jim O'Brien, who covered a clinic. "The circle with the one boy in the middle passing to the boys around him. It's good for passing and eye control, but more important, it gets them involved. That's my idea."

When he wasn't at the clinics, Connie was usually with his family. Hawk had little recollection of his own father, and thus had only a vague idea of what a father was supposed to do. But he was twenty-six, and increased maturity had brought a greater interest in his children. "All of a sudden," Connie recalls, "I really enjoyed being with 'em. Just watchin Keenan crawl on the floor, or helpin Shawna start to read, or seein her come home and show how she'd learned the Watusi, it gave me a good feeling."

The house on Charles Street was so densely inhabited, neighbors laughingly called it "The Hawkins Hilton." His wife's sisters, their boy friends, Nancy's friends, and a seemingly endless stream of visitors and hangers-on drifted in and out as though it were a public meeting place. The Litmans were never sure how many people actually lived in the house. No matter what time of day or night they telephoned, some were awake and others sleeping.

Hawkins wasn't overjoyed by the constant din and commotion in his home. But he had no strong desire to leave the ghetto. He was comfortable on the North Side, among people like himself, who spoke his language, shared his interests and values, and viewed him with respect. His friends included pimps, numbers writers, and freelance hustlers—the entrepreneurs of the neighborhood.

"The pimps are interesting," he says. "They can make a lot of money, but they live fast and they burn themselves out fast. They got to spend everything they make to keep up their fronts. There's a lot of pressure. After a while, they all seem to end up on dope. They lose their women and just become junkies."

But heroin affected more than pimps and hustlers. Hard drugs had reached out of the street into the schoolyard. When Connie returned to Harlem for the Rucker Tournament or visited his mother in Brooklyn, he was sickened. "That summer," he recalls, "I really began to notice it. When heroin started in Harlem, the athletes wasn't gettin hooked. But now drugs was everywhere. I'd see guys I used to play with—guys that once had great moves, fantastic bodies—and they'd be all sick and wasted. Some just stood around noddin. Maybe they'd hoped to play pro ball, but they never got a chance. So they gave up."

Then Connie learned about Eddie Simmons: he was on heroin.

Eddie had once been his closest friend, his mentor. But, with Hawk rarely in New York, they had drifted apart. "I began hearin stories about him," says Hawkins. "But I thought it was bullshit. I couldn't believe it. Not Ed. I knew he'd stopped playin ball, but . . ."

The stories persisted. Hawk went looking for Simmons. When Connie found him, he knew they were true. "He'd quit on himself," Hawkins says incredulously. "Ed, 'The Czar,' the guy who showed me everything, who got me into Boys High—he'd even lost interest in basketball. I was away. Jackie Jackson was gone with the Trotters. I guess Ed felt alone. He'd wanted to play pro, but the Rens fucked him and he never got another chance."

Simmons was still employed, managing a neighborhood youth program. "But," says Hawkins, "when I went to see him he was sittin with some junkies he'd hired. They were all high." Eddie greeted Hawk warmly. They spoke for several minutes, then agreed to meet in a bar that night.

Connie entered the bar to find Simmons talking with three men who were obviously high on drugs. "Ed had scratches on his hands and wrists like a junkie. He wasn't highed-up yet, but I could tell he was on something."

Simmons bought Connie a drink. Hawk looked into his eyes. They were glazed. Ed began talking of their days in the schoolyard, of the great games against Sanders, Ramsey, and Cunningham. For a moment, he seemed once more like "The Czar," the kid with a million angles and a beautiful set-shot. But the men around Simmons had begun to nod and scratch.

Hawk was uncomfortable. "Ed," he said finally, "I can't be seen with dudes like this, man. You understand?"

"Sure Hawk, I'll get rid of 'em. We'll go someplace."

Connie shook his head. The words did not come easily: "Man, I can't go with you either. We're still friends, Ed. We'll always be tight. But with you being around these dudes, I can't be with you."

Eddie said nothing. He stared at Hawk, a tiny smile on his lips. Then he turned toward the three junkies. Connie pushed hurriedly through the crowd and left the bar. On the street, he thought he was going to cry. But no tears came: "There's no way I can explain how bad I felt. Ed had done so much for me. But what could I do? After that, he'd call my wife or write me askin for money. For a while, I sent what he asked for. Then I stopped. I knew he'd only be usin it to buy drugs. It was three years before I saw him again."

Connie made fewer trips to the Rucker Tournament that summer. But one weekend he traveled to New York to play in the tournament's All-Star game. Hawk went one-on-one against Willis Reed, outscored the Knicks star, and won the Most Valuable Player Award. "Reed wasn't in real good shape," Connie admits. "He played a bad game. But it made me feel great to show the New York people what I could still do."

But while Connie was acclimating himself to Pittsburgh, the Pipers left town. Gabe Rubin had needed 5,000 fans per game to break even. He drew 3,289 and lost $334,532. Unable to find a radio station or sponsors to broadcast the games of his championship team in 1968–69, Rubin concluded that interest in Pittsburgh was too low. This may have been correct. But the franchise was moved to an even less promising location: Minneapolis.

The town was a pro-basketball graveyard. The sport was never popular in the north country. In the 50's, even before pro football and pro hockey (which had devoted followings) joined competition for the entertainment dollar, the Minneapolis Lakers barely broke even with a championship team. The franchise eventually moved to Los Angeles. In the ABA's first year, the Minnesota Muskies actually attracted fewer fans than the Pipers did in Pittsburgh. The Muskies, recognizing a hopeless situation, quickly departed for Florida.

Nevertheless, Rubin was able to unload 85 percent of his stock to Bill Erickson, a boyish-looking, thirty-eight-year-old Minnesota lawyer, who liked to wear red turtleneck shirts and sit in the stands shouting at the referees. Erickson was the ABA's general counsel. He had been encouraged to bring the club to the Twin Cities of Minneapolis–St. Paul by Commissioner George Mikan. The commissioner lived in Minneapolis. He had business commitments there. He didn't like the idea of moving the league offices. But it would have been awkward for the offices to remain, if the ABA had no franchise in the Twin Cities. So, when the Muskies moved away, Mikan helped convince Erickson to bring in the Pipers.

The move was even more disastrous than it first appeared. "We didn't have any fans," Connie recalls. The club required a staggering 8,000 spectators per game to cover costs. The announced attendance averaged 2,263—although each of the 14,500 seats at the Metropolitan Sports Center was offered for just $2 during the second half of the schedule. The Pipers went $772,589 in the red. Erickson was unable to keep up his payments to Rubin. All the stock reverted to Gabe. Then, to make matters more unfathomable, Rubin moved the team back to Pittsburgh the following season.

Although performing in virtual privacy in Minnesota, Connie played the best basketball of his career. Accustomed to his teammates, confident from the start, he took charge as he had done during the previous playoffs. Chico and Charlie were still reluctant to relinquish the ball (Hawk played just 46 games, yet led the team in assists). But Connie shot more than ever. His first instinct was to crash the hoop—and he did it time and again. His play was more aggressive. Even his defense was improved.

During one stretch, Hawkins scored over 30 points in sixteen consecutive games. He set an ABA single-game scoring record with 57 points against the New York Nets. Until a knee injury felled him in mid-January, Connie was averaging 34 points per game.

Hawkins reported more than a week late to the Pipers' training headquarters at the Parkway Motor Lodge outside Minneapolis. He had staged a short holdout while David Litman got Erickson and General Manager Vern Mikkelsen to give Connie a $5,000 bonus to cover his additional living expenses in Minnesota.

At first, the Piper management had not only refused to give Hawk a bonus, but wanted to add another year to his contract. Litman explained that the suit against the NBA made the extra year impossible. When Erickson needed more convincing, David added pointedly that since Connie had signed a non-transferable contract with the "Pittsburgh Basketball Club" and Erickson had formed a new corporation, Hawkins's contract might be void—and Hawk might already be a free agent. Rather than find out, the Pipers hurriedly agreed to the $5,000 bonus.

Connie arrived to find the team in a state of shock. Vince Cazzetta was no longer the coach. The man who meant so much to their success had resigned and left the coaching profession when Rubin and Erickson refused to give him a raise to cover moving his wife and six children to the Twin Cities. Rubin, who earlier had called Cazzetta a great leader and a wonderful human being, said, "He's a lousy coach. His role was overrated. In my opinion, the Pipers won in spite of Vince Cazzetta."

It wouldn't take long for Gabe to discover how wrong he was. By the time Connie got to training camp, the Pipers already knew. Hawk entered his room and found Tom Washington on a bed staring at the ceiling. Wash looked at Connie and shook his head.

"What's happenin man?" Connie said. "Ain't you glad to see me?"

"We're in trouble, Hawk. This team is in trouble. We got us a coach that's outta his mind. The dude don't like black guys. Man, he don't like nobody. The whole team's comin apart."

The coach was thirty-nine-year-old Jim Harding, hired by the Pipers' management because, as he was quick to emphasize, "Jim Harding is a winner." He had coached at Marquette High School in Milwaukee, Loyola University of New Orleans, Gannon College, and LaSalle, and he had never had a losing season. His teams had never lost 3 games in a row. They were constant tournament participants and won by staggering margins. His lifetime coaching record was 200 wins and 51 losses.

But in his wake, along with the victories, Harding had left a trail of NCAA violations, ineligible athletes, altered transcripts, tortuous three-hour practices, player resignations, and endless turmoil. While he was at Gannon, the school's officials discovered that no player on his starting team had higher than a D− average. While he was at LaSalle he threatened to take away scholarships if athletes performed badly ("They're fooling with my reputation") and followed through on his threat. Philadelphia columnist Bill Conlin dubbed him "Baron Von Harding," but that didn't bother him. Once the coach fixed a reporter with an icy stare and delivered what he considered the ultimate putdown: "You," Harding sneered, "are an idealist!" LaSalle was placed on two years' probation by the NCAA for numerous infractions—but, by then, Harding was on his way to Minnesota and his rendezvous with the Pipers.

When Harding told his players, "I know more about this sport than ninety-nine and nine-tenths percent of the coaches in the country," he was probably correct. He saw basketball as a series of precise, interrelated movements. He could talk for hours about how to save a single step while playing defense.

Through a lifetime of dogged study, Harding had reduced the game to a true science—which would have been lovely if he could also have gotten his players from test tubes. This being unfeasible, Harding set out to re-shape the athletes.

He was a living, shrieking example of what happens when all those coachly values of discipline, conformity, patriotism, and uncompromising insistence on victory are carried to the ultimate.

Harding seemed consumed by the need to mold his team into not just a cohesive unit, but into an extension of himself—shaped in his own image. He took every defeat personally. He demanded total conformity and abso-lute obedience. Years of working with frightened adolescents had con-vinced him that anything could be accomplished through shouts and threats and punishments. That was the philosophy he brought to the Pip-ers—a collection of fragile, sometimes unstable personalities, which had produced a championship only under the most sensitive leadership. If ever a coach and a team were not meant for each other, it was Jim Harding and the Minnesota Pipers.

The first day of training camp, the Pipers discovered why Harding's col-lege players had not considered him the ideal father-figure. "I don't care if you were champions last year," he warned. "This is a new year. You'll do things my way, and that's the only way you'll do things. I know this game. I've been a winner every place I coached. And it won't be any different here. You'll play as I tell you to play—or you won't play!"

Trainer Alex Medich, who found himself functioning as Harding's aide-de-camp, recalls, "He really got off on the wrong foot. The players were used to Vince being understandin of 'em. This guy comes in and lays down rules and fines for everything but pickin your nose."

Harding ran the Pipers ragged from the opening practice. The daily rou-tine usually consisted of three separate sessions of two and one-half to three hours each. "He went wild," Medich says. "He didn't realize that it's a long season, that guys weren't in shape yet. He went too fast, rushed everyone. Then guys started getting hurt. But he questioned every injury. He was always thinking somebody was trying to goldbrick. Harding felt that if a guy wasn't in the hospital, he could play."

A small, trim man in white shorts and T-shirt—his gray hair cut military-style, close to the scalp, to camouflage his increasing baldness—Harding conducted practice sessions that would have been the envy of a Parris Island drill instructor. His cold, anxious eyes missed nothing. Mistakes, es-pecially mental errors, were greeted by shouts of anger and were punisha-ble by laps around the court. Often his workouts were a succession of: "All right, you, you, and you—twenty-five laps! Right now, get going!"

"One of his best rules," says Medich, "was that when he yelled, 'Stop,' everybody had to stop what they were doing. If they was in the middle of a shot and they let that shot go, look out. It was twenty-five laps."

Like most pros, the Pipers were deficient in fundamentals. Their play was often careless and unintelligent. There was ample room for instruction. But, while Harding could spot the slightest flaw, his criticisms were so harsh and his advice so rigid that he rarely helped the players. In the Army, Harding would have been considered a "book man." He did everything by the book—his book.

"He wanted everyone to shoot foul shots the same way," Connie recalls. "He felt you had to raise up on your toes and release the ball with your hand at exactly a forty-five-degree angle to the basket. Guys would get so flustrated, thinkin about their toes and their hands, they'd shoot worse than ever. Poor Wash, he was a bad foul-shot to start with. But Harding would be yellin at him every practice and it fucked him up even more.

"Harding screwed up Wash's whole game. He pulled him away from the basket for picks and screens, had him too far out to be a good garbage man like the year before. And he messed with the way Charlie and Chico played defense. When we won, they worked together. They hung back till their men dribbled over midcourt, then they pounced up, stopped the dribble, double-teamed the ball and made a lot of steals. They knew each other so good they would switch without sayin anything. But Harding wouldn't let 'em switch and he made 'em play tight, press, the whole length of the floor. Nobody can do that all season in pro ball. It wore 'em out, and our defense was lousy."

"Harding had this image of *his* kind of ballplayer: strong little white guys who didn't have much natural ability but hustled and scraped and was great at fundamentals," Connie says. "Harding would praise Steve Vacendak and Jimmy Jarvis. Till he found out Steve Chubin was a wild man with broads, Harding was crazy about him too. We got Chubin from LA. He was tough, a fighter-type, and he played pretty good. Harding loved the way he hustled."

The type of ballplayer Jim Harding sought sounds suspiciously like the type of player Harding must have been in his youth. In high school he was an All-State football and basketball star in Iowa. He maintains he lettered in varsity basketball at the University of Iowa. But, according to *Sport* magazine, "a spokesman for the Iowa athletic department . . . reported that the only mention of a Jim Harding was as a freshman numeral winner in 1942," when the Pipers' Jim Harding was thirteen years old.

The coach constantly harassed George Sutor, the 6′ 9″, 250-pound rookie center. Sutor was muscular, handsome, and attractive to women. He propositioned anything in a skirt and set an ABA record by collecting seventeen telephone numbers while the team was changing planes in O'Hare Airport. But, although strong and well-conditioned, Sutor was not an accomplished player. His self-confidence evaporated when he stepped on the court. At practice sessions, even during the regular season, Harding appeared bent on humiliating and emasculating him. "George was very inexperienced; he'd make errors," Medich says. "Harding seemed to pick on him cause George was the biggest, strongest guy on the team. George tried. Man, he did everything Harding told him—jumped when he spoke—but the coach got satisfaction out of making an example of him. George ran more laps than anyone."

"O.K. Sutor," Harding would scream. "You did it again! I don't want it done that way! You did it again! That'll be five more laps Sutor. Get going. Run, run, run!" The more laps Sutor ran, the more exhausted he became, the more errors he made, and the more Harding screamed.

The black players suspected Harding was bigoted because he treated them so harshly. At the least, he was very uncomfortable around them. "I don't know about the bigot stuff," says Medich, "but he didn't like the way some of 'em acted. And he was always thinking *somebody* was out to stab him in the back. So he wanted to stab the other guy first." One player was cut when Harding—skulking behind the dressing-room lockers—overheard him say the coach was "a racist." Harding also dropped black center Ted Campbell because, in Medich's words, "it was rumored that there was marijuana, or something like that, in his room. Right there, the guy never had a chance."

Harding was most unsettled by Richie Parks, the square-jawed, 6' 8" black forward, who had been a Piper substitute the previous season. Parks arrived at training camp in top condition, and many players were sure he would make the team. But Harding used Parks almost exclusively on defense in the drills. "The coach didn't give him no opportunity whatsoever," says Medich.

Why was this? "Well," Alex explains, "Jim didn't like his looks. He was kind of rough-looking, and Harding was afraid of him cause of his features. He thought Richie was defying him with his expressions, with his eyes. I tried to tell Jim that's just the way Richie looks, but he kept thinking the guy would go for his throat."

The team ate at reserved tables in the dining room at the Parkway. One evening, after the players had left, Harding and Medich sat finishing their coffee. Harding was silent, brooding, his face clouded. Suddenly he looked up at Alex and rasped, "I'm gonna cut Richie Parks. Go get him right now!"

"Come on coach," Medich pleaded. "This ain't no place to cut a ball-player, not in no public dining-room. Wait till tomorrow, so I can get his gear and you can do it in private."

"I just don't like that guy," Harding persisted, "I want him gone now."

"Jim, Jim, come on. Save it till tomorrow. You don't want to do it here."

"O.K.," Harding sighed, "tomorrow he goes."

The coach ordered another cup of coffee and fell silent again. For five minutes he stared over Alex's shoulder. As Medich was about to leave, Harding slammed his hand on the table and said loudly, "I have to cut him now, he has to go tonight. He's got to be out of here."

"Jim, are you serious?"

"Yes, yes, I'm not going to wait. Right now!"

"It was like he'd built his strength up for that moment," Alex recalls. "So I went and got Richie. Harding starts telling him about his expressions, about noticing the way he looked at him. He said, 'Now I didn't like that Rich, and I just don't think you and I can get along.' He never mentioned his playing, just personal things. Richie keeps calm, but he says, 'You never gave me a chance, I came here to play ball but you never wanted me in the first place.' Harding goes wild."

"Don't you raise your voice to me," Harding shouted.

"Don't tell me what to do no more," said Parks, his voice now rising. "I'll raise my voice if I want. I got some things to say to you."

"No, no, you shut up. I'm the boss. I'm the boss in this restaurant, because it's part of training camp."

"You son of a bitch . . ."

Alex threw his arms around Parks's waist just as the player moved toward Harding.

"Rich was mad. He would have laid Jim out," Medich says. "I got him outside and he went back to the motel to pack. I came back in and Harding's wipin his forehead and sayin, 'I'm glad that's over.'"

Several black players, convinced they were not getting a fair chance to make the team, left training camp without waiting to be cut.

To the Pipers' astonishment, Harding approached the exhibition schedule as though it were the last great crusade. He wanted, needed, to win every game. He raged at the referees and loudly berated players for the slightest error. At Eau Claire State Teachers College in Wisconsin, when the Pipers were finally beaten by the New York Nets (formerly the Jersey Americans), Harding reacted as though his team had just lost the league championship instead of a meaningless exhibition-game. He sat alone in the empty stands, breathing heavily and grumbling to himself.

The players dressed and walked to the bus which would take both teams back to Minneapolis. Alex was loading the equipment when Harding burst from the fieldhouse door. "All the Pipers off the bus," he shouted. "Everybody off. Everybody off." It was close to midnight.

The Pipers trooped back to the locker room, then watched in disbelief while Harding screamed and cursed at them, denounced each man's playing ability, and stormed about the room, kicking lockers so furiously he left dents in several doors. Back on the bus, where the Nets had been waiting for over an hour, Connie whispered to Washington, "The man is crazy. He's completely nuts. He gonna crack up before the season's over."

Hawk even tried to warn Harding. "It's not like college," he told the coach the following day. "You can't push guys like this. You can't expect to win every game. This is a long season man. We got playoffs at the end. This ain't no twenty-five-game thing like college. We gonna play one hundred games. You gonna kill yourself, if you don't calm down."

"Thanks," Harding said, "but I can take care of myself."

"The coach scared the shit out of the players," Medich recalls. "They'd complain to me about the way he treated them and I'd say, 'Talk to the coach about it, I can't do anything. He's my boss, too.' But they kept quiet. They were afraid. They figured he'd start hollerin about twenty-five laps. The only one that wasn't scared of Jim Harding was The Hawk."

When he was younger, Connie might have been terrified by a Jim Harding. But now he had too much confidence in his ability and was too aware of his importance to the team and the franchise to be intimidated. He sensed instinctively that in a showdown between himself and the coach, management would have to side with him, like it or not. The Pipers had no other drawing card, could not be a winning team without him, and weren't worth much in sale (always a consideration in risky ABA ventures) if he wasn't part of the deal. Connie never pondered these specifics, but he knew his value and acted accordingly.

The coach, however, was anything but impressed by his initial glimpse of Hawkins. "*That's* the Most Valuable Player in the ABA!" he scoffed at Medich, as Hawk loped through his first workout. "I can't see it, his fundamentals are awful!"

When Connie continued shooting after practice, Harding decided it was an excellent time for some instruction. "You're off balance when you take that shot," he announced, as Connie lofted a jumper.

"I always shoot it this way."

"You'll have to change. I don't want you falling away and pulling your arm back so far. I want you to go straight up."

Connie looked down at the coach, puzzled. "I been shootin it like this since I was a kid."

"Well, I don't care about that," Harding bristled. "I don't care if you were MVP, you'll do things my way around here." When the coach stomped away, Connie shrugged his shoulders and continued shooting as he had before.

"Harding would always be telling The Hawk to do things and The Hawk would just ignore him," Medich says. "He wouldn't get mad, in fact, he wouldn't say nothing. He'd defy him by just being silent, starin at Harding. Then he'd keep doin whatever he wanted."

The next run-in came a day later, when Harding called Connie into his office to go over team rules and fines. Hawkins listened quietly until Harding stated that every player must wear a white shirt and a tie on the road at all times. Hawk never wore white shirts and ties. He dressed as young men did on the North Side and in Bed-Stuy. On the rare occasions when he used a suit, he wore brightly colored shirts. Most of his wardrobe consisted of turtlenecks, Banlon shirts, sweaters, slacks, and dashikis. "I can't do that white-shirt stuff," he told Harding.

"What do you mean?"

"I don't have white shirts. I don't dress that way."

"Everyone on my teams dresses that way."

"I don't."

"You'll have to," Harding sputtered. "You'll have to, or you'll be fined. I'll fine you plenty."

"Man," said Connie, "this ain't no college. I ain't no college guy. Why you want me to dress like one? I'm not gonna do that. You gonna buy me new clothes?"

"We'll see about this," said the coach.

Then Connie got his annual toe infection. When Harding saw him sitting out the practice before the Pipers' first exhibition game, he warned Medich, "Hawkins has to play." Alex constructed a special shoe, with a square front and plastic top, that Connie could slide his foot into. But, in the locker room before the game, Hawk refused to wear it.

"It's all funny-colored and outta shape," he told Alex. "It looks like a clown's shoe. Man, I was a Globetrotter too long. I ain't gonna be a Globetrotter no more."

Medich returned in several minutes with the red-faced coach. "What's this about you not playing?" Harding asked.

"I ain't gonna wear that shoe."

"Why, for Christ's sake?"

"Man, you ain't payin me to be laughed at, to have no clubfoot shoe. If I fall down with that shoe, people gonna laugh. I'm not havin nobody laugh at me."

"I don't think it looks so bad," Harding said.

"Well, you weren't ever a Globetrotter. It looks bad to me."

"You'll be fined for this," Harding warned. "Hawkins, I want you in this game. I want you to play."

"I'm not playin," Hawk said. He didn't play.

Things came to a head when the Pipers made their first plane trip of the exhibition season. Connie wasn't on the plane. Hawk arrived the following morning—the day of the game. Harding was furious, especially when he saw Hawkins wasn't wearing a white shirt and tie.

Everything about Connie's demeanor rubbed Harding the wrong way. Hawk was something of a prima donna. He had been treated with kid gloves by Cazzetta and, eventually, fawned over by Rubin. He had been allowed to move at his own languid pace.

But the other Pipers felt no resentment. They knew Hawkins was their meal ticket, were in awe of his performances, and admired him as a man. Connie wasn't a haughty superstar. He didn't boast (in fact, he rarely discussed his own game). He went out of his way to compliment teammates, offered advice to young players like Washington and Sutor, listened to Chico's problems, and took his captain's role seriously. The players were willing to overlook his tardiness. But Harding was not.

When they returned from the trip, the coach spent most of the next practice complaining about "big shots" and "guys who think they can get away with anything." Finally, in a state of great agitation, Harding called a meeting and informed Connie that he was to be fined.

Suddenly Heyman, who was having an awful time trying to adjust to the new coach, jumped up and began to cry. "You treat us like pigs," he wept. "We aren't animals. We're not fuckin pigs or dogs, we're human beings! We've got pride. Why do you treat us like pigs!"

The other players were embarrassed. Harding was unmoved. "I'm sorry Arthur," he said. "But Hawkins will be fined, because I say he will be fined."

Connie finally spoke. "This is a lotta shit. You talkin about how I'm so late all the time. So I'm ten minutes late here and there, it don't mess nobody up. I don't do it intentionally. On the trip, I was there for the game, what difference does it make what day I get there?"

"You'll be fined," Harding repeated.

"Fuck if I will," Hawk said calmly. "If you can get that fine, I'll give you a thousand dollars extra."

The Pipers had been bugging Connie, as captain, to talk to the management about Harding. Now Hawk felt he had something specific to discuss.

He met the next day with general manager Vern Mikkelsen and owner Bill Erickson. "I told them Harding was drivin the whole team crazy," Hawk recalls, "how he was trying to change the clothes I wear, and my shot, and trying to make me play with the shoe, and how he wanted to take my money even though I was there the morning of the game. They said he shouldn't be doin those things. They said I should try to be more prompt, but they weren't gonna fine me and they'd talk to Harding."

Erickson and Mikkelsen didn't want their superstar upset just before the season started. But they also defended the coach. "He seems to be doing a good job, Connie," Erickson said. "We've got a fine exhibition record."

"You can think about records now," Connie answered, "but the man is too rough on the ballplayers. He never smiles. There's no place on his face for a smile. There's gonna be trouble."

"He'll get better," Mikkelsen promised. "He's always been a winner, he just needs to get used to the pros."

Connie shook his head. "The players gonna break first."

"We'll talk to him," said Erickson, "but I'm sure everything will be all right."

Harding never mentioned the fine being rescinded. But it was clear Hawk had won the confrontation. The coach never threatened to fine Connie again—even when Hawkins interfered with the cutting of LeRoy Wright.

Harding cut Wright a week before the season began. Hawk telephoned Rubin in Pittsburgh and complained. Gabe was still a part-owner and chairman of the board. He contacted Erickson and, the next day, Harding grimly announced that Wright was to become an assistant coach—on the payroll and available to be activated if the Pipers needed him.

A few days later, Mikkelsen told Harding to relax his dress code.

Thereafter, the coach let Hawkins go his own way. He recognized Connie's ability ("the greatest player in the world") and could see management would not support him if he tried to push Hawk around. So he pushed everyone else around.

By the start of the season, Harding had driven the Pipers so hard almost every player was limping. They were far ahead of other clubs in conditioning, however, and got off to a fast start. Connie had a string of sensational performances, and the Pipers moved quickly into first place. But victory was not enough for Jim Harding. "He wanted us to win every game by fifty points," Hawkins says. "One time we were thirty ahead and Frank Card, who was a rookie, made a mistake. Harding had a tantrum on the bench. He was screamin and cursin at everybody. If a guy made one error he'd take him out of the game and yell at him. Guys got tense and nervous, afraid to make a mistake and be embarrassed."

The coach's histrionics rarely subsided. Spectators behind the bench complained about his foul language. "He told me when he says a profane word I should hit him in the thigh," recalls Medich. This led to an Abbott-and-Costello scene one night in Duluth, Minnesota: "He went nutty," Alex says, "cursin and screamin every word in the book. I'm like a machine gun, hittin him ratta-tat-tat in his thigh. But he's forgot why I'm doin it. He's slappin my hand and cursin more, and I keeps hittin his thigh and he keeps slappin me away and callin everybody 'bastards' and 'cocksuckers,' and jumpin up and down."

The players were soon convinced that Harding would sacrifice the season to win a single game—and would certainly sacrifice one of them. As injuries piled up, the walking wounded were forced to play unrealistic amounts of time, thus aggravating their injuries. "Charlie Williams had a groin pull," says Medich, "but Harding made him play. He limped for two months. If he'd sat out ten days it would have healed."

The second night of the season, Harding used only one substitute. Three games later, four Pipers went all the way. The team was exhausted and almost blew a 15-point lead. Hawk played the entire forty-eight minutes and scored 42 points. It was half an hour before he had enough energy to walk to the shower. On the way, he spoke to Harding. "Man, I'm gonna wear down if I keep playin this much."

"I'll play you when I need you," the coach answered, "and I need you all the time."

Despite the fast start, the players were increasingly ill at ease. They felt Harding could not be satisfied. After a victory, they would bustle, tired but happy, into the locker room, slump on benches, and begin sipping beer and joking with each other. Then the coach would march in, grim-faced, stand in the middle of the now-silent room, and snap, "Well, we won, but we didn't finesse the hell out of em." As he turned to walk out, Harding would add, "Practice at one. This team needs it!"

"I can't explain how much the players came to hate that coach," Connie says. "He fucked up the head of everybody on the team. Poor ol' Chico was even gettin drunk *before* games. Arthur and Charlie was goin out of their minds with him yellin at em and benchin em soon as they made a mistake. And Wash hated him most of all. Wash was so sensitive, he couldn't stand to be around the man."

During the first half of a game against Kentucky, the Pipers played poorly. Washington missed several layups. Just before the half ended, Vacendak made three costly turnovers. In the locker room, Harding could have berated Vacendak. Instead he went after Washington. Pushing his face close to Tom's, he shouted. "You're careless, you fall backward when you shoot a layup. That's stupid! Go up hard. Why can't you get that through your head?"

Suddenly Washington began to weep. "I'm tired of you pickin on me," he sobbed at the startled coach. "You always fuckin pickin on me."

"No Tom," said Harding, "I hope you don't . . . I don't mean . . ." He put his hand on Washington's shoulder. The player brushed it off roughly. "Don't touch me motherfucker," he shouted, running from the room.

Harding turned to go after him. Hawk's voice broke the silence. "Leave him alone man."

"I just wanted to . . ."

"Leave him alone."

Harding nodded. "Alex, go get him."

"He won't come back in here coach," Medich reported five minutes later.

"I'll get him," said Connie. He found Washington standing against a wall, two hundred feet down the hall. Wash was still crying, his body shaking. Hawk cupped Tom's face in his hands.

"Take it easy, man," he said gently. "Take it easy. Everything's all right."

"I'm not goin back to that man," Wash sniffled.

"The man's crazy, Wash. You know that. You can't let him run you out of your job. You got to ignore him."

Just before the team was to return to the court, Hawkins and Washington entered the locker room. "O.K. men," said Harding, "go out there." Then the coach moved toward Washington. Hawk grabbed his arm: "It's best you don't say anything to him. He's pretty upset."

Harding looked befuddled, almost contrite. "Sometimes I get carried away," he mumbled. "I hope you guys know that. I hope he doesn't think I mean everything I say."

"What else is he gonna think?" Connie said. He walked out, leaving Harding alone in the locker room.

The unstable atmosphere was more than Art Heyman could handle. His play and personality became increasingly erratic. He ping-ponged between shouting matches with Harding and thinly disguised attempts to butter him up. "Art would try to soft-soap him," says Medich. "He'd say good things about Jim in the paper, have his wife call Harding's wife, and give the coach a lift home from the airport."

"The coach must be your daddy, you're so nice to him," Washington teased. Chico called Art "Harding Jr."

With paranoia sweeping the club, some players suspected Art was a "Valachi." Connie made up the term. It applied to players who spy on their teammates and give information to management. Most pro teams have someone they suspect. Often it is the trainer, or a white substitute or marginal starter trying to protect his position by ingratiating himself with his bosses. During the first ABA season, Roger Brown told Connie that the black Indiana players felt Jimmy Rayl was a Valachi.

The information passed along usually concerns black players dating white women, the names and gripes of discontented athletes, and the identity of players who complain about the coach. For years, many players on the NBA Hawks felt they couldn't trust Bill Bridges, a black man, because he was so close to management.

The Pipers suspected Heyman after the front office somehow discovered that Washington's hatred of Harding had reached the point of wanting to be traded. Erickson called Wash to his office, promised that Harding would calm down, but ordered Tom to stop voicing his desire to leave. "A lot of guys thought Arthur must have told, because the only ones that heard what Wash said was Chico, Charlie, me, and Art," says Connie. "But we couldn't be too mad at Arthur. He's a good guy, and he was havin so much trouble with Harding I guess he had to try anything."

Cazzetta had taken advantage of Heyman's being a streak player. When Artie was hot, Vince gave him his head. But since Harding usually pulled Heyman if he made one or two bad plays, Art rarely got momentum, and his performance suffered. There were numerous profane exchanges in full view of the fans. "I'm playing good," Art would shout, "what the fuck's the matter with you, why don't you take out somebody else?"

One evening in Duluth, Heyman cursed the coach and Harding announced: "That'll cost you fifty bucks."

"Why not seventy-five," Art sneered.

"It's seventy-five."

"Try one hundred."

"It's one hundred," said Harding.

Heyman and Harding also exploded at each other in practice. Once Heyman became so incensed at the coach's picky criticisms, he kicked a ball into the stands. "That's gonna cost you," Harding yelled.

"Get fucked," Heyman screamed, raising his fist and heading for the coach. Connie and Wash held him back. They later agreed they'd made a mistake. In any event, Heyman spent much of the season yelling at, then apologizing profusely to, the coach.

The Pipers were playing drum-tight. The instinctive cohesion, the helter-skelter esprit de corps of the previous season was gone. Connie alone kept them winning. Night after night, he pulled out games they should have lost.

"We knew we'd never make it through the year with Harding treating us that way," Hawk recalls. "A lot of guys felt we had to get rid of him. A couple of times we talked about *losin games on purpose* till our record was so bad he got fired. No bullshit, it was discussed. Seriously. I kept tryin to make everybody relax. I'd say, 'Hang on awhile, maybe he'll get better.' But I didn't believe it."

Several meetings "to clear the air" only increased the tension. Harding laughed at the players' discontent. "During the first meeting, everyone got a chance to talk and get things out into the open. But in the second meeting, *I* did all the talking," he told the press. "I realize everyone can't be happy. But I'm not going to have gripers either. If I find a griper, he will be dealt with accordingly."

Connie twice met privately with Erickson. The owner was sympathetic. He didn't approve of Harding's tactics. But he wanted a winning team and Harding still seemed like a winner. "The club's in first place," Erickson persisted. "I'm sure Jim will ease up soon. You can't argue with his record."

"See what his record look like when the season's over," said Connie.

Berated by Harding, shivering in the cold Minnesota winter, and ignored by the sports fans of the Twin Cities, the players huddled together for mutual support. Off the court, there was a closeness that had not even existed in Pittsburgh. Nancy had remained on Charles Street. "She didn't think there'd be any black people and she don't like the cold," Connie says. "I missed her an awful lot, but I understood how she felt." Hawk shared a small, two-bedroom duplex with Washington. Chico Vaughn and Frank Card, a flaky newcomer from the Philadelphia schoolyards, also lived in the apartment complex.

Since Heyman was the only married player who had brought his wife to Minnesota, the players socialized together often. "The white guys came to our parties and everybody got along good," Connie says. "Some maybe thought Arthur talked too much, but he was a lot of fun; he just didn't think about what he was sayin. There wasn't any fightin among ourselves. We were together cause we all disliked Harding. We did a lot of drinkin and carryin on, tryin to forget how he treated us."

Mikkelsen strengthened the club in late November by trading for Steve Chubin, scrappy white backcourt man—who immediately became the apple of Harding's eye—and Tom Hoover, a strong, 6' 10" center. Hoover had been around. He had played in the NBA with New York, Los Angeles, and St. Louis; in the Eastern League; and with Denver and Houston in the ABA. He wasn't a good shot and lacked great speed, but Hoover could play defense and rebound. The Piper players were delighted to get him. "He knew his job," Connie says. "He was physical, he could set picks. I thought he'd take pressure off me under the boards. I was hopin they'd let him play center, so I could go to forward."

During Hoover's first game, Wash got into foul trouble. Harding sent Hoover into the pivot and moved Connie to forward. Hawk scored 33 points. He left the game with ten minutes remaining and Minnesota leading New Orleans by 26. Hoover rebounded well and stiffled the Bucs' inside game.

But the bearded Hoover was a tough, opinionated black man who sizzled if he thought whites were trying to push him around. When Harding yelled at him in practice, Hoover glared and grumbled. He saw little action thereafter.

Still, the Pipers were rolling. A 7-game winning streak brought their record to 14 wins and 4 losses. Hawk had a record-breaking 57-point game in New York; got 33 in Miami; scored 35 points, grabbed 22 rebounds, and blocked a shot to save a victory over Los Angeles; and drew raves wherever he played.

The winning streak seemed to relax Harding—slightly. One evening, however, he shouted at the team, "I'm not gonna let you guys screw around on me. I'll have discipline on this team. You won't put me in the hospital like you did to Cazzetta."

But after several months Harding's words were losing some of their effect. The players weren't as frightened. The coach had levied some fines and was ruthless in practice, but the starters realized the team couldn't afford to fire them en masse. They still despised Harding and allowed him to upset their play, but they weren't jumping quite as quickly when he screamed.

"Even during the winnin streak, the coach was edgy," says Medich. "He was drinkin an awful lot. I had to pull him out of a couple of bars before he got into fights."

The winning streak ended in Denver. On reflection, Hawk thinks it was then that Harding began to come unstrung. The coach was especially manic on the bench, but the Pipers played poorly. Only a 53-point explosion from Connie kept them in the game. With 1:21 remaining, Minnesota trailed, 119-115. Chico hit a foul shot. Steve Chubin, ever the hustler, stole the ball and fed Connie. Hawk put 3 fakes on forward Julian Hammond, then drove through a maze of arms to score his 20th field goal. The Rockets led by one. Harding was beside himself.

Denver stalled the 30-second clock. When the Rockets finally shot, Washington came out of a pile-up holding the ball and signaled for time out. There were 18 seconds left. "We've got 'em," Harding exulted in the huddle, "We've got 'em. Now just do what I say."

The Pipers cleared the left side of the court for Connie. Hawk drove along the baseline with ten seconds to go. Center Byron Beck slipped in front of him. Connie stopped and lofted a jumper. He says Beck hit his arm. The referee didn't see the hit. The ball hit the rim and bounced off. The buzzer sounded, and Minnesota had lost.

It was the Pipers' first defeat in two weeks. Yet Harding raged in the dressing room. He continued to show his displeasure with a grueling practice when the team returned to Minneapolis. The Pipers won their next three games, but the coach still seemed angry. "He banned our record player from the locker room," says Connie. "In Pittsburgh it was like a symbol of our winnin team. We'd play soul music, and we always played the Impressions' 'We're A Winner.' It got us up for games. But Harding started sayin to 'turn it down.' Then he wouldn't let us use it at all."

Harding brushed off an opportunity to get Roger Brown from the Indiana Pacers. Roger was feuding with coach Bob Leonard, and Indiana was willing to part with him for Steve Chubin. But Chubin was Harding's favorite, and Brown, despite great skills, had a justified reputation for arrogance and occasional lackluster play. "Brown isn't my kind of guy," Harding told Medich. "Mikkelsen may want this deal but I don't want Brown on my team. And my word is law." (Brown went on to become an All-League forward.)

A few days later, in Los Angeles, Hawkins, who had scored over 30 points in 14 straight games, was hurt. Scrambling for a loose ball, he felt a knee slam against the side of his elbow. Pain shot up his arm. Time out was called while Alex massaged the elbow. Connie pressed his eyes shut and fought back nausea. Harding looked on in silence. "He didn't even ask if I wanted to come out," Hawkins recalls.

Connie continued to play. The pain was so intense he couldn't bend his arm properly to shoot. But he grabbed rebounds one-handed, curled off-balance shots into the net, and led a rally that erased a 20-point Los Angeles lead.

Then turnovers, which had plagued Minnesota all evening, helped LA come back. In the final moments, Connie stood at the foul line for two shots with a chance to tie the game. He had already scored 47 points: "My elbow hurt so much I thought about tryin them left-handed or underhanded. But I did it the regular way, and I missed both shots." The Pipers lost.

Harding was livid. "We just played stupid basketball," he told reporters. "We made fundamental mistakes and we didn't rebound."

Connie sat nearby, his body hunched with fatigue. His elbow throbbed. The coach walked over and stared down at him: "If you made those foul shots we'd have won."

"My arm was fucked up," Connie replied. "I couldn't shoot right." Harding's face puckered, as though he were sucking on a lemon. He turned away without a word. "You motherfucker," Connie cursed under his breath. "Injuries don't mean nothing to you. Next time I'm hurt, you see if I keep playin."

"The curfew is twelve-thirty," Harding announced. "Everybody better be in their rooms. I'm not fooling around. You were rotten tonight." The players glared at him.

Alex checked the rooms at 12:30. Everyone was in. But as he walked through the hotel lobby, the trainer noticed an unusual number of young women standing around. He had an inkling where they were headed. But he shrugged his shoulders and joined Harding at the bar. The coach was in a foul mood. "We shouldn't have lost that game," Harding repeated. "Careless play, no discipline, no fundamentals . . ."

"He kept brooding," Alex recalls. "By one o'clock he'd had about five martinis and he says, 'I'm going up and checking those guys. I want a little visit with some of them. I've got some things to say.' But I talked him out of it."

Harding downed another martini, then announced: "I'm going up there, Alex. There are some guys who've got to be talked to."

The coach pounded on Steve Chubin's door. Chubin opened it without asking who was there. Harding marched into the room—and found himself in the company of several unclothed people, most of them women.

"Naked broads!" Harding shouted. "What's going on here? They aren't wearing a damn thing. An orgy!"

"Yeah," said Chubin, grinning as he pointed to a girl sprawled on the bed. "Want to fuck?"

"I don't believe it," cried the coach, rushing from the room, "I don't believe it!"

He knocked on another door—and found more naked women. Hawkins heard a commotion in the hall and opened his door just in time to see the coach reeling toward the elevator, mumbling, "They weren't wearing a damn thing, not a damn thing."

Back in the bar, Harding shouted at Medich, "You didn't check those rooms!"

"I did, coach. Honest."

"You should have seen what I saw in Chubin's room. Naked broads! Naked broads!"

Harding swallowed another martini, then said, "Let's go eat." Walking up the street to a diner, the coach was still excited and fuming. Suddenly, he stopped short and winced, clutching his side.

"During the meal he feels another pain," Alex says. "I tell him he better see a doctor when we get back. That's when all the stuff about his heart and the high blood pressure started. And that was also the end of Steve Chubin. Harding's big red apple became a crabapple and he traded him to Indiana right away. But we didn't get Roger Brown any more. All we got was Mike Lewis, who was a rookie and sat on the bench."

The next morning, the team traveled to Oakland to meet the Western Division leaders. The game was billed as the first confrontation between Connie and superstar Rick Barry, who had jumped from the NBA. The Pipers were far ahead in the East. Oakland was even farther ahead in the West. A large crowd was expected.

Connie's elbow was still very painful. All morning Harding kept asking if he thought he could play. "Alex is gonna take me to a doctor in Oakland," Hawk said coldly. "If I can get something to kill the pain, I'll play."

At the airport, Harding continued to pester him. "It feels the same, man," Connie replied. "There's a lot of pain in there."

"O.K. I don't want you to play with a bad injury," Harding said hurriedly. "But the team *does* need you. Even with a bad arm, you're more effective than George Sutor or that Hoover with two arms. Don't forget that, Connie."

Then the coach turned to watch two long-haired boys in beads and dungarees walking across the terminal, carrying guitars.

"Look at those weirdos," he said with disgust. "Look at that, will ya. I bet they're faggots. That's what's wrong with this country."

The Oakland physician found broken blood vessels above the triceps. He gave Connie a shot of cortisone, but told him not to play. Harding was upset. He badgered Hawkins to see another doctor. Connie finally hid in a teammate's hotel room to avoid the coach.

Even without Hawkins, the Pipers played well. With four minutes to go, they led Oakland by eight. Then Minnesota ran out of gas and was beaten. Connie sat on the bench in street clothes, watching Harding squirm and bellow. At one point in the tense game, however, Hawk almost fell over laughing. Big Tom Hoover had been arguing with the refs all evening. From the bench he began shouting, "Look at Rick Barry, look at what he's doing! You motherfuckin refs always protectin the Whities. You don't give a shit for us. You out to protect the Whities!"

Harding's mouth dropped open. "You can't say *that*," he yelped in dismay. "You can't say things like that!"

"It's true," Hoover said, waving his hand at the coach. "Them refs always protect the Whities."

"I don't want to hear you say that again," Harding said, very upset. "You can't say that on my team."

The team returned to the Twin Cities after the defeat. Harding looked pale and drawn. "I've never lost three games in a row in my coaching career," he informed Connie, "and I'm not about to do it now." The Pipers had three days off. Harding drilled them as though they were preparing for the playoff finals. Penicillin was poured into Hawkins's elbow.

The day before the game, Harding sent the team through a rugged scrimmage. His angry shouts rattled through the St. Thomas College gym where the Pipers worked out. After an hour, the players were dragging. Harding continued to push. As exhaustion led to more errors, the coach's anger mounted. Then he screamed, "Stop!" and began to criticize a defensive mistake by Tom Hoover. The hulking center listened for a minute then said, "Aw man, I didn't . . ."

Harding's face flushed. "They'll cost you fifty dollars for talking back."

"What are you . . ."

"You're *suspended*, suspended for one week *without pay!* " Harding shrieked hysterically. "Go take a shower! Get off this court!"

Hoover moved toward Harding. Alex grabbed him by the waist. "Take it easy Tom," Medich said. Then he whispered, "This is the moment you've been waiting for. There's reporters here. This time Harding's gone too far."

As Medich eased Hoover to the locker room, Harding noticed Tom Briere of the Minneapolis *Tribune* standing beside the court. "You're not going to print that, are you?" he asked.

"I've got to," said Briere, "that's my job."

"Will you keep it out of the paper if I drop the fine?"

Briere shook his head. "Then," threatened Harding, "I'll have to close all practices to the press. I did that at college."

While the players were showering, Harding announced, "I don't want anybody on this team talking to a sportswriter. I'll do all the talking for this team."

"Coach," Connie said, "we don't have any fans as it is. You fuck us up with the press, they're gonna blast us and we'll never draw."

"Don't worry," snapped Harding, "I know what I'm doing."

The story broke in the local papers. The Minnesota management, clearly embarrassed, refused to back Harding. The restrictions on the press were lifted. Hoover's fine was rescinded. His suspension was dropped.

The Pipers managed to defeat Indiana the following evening. But just before the team was to fly to Houston, there was an announcement: Jim Harding would not be making the trip. The coach's diastolic blood pressure was dangerously high. He would be taking an indefinite leave of absence. "The players," recalls Connie, "were happy as sissies in Boys Town."

On the plane, Chico Vaughn toasted the occasion. "I hope," he said, "the motherfucker don't ever recover."

16

FLOATING CARTILAGE

> "Though you have never had a knee injury before,
> you know immediately what has happened to you. It hurts
> so much it isn't even localized; every nerve in your body screams
> with pain. The pain is absolutely exquisite. So is the fear."
> —*Robert Daley*, Only a Game

Jim Harding's temporary departure hardly ended the Pipers' troubles. Illness and injuries—the inevitable result of the coach's sustained pressure—began to pile up. Most of the players were hurting. Charlie Williams and Art Heyman missed games with recurring groin and hamstring pulls. Five players were out intermittently because of flu. Connie was ill for a week, sat out one game, and had several mediocre performances.

And the Pipers lost Tom Hoover. When the team was in Houston, Alex Medich was awakened in his hotel room by a call at 5:30 A.M. It was the county jail. Hoover was a prisoner. It seems that when Hoover was traded from Houston to Minnesota, he skipped town without paying about five hundred dollars in debts. His creditors were slightly piqued. Medich had to use the Pipers' meal money to bail him out.

"Howdy jailbird," Washington said, when Hoover walked into the dressing room.

"Don't fuck with me Swoop," the big center grumbled.

"Shit, I'm staying away from you," Wash laughed. "You might be a bad influence on me."

The Minnesota management, in an uncharacteristic rush of righteousness, took those sentiments seriously and sold Hoover (a player the Pipers needed badly under the boards) to New York the following morning.

Although they had been unanimously delighted by Harding's leave of absence, the Pipers' play did not improve. In fact, under interim coach Vern Mikkelsen, the easygoing general manager, they were even less impressive. Harding had a multiplicity of faults, but he at least terrified the guards into passing to Hawkins. Now, many players reacted to Harding's departure like school kids when the teacher leaves the room. Chico, Charlie, Art, and Steve Vacendak took advantage of Mikkelsen's low-key approach to do an excess of shooting. Mikkelsen, a former NBA All-Star with the old Minneapolis Lakers, urged them to find Connie. But he rarely raised his voice, and the guards ignored him. The Pipers began to lose as many as they won.

On January 7, 1969, while Mikkelsen was still coaching, I began work on a story for *Life* magazine about Connie. We had grown up in New York at the same time. I had watched him often in the Garden. After the scandal, I developed an almost morbid fascination with his career. I intended to write a short article on the feelings of a great athlete doomed to exile. It had never occurred to me that he might be innocent of the DA's charges.

We met in the lobby of the International Motel near LaGuardia Airport and drove to Commack Arena. We talked in the car and in the dressing room. Later, while the team waited at the airport, we spoke for over an hour.

I was struck by how gentle and unassuming Connie was—not humble, but without the affectations, pomposity, or excessive sense of self-importance so common to great athletes. I'd been warned he was courteous but close-mouthed with writers. Instead, I found him talkative and open. I had expected an external bitterness, an understandable self-pity, but there was none. When I got to know Hawk better, I learned of the pain inside. But knowing this only made his outward demeanor seem more remarkable. Hawkins had reached an accord with his situation and was trying to make the best of it.

Hawk could even joke about his lack of recognition. Before we left for the Arena, we grabbed a sandwich with Alex Medich. Connie thumbed through the Long Island *Press*, searching in vain for a story about the game. Finally he spotted a tiny three-by-two-inch ad at the bottom of a page: "See Connie Hawkins and the Pipers meet the New York Nets." It was the only mention of Hawkins in any of his hometown papers. "Real big, ain't it," he laughed. "I'm a real big man in New York!"

I found it easy to talk with him—although it would be a while before I saw past his plodding, ghettoized, sometimes ungrammatical speech to realize this was an intelligent man. We spoke about the Rucker Tournament, players from our high school days, and the Piper franchise ("I wish they'd move it someplace warm, where they've got some fans").

Neither of us mentioned the scandal or the blacklist.

Three nights later in Minneapolis, Connie erased any doubts I may have had about his ability. Several hundred half-interested Minnesotans were sprinkled among the 14,500 pastel-colored seats. There was no crowd noise, except for the munching of popcorn. Every shout from the bench rattled through the building. Outside, the wind howled in the empty parking lot. The thermometer was below zero. It was like watching a private scrimmage. But in these drab surroundings Hawk put on an incredible performance.

Guarded by two of the ABA's best big men, 6' 9" Mel Daniels and 6' 8" Bob Netolicky, Hawkins scored 47 points against Indiana. Almost every basket was a sensational shot. The Pipers got him the ball twenty feet from the hoop. If Daniels hung back, Hawk swished fallaway jumpers. If Daniels challenged him, Connie drove, wriggling between defenders, controlling the ball with one hand while fending off bodies with the other. If an opponent grabbed his arm, Hawk shifted the ball to his other hand and dunked while the man was still holding on.

Early in the fourth quarter, Hawkins took the ball on the left side of the court. He waved it over his head one-handed, then dribbled between his legs and behind his back. A defender stumbled as Connie glided toward the corner, then suddenly drove the baseline. As he reached the congestion under the basket, Hawk left the ground, shifted the ball from his left hand to his right, and stretched out the far side to begin a hooklike reverse layup. But Netolicky was off his feet and waiting to block it. Somehow, while still in the air, Hawkins made a 150-degree turn and—as Netolicky crashed into him—flipped the ball over his shoulder, while going back in the direction he'd come from. The ball rolled around the rim and went in. Every player on both benches leapt to their feet, screaming or holding their heads in disbelief. It was probably the most amazing shot any of them had ever seen.

From then on, every time Indiana got close, Hawkins made an off-balance field-goal with someone clinging to him. With the score down to 101-95, he hit a driving stuff Netolicky on his arm—for a 3-point play. At 104-97 he hit 2 foul shots. At 109-104 he swished a 20-foot one-hander, and with the score 111-106, and the entire Indiana defense waiting for him, Hawk drove through for his third 3-point play of the quarter (and fourth of the game).

His teammates seemed bent on undoing his heroics. They fumbled passes and missed shots. Indiana finally tied the score, 116-116. But in the closing seconds Hawk intercepted a pass and set up rookie Arvesta Kelly's game-winning jumper.

Indiana missed a desperation shot. Connie's huge hand rose above the jumble of limbs beneath the hoop to snare the rebound. Charlie Williams and Steve Vacendak had lost the ball three straight times against the Pacers' press, so this time Hawk took it himself. He dribbled behind his back, slid through the defense, and was still dribbling when the buzzer sounded.

Nancy and the children had come from Pittsburgh and had been staying at Hawk's apartment for several weeks. Washington was sleeping on the couch. But that night nobody planned to sleep. They were having a party —an every-other-night occurrence, I discovered.

It was a loud, bustling scene with soul music blaring from a stereo, Chico marching about waving a huge brandy snifter filled with Catawba pink and intoning, "I'm The Chic from Puerto Ric," and Frank Card hiding in the closet, bouncing out "Laugh-In" style, imploring girls to join him.

Connie, tired and aching, sat in a corner gazing out at the merriment. He spoke eagerly about the league ("We got guys who could play in the NBA") and the schoolyards ("People never forget what you do there"), and surprised me by asking to see some of the stories I'd written.

Then Chico wandered over and began regaling us with tales of his former teammate and drinking companion Reggie Harding. A 7', 250-pound teenage sensation in Detroit, Harding hadn't come close to graduating, but signed an NBA contract with the Pistons in 1963 when his high school eligibility expired.

Reggie was talented enough to average in double figures. But his name appeared on almost as many police blotters as NBA scorebooks. During one particularly active period, he was accused of assaulting a police officer, arrested when the cops raided an after-hours joint, and charged with "loitering in a place of illegal occupation." The NBA suspended him for two years. But the league eventually took him back.

Harding's attitude still left something to be desired. He was regularly overweight and tended to miss things—like practices and games. He was finally cut by the Chicago Bulls in 1967.

"Last I heard," noted Chico, "Reggie in jail someplace. He got shot in the knee tryin to rob an after-hours club."

"I met him when I was with the Trotters," Connie recalled. "He always wore those real long, belted trenchcoats, like a gangster."

"That's what he wanted to be," said Chic. "But he too stupid. In high school, he want to rob this store in his neighborhood. He put a mask over his head and walked in with a gun. The man in the store just laugh: 'Come on Reggie, I know it you. Ain't nobody else around that big.' But Reggie say, 'Naw, it ain't me. Now give over that money.' He got caught real quick."

With the Pistons, Harding enlivened training camp by bringing a gun. "Reggie'd shoot at Sonny Dove's feet to make him dance," Vaughn drawled. "He a rough dude. One time, at this hotel, a broad don't want to put out for him. Reggie pick her up over his head and take her to this open window. He say he gonna throw her out—ten floors—if she don't do her thing. Man, she did her thing that night."

With a reminder that "all girls love The Chic," Vaughn rejoined the party. "Hawk," I asked tentatively, when we were alone, "how does it make you feel, when the NBA reinstates a guy like Harding—with a police record—and they bar you for just being an intermediary eight years ago?"

Connie's eyes narrowed. I was afraid the question had turned him off. Then he sighed and stood up. "I feel shitty. Let's go upstairs a minute. The kids should be asleep. I want to look in on 'em."

In the darkened room, Hawk looked down at Shawna and Keenan. He moved to the edge of the bed and pulled the cover up to his son's neck. His fingers pressed gently against Keenan's billowing natural hairdo ("The Hawk's nest," he said later). Finally he closed the door.

Still in silence, we sat at the top of the stairs. His thoughts were far away. "Hawk," I struggled, "about what I said downstairs. About the scandal. I don't know how to say this, but I want you to know, even if you were in it, I can tell you're a different person now. I don't think that something you did eight years ago should be important any more."

He rose and walked into an empty bedroom. There was a bottle of rum on the bureau. Hawkins filled a drinking glass, then washed it down, sprawled across a double bed, and stared at the ceiling.

"I never talk about the scandal," he said, his voice flat, pained. "It's been eight years since I really talked about it to anyone but my lawyers and my wife—and I don't like to do it with them. The players understand. They never mention it."

Suddenly Hawk sat erect. His eyes were watery, and the words came in a rush: "You wanted to know how I felt. How do you think I feel? I know how good I am. But ain't no way I can get a chance. It's like havin the water runnin and your hands tied so you can't turn it off. I know what you think. You think I was mixed up in it. But I wasn't, man, I swear I wasn't. I was just so scared. I told those DA's things that didn't happen. I thought they was gonna put me in jail!"

"Is there any way I could prove that, Hawk?"

"I don' know man, I don' know. My lawyers workin on it."

"Would you mind if I called them? Maybe they can give me some leads. If you're telling the truth, I want to look into this. But I want you to know one thing . . ."

"What?"

"If I start digging, and I find out you were guilty, that you did introduce people, I'm gonna write that too."

"Man, I didn't introduce nobody to nobody."

I liked Hawkins. I was flattered by his faith in me. But it would be several months before I was sure he was telling the truth.

The following day, I called David Litman in Pittsburgh. At first he was disturbed that Connie had spoken with me. But when he realized I was going to investigate, regardless of his cooperation, he agreed to meet me in New York when I returned from Minnesota. "Connie has been hurt irreparably by the NBA's blindness," he said over the phone. "He's never had an endorsement, he's earning a fraction of what he's worth and, with no widespread reputation, what kind of job opportunities do you think a person like him will have when he can't play any more?"

During the next week in Minnesota, I often thought of the scandal—and Hawk's alleged involvement. I think Connie sensed this. But the knowledge that I planned to probe his past didn't seem to affect him. Hawkins was no more or less friendly, no more or less cooperative. He remained hard to pin down for interviews, and he slept through several appointments. But, wearing only his thin Piper warmup suit and sneakers, Hawk stood in an open, snow-covered field for thirty minutes, palming basketballs in his naked hands while a *Life* photographer snapped roll after roll of film. Twice Connie's fingers became so numb he couldn't grip the balls. Once he shivered so violently we took a ten-minute break in the car. Yet there was no word of complaint.

As I spent more time with him, I found that Hawkins had a droll, sometimes biting sense of humor. A sly, foxlike smile would crease the corners of his mouth. His large, sleepy eyes seemed to say he was keeping part of the joke to himself. One afternoon, while some teammates lay about his living room watching television (boredom is the pro ballplayer's constant companion), Hawk turned to Chico, who sat glumly in a corner. "You know why you drink so much, Chic?" he said, grinning. "You drink because it gives you a nasty personality."

"Why does he want a nasty personality?" asked Frank Card.

"Cause it's better than nothing," Connie said. "And when Chic ain't drinkin, he ain't got *no* personality at all." Even Chico laughed.

Hawk could be silly as well as cutting. He and Washington often strolled about in purple plantation hats, imitating slave masters. "I treats ma colored same as I treats ma Mexicans and ma animals," Connie would declare. W. C. Fields routines were an inevitable part of each day.

Connie and Tom attended every Fields film in the Twin Cities. They were ejected from the University of Minnesota theater for laughing too loud and waving their feet in the air.

"Who's got the best sex life in pro ball?" a player asked Hawkins one night.

"The referees," he answered, straight-faced.

"Come on."

"I ain't kiddin. The referees fuck the ballplayers every night!"

But beneath the laughter, there was pain. Hawk's teammates respected him as a man. No one brought up the scandal. Yet Connie knew it was never far from their minds. "I hear," said one player, "the New York DA has a lot of stuff on him."

Added another, "If Hawk didn't do anything wrong, how come he's in this horseshit league?"

Even ABA Commissioner George Mikan spoke about Connie as though he were a reformed ex-con. I met with Mikan in the league's Minneapolis offices. "Hawkins made a mistake," he told me. "We don't dispute that. But we looked into his background and saw dire need. The thing I was concerned about was, Would he do it *again?* We investigated and found he's a totally rehabilitated family man."

"If there's a merger," I asked, "would Hawkins and the other ABA players on the NBA blacklist be left out?"

"Hell no," Mikan thundered. "All them boys would come along. We won't let 'em down. The NBA has some rotten apples. Look at that big spook that played for Detroit, Reggie Harding. He was a convicted second-story man."

As I was leaving, Mikan, who badgered Connie throughout the season to shorten his natural haircut, added, "What I like about Hawkins is his patriotism. When the national anthem plays, some guys are scratchin their ass. But Hawkins has got his hand over his heart where it belongs. Our players are supposed to be setting an example for youth to identify with."

Actually, the youth of America would identify more readily with pro basketball players if the people who run both leagues stopped trying to pass off their athletes as super-eunuchs. Ballplayers are more in tune with their age group than their bosses want known.

One evening I walked into the Pipers' locker room, just after the team had gone out to warm up. Along with the odor of liniment, was the unmistakable scent of marijuana. I later learned that at least one of the Pipers got slightly stoned before games. "You could tell by his eyes when he'd had the weed," Medich laughs. "He'd get that faraway look."

It's questionable whether any other pro basketball players smoke before games—although several big-league baseball pitchers won't work the first inning without a little grass. Outside the locker room, however, marijuana is common in both the ABA and NBA. This should hardly be surprising. If twenty-five-year-old account executives and twenty-five-year-old college instructors turn on, why not twenty-five-year-old ballplayers?

Both leagues prefer to hush up this sort of thing. But they have already come very close to being unable to. During the 1969–70 season, there were near pot-busts on two teams. In both cases, players were smoking in hotel rooms and just cleared out before the house detective arrived.

Jim Harding returned January 12. Doctors reported his blood pressure normal. But he would continue taking pills. He'd been out twenty-five days. The Pipers' lead over second-place Kentucky had risen from $4\frac{1}{2}$ to 5 games, but they had lost 7 of 13. Connie thought Harding might help the floundering club. "If he's learned to control himself," Hawk said, "maybe he can stop the individualism before it's too late."

The other Pipers were less optimistic. When George Sutor suggested that "we make the games close and give him another heart attack," heads nodded approvingly.

It seems Harding also considered that possibility. Before his first game, he pulled Connie to the side. "Go hard right away," he said softly. "Please. I'm asking you. Win big so I won't feel any strain for a while." Hawk looked down at Harding. The face was smiling, trying to mask his concern. But the eyes were frightened, pleading.

"I'll try," Connie said, disliking the man, yet feeling sorry for him, and not really knowing what else to say.

The Pipers beat Dallas, 116-105, in a fairly casual game. Connie controlled the tempo and scored 29 points. Dallas, which had lost nine straight, was squabbling and disorganized. Harding wasn't the only unpopular coach in the league. Cliff Hagan, the former St. Louis Hawks star and the Chaparrals' player-coach, cursed and glared at players who didn't pass *him* the ball. "Hagan," said one Chaparral, "thinks the sun sets on his ass."

Harding was comparatively subdued. He fidgeted on the bench, gnawed on his lips, and bounced to his feet nineteen times in the first quarter. But he did little shouting. It was the calm before the storm.

He called a practice the next day, and kept his composure for about fifteen minutes. Chico showed up with "the flu" and couldn't work out. Then Arthur bounced a careless pass off Vacendak's foot. The volcano erupted. "Goddamn, Art," Harding yelled, rushing across the court, waving his arms, "what the hell's the matter with you?"

In Duluth the next evening (the Pipers transferred several home games, but drew only empty seats), Dallas and Minnesota played a spine-tingler. Hawk was magnificent. He scored 30 points in the second half, including a 3-point play on a spinning jumper that sent the game into overtime. Harding, his forehead glistening, raged and shouted, burying his head in his hands and stamping his feet. By the overtime, the coach was exhausted.

The teams traded baskets. With the score tied and sixteen seconds remaining, Steve Vacendak stepped to the foul line for one shot. Harding turned his head away and hissed to Alex, "I can't look. Tell me what he did. Did he make it? Did he make it?" Vacendak made it.

Dallas worked for the final shot. "Please God. Please God, help me. Help me," Harding whispered. Cincy Powell swished a jumper at the buzzer. Minnesota lost, 102-101.

On the plane to Minneapolis, Harding sagged in a window seat, tie open, eyes dull, breathing heavy. "He can't take much more," Connie said to me. "But he's gonna be murder at practice tomorrow."

Hawk was right. In the previous eight days the team had played six times and practiced once. But Harding sent them through a tough two-hour workout at St. Thomas. "Watch him," Sutor whispered to Hawk, while Harding demonstrated a defensive stance to Frank Card. "You can see why he loves practice. He's over on the side, moving his body along with the guys. It's like *he's* out there instead. When we make a mistake, he's pissed because we're acting out his part—and fucking it up for him."

When the practice ended, Connie continued to play one-on-one with Card. "That's how he is," said Alex as we walked down the stairs to the dank, clammy dressing room. "Hawk's always workin on those moves."

I spoke with Harding while he dressed. The coach seemed more relaxed. I could almost see why administrators and owners hired him despite his troubled record: when not confronted by immediate pressure, Harding can convey an air of impressive self-confidence and determination—almost of missionary zeal. He projects victory. "This team can go all the way," he said, knotting his tie. "We'll hold on. There may be trouble now, but it's nothing hard work can't handle."

A conservative, meticulous dresser, he spent several minutes adjusting the knot in the mirror. His face was tired, filled with lines that didn't appear in his press-book photo. But his voice was strong: "There isn't a greater player than Connie. There are some things he's still learning. His defense is behind his offense. His habits reflect a lack of coaching, but for pure talent, no one is better. With him, we *will* hold on."

A shout came from the stairs: "Alex, Alex, get up here quick, Hawk is hurt!"

Harding's jaw tensed and trembled. At first, he didn't move with the others who rushed toward the stairway. "Christ," he said under his breath, "this is all I need."

Hawkins and Card had been driving on each other. Connie had faked

Frank left, then burst quickly to the right. "I took two steps," he recalls, "got past him, and then I felt this pain cutting into my leg. I fell down under the basket."

His mind blurred. Groveling on the court, Hawk tried to straighten the leg. He couldn't. The knee was locked. "Get Alex," he shouted at Card. But there had been no body contact and Card thought Hawkins was joking. "Frank," Connie shrieked again, "I'm hurt, I'm hurt, I ain't kiddin, get Alex!" This time Card bolted toward the stairs.

"The leg was stuck at a forty-five-degree angle," Connie says. "I thought all kinds of things. Was this the end? But I couldn't think clearly cause the pain stuffed up my mind."

When I reached the gym, Hawk was still writhing on the court. Alex, his face nervous and uncertain, gripped Connie's ankle and began twisting the leg, trying to loosen the knee. "No, no," Hawkins screamed, "don't do that Alex! You don't know what you're doin. Get me a doctor!"

Sutor and Mike Lewis helped Medich carry Hawk down the stairs to the closet-sized trainer's room. "Stan Wilson is down there," Alex reassured. "He was the Muskies' trainer last year. He's a salesman for Three-M. He was selling me some stuff. He'll help you."

They stretched Hawkins on a rubbing table. Wilson, a short middle-aged man in horn-rimmed glasses and a checkered sport-coat, ran his hands over the knee. Connie's features were contorted with pain. "You've got a floating cartilage right in the joint," said Wilson.

Harding, hovering above the trainers, his hands thrust into his pockets, snapped, "Well, how do you get it out?"

Connie's large eyes riveted on Wilson as the trainer gently kneaded the joint. Hawk let out a loud gasp, then a groan. "There it is," said Wilson, "it's out. But it'll slip back. There's a piece of cartilage broken loose. It can keep floating back into the joint. It's like a rock caught in a door hinge."

"What now?" Connie asked, still looking into Wilson's eyes.

"Maybe an operation. I don't know. A doctor ought to see this right away. He might say you can go through the season with it."

Harding had left the room. He was standing outside the door, inhaling deeply, when I stepped out to get Connie some water. "Is he all right?" Harding asked.

"For now, but Wilson says they won't know for a while."

"Well," Harding said bitterly, "he better be all right for that game tomorrow night!"

Wilson and Medich helped Connie to his locker. As Hawk pulled off his shirt, the knee locked again. He moaned and crumpled backward onto a narrow wooden bench that separated two rows of gray metal lockers. Three students, dressed for their gym class, faces a mass of acne, peered open-mouthed at the long, thin figure writhing on the bench—chest heaving, ribs glistening in the dim light of an overhead bulb. "Oh shit," Connie moaned, "oh shit."

Wilson again worked on the knee. Hawk's fingers clutched the bench. The cartilage was finally dislodged. But Hawkins was still in great pain.

Alex and I helped Connie dress. Wilson made a splint to hold the knee straight, then wrapped it in ace bandages. Harding, already in his felt-collared overcoat and hat, stood at the end of the row of lockers. "Jesus Christ," he mumbled through clenched teeth. "Jesus Christ, this is all I need. This is the final blow." Then he left.

It took half an hour to get Connie into his clothes and coat. Every movement was agonizing. He said almost nothing. At last he leaned down and dropped his arms over Alex's and my shoulders. We walked gingerly to Medich's station wagon for the drive to St. Mary's Hospital. "Thanks for helping me," Connie whispered.

The hospital—quiet, yellow-walled, and antiseptic—became a montage of waiting rooms, staring interns, X-ray machines, white coats, morphine injections, and hushed voices. All the time Connie's eyes were growing wider, more concerned, and Alex's dark brows were pressing closer together, his voice repeating, "I don't know, I just don't know."

"I tried not to worry," Hawkins recalls, "but those doctors would poke at me and every time somebody said 'operation,' I got all tense. All my life I've been frightened of operations. Then the morphine relaxed me."

He tried to put up a brave front, flirting half-heartedly with the nurses. "Is the morphine working?" one asked.

"Yeah, I'm gettin high," he said.

"That's not the idea."

"Well, maybe you better give some more."

It took several hours for Hawkins to reach a private room. Then the bed was too short. His legs hung far over the edge. "Are you allergic to anything?" asked a nurse.

"Yeah, Rakel."

"What's that?"

"He's a referee. Every time I see him I break out in six personal fouls."

A doctor, Harvey O'Phelan, examined his leg. "It's a torn cartilage," he said. "You could call it floating. If it doesn't heal, then it'll have to come out. If it locks again, you'll need an operation. But if we don't need to operate, you could play pretty soon."

"I don't want no operation," Hawk said.

"Let's see what happens."

Later two of Dr. O'Phelan's associates inspected Connie. They were maddeningly indecisive and contradictory. One leaned toward an immediate operation, the other thought the leg would heal with rest. "You'll find," said a Dr. Wilson, "that we all have different ways of doing things. But let's not rush. This is a big decision."

"I didn't know what to think," Hawk remembers. "If the doctors couldn't make up their minds, that was frightening. One doctor'd get my hopes up, then the next one would scare me."

We had reached the hospital about 2:00 P.M. Alex left at 6:30, when Hawk seemed settled. There had been no sign of Harding, Mikkelsen, or Erickson.

I sat in an armchair at the end of Connie's bed and set up the portable tape recorder I'd been carrying all day. "This is a break for me," I kidded. "Now you can't escape. I'll finally get some real interviewing done."

"It might ease my mind."

We talked about the Globetrotters and the Rens and Boys High, and then I could see that the morphine was wearing off. A larger bed was rolled in, the leg was placed in traction, and we continued to talk. "Hawk, I've got to ask this: Are you scared?"

He nodded.

"What if something went wrong, if the leg didn't come around?"

Hawk bit his lip in silence.

He had been thinking about the same thing. "I don't know, I'd try to stay in basketball, a coachin job maybe," he groped. "But I don't have no experience. I just have an unbelievable commitment to basketball. If I couldn't play no more I think that would just be the end of Connie Hawkins. There wouldn't be no more me."

The nurses threw me out at one o'clock in the morning. They gave Connie two sleeping pills. That night he dreamed that his son had drowned in a swimming pool.

The next morning Hawk's initial fear subsided. There was less pain. Dr. O'Phelan reexamined him and said that for the moment an operation was unnecessary (though Hawk would probably need one at the end of the season). Conceivably, Connie might even be able to play in Saturday's game —provided the knee felt strong enough. Hawk would likely be the judge of that.

Saturday's game was against Oakland at the Sports Center. There was to be great pressure on Connie to play. The Oaks had won fourteen straight. A victory in Minnesota would tie the Pipers' league record, set the previous season. The Minnesota management had billed the game as the ABA's finest attraction: Hawkins's first clash with Rick Barry, a confrontation of the league's best teams. The game, they had predicted, would prove Twin Cities fans could support basketball—and that the Pipers were superior.

But the promotion was in trouble. Barry would not play. He'd been injured in the East. The Pipers had lost two straight. Erickson was desperate that the event not flop at the gate and that his team perform well before a large crowd. He needed Hawkins.

I arrived at the hospital at 9:00 A.M., carrying a newspaper which already quoted Mikkelsen as saying, "Dr. O'Phelan took a look at him and said he should be O.K. for Saturday." It was Thursday.

Connie spent much of the morning with a physical therapist, getting whirlpool and ice massages. His legs were so long he couldn't sit in the whirlpool and get his knee under the water. He had to balance on the edge of the tank and lean down until the knee was submerged.

"There isn't as much pain," he said. "I really feel better. I'd like to play. It's a big game."

"Sounds stupid. Why risk the leg so fast. Wait till it's stronger."

"Let's see what happens," he said.

We spent the rest of Thursday with the tape recorder. I was getting to know him much better. "With your moves," I asked, "do you sometimes feel you're an artist, doing something creative, as well as being a ballplayer?"

Hawkins smiled. "When you say it that way, yes. I try to be creative. A lot of it is just natural. But I also try to do things that are artistic with my body and my moves. I get pride being able to do things nobody else can do. It gives me confidence about myself when I can be special."

We listened to the Pipers' game from Houston on the radio that night. Minnesota was soundly beaten. "Harding gonna be freakin out soon," Connie said.

By Friday morning Hawk could limp about the halls. The pressure for him to play was growing. "Harding wanted Hawk back fast," Medich recalls. "Probably too fast. When Hawk first got hurt, Jim disappeared. Nobody could find him till we left for Houston. After we lost down there, he was a mess. He knew he needed The Hawk."

Mikkelsen called Connie and—in the process of inquiring about his health—stressed the importance of the game. Alex, too, was pushing Hawk to play. He may have known better, but he was at the mercy of management. Trainers are never highly paid. They have no job security. It's a rare trainer who'll flatly veto a player's participation if the owners press him. Alex was obviously being pressed. And he was pressing Hawk.

Dr. O'Phelan again told Hawkins that, *if the knee felt strong enough,* he could play Saturday night. "He said I shouldn't play if it didn't feel right yet," Connie recalls. "He said if it locked again, I'd have to have an operation right away."

Mikkelsen and Medich were tantalizing Connie. They didn't order him to play, but they reminded him it was *possible*. They took advantage of his competitive instinct and his pride, and they harped on how much he was needed. Hawkins may sometimes shade toward hypochondria. But he can be challenged and flattered into disregarding real pain.

"If I wear a brace and they wrap the leg real tight, I could do it," Connie said Friday night.

"What the hell for?" I asked. "Wait till the whole leg is a little stronger."

"I know," he admitted. "I probably won't play, not unless I'm sure. Right now, there's still pain in there."

That night, with the tape recorder running, I brought up the blacklist. "I don't feel no disappointment or animosity toward the NBA," Hawk said at first. "I don't miss all the publicity Elgin and Oscar got. I have my personal satisfaction."

"Bullshit," I said. "I can't believe that. You've got too much pride in your game to be happy playing in Commack and Duluth."

Connie turned his head from the microphone and stared at the blank wall. "O.K.," he sighed. "I retract my statement. There is some animosity and there is a *great deal* of disappointment. I feel the NBA has really hurt me. If I'd had a chance, I think my family would have security now, instead of nothing. I wouldn't be worryin so much about what happens to my leg. I know I've missed out on the fantastic salaries. There are guys makin ten times as much as me. It demoralizes me. Every now and then, I just can't help it."

Hawk was checked out of the hospital a few hours earlier than planned on Saturday. Instead of driving him home, Alex headed for the St. Thomas gym, so Connie could "loosen up the leg" with a light workout.

That afternoon, at his apartment, I expressed surprise. "I just wanted to get the leg unstiff," Connie said.

"You aren't still thinking of playing."

"No," he mumbled evasively. "It still hurts."

Alex called around 3:00 P.M. He suggested he drive Hawk to the Sports Center and tape him, "just to see how it feels." When I arrived for the game that night, Hawkins was sitting on the bench in uniform. The knee was tightly bound. The leg could not be fully extended.

Everyone, of course, still said Connie wasn't really going to play.

The crowd of 4,722 was large by Piper standards, however, and Erickson wanted an impressive showing from his team. Harding, who had lost two straight, wanted one even more. With six minutes left in the first quarter, the coach sent Connie into the game.

Hawk couldn't run. He hobbled about, dragging the leg. Yet somehow he managed to score 14 points in the next eighteen minutes, holding the team together during an Oakland hot streak.

In the locker room, Connie, lost in the excitement of the game, asked Alex to remove part of the tape. Minnesota trailed, 55-49. With a bit more mobility, Hawk sensed he could score enough to produce the upset. "I took off the part of the tape that was holding him back," Medich admits. "Hawk said he felt good, so I let him stretch out."

Still wearing his hospital identification bracelet ("In case they have to cart me back," he joked before the game), Connie reeled off 7 points as the second half opened. The Pipers cut the lead to three.

Then Vacendak missed a shot. Hawk leapt for the rebound. He came down without the ball—and his knee locked. He crumpled to the floor, clutching at the pain, unable to stifle his screams. He was carried to the bench, where the knee was unlocked. But he played no more, and Oakland won, 111-108.

Harding stormed toward the locker room at the buzzer, his face a mask of fear and fury. Soon the arena was empty. Hawkins was still too weak to walk. He, Alex, and I remained on the bench. "I don't want an operation," Connie said, with more pleading than conviction. "All I need is a little rest."

The next morning I flew to New York to meet the Litmans. Connie called a week later. He was in the hospital. "I tried to talk 'em out of it, but it's no use," he said. "They're givin me the big 'O.' And I'm scared."

17

WOUNDED HAWK

"This has to be the worst season ever."
—*Connie Hawkins, April, 1969*

The professional athlete often endures a special paranoia when confronted by major surgery. Unlike a lawyer or teacher, the athlete can't function slightly crippled. His body is responsible for his income, status, and self-image. If anything goes wrong, if there is irreparable damage, his life may change radically. Even when surgery is over, he faces an indefinite period of uncertainty. He can never be sure his body will function as before.

The operation, though a harrowing experience, turned out to be the easy part for Connie. Recovery was slower than anyone anticipated. The psychological problems were as serious as the physical. It would be almost a year before Hawkins was convinced the knee was sound.

After the knee locked again in the Oakland game, Hawk pleaded for time to allow the injury to heal. But the Pipers brought in Dr. Don Lannin, a respected surgeon who worked with the Minnesota Vikings football team. He said there was no choice but to operate. "You could play," Dr. Lannin told Connie in late January, "but it would lock again. That piece of cartilage has to come out."

"Please," Hawk begged, "could we wait one more week? Maybe it'll . . ."

"It won't make any difference," said the doctor. "But relax, this isn't a serious operation. You could be back playing in six or eight weeks."

That night Connie sat in his living room and sobbed. Then he drank rum and wine until he passed out. The next morning, he showered and went to the hospital.

The idea of surgery was hard to accept. Since Hawk hadn't exercised for more than a week (and the knee hadn't locked), he felt no pain in the leg. It was still weak, but he could walk on it: "In the hospital, I kept thinkin 'I could run outta here while the nurses ain't lookin.' "

The night before the operation Connie began to panic. He needed extra sleeping pills. Then he had a nightmare: "I dreamed coach Harding wanted me to play the day after surgery. They dragged me out on the court and my leg fell off. When I woke up the next morning I was so scared. Rollin into the operating room, I thought, 'This is it, complications are gonna set in and I'm gonna bleed to death!' "

The operation went smoothly. But when Hawkins was being placed back in his bed, he awakened from the ether prematurely and became hysterical. He struggled to get up. Nurses and orderlies had to lean on his shoulders and pin his arms to force him down. Then he passed out.

Hours later, Hawk woke to see a cast running from the bottom of his shin to the midpoint of his thigh. He felt a stinging sensation in the leg and buzzed frantically for a nurse. "Oh, that's nothing to worry about," she told him. "It won't hurt after a while." She gave him an injection and he fell asleep.

Hawkins was in the hospital a week. He was released with the cast still on his leg and moved about on crutches for three days. Then he went to Dr. Lannin's downtown office. While Connie lay on a table, the doctor removed the cast.

Hawk stared in horror at the leg. He had expected it to be unchanged except for a large scar. Instead he saw a thin, wrinkled limb that looked nothing like his own. The muscles were shrunken and soft. It had almost no color. "Oh my God," he cried. "Oh my God, look at it!"

"Take it easy," Dr. Lannin said. "It's expected to atrophy in the cast. You weren't using the muscles. You'll have some physical therapy, lift weights, and it'll be normal in no time."

Connie didn't believe him. When the doctor left the room, he lay back and tried to lift the leg. It didn't move. He gathered his strength and tried again. He still couldn't raise it off the table. "It just lay there like a piece of wood," he recalls. "I started cryin. I thought the doctor was afraid to tell me I'd never play again. I thought, 'I'm gonna be a cripple!' "

Dr. Lannin found him in tears. "Don't worry, please Connie. This is normal, try to understand that. In a month or two you'll be fine." Hawk wanted desperately to believe him. But as long as there was no strength in the leg, he couldn't.

Lannin set up a physical-therapy program with Fred Zamberletti, the Vikings' trainer. The first day, Zamberletti placed Hawkins on a table and asked him to raise the leg to a forty-five-degree angle. Connie couldn't do it. "You aren't trying hard enough," said the trainer. "The operation is over. Get it out of your mind. You can do it."

Hawkins tried again. Not only was he still unable to raise the leg, but he felt a searing pain at the spot of the incision. He fought back a scream of frustration.

"It's in your mind," persisted Zamberletti. He placed his index finger under Connie's heel. "Try it once more."

The leg remained motionless. "Man," Hawkins cried, "you see! You see, it ain't workin. Something is *wrong* with it!"

"Take it easy," said Zamberletti. "I'll help you." He lifted the leg with his index finger and held it at forty-five degrees. Connie's eyes were shut tight.

"Now lower the leg and lift it again," said the trainer. "I'll keep helping you." Hawk did as he was instructed—unaware that Zamberletti had removed his finger.

"As long as I support it with my finger it's not too hard, right?" Zamberletti asked. Connie nodded.

"Then open your eyes."

Hawkins gasped. He was holding the leg up by himself.

There was still pain, but Connie found he could repeat the movement a dozen times. "Tomorrow," said Zamberletti, "we'll put a weight on it, then add one pound each day. You're gonna be all right."

"When I left his office I felt like a rock had been taken off my head," Connie recalls.

But Hawkins was in no rush to rejoin the Pipers. The team had fallen apart. The first to fall was Jim Harding. "When the Hawk got hurt again," says Alex Medich, "Jim couldn't take it. He said, 'I'm finished. Now we'll never win.' "

The Pipers beat the hapless New York Nets in their first game without Connie. But they looked ragged. Three nights later, they committed 22 turnovers, blew a 19-point lead, and lost to Miami. "They're going to investigate us for throwing games," Harding said, kicking aimlessly at the locker-room door. Then he turned toward Charlie Williams, who had been resting a severe hamstring-pull: "Charlie, you better be ready tomorrow night, cause you're starting!"

The Pipers could manage just 90 points in losing to Kentucky. The team hit only 29 of 107 shots. Harding was his volatile, profane self on the bench. But, after the game, he seemed subdued and vanquished. The Pipers had lost 5 of 8 since his return. Their lead over Kentucky was down to 2. Fourth-place Miami was just 5 games back. Only the ineptness of the Nets, 13½ behind, guaranteed the Pipers a fourth-place finish—and a playoff spot—in the five-team division. "Without Hawkins," Harding said, "we can't score enough. This team is going to finish fourth, and there's nothing I can do about it. I've never had such a frustrating season."

His frustration peaked the next evening in Louisville, where he had gone to coach the East squad in the ABA All-Star game. At the official banquet, Harding was introducing the players. He called Tom Washington's name (Wash was replacing Hawkins). There was no response.

"He's not here, coach," called Art Heyman, standing near the head table. "He's sick."

Harding's eyes flashed. "Sick? What do you mean, sick?"

Heyman shrugged. "We'll see about this later," Harding said. Then he introduced Charlie Williams.

"He's sick too," said Heyman.

"Those guys aren't sick," Harding cried. "This is going to cost both of them one hundred and fifty dollars. They'll be able to pick up their checks with a teaspoon next week!"

After the banquet, Harding angrily called the players' rooms. They were there. "Meet me in the lobby," he demanded. The punishment had risen with his anger. He said they would be fined five hundred dollars apiece.

But Erickson and Mikkelsen immediately overruled him. Now Harding was boiling. "Those two are gutless," he stormed. "They may be able to get those players off now, but they can't tell me how to coach. I guarantee they won't play in the game."

After midnight, a martini in hand, Harding stood at the bar during the postbanquet ball, deriding the Pipers' board chairman, Gabe Rubin, to Bob Fowler of the St. Paul *Pioneer Press*. Harding despised Rubin. He knew that some of the veteran Pipers—especially Chico—telephoned Gabe regularly to complain about the coach, and that Rubin had gone to Erickson several times.

Erickson had sided with Harding on every issue but the cutting of LeRoy Wright. Yet the coach was still bitter. He felt Rubin was out to get him. "Last week I fined Chico Vaughn and I told him, 'Go tell your Pittsburgh benefactor,'" he boasted.

Harding's eyes searched the ballroom. "Where's Rubin?" He spotted Gabe at a table with Mikkelsen. "I'm going to talk to him."

Harding marched to the table. They exchanged words. Moments later the thirty-nine-year-old coach was fighting with the chubby, fifty-seven-year-old chairman of the board. He tore the breast pocket from Rubin's suit and left a welt on his temple. Rubin cut Harding's face with his fingernails.

They were dragged apart. But Harding was still in a fury. Twice he broke loose and charged Rubin. Finally, blood pouring down his face, the coach was ushered from the room by Mikkelsen.

It was 1:30 A.M. By 2:00 o'clock Harding had regained his senses and realized he was in trouble. He called Art Heyman's room and begged the player to help him. "I'll lose my job, I know it," he said. "Talk to Rubin for me. Talk to Erickson. You've got to help me."

Heyman said he'd see what he could do. Then he hung up and went back to sleep.

The next morning, Mikan announced that Harding had been dismissed as the All-Stars' coach. "Things like this shouldn't be done in a public place," the commissioner explained sagely. Two days later, Erickson fired Harding as coach of the Pipers.

(But this by no means spelled the end of Jim Harding's coaching career. That summer, the University of Detroit decided Harding had much to offer young adults. "As an educator," said Detroit dean of students Fred Shadrick, upon giving Harding a four-year contract, "I will say that if you look across the country in athletics, you will see the need for this kind of man." That season, half the Detroit players saw the need to quit the team. The following year, nine freshmen and sixteen varsity players boycotted practice, charging that Harding's "failure to recognize us as human beings with human feelings, wants and desires has driven us to the point of psychological depression."

"I'm a demanding coach," Harding responded. "Nobody ever said I wasn't. These kids are a pack of liars, all twenty-five of them. They don't want to pay the price for success. This is their way of avoiding discipline." The school's Athletic Board of Control backed Harding to the hilt and crushed the revolt.)

Since Erickson could no longer deny rumors that the Pipers were going to move, he didn't waste money hiring an outside coach. Instead he appointed the team's director of special promotions, one Verl (Gus) Young. Gus had prepared for the job by running a bowling alley for the past twelve years.

Bald and bespectacled, the fifty-nine-year-old Young looked like a junior high school English teacher. He had coached at such basketball hotbeds as Carleton and Gustavus Adolphus colleges, but retired to his bowling alley in 1957.

"Gus was a happy-go-lucky old fella," recalls Alex Medich. "He knew about basketball—but it was basketball from twenty years ago."

Young tried to revive the team by creating a casual atmosphere. He promised basketball would be "fun again," returned the record player to the locker room, and reacted peacefully to defeats. "His only big trouble," notes Connie, "was incompetence."

The players were punchy after bouncing from Harding's tough rule to the easygoing Mikkelsen, back to Harding, and then to Young. Once they realized that Gus had neither the desire nor the authority to discipline them, chaos became the Pipers' norm. Players shouted down the coach at team meetings, ignored him at practice, and made substitutions without bothering to let him know.

The team collapsed under Young, losing five of its first six. "We're really misfits now," Washington told Connie when he visited the hospital. "Everybody grabs the ball and shoots. I never see it. Charlie throws up thirty a game. Gus is so out of it, Chico came to practice blind drunk and Gus couldn't even tell."

"The team went to pieces," recalls Art Heyman. "Gus had no curfew, no discipline. After four months of Jim Harding it was like getting out of jail. Everybody went wild." Heyman, of course, did little to restore discipline when he regularly told the coach to "go fuck yourself."

But Young didn't enhance his own position by diagramming plays with six men on each team, falling asleep on the bench, and making such curious statements as "We're the losingest first-place team you've ever seen."

Soon, the Pipers were the losingest *fourth*-place team you've ever seen.

At a pregame meeting Young solemnly told his charges, "Last time we faced them, Louie Dampier beat us. We've got to stop him tonight."

"Gus, Gus," cried Heyman. "Dampier is with Kentucky. We're playing Dallas tonight."

When the coach revealed his confusion with modern rules by demanding a referee give Minnesota a second technical foul shot because the team was in a bonus situation, the players guffawed openly. Heyman fell off the bench and rolled about the floor shaking with laughter.

The day Hawk left the hospital, Chico went to his apartment. "The team all fucked up," moaned the Chic. "Charlie and Art do what they want. Art causin dissension. He ignore Gus and laugh at him."

When Chico had left, Washington chuckled. "That motherfucker should talk. He ignore Gus and laugh at him too. And he shoots his Goddamn three-pointer every time he touches the ball."

Connie visited practice and saw players going through the motions, some laughing, others becoming angry. "Nobody had respect for Gus," Connie says. "He'd lost control in two weeks. At meetings guys didn't pay no attention to him. They paired off and talked strategy with each other. They'd end up with five or six different opinions. Then they'd go out and do whatever they felt like.

"Vince Cazzetta was a nice guy too. But we had respect for him. He could be tough when he had to. He could handle men. How can you get turned on by a coach who says, 'Now boys, what we need is more giniger'?"

Four weeks after the operation, Hawk began light workouts. His first tentative steps were not encouraging. There was a slight puffiness. Fluid developed. "They tell me I'll be able to play by the end of the season," Connie said, "but I don't think so."

Minnesota doctors maintained Hawk would not aggravate the injury by returning to action. But, that summer, doctors for the Phoenix Suns told the Litmans that Connie should never have been allowed to play.

Erickson needed Hawkins—even half of Hawkins—if the Pipers were to survive in the playoffs. And a successful playoff showing would bring a better price when Erickson sold the team. So the owner pressed Hawk to return quickly.

On March 19, less than eight weeks after the operation, Connie played against Oakland. His performance was disturbing. Hawk could still shoot, but he seemed weak and immobile. When I saw him play at Commack two weeks later, I couldn't bring myself to tell him how bad he looked. But he knew. Hawk was dragging the injured leg—a limping, awkward caricature of himself. His game is dependent on quickness, balance, and spring. He had none of these.

Connie was scoring twenty points per game, but his stamina was so low and his knee so painful, he contributed nothing on defense.

Hawk was worried. "It's supposed to be gettin better," he said, "but it ain't."

The Pipers weren't getting better either. Only their various neuroses were running wild. Hawk rarely saw the ball. Charlie Williams was shooting so much, Connie finally said, "Man I'm not knockin you, but you're takin thirty, thirty-five shots a game. And you ain't even making forty percent. That don't help us."

"Shooting is what basketball's about," Charlie replied. "My money comes from my points."

"Someday," said Hawk, "your arms gonna fall off."

"Not from passin." Charlie laughed.

Hawkins began snidely referring to Charlie as "The Rifleman." But Williams continued to fire away.

One night, after a particularly harrowing defeat, Heyman approached Connie. "All these guys are becoming creeps, Hawk. Why don't we room together?"

That was all Hawkins needed. But, to get Heyman off his back, he said, "I'll talk to the coach about it, but keep quiet. Don't you say nothing to nobody."

"Sure Hawk, whatever you say."

The next day, as they sat on the plane, Washington glared at Connie.

"What's the matter Wash?"

"I thought we were tight."

"We are. What is it?"

"I hear you don' want to room with me any more. You're going to room with Arthur. He's been telling everybody on the club."

The players—once close-knit away from the court—stopped socializing together. There were few parties. "Everything's gone," said Wash. "We've got to do something before the playoffs. We've got to get rid of Gus Young."

Connie felt sorry for the hopelessly misplaced coach. "Gus wasn't mean and ruthless," he recalls. "It wasn't his fault the front office stuck him there. He just didn't know basketball. I tried to get the guys to quit pickin on him, and I always put my arm over his shoulder to try and make him feel better."

Connie could easily have lost interest. Instead he attempted to pull the team together. His first hope was assistant coach LeRoy Wright. Neither Harding nor Young had given him much responsibility. The black players thought Wright should have been named coach when Harding was canned. "The owners," says Connie, "didn't want a black coach. We were sure of that."

Hawkins was convinced, however, that LeRoy could coach the team. They often spoke in Hawk's hotel room late at night. "Talk to Gus," Connie would say. "Tell him to let you give some pregame talks and give instructions in the huddle."

Wright approached Young. He got nowhere. "Gus says he's coached for years and he knows the game," LeRoy told Connie. "He'll listen to my suggestions in private, but he wants to run the whole show."

Wright was reluctant to pursue the issue. He feared for his job. Connie had no such fears. Many players were begging him to speak with Mikkelsen. So Hawk found himself in the Pipers' offices complaining about another coach. "Gus don't know what's goin on," Connie said. "Why don' you come back? Or let LeRoy coach? Gus is a farce."

"He'll be all right," Mikkelsen said. "He just needs some time to get reacquainted."

"We ain't got a hundred years."

But Hawk saw it was hopeless: "Mikkelsen was a Goddamn puppet. Erickson made all the decisions. He thought he'd look bad if he got rid of Gus. So we were stuck with him."

Heyman had an idea: "I went to Erickson and begged him to let *me* coach. But he didn't go for it. So I told him he should let Hawk coach. He didn't go for that either. He knew Gus was incompetent. But he just wanted to get the season over with."

One evening, after the Pipers had been slaughtered at Miami, Jim O'Brien, then with the Miami *News*, tried to enter the locker room. Gus Young blocked the door. "You can't come in here," he said. "We have too much dissension already." The quote looked beautiful in the next day's papers.

The regular season ended in Kentucky. One of the Colonels persisted in kicking and bumping Connie's injured knee. Hawk was knocked down four times without a foul being called. "You can go fuck yourself," he finally said to the referee. "If you ain't gonna protect me, I ain't playin." He walked to the bench and sat out the rest of the game.

The Pipers lost. They finished in fourth place with a 36-42 record. Since Connie's injury they were 16-33. Under Gus Young they had won but 10 of 32 games.

Connie had hoped his leg would be sound for the playoffs. It wasn't. He had several high-scoring nights and was primarily responsible for Minnesota carrying Miami seven games, but Hawk still looked clumsy. After each game the knee was swollen and throbbing.

The rest of the Pipers bickered among themselves. Twice Gus Young tried to give defensive assignments in the locker room but was loudly overruled by Heyman and Williams. Washington cursed Charlie for shooting too much. But Williams ignored him.

As they dressed for one game, Heyman, who wasn't seeing the ball much, cornered Connie. "Tonight let's you and me work together," Art said. "Screw the rest of those guys. They aren't doin a thing anyway."

When Hawk had agreed, Heyman slipped over to Washington: "Wash, tonight let's you and me work together. Screw the rest of those guys. They aren't doin a thing anyway." He had similar conversations with Chico, Steve, and Charlie.

"It didn't take long to figure out what he was doin," Connie laughs. "We checked and found out he'd fixed himself up with everybody. But no one mentioned it to him. We understood Art. He just wanted to be more involved."

The night before the seventh game, Connie and Art were sitting in the lobby of the Cadillac Hotel in Miami, when Gus Young staggered through the door. He was very drunk. "Coach," Heyman called out, "what time is the game tomorrow night?"

"Game?" mumbled Gus, lunging into the elevator. "Game? I don't know. Ask Alex."

The seventh game was a fitting conclusion to a pathetic season. The Pipers fell far behind. But Vacendak led a rally in the third quarter. Then, just as they moved within striking distance, Charlie grabbed a rebound, dribbled over midcourt, and fired a wild shot. The ball slammed off the backboard, Miami started a successful fastbreak, the momentum turned, and the Pipers were finished. Connie signaled for time out. "Now boys . . ." Gus began in the huddle. "Shut up," shouted Washington. "Listen Charlie, you been fuckin us up all year with your shootin. You done it again! What's the matter with you?"

"Get off my ass Wash," replied Williams. The argument persisted through the time out. They were still shouting when they returned to the court, and continued to do so until the final buzzer. Miami won easily. The season was over.

Hawk's knee had been especially painful that night. He had not played well. He sat in the dressing room and listened to his teammates curse each other.

Heyman stood by the door. He was planning to punch Gus Young as soon as he entered. "I felt he'd screwed up the team with his rotten leadership," Art explains. "He should have taken charge or stepped down. I was mad. But he walked in, came up to me, and started to cry. You can't punch out a guy who's hugging you."

"You guys were just great," Gus wept. "Being associated with you has been the most wonderful experience of my life." Connie embraced the coach.

"I felt sorry for him," Hawk recalls.

Hawkins and Washington drank themselves into a stupor that night. "This is a season I'd like to forget," Tom said.

Connie was drinking to forget more than the season. "If my knee don't get any better," he confessed, "I'm in trouble. On this leg, the way it is now, I'm not the real Hawk."

HAWKINS V. NBA

"There is a possibility of a suit. We've had them before."
—*J. Walter Kennedy, NBA Commissioner, May, 1966*

"As a lawyer, I wouldn't give five cents for Connie Hawkins' lawsuit."
—*George Mikan, ABA Commissioner, January, 1969*

"You have a gut reaction that the law is what it should be.
You feel that if somebody has been fucked there's a remedy somewhere."
—*Howard Specter, Attorney for Hawkins,*
Following million-dollar settlement, June, 1969

Connie came back to Pittsburgh in April of 1969. He was trapped in a second-rate league, fearful his knee might never heal and convinced he had nothing to look forward to. But the tide was turning in his suit against the NBA. Beginning with no legal precedents on their side, the Litmans and their partner Howard Specter had spent more than forty thousand dollars and worked over ten thousand hours on the case. They had contended not only with the wealth and influence of the sports establishment, but also with the hostility of the prestigious New York County DA's office. Yet their preparation had been exhaustive, and they had outhustled and outsmarted the men from the league's nationally known New York law firm. One by one, the foundations of the NBA's case had been toppled. The stage was set for an astonishing legal victory.

When the Litmans had filed suit, on November 3, 1966, their friends in the legal community chuckled. No athlete had ever recovered extensive damages by suing a professional sport for excluding him. Baseball wasn't even covered by anti-trust legislation. Basketball, it was thought at the time, might also be exempt.

The only similar case was hardly an encouraging precedent: Jack Molinas's suit for reinstatement in 1960. District Judge Irving R. Kaufman had tossed it out with a scathing opinion. The NBA, he said, was justified in avoiding "even the slightest connection with gambling, gamblers, or those who had done business with gamblers."

During Hawkins's suit, the NBA lawyers constantly referred to Judge Kaufman's decision, which carried with it the unspoken reminder that Molinas—supposedly reformed and a respected member of the bar—was next heard from in the 1961 scandals.

"At the time we first contemplated redress," David Litman recalls, "we really didn't think there was much hope. We were talking to Connie more as friends than lawyers. In the fall of 1963 I thought I'd try to help, so I wrote a letter to Kennedy and every NBA club."

"Mr. Hawkins," read the letter, "becomes eligible to play with the NBA by virtue of his class graduation. He is desirous of playing professional basketball . . ."

Kennedy curtly replied: "Please be advised that this office does not maintain a draft list. The drafting of players is an individual club responsibility."

No team drafted Hawkins in May of 1964.

David tried again the following fall. "In view of the fact that your league is the only professional basketball league in existence today," he wrote, "a failure on your part to give Mr. Hawkins an opportunity to show his ability does, in fact, deprive him of his basic right to earn a livelihood in his chosen profession . . . a continued refusal on your part to give Mr. Hawkins an opportunity . . . will create a cause of action. . . . However, at this time, Mr. Hawkins has no desire to institute any litigation. He merely desires to have an opportunity to determine whether he is competent enough to play in your league."

Kennedy and the club owners didn't even bother to write back.

When another year passed and Connie was again ignored in the draft, the Litmans were convinced that Hawkins was blacklisted. "We suspected it for some time," David recalls. "Commissioner Podoloff said as much to my brother Eugene, when they were discussing the Pittsburgh Rens coming into the NBA back in 1962. After a few years, there was no doubt."

The Litmans had long been involved in local civil-rights and civil-liberties cases. They were active in the American Civil Liberties Union. Roslyn was then general council for the Pittsburgh ACLU. As the nature of Hawkins's plight became evident, they began to think more seriously of attacking the NBA through the courts.

"A successful lawyer," says David, "must be driven by a certain feeling of indignation, and that's what we began to feel. We hadn't spoken much with Connie about the scandal, but he'd told us he was innocent and we believed him. We felt he'd been wronged. And I believe that if somebody is wronged, a cause of action can be found for it."

The Litmans hired a law student named Wayne Bradley to do fulltime research into possible grounds for an anti-trust suit. Then, on April 29, 1966, David wrote Kennedy once more. This time he warned, "Unless Mr. Hawkins is permitted the opportunity to play . . . legal proceedings will be instituted . . ."

Kennedy telephoned Litman. "I got your letter," he said. "I'd like you and your client to see me at my office."

"My client is in Europe with the Globetrotters," said Litman, "but I'd be happy to meet with you."

"That," said Kennedy, "would be fine."

Litman believed, from Kennedy's tone, that the NBA was having a change of heart. "I had a good feeling going into that meeting," he recalls. "I wanted to get the questions about Connie's reputation cleared up and I wanted to get him into the league. I thought that was their intent."

Evidently it wasn't. In Kennedy's office was Steven Kaye, an attorney from Proskauer, Rose, Goetz and Mendelsohn, the NBA's law firm. "They were on a fishing expedition," Litman remembers bitterly. "Kaye sat there taking notes while they asked me questions like, 'Who did Hawkins associate with?', 'Did he ever accept money?', 'What does he know about bribes?'. They were trying to prepare their case against him. They weren't interested in fairly judging his story. When I asked if they *thought* he'd associated with gamblers, and if so, *what* gamblers, they refused to give me any information. They wouldn't even tell me why Connie hadn't been drafted. I left there completely disgusted. They had deliberately misled me."

The following week, the Litmans received a letter from Kennedy dated May 18, 1966. The Commissioner reiterated that individual teams—not the NBA—draft players, and that no club had drafted Connie.

Kennedy didn't bother to add, however, that in 1965 the St. Louis Hawks, New York Knicks, and Los Angeles Lakers had quietly requested permission to negotiate with Hawkins. Each club wired the league office, asking that Hawk be placed on their Professional Negotiation List. Kennedy had turned them down—because, as he later explained, "there was some question in my mind about his desirability to play in the National Basketball Association."

The Commissioner also didn't inform the Litmans that Connie Hawkins had, by then, been *officially* barred from the NBA. Two days after Kennedy's meeting with David, the league's Board of Governors had passed a resolution placing Hawkins off limits—pending the conclusion of an "investigation" Kennedy was supposed to have already begun.

Kennedy's letter did state that "information has come to my attention that Mr. Hawkins has been accused of consorting with known gamblers and of accepting money from at least one known gambler." David Litman was invited to bring Connie to Kennedy's office, where Hawkins was to be questioned by the Commissioner and NBA attorneys, and then permitted to make any statement he wished. Then Kennedy would "continue" his investigation and "issue a ruling."

Litman agreed to a hearing, but insisted that it be "fair and impartial." He offered the NBA two proposals: that the league inform him of the specific charges against Hawkins, give him time to investigate, and then hold the hearing; or that the NBA allow him to cross-examine Connie's accusers, then let him investigate and present a defense.

Kennedy flatly rejected both proposals. He announced he would proceed with his own investigation. Then he sent Litman a letter containing four questions—pertaining to the counts in the Joe Hacken indictment—which Connie was asked to answer in writing and under oath.

1. Did Connie Hawkins testify before the grand jury of the County of New York and, if so, what was the substance of the testimony given by him?
2. Did Connie Hawkins ever meet with Joseph Hacken and, if so, when and where did each meeting or conference take place and what transpired at each meeting or conference?
3. Did Joseph Hacken ever offer Connie Hawkins any sum of money for an introduction to amateur basketball players and, if so, when and where was each offer made and what were the circumstances of each offer?
4. Did Joseph Hacken ever give Connie Hawkins any sums of money and, if so, when and where were such sums given, what were the amounts given, and what were the circumstances under which each sum of money was given?

"When we got the questions in that form we knew it was a setup," says Roslyn Litman. "First they offer a hearing without any provisions for due process—a virtual Star Chamber proceeding—then they send those questions. We knew they'd take Connie's answers and say, 'You're out, and now we're going to tell you *why* you're out.'"

David—noting that Hawkins still had not been informed of the specific charges against him, nor told who his accusers were, nor informed on what basis he would be judged—advised Connie not to answer the questions.

Litman's last letter to Kennedy warned, "My research on this matter indicates that your organization has committed a number of criminal and civil offenses which could very well result in a number of adverse verdicts against your organization and each of its members."

There was no reply from the NBA.

The Litmans still had not pressed Connie for precise details of his relationship with Hacken and Molinas. They knew little of what happened to him in the DA's office. Now they had to find out. When Connie returned from Europe in the fall of 1966, he and Roz sat in the Litmans' living room one night and talked for hours. Hawk was uncomfortable, ashamed; these were memories he'd tried to force from his mind. But Roz persisted, her tone gentle but firm. "I subjected him to a pretty tough cross-examination," she recalls. "Finally, I was able to learn that he'd made a number of statements in the DA's office that weren't true. He didn't remember what he'd said, but he knew he'd been so frightened he told them what they wanted. By the time we were finished, I had no doubt of Connie's innocence."

Wayne Bradley had found enough information to convince the Litmans that an anti-trust suit had a chance of success. But the time had come for their firm to take over the case. Until then, Roz and David had financed it from their own pocket. They had already spent over $15,000. Connie, of course, had no money to pay legal fees.

They met with their partners, Steve Harris and Howard Specter (who was then just twenty-six years old). "The case has great merit," David told them. "But it's a long shot. It could become very big, and could become financially prohibitive." Harris and Specter agreed that the firm should handle it, with Howard joining Roz and David in the actual work.

This was the Litmans' contention: The NBA was a closed organization which, by virtue of being the only major league in pro basketball, had a monopoly on all jobs in that field. The NBA teams and the league itself (through the commissioner) had conspired to arbitrarily blacklist Hawkins, in violation of Federal anti-trust laws which prohibited restraint of trade. An agreement—possibly tacit—existed among NBA clubs, as early as 1964, not to draft Connie. This had damaged Hawk's reputation and deprived him of the salary, endorsements, job opportunities, and future employment that his status as a star player would otherwise have brought.

"Our position," explains Roslyn, "was that when your organization occupies a substantial portion of the market, you've got to give applicants some reasonable way to get in. And if you exclude them, you've got to afford them due process of law. That means notice of the charges against them and a fair and impartial hearing. We never received notice of the specific charges. As far as the hearing Kennedy offered, we believed it wasn't a *fair* hearing because it lacked due-process standards: Connie didn't know what he was being accused of, and he didn't know who was accusing him. We felt Kennedy's 'hearing' was just a cover for exclusion."

In addition, the Litmans emphasized, the hearing wasn't offered until 1966, two years after Connie became eligible for the NBA. (And, they would later discover, a week *after* Hawkins had been officially barred.)

To make their argument stick, the Litmans first had to establish that what the NBA had done to Connie fell within the realm of an anti-trust violation. "No one had ever applied the principal of group boycott to a sports case," says Roz. "At the time, there was a question of whether basketball was covered by anti-trust laws."

The question was not fully answered by the Hawkins suit, since the case was settled before it reached actual trial. But the presiding judge, Rabe F. Marsh, didn't dismiss the suit, and the NBA—strangely—never challenged it on the basis of pro basketball being exempt from anti-trust regulations. Subsequently, many suits against pro basketball were filed, using *Hawkins v. NBA* as a basis. (The NBA eventually conceded it was not exempt. When the league sought to merge with the ABA in 1971, it approached Congress, seeking passage of a law granting pro basketball an exemption.)

But anti-trust was just the first small hurdle. The Litmans also had to establish that Connie was good enough to play in the NBA, that he was available to play, and that he had suffered damages by being excluded. This would take time, but was eventually done.

Their toughest task was to prove that there was a *conspiracy* to keep Hawkins out of the league. It wasn't enough to show that Hawk hadn't been drafted. They had to convince the court that there was some sort of agreement, understanding, or policy among the NBA clubs not to take him.

All this was probably irrelevant, however, if they couldn't also show that Hawk was innocent of the "intermediary" charges. The NBA was almost surely in the clear, if it could establish that Hawkins was knowingly involved in the 1961 scandals—and that it was on the basis of this immoral involvement that the league chose to bar him.

The NBA's position was less complex. First, it denied that there had been any conspiracy to bar Connie. It maintained that his not being drafted in 1964 was a matter of coincidence, that each team decided unilaterally it didn't want him. The league conceded that Connie was now off limits. But it argued that the Molinas case proved the right of the NBA to bar those involved with gambling and that Commissioner Kennedy—who had information that Hawkins had been associated with gamblers—was correct in ordering an "investigation" before any team could negotiate with Hawk. This investigation was in good faith, the league maintained— the NBA had nothing against Connie—but it could not be completed because Hawkins refused to answer the four questions or submit to a "hearing."

The first major skirmish came in December of 1966 when the NBA rolled out its big gun, George G. Gallantz, a trim, erudite attorney who had been the league's chief counsel since its inception in 1946. Gallantz's courtroom delivery was so smooth and convincing, Roz was afraid Judge Marsh would dismiss the suit immediately. "It was the first time I'd ever heard him speak," she recalls with a shudder. "It was painful to listen, he was so good. He sounded as though everything was on his side, the flag and the great sport of basketball, which they just wanted to keep clean for American youth. And here I was with this 'fixer' trying to ruin the whole game."

"I would like to say categorically that the National Basketball Association has never had among its members anyone who has been so much as accused of being a gambler or of having anything to do with gamblers, or of fixing . . ." Gallantz intoned.

The NBA wasn't going to quibble over Connie's ability (although later in the case, numerous NBA officials did). Gallantz stressed the moral issue: "We may very well concede that he is a skilled basketball player. My own suspicion is, were it not for the record that he made with the grand jury of New York, he might very well be one of the most skilled players in the National Basketball Association. [But] what is going to be relevant is the events that are hinted at in the 1961 indictment. Is he a corrupt man who has taken money to corrupt others—kids—playing on college basketball teams? That is the issue in the case. And, if we prove that he is so corrupt, then under the Molinas case, that is the end of the case. It doesn't make any difference whether he is the best shot in the world."

Gallantz immediately requested that Judge Marsh throw out the suit because the Western District of Pennsylvania was improper venue: he maintained that since the NBA practiced no business, and had no team, in the Western District, the trial did not belong there.

Judge Marsh reserved a decision and gave the Litmans time to research. "With anti-trust law," explains Roslyn, "the definition of 'doing business' is less rigid. You don't necessarily have to have an office or even sell goods. This is to help the little guy who wants to bring suit near his home against a big company."

After months of exhaustive investigation, and court-ordered interrogatories (written questions and answers) and depositions (face-to-face interrogation under oath), the Litmans were able to show that the Zollner Piston Company, which owned the Detroit team, did business in the Western District; the Philadelphia 76ers had played several games in Pittsburgh; Jack Kent Cooke, owner of the Lakers, had a minor-league hockey team in the district; Madison Square Garden, which owned the Knicks, had a minor-league club that played against Cooke's team; and the NBA itself televised games into Pittsburgh.

Judge Marsh ruled in the Litmans' favor.

Then, however, Gallantz presented a motion to transfer the case to New York. He cited a Federal rule that the convenience of witnesses and parties to the case, and "the interest of justice," should be considered when deciding the place for a trial. The NBA believed the suit would revolve around what happened in the 1961 scandals and witnesses would thus be fixers, detectives, and players living in the New York area. Gallantz also noted that the league's offices and a franchise were in New York. He added, in passing, that the case should be tried in front of a jury which understood the grave consequences of fixing.

"A move to New York would have murdered us," says Roz. "The NBA could have out-financed us something fierce. They could have used the prestige of Hogan's office, and the fact that this was the district where Judge Kaufman decided against Molinas. And the docket there is so crowded, the NBA could have postponed the case until the end of Connie's career."

More research, more depositions, more interrogatories, and once more the Litmans won their point. "The NBA thought in terms of the scandal," David says. "But we maintained the case dealt with broader issues. The first was our allegation that there was a conspiracy or combination to keep Hawkins out of the NBA. That meant witnesses would include owners and general managers who were at the draft meetings and the Board of Governors meetings. These people would be coming from all over the country— not just New York City." It was also relevant that Connie was a resident of Pittsburgh and that David Litman, because of his meeting with Kennedy, would be a witness.

Judge Marsh eventually ruled that the NBA had not established that more people would be inconvenienced coming to Pittsburgh than coming to New York. The decision was very close. The judge admitted he could have leaned in either direction.

As would often happen during the case, the Litmans' thoroughness was a crucial factor. During the winter of 1968–69, while the motion to transfer was being argued, George Gallantz alleged that Hacken and Molinas were potential witnesses for the NBA. He said they were in New York State prisons and, therefore, more accessible to a New York court.

But Gallantz had never spoken to Hacken or Molinas. David Litman had been interviewing them since late 1966. He knew Gallantz's information was wrong. Litman presented the court with affidavits from Hacken and Molinas, stating they were, in fact, out of prison and—although living in New York—willing to testify in Pittsburgh. This led Judge Marsh to conclude that "their inconvenience and unavailability as witnesses for the defendants (NBA) is to be disregarded," and helped swing the venue decision in the Litmans' favor.

The legal hassling for home-court advantage took more than two years to resolve. By the time the Gallantz motion to transfer was denied and the suit was safe in Pittsburgh, the Litmans had learned a great deal about the two central issues of their case: Connie's innocence of the intermediary charges, and the existence of an NBA blacklist.

They had begun serious investigation in late December of 1966. David visited Hacken in Wallkill Prison and secured a signed affidavit stating that Connie was completely innocent. "The kid," Hacken told him immediately, "got a raw deal. I never mentioned fixed games to him. He never introduced me to anybody."

The same week, Litman went into the Tombs, the Manhattan prison, and met with Molinas. Again he was told that Connie was innocent. Again —after some haggling this time—he secured an affidavit.

But things went less smoothly several days later, when the Litmans met with Assistant DA Peter D. Andreoli, who had been in charge of the basketball case. They arrived for an appointment at the DA's office to find that Andreoli wanted to conduct the entire interview over an intercom, with the Litmans getting no closer than a receptionist's desk. When they insisted on meeting him in person, he made them wait over an hour.

Pete Andreoli is a burly, aggressive veteran of the DA's office. He likes to project an image of toughness and self-importance. But he gets jumpy in the tight spots. "When he's going to trial he's always sure he's gonna lose," says a detective who has worked with him often. "Pete'll start talking on and on about how he used to fly these bombing missions over Germany during the war. As soon as you start hearing about those Goddamn missions, you know he's getting tense."

In his first meeting with the Litmans, Andreoli was abrupt. "I have nothing to do with this. It's a civil matter," he said. "I'll tell you what I tell everybody—look at the indictment."

"We'd really like to help this kid," Roslyn tried to explain. "We think he's been hurt badly."

Andreoli's face reddened. "If you think I'm going to let any fraud be perpetrated on the court, you're wrong," he threatened. "This Hawkins was no babe in the woods. If there's any fraud, the grand jury minutes can be released. I'll see to that."

"Andreoli implied he had enough information somewhere in the DA's office to prove Connie was a rogue of the worst kind," remembers David. "We left there depressed. He'd been arrogant and unfriendly. But we assumed we at least had the commitment of a fellow lawyer that he wasn't going to involve himself."

Two years later, in late 1968, the Litmans discovered that Andreoli was very much involved. While taking one of several depositions of Walter Kennedy in New York, they learned that the NBA commissioner had met with Andreoli as early as 1963. The meeting took place several days after Kennedy received Litman's first letter about Connie.

In 1966, Kennedy and Andreoli spoke on the phone just prior to the Board of Governors' vote to ban Hawk. In 1967, the NBA's lawyers had been permitted to meet with detectives Kenneth Wheaton and Nat Laurendi. They were given information concerning Hawkins's "confessions."

Surprised and shaken, the Litmans called Andreoli. "Don't blame me if other counsel is more enterprising," said the DA.

"Right there," recalls David, "we knew Andreoli had chosen sides."

David and Howard rushed to the DA's office. "Andreoli was very cold and officious," Litman says. "He always tried to appear very impressive: constantly getting ready for trial or just finishing trial. He kept telling us about all the lawyers he'd wrapped up for fraud or subornation of perjury. I suppose it was a mild threat. But I was too stupid to realize he thought I might be doing something out of line."

David, who can be extremely persuasive when he's angry, demanded to know what was in the notes Detective Wheaton had discussed with the NBA's lawyers. Finally, Andreoli allowed Wheaton to read the notes aloud. David and Howard heard, for the first time, Connie's supposed admissions that he'd introduced Wilky Gilmore to Molinas and that he knew Molinas and Hacken were fixers.

As Wheaton read, Andreoli's smile broadened. "It shook me when I heard those notes," says David. "Andreoli looked so happy, as though he'd been vindicated. In fact, he gave the impression of just having had an orgasm."

A few months later, in early 1969, during the deposition of Detective Laurendi, who had kept the files on the case, the rest of Connie's statements became public. Now everything was in the open, every damaging "confession": Hawkins's alleged admission that he and Vinnie Brewer had discussed fixing games for Molinas, the assorted (and contradictory) confessions of the Gilmore introduction, and the unsigned, undated notes which described the two hundred dollar loan from Molinas as a gift.

While the "confessions" were trickling out, I had my first meeting with the Litmans. It was January 25, 1969. They were cautious, worried that I might hurt Connie with a sensationalized story. But when I remarked that "Hacken and Molinas are out of jail, and Connie is the only one who's still being punished," I could feel them relax.

They agreed to give me some leads. Legal ethics prevented them from cooperating more closely (lawyers aren't supposed to try their cases in the press), but they helped me reach several key sources and directed me to the Western District courthouse where the depositions were filed.

They had divided the work on the case. Roz and Howard were handling depositions and would do the court work, while David—an expected witness—was doing the investigating. Our trails crossed constantly in the next three and a half months as David and I duplicated scores of interviews, sometimes exchanging leads and information.

A few weeks after my initial meeting with the Litmans, they flew Connie from Minnesota to New York. He was still recuperating from the knee operation, hadn't played again yet, and was limping badly. In the Litmans' suite at the Pierre Hotel, Hawk and I had the first of many long discussions of the scandal. It wasn't easy for Connie. It hurt his pride to admit how confused he had been and how thoroughly the detectives had intimidated him. Even then, his story was almost too incredible to believe. As Hawkins spoke of his contacts with Molinas and Hacken, I was hard-pressed to imagine how this now mature adult could have been so naïve. It was only when I began to explore Connie's background—to learn what he had been like as a teenager—that his explanations became entirely believable.

The meeting at the Pierre lasted four hours. That night we went to watch the Knicks at the new Madison Square Garden. It had been nine years since Connie played in the old one. The memories came in a rush. "I'll never forget it," he said, gazing around the shiny new lobby. "Playing for the city championship in front of eighteen thousand people. It was Cloud Nine. The noise, the fans, the smoke—I'll never forget the smoke—it kind of hung over the court, but never touched it, just hanging there like a halo."

Hawk stretched his injured leg into the aisle and stared at Willis Reed and Guy Rodgers and the others he played with in the summer. He hardly spoke during the first half.

At the concession stand, the fans—New York fans—recognized him immediately. "Connie Hawkins," they yelled, "how ya doin, Hawk!" A husky young man in a rumpled suit tugged at Connie's arm. "You're the greatest in the world," he said. "Been watchin you since Boys High. How's Roger Brown? Where's Tony Jackson playin?"

"You a real New Yorker, man," Connie grinned.

"Listen," said the fan excitedly. "I don't care what you guys did in the past. The ABA ought to put a franchise in Brooklyn. They could have Roger Brown and Doug Moe and Tony Jackson and you, all on the same team."

A sad smile played around Connie's mouth and he looked down at the man for what seemed like a long time. Then he sighed, "Yeah, they could call us The Fixers."

My own investigation began at the DA's office. I found the same hostility the Litmans had encountered. "I'm too busy to meet with the press. I'm in the middle of a trial," Andreoli said icely over the phone. "I might be free in a few months. But I'll tell you this, Hawkins was no babe in the woods."

I was directed to Hogan's PR man, Jim O'Leary, who informed me, "Hawkins showed knowledge of the fixes and what the contacts were for. He's admitted taking two hundred dollars to make an introduction."

He suggested I submit a list of questions, since Andreoli was much too busy to meet directly with writers. But when I handed O'Leary a sheet with forty-one questions—including "Did Hacken or Molinas make any statement concerning Hawkins, and, if so, what did they say?" and "How often was Hawkins questioned?"—I was told Andreoli had no comment because the DA's office wasn't getting involved in a civil matter.

"I think you're barking up the wrong tree," O'Leary cautioned. "Al Scotti, the head of the Rackets Bureau, wants me to tell you Hawkins was involved. Look, Hawkins was allowed to call his family. He admitted introducing Gilmore to Molinas. He even admitted talking to Vinnie Brewer about fixing games. This kid was no babe in the woods."

I wondered where I'd heard that phrase before.

Once the detectives' notes of all Connie's "confessions" were made public, it was clear that if the statements couldn't be refuted, Hawkins was in serious trouble. The Litmans' case was dead. I still had a story—but it was a story that would have driven Connie even from the ABA.

David Litman and I separately located and interviewed dozens of gamblers, former players, and detectives. Almost immediately, the validity of the confessions began to pale. All players mentioned in the notes maintained Hawkins had done nothing wrong, that the statements attributed to Connie were untrue. Both David and I spoke to players who had been actively involved in the scandal—some who were caught, others who'd escaped detection—and each said Hawkins knew nothing about the fixed games.

It took a week to locate Wilky Gilmore in Stamford, Connecticut. But it was worth the effort. "Did Hawkins introduce you to Hacken or Molinas in Rockville Centre?" I asked.

"It wasn't Connie," Gilmore said. "In fact, Connie wasn't even there."

Then he added, "Funny thing, a lawyer from the NBA was here. He had all the facts mixed up. He thought Connie introduced me to Molinas at the Holiday Festival. First he said they wanted me to be a witness. But, when I told him what really happened, he said it wouldn't be necessary."

I found Vinnie Brewer working for the Youth Board in Harlem. He laughed when I told him the DA claimed he'd told Connie that he fixed games. "If that was true," Brewer asked, "why didn't the DA bring me in? I was never contacted. Nobody questioned me. And Connie never even spoke to me about Molinas. He didn't have to. I knew Jack from the schoolyards."

I called O'Leary and asked if Brewer had been questioned or had testified before the grand jury. The DA's man conceded he hadn't.

With each interview, the realization kept growing: Connie was really innocent. But the two hundred dollars Hawk got from Molinas still bothered me. Was it actually a loan?

I finally found Fred Hawkins in Bed-Stuy. He confirmed Connie's story, emphasizing that he had returned the money to Molinas while Hawk was still at Iowa. The next day I met Molinas. If Jack's version had differed vastly from Fred's, there would have been a gaping hole in Hawkins's defense.

Molinas, then on parole and living in Brooklyn, placed his glistening shoes atop his attorney's desk, and puffed a thick cigar. Wearing an expensive suit, wide paisley tie, and infectious smile, Jack was the same picture of confidence and charm he had been until the closing days of his trial. He had abandoned his pretense of innocence, but not his sense of humor. "I don't need the publicity," he joked. "What can you write about me except that I corrupted the youth of America?"

"Allegedly corrupted," reminded his lawyer, a Runyonesque figure in sharkskin suit, pink shirt, and huge purple cuff links.

"Of course," said Jack, laughing.

But Molinas didn't laugh about Hawkins. His explanation of the two hundred dollars he gave to Hawk coincided with Fred's and Connie's: The money, Jack said, was given as a loan. It was an investment to soften up

Hawkins for a future approach: "I never expected to see the money again. Then one day, this guy walks into my office and puts two hundred dollars on the desk. He says he's Connie's brother. And that was well before the scandal broke."

The clincher was Detective Anthony Bernhard. He told Litman and me that when he picked up Hawkins at Iowa in 1961, Connie couldn't even comprehend what the scandal was about. He described how Hawkins had maintained his innocence for almost a week.

Why had Connie made false confessions? Again Bernhard was crucial. He defended his former colleagues but gave vivid descriptions of the pressure put on the players, the chaos in the DA's office, and Connie's broken, terrified condition when he confessed. Bernhard also reluctantly admitted that, while in the DA's custody, Hawkins had never been informed of his legal rights.

Litman secured a signed statement from Bernhard and recorded him on tape.

But I needed confirmation. Bernhard had left the DA's office honorably in 1966, but had been on very unfavorable terms with his superiors. As a private investigator, he was not doing well financially. He was anxious for notoriety and hoped to ingratiate himself with the Litmans. His story had to be checked.

In several instances, I found that Bernhard had exaggerated or even possibly lied. But on every important point, the detective had extensive notes and memoranda confirming what he said. Later, I obtained other notes, filed at the DA's office, which substantiated his contentions. In addition, Litman and I spoke with many other detectives. Most were still on the force. They were tough, dedicated men with enormous pride in their work. Many refused to believe that Hawkins had been badgered into false confessions. They didn't trust Bernhard. But, in the process of attempting to refute him, they actually supported most of what he said.

"We were being pushed to break kids fast, to get confessions," said one detective. "But nobody used rough stuff. I thought the kids were well treated. Of course we had to frighten them with talk about jail and perjury, but how else were we going to get Molinas?"

None of the detectives could be quoted in my story. But their words on the same subjects allowed me to quote Bernhard without hesitation.

Meanwhile, Roslyn and Howard were taking the depositions of Kennedy and many NBA executives. What they discovered was incredible. The decision to blacklist Hawkins, it turned out, had been totally arbitrary, made without the vaguest idea of the facts involved. The league never made a serious investigation. No thought had been given to due process of law or the presumption of innocence. Everyone in the NBA assumed they had the right to keep out Hawkins simply because they didn't want him.

It never occurred to these respected administrators and businessmen that before they barred Connie Hawkins for life from doing the only thing he knew, they had a legal—not to mention moral—responsibility to confirm the accusations made against him.

When Kennedy decided to stop the Knicks, Hawks, and Lakers from negotiating with Connie in 1965, and when the NBA Board of Governors voted to bar him in 1966, they didn't even know about the "confessions" he was supposed to have made in the DA's office. (It was only after the Litmans filed suit, and the league had to justify its decision publicly, that the NBA lawyers scurried to meet Hogan's detectives.)

The league barred Hawkins simply because of what had been written about him in the newspapers—and, possibly, because of some damaging but completely unsubstantiated statements from Assistant DA Peter Andreoli.

In 1963, Kennedy had met for one hour with Andreoli. There is almost total disagreement about the substance of their discussion. Testifying under oath, during his deposition, Kennedy swore that the assistant DA told him District Attorney Hogan's public labeling of Connie as an "intermediary" was accurate. The commissioner also claimed that Andreoli informed him that "the allegations [against Hawkins] in the [Hacken] indictment are basically so," that Molinas and Hacken were "well known" to Connie, and that Hawk did attempt introductions for the purpose of fixing games.

Andreoli denies all this. Also testifying under oath during a deposition, he swore he did no more than *show* Kennedy the indictment.

But, even assuming that Kennedy's recollection of the conversation is correct (and that Andreoli is trying to weasel out of any responsibility for Hawkins's being blacklisted), the NBA has no excuses. No attempt was made to confirm Andreoli's supposed accusations against Hawkins. In fact, Kennedy was so uninterested he didn't even bother to ask Andreoli *what* players Hawkins was alleged to have approached. In making his "investigation," the commissioner spoke to none of the detectives and read none of their notes.

The rest of his inquiry consisted of hiring the Pinkerton Agency for several months in early 1966. He admits he got no new information.

"We suddenly realized," says Roslyn, "that they'd excluded Connie for *nothing.* In 1967, when Gallantz met with the detectives, he was scratching around for evidence to support something the NBA had done years before. They hadn't drafted Connie because his name appeared in a newspaper article about the scandal. It was astonishing!"

Like the other NBA officials, Kennedy had been cocky, almost condescending, when the case began. But by the time his final deposition was taken, on March 11, 1969, the commissioner was squirming. He was forced to admit that almost five years after Hawkins became eligible for the NBA draft—and three years after Connie was officially barred—he didn't even know that Joe Hacken and Jack Molinas had separate indictments.

Kennedy's ignorance—and lack of curiosity—about Hawkins was embarrassing. When Roz asked if he knew that Hacken had *not* been found guilty of the indictment count in which Connie was named, Kennedy said, "I was not aware of it, and I am not aware of it now."

MRS. LITMAN: "If you were made aware of that fact at this time, would that influence your decision with respect to Connie Hawkins . . ."

MR. KENNEDY: "No."

MRS. LITMAN: "Did you ask Mr. Andreoli at your meeting whether Hacken had been found guilty of these accusations [in the indictment]?"

MR. KENNEDY: "No."

MRS. LITMAN: "Did you understand . . . the facts set forth that you read . . . were just that, accusations?"

MR. KENNEDY: "Yes."

Later, she asked the commissioner if he'd inquired whether Hawkins had *accepted* the five hundred dollars Hacken was alleged to have offered.

MR. KENNEDY: "No."

MRS. LITMAN: "Did you consider it to be of any importance?"

MR. KENNEDY: "Not at that point."

When Mrs. Litman asked Kennedy if he felt it was "important" to know what Connie was supposed to have done in order to get $210 from the fixers, the commissioner answered, "I think it is now."

MRS. LITMAN: "But you didn't then, is that correct?"

MR. KENNEDY: "I don't recall. I never gave it any thought at the time."

In a document submitted to the court, the NBA had named Wilky Gilmore as a player Hawkins had introduced to gamblers. During the deposition, Roslyn forced Kennedy to admit that Gilmore was the only name the NBA had. (Gilmore, of course, had already signed a statement for the Litmans swearing that Connie was not the player who introduced him to Molinas. By then, the NBA's lawyers had also visited Gilmore. They knew Wilky would not support their contention. But they apparently hadn't bothered to inform Kennedy.)

MRS. LITMAN: "How many such attempted introductions do you believe there have been?"

MR. KENNEDY: "I don't recall how many."

MRS. LITMAN: "Was it more than one?"

MR. KENNEDY: "I have no idea."

MRS. LITMAN: "And the only one you know anything about, as you understand it, is the one involving Wilky Gilmore; is that correct?"

MR. KENNEDY: "Yes."

MRS. LITMAN: "But you have not felt impelled to inquire of [your] counsel as yet what Gilmore has to say about that?"

MR. KENNEDY: "That is correct."

The NBA's investigation had been something less than exhaustive.

MRS. LITMAN: "Prior to March, 1967, did you ever attempt to contact detectives Wheaton and Laurendi?"

MR. KENNEDY: "No."

• • • • •

MRS. LITMAN "Did you ever contact Hawkins's coach where he had played ball?"

MR. KENNEDY: "No, I did not."

• • • • •

MRS. LITMAN: "Did you speak to any members of Hawkins's family?"

MR. KENNEDY: "No."

• • • • •

MRS. LITMAN: "Did you ever check the police records on him?"

MR. KENNEDY: "I don't recall any checking."

MRS. LITMAN: "Did you speak to Hacken or Molinas?"

MR. KENNEDY: "No."

MRS. LITMAN: "Did you check the transcript of the Molinas trial?"

MR. KENNEDY: "I don't recall."

The league's attitude toward "tainted" players also turned out to be inconsistent. Kennedy cited Hacken's indictment in barring Connie. At the deposition, however, he admitted that, until recently, he had *never* checked the document to see if it also mentioned any current NBA players.

In fact, the *first* player named in the indictment was Fred Crawford, who was with the Los Angeles Lakers of the NBA. Hacken was charged with offering Crawford, then at St. Bonaventure University, a $1,000 bribe which the DA said Crawford didn't report.

Kennedy maintained he didn't know Crawford was in the indictment when he first approved the player's contract in 1967. But, said the commissioner, it wouldn't have mattered; he still wouldn't have held a hearing or investigation. Why? Because St. Bonaventure—which never held a hearing—allowed Crawford to continue playing, after he spent one year in the hospital with tuberculosis.

In 1967, *Life* magazine's crack investigative team had published an article accusing Bob Cousy of knowingly associating with bookmakers and gamblers while he played for the Boston Celtics. "Cousy," the article read, "conceded he had been warned about his associates by Boston police as long ago as 1963. But he refused to end the relationship . . ." *Life* also maintained that the FBI had found Cousy's name in the notebook of Gilbert Beckley, the nation's largest bookmaker. It was scribbled next to the word "Skiball," the nickname of Francisco Scibelli, a bookmaker Cousy admitted knowing.

"In this hypocritical world we live in," the article quoted Cousy as saying, "I don't see why I should stop seeing my friends just because they are gamblers. How can I tell Andy (Andrew Pradella, Scibelli's bookmaking partner) when he calls and asks about a team that I won't talk to him about that?"

When the story appeared, Cousy held a tearful press conference. He denied ever giving gamblers information, and said, "I suppose I'm guilty of indiscretion. But I'm not guilty of anything else."

That was enough for Walter Kennedy and the men who run the NBA. In 1969, when Cousy was named coach of the Cincinnati Royals, the commissioner made no attempt to check the validity of the charges against him, held no hearing, and didn't even discuss the matter with Cousy. He simply approved his contract.

Of course, Cousy was an all-time NBA All-Star—not a black schoolyard player from Bed-Stuy.

The NBA denied there was an understanding among its teams not to draft Hawkins in 1964. But the league's argument was hardly convincing. During the depositions, Kennedy conceded that, just before the draft, he told Los Angeles general manager Lou Mohs about his discussion with Andreoli. Roz got other NBA executives to admit they had been aware that a player—specifically Connie—mentioned in the scandal was taboo. Howard Specter got Red Auerbach to go even farther.

Specter asked Auerbach if the NBA had a specific policy regarding athletes who were approached with bribe offers but didn't report them. Red answered, "I don't know the details of it. All I know is that if a man was involved, he was therefore ineligible."

MR. SPECTER: "Is it your understanding he [Celtics owner Walter Brown] received information from the League that certain players had been involved in the scandal?"

MR. AUERBACH: "Oh, I would think so, yes."

MR. SPECTER: "Because of your recollection that he advised you he had received such information?"

MR. AUERBACH: "Yes."

MR. SPECTER: "Do you recall the names of any specific players?"

MR. AUERBACH: "Well, you had guys like Hawkins, Brown, the name Doug Moe was brought up. That's all I know offhand."

The NBA executives constantly contradicted each other's *sworn* statements. Former commissioner Maurice Podoloff maintained he never made "any kind of ruling" concerning Hawkins. However, when Ned Irish, the Knicks' former general manager and currently operating head of Madison Square Garden, was asked, "Were Hawkins and Brown players whose names, as you understood it from Mr. Podoloff, would not be approved?" he answered, "Yes."

Kennedy was asked, "Was any ruling made from 1961 on (excepting the Hawkins ban in 1966) concerning persons who were involved in or named in the basketball investigations. . . ?"

"None," he answered, "not to the best of my recollection."

Irish told a different story: ". . . the commissioner reported that certain people—he wouldn't approve certain contracts if they were submitted . . . I don't know whether Podoloff was commissioner then or Kennedy . . . I know that both of them have made similar statements."

"Just to be clear," Roslyn asked him, "is the statement that they, as commissioners, would not have approved of certain contracts if they were submitted?"

"Correct," said Irish.

"And what certain contracts were they referring to?"

"Referring to players whose names had been in print—associated with the gambling activities."

Howard Specter, heavy-set and mustached, owned part of a boutique called Fringe Benefits. He "fucked around and drank a lot" while working his way through the University of Pittsburgh, and was told by the dean of Pittsburgh Law School he would "never be a successful lawyer." The dean was wrong. Howard became a full partner in the Litmans' firm in 1969. He has no interest in sports, never went to a pro basketball game until the suit was filed—and was consequently amazed when he encountered the NBA officials. "Some of them could look you in the eye and say the sun was shining in the middle of the night," he recalls. "These guys, who were supposed to make their living from basketball, sat there and told us they'd never heard of Hawkins, or didn't know much about him, or didn't think he was good enough to play in the NBA."

Red Auerbach, who once offered to pay Connie under the table to go to Providence College, had some interesting explanations for not drafting Hawk in 1964. At one point Red said, "We had a world championship team . . . we didn't want any situation where there was any smoke or any question of anything." Later he claimed, "Actually, I wasn't that well informed on Hawkins because I wasn't interested in him."

Still later: "I didn't see Hawkins play. How could I draft a man I didn't see play . . ."

But when Specter asked him why he drafted a player named Jeff Blue in 1964, Red answered, "Never brought him to camp, never even saw these guys play. We just throw in names, sometimes we needed bodies."

MR. SPECTER: "You didn't see him play?"

MR. AUERBACH: "No."

Dick Klein and Marty Blake, then with the Chicago Bulls and Atlanta Hawks, claimed scouting reports on Hawkins showed, in Klein's words, "that we shouldn't waste any time or money looking at him."

Ned Irish was more to the point: "I wouldn't consider Connie Hawkins to be an asset regardless of his basketball ability."

"Is that because of what you read in the newspapers about him?" Roz asked.

"Not because of what I read, but what many millions of people in the City of New York have read."

"Are you referring now to the fact that he was involved in newspaper publicity?"

"Adverse newspaper publicity," said Irish.

But, at another point in the deposition, Roz asked, "Wasn't there an earlier basketball scandal in approximately 1945?"

MR. IRISH: "There could have been, yes. Yes, there was."

MRS. LITMAN: "And, in fact, you were a witness before the grand jury in the 1945 investigation, were you not?"

MR. IRISH: "Yes, I was."

• • • • •

MRS. LITMAN: "Do you recall whether or not Commissioner Valentine made certain allegations concerning your knowledge of gambling activities at that time [1945]?"

MR. IRISH: I do. . . . He made an allegation that I had asked for protection and that I made certain statements in asking for it which to the best of my knowledge I did not make. . . . I made a request for police protection and coverage [in the building], but I did not say that I had known about these activities or who they were."

Mrs. Litman: "And was there newspaper publicity attendant with your appearance before the grand jury at that time?"

Mr. Irish: "Considerable."

A pretrial hearing before Judge Marsh was scheduled for July, 1969. Although the case was going exceptionally well, the Litmans still weren't confident. The evidence was piling up on their side, but juries are always unpredictable. The primary worry, however, was Connie. His deposition had not yet been taken. This was the NBA's chance to reverse the momentum of the case. If Hawk did badly—if George Gallantz was able to confuse him into contradicting himself, admitting to perjury before the grand jury, or conceding that some of his confessions were true—the NBA still had a chance.

"Connie had given a deposition the previous fall on the limited question of venue," Roz recalls. "We were trying to show that although he played in Minnesota, he was a resident of Pittsburgh, which was the truth. But he did so badly it appeared, by some of his answers, that he didn't live here at all."

Hawk had been confused and nervous. He misunderstood questions, blurted incorrect answers, and came across as almost laughable. Questioned by Bruce Bowden, the junior lawyer from the Pittsburgh firm helping the Gallantz firm on the case for the NBA, Hawk had even managed to forget the name of his next-door neighbor. When Bowden asked what personal property Connie's family had in their Charles Street home, Hawk should have enumerated many items to show he was settled there. Instead, he simply mumbled, "We have TV." This was damaging, because Hawkins lacked the usual indicators of residence:

Q. Do you have a driver's license, Mr. Hawkins?
A. No, sir.
Q. Are you registered to vote anywhere?
A. No, sir.
Q. Do you own any land, any real property or houses . . . ?
A. No, sir.
Q. Are you involved in any business enterprise other than professional basketball?
A. No, sir.
Q. Do you own any securities, stock or bonds?
A. No, sir.
Q. Do you have any bank accounts, Mr. Hawkins?

A. No, sir.
Q. Do you have credit cards or credit accounts?
A. No, sir.

The most devastating moment came when Bowden asked Hawk to name people who could testify to his moral character. The Litmans were arguing against shifting the case to New York. Connie should have listed people in Pittsburgh. Instead he had announced, "It would be some friends I grew up with in Brooklyn."

His comments were so obviously muddled, they made little impression on the judge. The case stayed in Pittsburgh. But if Hawk butchered the upcoming deposition—which would deal with every aspect of the suit—the results could be disastrous. And Connie wouldn't be facing a young, inexperienced lawyer. George Gallantz would be asking the questions.

When Connie got back to Pittsburgh, after the horrendous playoffs against Miami, Roslyn explained the situation. They had less than two weeks to prepare for the deposition. Hawk was frightened. His future depended on his performance. But he could rely on nothing but his mind.

Roz, Howard, and David shelved all other business to work fulltime with Connie. "Against a skilled attorney, having the truth on your side often isn't enough," says Howard. "Especially if, like Connie, your memory is genuinely hazy about many of the specific events. You must be prepared. We went over everything that had happened from the date of his birth. We explained the history of the case, the nature of the NBA's defense, and what they would try to prove—primarily by getting admissions from Connie. We reviewed every fact. Then we interrogated him over and over."

Hawk threw himself into the preparation. He even arrived at meetings reasonably on time. "It was unreal," he remembers. "I never worked so hard for anything in my life."

The three lawyers took turns questioning him, pretending they were George Gallantz. At first, Hawk could be led so easily, it was embarrassing.

"You're 6' 10", right?" Howard would say.

"Right. No, wait. I ain't 6' 10". Why did I say that?"

"Because you aren't concentrating hard enough!"

Sometimes all three questioned him at once, hitting with unrelated queries. His head was spinning. "They were like ballplayers," he says. "Each one had a different style. Roz was soft and feminine, nodding her head. The next thing I know, I'm nodding my head and saying Yes, when I should be saying No."

"Connie had to understand the importance of admitting that he didn't remember everything, especially what happened at the DA's office and the specifics of his meetings with Molinas and Hacken," says Howard. "We showed him Kennedy's deposition so he could see how many times Kennedy said, 'I don't recall.' Connie seemed to feel that not remembering was a reflection on his intelligence, and he was very defensive. But when he tried to say more than he was sure of—to fill in blanks—he always tripped himself up, because he *really* didn't remember."

Connie also had trouble accepting the fact that he had been duped by the fixers. For a while, he attempted to gloss over and explain away his relationship with Molinas and Hacken—and was constantly trapped in the questioning.

Everyone was tense. Tempers flared daily. "After the first few times," Connie recalls, "they really questioned me rough. David got me so mad I wanted to punch him in the mouth all the time."

Slowly Hawk began to catch on. His answers became more precise. He wasn't trapped as easily. The lawyers showed him how to throw the ball back to his interrogators. When a simple Yes or No would have hurt, he learned to say "Yes but . . ." and then elaborate.

Connie took notes on a large yellow pad which he carried everywhere. He never allowed the lawyers to see it, but each morning he arrived with new questions, asking how he should respond to things Gallantz might ask. When the lawyers wanted to quit for the day, he invariably pressed them to continue.

As the deposition approached, Roz, David, and Howard alternated being Connie, showing him how the rough spots should be handled. Hawk got great pleasure when Howard caught David in errors four straight times. "That gave me more confidence," Connie says. "If a fuckin smartass lawyer like Dave could mess up, I shouldn't be so tense."

But Hawkins was still far from perfect himself. During one session, David, playing Gallantz, asked him, "Did you just take money from everyone who offered it?"

"Yes, sir," Hawk responded. Roz went through the ceiling.

"Did you really?" she shouted. "Think before you answer. *Think!*"

Nevertheless, Connie continued to improve. By the eve of the deposition, the lawyers felt he was ready to answer questions. "The key was for him to stay relaxed, not be scared by Gallantz," Howard recalls. "He had to remember to tell only what he really knew, only the truth. If he didn't understand a question, he had to ask, not be embarrassed about his vocabulary."

That night, the children were sent to bed early. The house was quiet. Connie sat in his living room, eyes fixed on the yellow note-pad. It was after midnight when he climbed the stairs to the bedroom. Hawk rarely has trouble sleeping, even before an important game. But this was different. He lay awake for what seemed like hours, listening to Nancy's soft breathing and staring into the darkness.

The morning of May 1, Roz, Howard, and Connie went to the law offices of Buchanan, Ingersoll, Rodewald, Kyle and Buerger, the Pittsburgh firm assisting the NBA's New York lawyers with the case. "Connie was as ready as possible," remembers Howard. "But we weren't sure what would happen to him under pressure."

Hawk's hands were sticky. His freshly pressed suit felt scratchy and ill-fitting. In the elevator, Roz whispered, "Just relax, be yourself." The elevator door opened into Buchanan's offices. Directly in front of them sat a matronly secretary in an ankle-length dress. "I thought, 'She looks like a lady who runs concentration camps,' " Connie says. "That frightened me. I was in a daze."

Gallantz arrived moments later, cold and businesslike. There was some small talk—during which Connie was surprised to learn the NBA's top lawyer didn't know Jerry West was white. Then they moved to a long wood table. Roz sat next to Connie, with Howard on her left. Gallantz sat across from Hawkins, looking into his eyes. "This," Hawk thought to himself, "is it. I can't be stupid now."

"Connie came across as gracious, warm, and intelligent," says Howard. "He handled almost everything beautifully. A couple of times he elaborated too much. Once he said he owed the Litmans twenty-five thousand dollars when he really didn't know what he owed them. But over all he did excellently."

During the morning session, Gallantz asked about Hawk's early years, the teams he'd played for, and his previous earnings. It was only a warmup. After an hour's lunch break, the lawyer directed himself to the scandal. Hawk stayed cool.

Mr. Gallantz: "Did he [Detective Bernhard] ask you who Molinas was; whether he was a gambler?"

Mr. Hawkins: "I don't recall what he stated."

Mr. Gallantz: "Did you know that Molinas was a gambler?"

Mr. Hawkins: "No, sir, I did not."

Mr. Gallantz: "Did you know what his background was?"

Mr. Hawkins: "I knew he was a basketball player."

When he realized he could handle the questions, Connie's confidence grew. There was nothing unexpected. The Litmans had covered everything. "It's like when you make your first three or four shots," he says. "You start believin in yourself."

MR. GALLANTZ: "How much can you recall about what you were asked and what answers you gave [in the grand jury]?"

MR. HAWKINS: "I can't recall anything."

MR. GALLANTZ: "Were you asked whether you ever met Joseph Hacken?"

MR. HAWKINS: "I don't recall."

• • • • •

MR. GALLANTZ: "Did Andreoli [in the grand jury] . . . go through with you each meeting which you had with Joseph Hacken?"

MR. HAWKINS: "I don't recall, sir."

Connie's responses were more than a cascade of "I don't recalls." When Gallantz sought specifics of his contact with the gamblers, Hawk's answers were so simple and forthright that even the NBA's lawyer seemed disinclined to challenge him.

MR. GALLANTZ: ". . . Tell us in the best way you know how, where and when and how it [a conversation with Molinas] happened."

MR. HAWKINS: "Well, the place was at my house. I called him up. I don't—it was during the Christmas holidays when I was home I called him up and I ask him if I could borrow some money off of him and he told me he would lend me the money. And right before I got ready to go back to school, he came by my house and he brought me—I told him I wanted to borrow two hundred dollars and he lent me two hundred dollars to get back in school."

MR. GALLANTZ: "In cash?"

MR. HAWKINS: "Yes, sir."

MR. GALLANTZ: "Did he ask you for a receipt?"

MR. HAWKINS: "No, sir, I don't think so."

MR. GALLANTZ: "Did you have any other conversation about it at all?"

MR. HAWKINS: "Yes, sir."

MR. GALLANTZ: "Can you recall the conversation?"

MR. HAWKINS: "Yes. He asked what did I need it for and I told him I needed it for my tuition at school, for my room and board and so forth. And I told him that, you know, the job that I had that they paid me for, my job that I was working on, and I came home with the money and during the Christmas holidays I had spent some. Instead of saving the money to pay my tuition, I spent the money on a gift to my mother and my brother and I splurged. When I say splurged, I mean I was picking up tabs and things of that nature. And I told him I need two hundred dollars to get back in school and pay my tuition."

MR. GALLANTZ: "This was on the phone or face-to-face?"

MR. HAWKINS: "This was face-to-face."

MR. GALLANTZ: "Anything more?"

MR. HAWKINS: "I don't think so."

MR. GALLANTZ: "Any talk of paying it back?"

MR. HAWKINS: "Yes, sir. He told me to pay it back as soon as I could."

MR. GALLANTZ: "Did you ever see Molinas again after that?"

MR. HAWKINS: "No, sir."

. . . . .

MR. GALLANTZ: "Did you ever repay Molinas the two hundred dollars?"

MR. HAWKINS: "I didn't pay him, but my brother did."

MR. GALLANTZ: "Your brother told you he paid it?"

MR. HAWKINS: "Yes, sir."

MR. GALLANTZ: "When?"

MR. HAWKINS: "I found out later on that he paid it a couple of months after he lent it to me."

Later, Hawkins's confidence got out of hand. Gallantz tried to establish that the Litmans stopped Connie from answering the four questions sent by Kennedy in 1966. He tried to create the impression that Hawk would have cooperated with Kennedy's investigation had he known of it.

Roz had cautioned Connie against answering questions he did not understand. She'd told him that if it seemed he was getting into hot water because he was misunderstanding what Gallantz asked, she would warn him. But, when the warning came, Hawk was feeling so cocky he ignored it.

MR. GALLANTZ: "Mr. Hawkins, were you ever told that Mr. Kennedy wanted you to file an affidavit saying whether or not you had ever testified before the grand jury?"

MR. HAWKINS: "I don't recall."

MR. GALLANTZ: "Were you told that your lawyer had refused to file such an affidavit on your behalf?"

MR. HAWKINS: "I am not sure. I don't recall . . ."

MR. GALLANTZ: "Do you have any objection to filing such an affidavit?"

MR. HAWKINS: "No, sir."

MR. GALLANTZ: "Were you told that Mr. Kennedy had asked that you file an affidavit saying whether you had ever met with Joseph Hacken . . . ?"

MR. HAWKINS: "No, sir, I don't think so."

MRS. LITMAN: "Excuse me. . . . Would you please inform the witness that filing an affidavit and furnishing a statement under oath is one and the same thing. . . . I want to be sure the witness is understanding your question . . ."

MR. GALLANTZ: "Do you know an affidavit and a statement under oath are the same thing?"

MR. HAWKINS: "Yes, sir."

The first day of questioning ended moments later. Connie felt good. "Is that all there is to it?" he said in the elevator. "You guys were harder than that."

"Tomorrow will be rougher," Howard warned. Roz was silent.

When they reached the Litmans' office, she began screaming at him. "That was a stupid thing to do, how could you do it? You have to be perfect. This is the most important thing in the case. You didn't know an affidavit and a sworn statement were the same thing. Why did you say you did? What are you trying to prove? Whose side are you on?"

Connie walked into the men's room. Howard opened the door five minutes later and found him weeping, his face in his hands. "I blew it," Hawk cried. "I blew the case."

By this time Roz had calmed down. Connie's error hadn't been fatal. In fact, most of his performance had been excellent.

They spent the rest of the evening trying to reassure him and get him psychologically ready for the final day of interrogation.

"When we went in there, that second day, I knew I'd have to do real great. I had to make up for the way I screwed up before," Connie recalls.

For almost two and a half hours, Gallantz picked and probed, attacking Hawkins's claim that he didn't remember what happened in the grand jury room. But Hawk, even today, doesn't remember what happened—and he refused to let the lawyer shake him.

MR. GALLANTZ: "In 1961 when you read these newspapers and found yourself referred to as an intermediary, did you feel it was not true?"

MR. HAWKINS: "Yes, sir."

MR. GALLANTZ: "Did you also feel it was inconsistent with what you had testified before the grand jury?"

MR. HAWKINS: "I don't recall what I said to the grand jury."

Gallantz kept trying, hoping to establish that Hawk had committed perjury. But Connie's story held up. As the NBA's attorney continued to press fruitlessly, Roz said across the table, "I don't want to impede you, but I would appreciate it if you would . . . attempt not to be so overbearing in your manner [of] questioning."

MR. GALLANTZ: "Mrs. Litman, when you say a thing like that—"

MRS. LITMAN: "I want the record to indicate that action now."

MR. GALLANTZ: "I just slammed the file on the table and . . ."

"Rozzie always told me that once a good lawyer gets too angry he's lost his case," Connie says. "When Gallantz got mad, I felt great. I figured it must be cause I'm doin a good job."

He was doing a good job. With neck straight and eyes fixed on Gallantz, Hawkins admitted he had been frightened into false confessions: "There were times when they were questioning me, [and they] wouldn't accept the truth, and then I started admitting to things . . . I shouldn't have admitted."

MR. GALLANTZ: "You had the idea that the detectives were trying to get you to say things that were not so?"

MR. HAWKINS: "Yes, sir."

MR. GALLANTZ: "And you think from time to time they succeeded in getting you to say things that were not so?"

MR. HAWKINS: "Eventually they did."

As the deposition drew to a close, the lawyer made a final thrust at Connie's grand jury story. "Mr. Hawkins," he asked, "you have indicated you gave some information to detectives that you now believe wasn't the truth, because of the compulsions you were under, isn't that right?"

"Yes."

"Did anything like that happen in the grand jury room?"

"I don't recall what happened," Connie said.

"In other words," said Gallantz, setting a trap, "you may have felt under some compulsions in the grand jury room too?"

"Could you explain compulsion to me?" Connie asked. Roz and Howard couldn't help smiling. Connie wasn't going to stumble into a semantic snare.

"Well," said Gallantz, "compelled to say things that you knew weren't the truth, as happened when you were being interviewed by the detectives."

"I don't recall what I said," Connie repeated once more.

When Gallantz continued his line of questioning, Roz engaged him in a bitter argument. As she leaned in front of Connie to speak to the court reporter, Hawk pressed forward and planted a soft kiss on her cheek. "*That's* never happened in a deposition before," she laughs. "I was horrified that one of their attorneys had seen it. But they hadn't. Connie was just feeling very proud of himself. And he had every reason to feel proud."

Soon they were in the elevator and she threw her arms around him. The deposition was over. The NBA had come away even weaker than before. "You were great. Connie, you were wonderful!" Roz cried. "You really showed that Park Avenue lawyer."

"I was breakin out with the shines," says Hawk. "I felt good inside.

When they said, 'No more questions,' I wanted to go on. I knew I'd done good, and this was something I'd done with my head, with my brain, by thinkin."

MILLIONAIRE

> "Evidence recently uncovered indicates that Connie Hawkins
> never knowingly associated with gamblers, that he never
> introduced a player to a fixer, and that the only damaging
> statements about his involvement were made by Hawkins himself—
> as a terrified semiliterate teenager who thought he'd go
> to jail unless he said what the D.A.'s detectives
> pressed him to say. Hawkins, in other words, did nothing
> that would have justified his being banned by the NBA."
> —Life *magazine, May 16, 1969*

When my article asserting Connie's innocence appeared in *Life*, it got good play from the wire services, but no comment from the NBA. The first reaction came from Senator Edward Kennedy, who invited Connie to an athletes' memorial dedication of Robert F. Kennedy Stadium in Washington. Still unsure of himself, Hawk spent much of his time in the capital asking people why he'd been invited.

"The great thing that happened there was that NBA players said they wanted to help with my lawsuit," he recalls. "Don Nelson was fantastic. He said, 'What can I do that's constructive?' Tears almost came to my eyes. I'd hardly seen him since Iowa. He said he'd testify at my trial if they needed proof I was a good ballplayer. And he said he was gonna get other players to speak for me. Ray Scott said the same thing. It was unbelievable."

On Friday, June 6, the day Connie left for Washington, something even more unbelievable began to unfold. Roz was in her office, preparing for depositions scheduled on the West Coast the following week, when the phone rang. It was David Stern, a young lawyer at Proskauer, Rose, Goetz and Mendelsohn, who had been working on the case with George Gallantz.

"Monday," he said to the startled Mrs. Litman, "Mr. Gallantz will be calling to discuss a possible settlement."

Roz's hand shook so furiously she could hardly keep the receiver to her ear. "There's a league meeting in Detroit," said Stern. "The matter will be discussed. Maybe in this light you might want to postpone the depositions in California?"

"I almost dropped dead," Roslyn recalls. "But I had to act as though I wasn't impressed. I said I wanted to proceed with the depositions because it was hardly likely that one telephone call would result in a settlement. But, as soon as I hung up, I ran into David's office jumping up and down and shouting, 'Guess what, guess what, oh, oh, guess what?' For a moment, I was so excited I couldn't tell him what."

George Gallantz called at 10:50 Monday morning. "I suppose," he said, "you know the purpose of my call."

"Yes," said Roz, "Mr. Stern informed me you would be calling to discuss the possibility of settlement."

"That's correct. What did you have in mind?"

"First, does this settlement include a contract for Hawkins to play in the NBA?"

There was a pause at Gallantz's end of the line. Roz held her breath. The Litmans feared the NBA might be offering nothing more than a token cash payment to get Connie off its back.

"A contract," said Gallantz, "is feasible." Roz's hand started shaking again. "The rights to Hawkins have been assigned to Phoenix. The team's ownership is complicated, but the man you'll be dealing with is Richard Bloch of Beverly Hills."

"It was like a fairy tale," says Roslyn. "I couldn't believe it was real. We'd waited so long, it just couldn't be happening. Finally, I asked if we could get clearance for Connie to play with any team he wanted."

"No, Phoenix already has rights to him," said Gallantz. "He's being treated in the same fashion as Lew Alcindor, like the great basketball player you say he is."

That weekend, Phoenix, which had won but sixteen of eighty-two games in its first season as an expansion franchise and had recently lost a coin flip for Alcindor to Milwaukee, had gained rights to Connie via another coin flip with Seattle. The Detroit meeting had been stormy. Several NBA executives were vehemently opposed to settling the case. But, as an NBA general manager told me later, "It was damn clear we were going to lose if we went to court." The league planned to save face by claiming that, in the process of Connie's deposition, he finally answered the four questions Kennedy had asked in 1966.

Roz and Gallantz haggled over terms. She proposed a million-dollar figure, which he called "out of the ballpark." He eventually agreed to report to the NBA that the case could be settled for something in the vicinity of $850,000, plus a contract. It was agreed that the Litmans would meet with Richard Bloch while they were on the Coast for the depositions.

Before leaving that night for Los Angeles, Roz called Connie. "There's a chance, a slight chance, that we might settle the case. Don't get your hopes up. Don't say anything to anyone. We'll be in touch as soon as we know something."

"I had no feelings," Hawkins says. "I'd formed a mental block in my head. I didn't believe it could ever happen, so I sort of shrugged my shoulders and forgot about it."

When the depositions were completed, Richard Bloch invited the Litmans to his Beverly Hills home for breakfast Thursday morning, June 12. "As soon as we arrived, we knew this wasn't going to be the usual NBA crap," David says. "The very fact that we were meeting in his home instead of an austere office indicated something. Dick Bloch turned out to be an especially warm, homey type of guy. He's a big real-estate developer, but a very down-to-earth person. He said he didn't know about Connie's ability, but if he was half as good as we said he was, Dick wanted him on his team."

After three hours of earnest but amiable negotiations, a tentative agreement was reached. Hawkins would get an annuity of $600,000 ($30,000 per year for 20 years starting at age forty) and a five-year no-cut contract totaling $400,000. His salary would start at $50,000 and increase by $15,000 annually. Connie would also receive $250,000 additional damages for settlement of the case—$125,000 immediately, and $25,000 a year for five years. The lawyers would take part of that as legal fees. They would also get $35,000 from the NBA for their expenses on the case.

Under a contract they had with Connie, the Litmans' firm was entitled to a large percentage of the settlement. They chose to take much less.

A request by David Litman that the settlement include an option to buy a percentage of the Phoenix franchise, was left to further negotiation.

"When we left Bloch's house," says David, "everything seemed great. But we got back to the hotel to find that all hell had broken loose. There were messages from my office and from the media. Somehow the story of the settlement was already out."

The leak had come from New York. Chip Cipolla, the sports director of radio station WNEW, had announced on the air that Phoenix had rights to Hawkins and that Connie had "signed or is about to sign." Cipolla's source was an NBA owner.

Roslyn was almost hysterical. Convinced that the premature disclosure and unfavorable publicity would frighten off the NBA, she burst into un-characteristic tears. "All our work," she cried, "ruined by a radio broad-cast!"

They were particularly concerned that Connie might already have confirmed the story if contacted by the press. Hawk, in fact, had been del-uged with phone calls. But he had correctly sized up the situation and had kept his mouth shut. "It's the first I've heard the story," he told the Associ-ated Press. "Just say I deny it."

Gabe Rubin had also called Connie. Rubin was in the process of moving the Pipers back to Pittsburgh. The Litmans had bumped into him and his lawyer Skip Kaufman several times that spring. Gabe had promised to visit their office soon to discuss a new contract for Hawkins. But he'd never shown up. Now he frantically phoned Connie and begged him not to do anything until the Pipers made an offer. Hawk told Rubin he didn't know what was going on—which was basically true.

By the time the Litmans got back to Pittsburgh that night, the story had died down and the first of many crises was over. Kennedy, Mikan, Rubin, and Phoenix general manager Jerry Colangelo had all issued denials. David called Bloch from the airport. "I've talked to the people involved," said the Phoenix owner, "and we're ninety-nine percent sure this thing will work out. We'd like you to come to Los Angeles next week. Kennedy is in Hawaii, but he's cutting short a tour of the Far East to fly back here. There's going to be a meeting of the Board of Governors. It looks very good."

"We were floating," says David. "We explained the details to Howard. Then I called Connie and told him we had a settlement proposal to present to him. He was to meet us in our office at nine-thirty the following morn-ing. But he didn't show up. I called his house at eleven o'clock and was told he'd gone to have his *car washed!* I couldn't believe it. We've got a million-dollar proposal to make, and he decides to wash his car!"

"I was stallin," Hawk admits. "When they said there was a real chance I'd get into the NBA, I was scared to relate to it. I was afraid of bein let down—that was the big thing—and I guess I was also scared of facin the challenge."

He arrived at the firm around noon. The lawyers took him into David's office and explained the NBA's terms. Hawk listened in silence while David told him that—if the settlement came through—he would not only be accepted by the NBA but would eventually receive $1,000,000.

"It was like his words didn't make sense," Hawkins says. "I didn't feel nothing at first. I couldn't relate to the money at all."

When David finished speaking, Connie was still mum. "Well," said Roz, impatiently, "what do you think?"

"I don't think I want to play in the NBA," said Connie.

Howard stood up and staggered from the room. "The fuckin guy is crazy," he mumbled, "absolutely crazy."

The Litmans stared open-mouthed. Then Connie grinned. "I'm just kiddin," he said, "I accept." Still, he showed no real emotion.

They took him to lunch at the Carleton House, and he sat quietly while they laughed and kidded and called him their "favorite millionaire." Then, suddenly, he sighed, lowered his head and sobbed into the tablecloth: "The NBA, the NBA, after all these years . . ."

They phoned Dick Bloch that afternoon. "While I was talking," says David, "Connie wrote me a note saying he wanted sixty thousand dollars the first year instead of fifty thousand dollars. I think sixty thousand dollars was a magic figure to him: it conveyed a certain status he wanted very much. I told Dick we'd take only a five thousand dollar raise the second year, so the total would be almost the same. He agreed without even asking Connie's reason. Then he said he wanted to talk to his player."

"Connie," said Bloch, "I know you've been wronged. I just want you to realize that I wasn't a member of the league when these things were done to you. I'm sorry for what's happened, but I'm very glad you're going to be in the NBA now and delighted you'll be with Phoenix."

Life assigned me to do a followup story, if the settlement came through. I spent that weekend with Connie in Pittsburgh. Hawk was hardly behaving like a man about to receive a million dollars. He joked a lot and partied a lot, but he was too nervous to eat properly and lost eight pounds. He was trying to shield himself against another disappointment. Yet it was more than that. He was doubting himself. "I was concerned about my playin ability," he said. "It wasn't like before, when I was young with two solid legs and a lot of energy. I was older and I'd had the operation. All these people talkin about how great you are—about all the things you'll be able to do if you only get a chance—it puts a lot of pressure on you. I knew everybody would say, 'O.K., now do it.' But, with my leg, I didn't know if I could."

One moment Hawkins would extol the ABA (". . . because I just like the league"). Then his tone would change, and he'd speak of the debt he owed Roz, David, and Howard: "They always believed in me. I thank God for puttin them on this earth."

Late Sunday night, as we leaned against the jukebox in the crowded

Louendi Club, he said, as matter-of-factly as he could, "What would happen to you if I got in the NBA and then fucked up?"

"What do you mean?"

"Would you be in trouble? I mean, you wrote in the article about how great I was. Suppose I didn't play so great?"

"Nothing would happen man, don't worry about it."

"I'm worryin about everything now," he said.

Roslyn was fearful that another news leak would kill the settlement. She prepared us for Monday afternoon's plane trip to LA as though we were attempting a passage through enemy lines. "We can't let the press find out Connie's in Los Angeles," she stressed. "They'll put that together with the Board of Governors meeting and realize what's about to happen. We mustn't all sit together. And Connie, if anyone asks if you're a basketball player, say No."

We were about as inconspicuous as a herd of buffalo. I had brought along a photographer, who proceeded to rush about the plane snapping pictures. When a stewardess asked who the tall fellow was, he said, "Oh, that's Connie Hawkins." The lawyers soon forgot they weren't supposed to be noticeable. Roz and Connie engaged in a loud, giggle-filled card game. David drank wine until he fell asleep, with his feet protruding far into the aisle. Howard got stumbling drunk and threatened to undress in front of the stewardesses unless they gave him more liquor. Just as we were about to land, he stood up and addressed the other passengers in his most dignified courtroom tone. "There's no cause for alarm," he proclaimed, "but I must inform you that, several hours ago, this plane crashed over Memphis."

Tuesday and Wednesday, Roz, David, and Howard were closeted with attorneys for the Suns. The negotiations were tense, emotional, and often heated. "It was very tiring," says David. "We argued back and forth for hours. We must have debated everything: the terms of the annuity, the length of the contract, the no-cut clause. They were continuously requesting minor revisions. My most profound memory of those two days is utter and total fatigue."

It turned out that the contract and settlement still had to be approved by the NBA's Board of Governors, where each team had one vote. The Board would hold a special meeting on Thursday at the LA Forum. Kennedy and Gallantz now favored settling the case, but there was concern that Ned Irish, Red Auerbach, and representatives of some of the older franchises would try to torpedo the agreement.

The Litmans demanded—and got—Kennedy's advance approval of the contract. But they knew the Board of Governors could still overrule him.

Meanwhile, Connie sweated it out at the Beverly Wilshire Hotel. "I tried to act real calm and kid around with everybody, but this nervousness kept buildin up inside me," he says. "I was startin to feel maybe there was a chance. But soon as I started to feel that way, I'd worry it would fall through."

At four o'clock Wednesday morning Connie and I walked down a deserted Wilshire Boulevard trying to talk ourselves to sleep. "The money would be beautiful, but I can't imagine what a million dollars really is," he said. "The big thing is clearin my name. I want people to know I'm an honest ballplayer."

For a long time we stared through a showroom window at some expensive sports cars. Then Connie laughed. "See that," he said, pointing to a glistening Maserati. "In a couple of days I might be able to buy that if I want. Wouldn't that be outtasight?"

We crossed the street to a gas station, intending to get two Cokes from a vending machine—but we didn't have forty cents between us.

An agreement was reached with the Phoenix lawyers—Don Pitt, Marvin Meyer, and Larry Kartiganer—Wednesday evening. Two separate player contracts were drawn up. One was for five years at $100,000 per year. Phoenix would attempt to use it if the Board of Governors *refused* to settle the lawsuit. If the Governors agreed to the entire settlement package, the second contract—calling for a total of $410,000 over five years—would go into effect. "The Phoenix people told us they wanted to use the five hundred thousand dollar contract as a wedge against the Board of Governors," says David. "They wanted Connie even if he was still suing the league. They intended to say, 'We're signing him with or without you, and there'll be another lawsuit against you if you don't approve the signing.'"

The terms of the proposed settlement were almost identical to those reached by Bloch and Litman the week before. Connie would get a $600,000 annuity, starting at age forty-two. It would pay him $30,000 a year for twenty years. He'd also get the five-year no-cut contract for $410,000. There would be a cash payment of $250,000—payable 50 percent at the signing and the balance over 5 years—plus $35,000 for legal costs. Phoenix also agreed to grant an option to buy a percent of the team at the same price paid by original investors.

"Connie signed the contracts late Wednesday night," says Roz. "We were all happy, but he knew—as we did—that he wasn't in the NBA until the Board of Governors approved him. If they rejected the contracts, the chances of our eventually winning the suit would have been vastly improved. But so much bitterness had been built up, we still had no absolute guarantee of approval—no guarantee he'd ever play in the NBA."

After the signing, Connie and I went to a night club called The Factory with the Suns' general manager Jerry Colangelo and coach John Kerr. The atmosphere at the table was breezy, but Connie was subdued. "We're all smilin now," he whispered to me. "But this thing ain't sure. Those guys could still fuck me tomorrow."

The Board of Governors meeting was scheduled to begin at the Forum shortly before noon on Thursday, June 18. That afternoon, Connie, Kerr, and Colangelo sat in the Litmans' suite playing Hearts with Phoenix writers Joe Gilmartin and Vern Boatner. The journalists had been flown in by the team and were waiting to write stories as soon as the settlement was approved. "I sat by the telephone," says Roslyn. "I was so nervous I jumped every time it rang. David and Howard were pacing about. But Connie was so cool. He was laughing and shouting, 'I'm winnin, I'm killin 'em'—and there he was with his whole future on the line."

Bloch's first call came at 2:00 P.M. There was an air traffic controllers' slowdown. Planes were delayed. The meeting had been put off until late afternoon. An hour later he called again. The plane from New York still hadn't arrived. Then, for several hours, there was no word. At six o'clock Bloch's wife phoned the room. Somehow, the story of the signing had broken on the East Coast. Early editions of the next day's newspapers in Pittsburgh and New York were already announcing that Connie had jumped to the NBA. The Litmans were afraid the news would reach the Forum and unnerve some of the Governors to the point of rejecting the settlement.

"By seven-thirty we knew something had gone wrong," says Roz. "Spirits had begun to pale. Connie wasn't joking and laughing any more. At about eight, Don Pitt, the Suns' attorney, telephoned from the Forum. He said, 'There's a problem out here. The meeting's been adjourned. Dick and I will meet you back at the hotel. Tell Colangelo and Kerr to leave the room.'"

"Will the meeting be resumed?" Roz asked.

"No," said Pitt.

Bloch and Pitt reached the Litmans' suite at nine. They entered solemn-faced, shaking their heads. "We just couldn't sell them," said Bloch. "They've adjourned. They're not going to approve the contract."

Connie had gone to his room to watch television. Roz found him laying on the bed, staring at the screen. "It looks like the whole thing's kaput," she said, fighting back tears of anger and disappointment. "I'm so sorry, Connie."

Hawk nodded his head. "It's all right. Don't worry about it. They been doin this to us all along."

"He was so stoic, so beautiful," she recalls. "There was no bitterness in his voice."

Inside, Connie was aching. "I didn't want her to know how bad I felt, cause I knew she felt bad already. But when she left I was awful depressed. It'd been so close . . ."

By the time Roz got back to her suite, Dick Bloch had received a call there from his wife. The Governors were at the Beverly Hills Hotel. There was now a chance an executive committee might reconvene. Bloch and Pitt left hurriedly. Roz, David, and Howard sat and waited, too tired to talk.

Pitt came back at midnight. The NBA wanted more revisions in the settlement agreement. "Pitt asked if we'd change the annuity from thirty thousand dollars a year for twenty years to twenty-five thousand dollars a year for twenty-four years," says David. "I was happy to do that. Then he asked for several more changes in the wording and a couple of alterations in the timing of payments. After that, he said they wanted to give Connie less salary—maybe forty thousand dollars the first year—and he asked if we'd agree not to represent any other blacklisted players who might sue. Finally, he wanted us to guarantee we would not have anything to do with any books that were published about Connie."

Roslyn had been lying on the couch in a near stupor of exhaustion. "But," she says, "when I heard Pitt saying, 'Maybe Connie will agree to this or maybe he'll accept that,' I became furious."

She rose up to her full 5′ 2″, jabbed her finger at Pitt, and shrieked, "We've committed ourselves to you, but you've kept us dangling. For three days you've been asking for changes and we've been going to Connie and asking him to agree to revisions. Then you come back and tell us, 'No deal.' Now you're asking for more changes. I'm not going to talk to Connie. I'm not going to present any more revisions to him. I'm not going to get his hopes up again, until I have a guarantee that this is the NBA's final, official offer—and that if we accept it, everything is settled. We're tired of your bullshit. If the NBA doesn't like that, then *fuck the NBA!*"

For a moment, Pitt was speechless. Finally he stammered, "I, I'll, I'll report back to them and be back here as soon as I can. Don't go to sleep. I'll be right back."

Pitt called an hour later. The NBA was willing to settle the case. He said he was bringing a final proposal.

Roz rang Connie's room. Hawk was still lying on the bed. For three hours, his mind had been almost a total blank. "I felt so let down, I couldn't get my hopes up again," he recalls. "It was all too much by then. I went to Roz and Dave's suite. They shut me in the bedroom. I stood by the door listenin. I could hear Pitt come in. He started givin them an offer."

Strangely, the league's last proposal was almost identical to what had been agreed upon the previous day: a $410,000 five-year no-cut NBA contract, a $600,000 annuity starting at age forty-five, $250,000 in cash (half at once, the rest paid over five years), $35,000 for the firm's out-of-pocket expenses, and an option on a percentage of the Suns. Part of the cash payment went to the Litmans for legal fees. The total value of the package, minus the option, was $1,295,000.

When Pitt finished speaking, Roz walked into the bedroom and again went over the offer with Connie. "I could hardly hear her," he recalls. "I knew they was gonna let me in the league, but my head was foggy and couldn't follow the details. It was like I was an outsider watchin the whole thing."

"Well," she said, "do we accept?"

"Yes."

Roz returned to the suite's living room, where David, Howard, and Pitt were waiting. "Connie will agree to the settlement," she said.

David approached Pitt. "Are you *completely* authorized to bind your client and the NBA?" he asked, almost fiercely. "If I tell you it's a deal right now, does that mean we have a deal that is binding and there will be nothing but the formality of signing tomorrow? The deal is right now?"

"Yes," said Don Pitt. "Right now."

Five minutes later, David and Connie burst into my room. I had written a story in anticipation of the settlement, but *Life* was going to press that night and I had just phoned New York to tell the editors not to print the article, that the NBA had backed out. "It's settled," David cried breathlessly. "Call them back. He's a millionaire!" Connie said nothing. There was a grin on his face, but he seemed numb.

I called New York. The story announcing the settlement was put back into the magazine, just as the presses began to roll. While I was on the phone, David returned to his suite. Connie slumped in a lounge chair. When I hung up, I turned to see that he had begun to cry. In moments, his body was shaking, the tears washing down his cheeks. He slid off the chair and knelt on the floor, his huge hands cupping his face. The sobs were from deep within him—loud, almost agonized. "Oh thank you. God, oh thank you Father, oh Jesus, oh God thank you," he moaned, rocking back and forth on his haunches. "Oh Jesus, it's over. Thank you Father, thank you."

It took fifteen minutes for Hawk to get himself together. Then we went to the Litmans' suite. Everyone was hugging and kissing and yelling and swinging each other around. "I," announced Connie, "need a drink."

"We've got Scotch," said David, "but only half a bottle of soda and no ice or glasses."

"I'll take care of it," said Hawk. He left the room and found a bellman.

"Can you still get us some glasses and some ice?" he asked.

"I can for you," said the bellman. "You're Connie Hawkins aren't you?"

"How you know who I am?"

"I just sent out a telegram about you."

"But you didn't see my picture or nothing. How'd you know?"

The bellman grinned. "I knew," he said. "I just knew."

Back in the suite, Connie couldn't wait for the ice. He took the Scotch and gingerly poured it into the half-empty bottle of soda. Then he shook it lightly and drank from the bottle. "You look pretty silly," said Roz.

Connie cocked his head to the side and smiled. "That's how all us millionaires do it," he said softly.

SETTLEMENT POSTSCRIPT

"Nowhere have I heard anything coming from the Litmans
or from Connie to the effect that
Connie has been grateful for two years in the ABA,
grateful for the opportunity to be playing somewhere."
—*Gabe Rubin, June 27, 1969*

The ABA and NBA vied for the most graceless response to the settlement.
NBA Commissioner Walter Kennedy, with an opportunity to express genuine regret for what he and the Board of Governors had done to Hawkins,
tried to squirm out of any admission of guilt. He even refused to admit that
Connie received a financial settlement—much less a million dollars—in exchange for dropping the suit.

Kennedy's official statement read, "I am approving today a player contract under which Connie Hawkins will play for the Phoenix Suns beginning next season. Shortly after I became commissioner, I attempted to look
into the serious charges against Hawkins . . . in 1961 . . . in connection
with a basketball scandal. Because I had no way of compelling answers to
questions from those who might know the facts, I was unable to conclude
the investigation. However, the lawsuit just terminated did afford us an opportunity to learn what facts were really available.

"It has always been the policy of the NBA to make every effort, consistent with fairness to the player involved, to keep itself free of any contact
with anyone who has been associated with gambling or fixing.

"The NBA counsel now has advised me, on the basis of the evidence so
developed, that the employment of Hawkins as a player by an NBA team
will not be inconsistent with that policy."

Later, some NBA people tried to make it appear that admitting Hawkins
was simply a tactic to weaken the ABA, and had nothing to do with the
merits of Connie's suit. Many sportswriters fell for this smokescreen because getting Hawk did help the NBA in its money war with the younger
league. But the fact is, the NBA didn't have to settle the suit to sign

Hawkins. The Board of Governors could simply have approved his contract with Phoenix (five years for $500,000) and continued to fight the case in the courts. The NBA settled because it didn't have a leg to stand on— and the league officials knew it. As a member of the Board of Governors conceded to West Coast writer Bill Libby, "We simply had an indefensible stand. We had wronged this boy, if not by being party to the original act, by supporting it later. I'll be honest: We probably would never have acted if our top legal advisor had not warned us we were likely to lose. We really were not too concerned with the ABA. We wanted to right a wrong and get out of a heavy loss at a reasonable price."

(There may have been another factor in the NBA's decision to settle. I can't substantiate the story, but it was told to me by a law-enforcement source. He says that my article in *Life* so infuriated Assistant DA Peter Andreoli that he arranged with a judge for the NBA to receive permission to view Hawkins's hitherto-secret grand jury testimony. Andreoli believed the testimony would convince the NBA lawyers of Connie's guilt and that the league would move to introduce the grand jury minutes as evidence in Hawkins's Pittsburgh trial. This, Andreoli felt, would vindicate him.

But his plan backfired. The NBA attorneys were hardly elated when they saw Hawkins's testimony. Connie's statements to the grand jury were as confused and contradictory as his "confessions" to the detectives. It was obvious from reading the minutes that Hawkins was scared, mixed-up, and being led by his interrogator. Introducing the grand jury minutes in Pittsburgh would actually have substantiated Connie's claim that he was frightened into the false confessions. After reading the minutes, the NBA, to Andreoli's dismay, concluded that its case was hopeless and decided to settle.)

The ABA's response was to accuse Connie and the Litmans of everything from deceit to treason. "If it hadn't been for the ABA," said Mike Storen, then Indiana's general manager, "he never would have had a shot at the NBA. We gave him his chance when nobody else would. We made him a star and now he deserts us. My players here feel that Hawkins sold them out. They're all disgusted with him. He took the back door, took the money, and ran."

Bill Erickson said, "I was conned into letting Connie play out his option with the Pipers last season." Gabe Rubin, while admitting a "feeling of excitement for the boy," was angered that the Pipers had not been given a chance to bid against the NBA for Hawk's services.

All this was verbal trash. Connie had been a star with Boys High, Iowa, the Pittsburgh Rens, and the Harlem Globetrotters. He was a legend in the schoolyards. The NBA was well aware of his ability. The American Basketball Association hardly made Connie Hawkins.

The ABA's decision to sign Hawk had nothing to do with altruism. The only motive was money. They took Connie even though, as George Mikan made clear, they thought he *was* guilty of the intermediary charges. The league needed players, and Hawkins was the best available. The salary they paid him was absurdly low for a Most Valuable Player. When they finally got around to sending him his MVP trophy, it arrived broken.

Despite Mike Storen's claims, no resentment toward Connie was voiced by any ABA players. Many called to congratulate him. Storen's own star at Indiana—Roger Brown—flew to Pittsburgh for a party in Hawk's honor.

Bill Erickson had no beef at all. He didn't *allow* Connie to play out his option. That had been agreed upon prior to the 1968 season—before he owned the club—when David Litman negotiated a two-year (no-option) contract with Gabe Rubin.

The Litmans had given the Pipers plenty of time to make an offer. Rubin constantly promised to visit their offices to talk contract, but never showed up. David had one discussion with Erickson but—because the Pipers' finances and location were uncertain—the meeting produced, in David's words, "nothing of substance."

This was academic anyway. Hawk could never have seriously considered an ABA offer. "The NBA was my dream," he says. "All those years of hopin, of being kept out, I couldn't have walked away from it."

The Pipers made a last pathetic jab at Hawkins. They didn't send his final paycheck for $801.63. Then, on August 1, three months after the season ended, the club (which had lost over $700,000) mailed him a bill for $108.93. This included $60.90 for a plane ticket between Minneapolis and Pittsburgh, where Connie had gone, with the team's consent, to have a specialist examine his knee.

Hawkins sent the Pipers nothing. But he never received the money they owed him.

Connie's departure, following on the heels of disastrously unsuccessful negotiations with Kareem Jabbar (then Lew Alcindor), was the straw that broke George Mikan's back. The night of the settlement, Big George sent Hawkins and Litman a desperate telegram—which he also released to the press. Mikan offered to "beat any offer for your services made by an NBA team or the NBA itself." The wire arrived thirteen hours after Hawk's NBA contract had been approved.

"Both the Minnesota Pipers and the ABA league office mishandled the whole thing," said Alex Hannum, then coaching Oakland. "They knew he was a free agent, but they did nothing until it was too late. There are a lot of people in the league who are upset."

One month later, Mikan resigned.

For Hawkins, the settlement brought more than financial security. It gave him an opportunity to blossom as a man. For the first time in his adult life, Hawk was truly proud to be himself. The whispers and sidelong glances were gone. He no longer lived in the shadow of the scandal. "I'd been dead for eight years," he says. "But the stigma was off me. I was gettin treated with more respect. I didn't realize what a deep shell I'd been in till I came out of it."

In almost every way, Connie projected more self-confidence. His speech was still hard-core ghetto, but he found it increasingly easy to converse with strangers. His newspaper and television interviews were no longer exercises in caution and monosyllabics. He appeared with Flip Wilson on the *Tonight* show and did well. Early in his initial season with Phoenix, the *Life* advertising department invited him to a luncheon. "How could anyone have thought he was an idiot?" an adman whispered to me, as Hawk bantered casually with several dozen Madison Avenue types.

"What do you think of the Knicks being ten-and-a-half-point favorites over Phoenix?" asked an advertiser.

Hawkins arched an eyebrow. "Man," he chuckled, "I don't think nothing about *that*. Don't you-all think I'm the last guy in the NBA that oughta be wonderin about point spreads?" His audience laughed loudly.

In personal relationships, Connie became more assertive. Once easy to manipulate, he now bristled at any hint someone intended to use him. At the Rucker Tournament, the summer after his first season in the NBA, a Bedford-Stuyvesant organization distributed flyers announcing a gala birthday party and dance for Hawk at a Brooklyn hotel. Connie was never notified of the event. He didn't see a flyer until five days before his birthday. It was simply assumed he would show up.

But Hawkins investigated. He found the promotion was being staged by a local youth organizer with a reputation for helping himself more than he helped youth. The promoter was charging five dollars per person. There was no indication where the money would go.

When Hawk decided to spend his birthday at home, the promoter dispatched several of Connie's old friends to dissuade him. "The community goin to honor you and you ain't gonna be there," said one. "That don't look good, man."

"Fuck what it look like," Hawkins snapped. "It ain't the community honorin me. It's some jive dude out to make himself some bread. Well, he ain't makin it off me. Next time somebody plans a party for me, they can ask me about it first. Don't nobody need to spend five dollars to tell me happy birthday!"

Connie was still an unparalleled sleeper. Punctuality remained an unacquired trait. But, he says, "I started thinkin more." He could afford the luxury of introspection and the time to wonder what he really believed. This resulted in many subtle changes, most notably an increased consciousness of—and pride in—his blackness.

As recently as the previous winter in Minnesota, Hawk had been the kind of black man who described himself as "colored." One night, after much prodding, when he had finally asked a waiter to stop calling him "boy," Connie whispered, as the old man walked away, "I hope I didn't hurt his feelings."

After the settlement, Hawkins didn't construct an elaborate personal racial philosophy, but he became more sensitive to the subtle racism that abounds in pro sports ("When Mikan told me to cut my natural, I should have told him to go fuck himself") and began to reappraise his past experiences ("I know why I wasn't happy with the Globetrotters—I wasn't actin like a man"). Today, if someone calls him "boy," Hawk turns cold and moves away.

"I talked more with guys about black things, what people were doin," he says. "I got these records where Dick Gregory does long raps about blackness and how the black man gets treated. I didn't become, like, a militant—I don't feel hate toward white people—but I started gettin my own black thing together."

In Minnesota, he had worried that his wife's Afro wig was "too black-powerish." Less than a year later, he would tell her to take off a blond wig because "it looks like you got no pride."

One evening, while we were watching TV, Hawk saw a Wheaties commercial in which Henry Aaron makes an error, strikes out, and hears a white fan yell, "Hey Aaron, you forgot your Wheaties!"

"Would you do that ad?" Connie asked.

"I don't know. I suppose, if they paid enough. Would you?"

"No," he said. "That ain't for a black man."

During the case, it had been necessary for Connie to keep his public image good-guy clean. Now, slowly, Hawkins began to act as he felt. His natural haircut grew high and bushy. He sprouted wide Edwardian sideburns that covered his cheeks.

In Phoenix, Connie continued the habit of cupping his cigarette in his palm while walking through the crowds, because he didn't want youngsters to know he smoked. He still stood outside dressing rooms patiently signing autographs for the young fans. But Hawkins no longer stood at stiff attention or sang along during the national anthem ("I don't really feel it"). He was more outspoken in the press. His willinginess to buck management, building since his late Globetrotter days, continued to grow (although his organizational deficiencies remained). When Hawkins thought the Suns were short-changing their trainer on pay during the playoffs, he unsuccessfully proposed the players complain en masse. A year later, when several blacks discussed boycotting games if the NBA barred Seattle's Spencer Haywood, Connie readily supported the move.

Hawk was no longer semiliterate. Although hardly a voluminous reader, he had shaken his fear of the printed word. He looked at the sports pages with a more critical eye, even noticing bylines and recognizing which writers covered pro basketball most competently.

Connie read *The Peter Principle* and was reminded of many people he had encountered in sports. After finishing a complimentary article about himself in *Ebony* magazine, Hawk said, "It's nice, but it wasn't written good. There wasn't anything in there somebody else didn't write before. And the writer didn't try to tell what kind of person I am. If he doesn't do that, how can he write a good story on me?"

Hawkins also pondered things he would previously have dismissed. Once, during the summer, he asked me, "Why do people say Hemingway is a good writer?" Later he said, "Did you ever wonder who you really are?"

"Are you wondering?" I asked.

He nodded. "I guess I don't know. I'm black and I'm a ballplayer. Past that, I think I'm just startin to find out."

Connie became much less sensitive about his past, more able to laugh at himself. When the Suns sent him a publicity questionnaire, he filled it out thusly:

Q. What were the honors you won in college?
A. I won the honor to leave.
Q. What nickname do you want to be called?
A. Superstar.
Q. What was your grade-point in college?
A. 0.0.
Q. What was your minor in college?
A. Sports.
Q. What was the highest degree you attained in college?
A. 50 points.

When reminded how hurt he had been by my *Life* article describing him as "a semiliterate teenager," Connie laughed and said: "Yeah, but now I'm a semiliterate millionaire."

21

A TROUBLED SUMMER

"It is reliably reported Hawkins can throw a ping-pong ball across the Mississippi against the wind—with either hand."
—*Joe Gilmartin, Phoenix* Gazette, *July, 1969*

The ostracism was behind him. Hawk was vindicated, financially secure and a nationally known star. But the aftermath of the settlement brought new pressures and problems, with which—despite his personal growth—Connie couldn't always cope. "I thought when I won my suit," he recalls, "everything was gonna be peaches and cream. But it wasn't. It seemed like everything went wrong. I was tryin to get myself together to face the biggest challenge of my whole life. But that summer, all I had was trouble."

Hawk would have been comfortable remaining in the ghetto. But Nancy wanted to get out—and Connie wanted to make her happy. They bought a $45,000 home in a predominantly white residential section of Pittsburgh. They had ten rooms, a garage, and a large lawn. But their next-door neighbors took one look at them and moved. A year later, the house next door had not been sold.

Several women in the neighborhood invited Nancy to tea. But now Connie was wary. He told her not to go. "I don't want you socializin with them," he said. "We had plenty of friends before we had money—and those are gonna be the friends we have now."

Many of those friends, however, began to treat the Hawkinses differently. "They changed their whole outlook on us," Hawk says. "There was a lot of jealousy. I guess when poor people see another poor person get money they can't be happy for them, cause they are still poor. My so-called friends started tellin us *we'd* changed, taken on airs. They'd say, 'Now you a millionaire and you don't want to talk to nobody.' They'd say it as soon as they saw you, before they had a chance to find out if you wanted to speak to them. It really upset my wife."

For all the talk about a million dollars, Connie didn't have much money.

· The down payment on the house, and some new furniture, used up most of the NBA's first settlement check. The Litmans badgered him to save enough to pay his taxes. At first, Nancy, who had also known nothing but poverty, had trouble managing their money. Savings accounts, checkbooks, and mortgage payments—everything was new to them.

"Even the kids thought we were rich," Hawk laughs. "Shawna had a tooth come out, and instead of the dime I used to leave, I put a dollar under her pillow—so she tried to pull out the rest of her teeth."

Connie went out of his way not to change his lifestyle. He drank at the same bars and continued to work in the mayor's ghetto basketball clinics. He bought little for himself. The only sign of his new affluence was an improved wardrobe. Even that was moderate. Hawk still wore body shirts, bellbottoms, and dashikis.

"It was a year before we even bought a car," he says. "Then we got a secondhand station wagon for five hundred dollars. But people kept sayin, 'When you buyin your Cadillac?' And, that first summer, everybody started askin to borrow money, a hundred here, two hundred there. My brothers in Brooklyn wanted money. Earl wanted me to set him up in a business. Nobody would believe I didn't have the whole million dollars right in my pocket."

In Pittsburgh, and later in Phoenix, strangers phoned or approached him on the street asking for money. He received weird letters from people who wanted him to pay their legal fees or put their children through college. One woman followed Hawk around asking for five hundred dollars to get an abortion. "Everybody thought I was a black Michael Brody," he says. "Guys I thought were my friends would start talkin to me, and next thing I know they're makin a business proposition. At Ruckers, I'd be watchin a game, and guys who hadn't said 'Hello' to me in eight years would start crowdin around, shakin my hand and wantin me to invest in something. When I told 'em they had to speak to my lawyer, they'd start tellin people I'd gotten stingy.

"Also at Ruckers, people I didn't know, or maybe I'd met once, would stick their face in my face and say, 'You don't remember me do you?' If I didn't remember, it hurt their feelings, and they'd go around sayin, 'Hawkins thinks he's too good for his old friends.'

"There was a time when I'd have liked all the attention. But I was seein through to the phoniness, and it was depressing. Sometimes I wonder if I wasn't better off when I didn't think so much about people and what they were up to."

Connie had hoped that the settlement money might pay for an operation to restore his mother's sight. She was not only blind, but suffering from obesity. Hawk brought her to Pittsburgh for observation at Presbyterian University Hospital. He visited her every day. Her shortness of breath and her compulsive eating frightened him.

The doctors said nothing could be done for her eyes. Hawk's sightless fan—she attended every game in New York and got play-by-play accounts from his brothers—would remain sightless. But the obesity was partially checked. When she was released from the hospital, Connie took his mother into his home. "But even that was a problem," he says sadly. "She didn't get along with Nancy. They had all these misunderstandings about things." Hawk was always in the middle, loving them both and not knowing what to do. Eventually his mother went back to Brooklyn.

Connie's biggest problem was his knee. Shortly after the settlement, the Suns had sent him to Dr. Robert Kerlan, the Los Angeles specialist famous for treating Sandy Koufax, Elgin Baylor, and numerous other top athletes. "Dr. Kerlan said Connie will be able to perform up to one hundred percent," reported Phoenix general manager Jerry Colangelo. "His knee is now as strong as the other one. Dr. Kerlan did say that there will be soreness and discomfort, and that Connie might need rest from time to time, but the overall report was very encouraging."

The team set up a program of physical therapy for Connie in Pittsburgh. Each day that summer he took a cab to the Arena and worked out under the supervision of Ken Carson, the trainer for the Pittsburgh Penguins of the National Hockey League. Hawk worked for ten minutes on a stationary bicycle, then strapped weights to his shoe, lay on his back, and raised the leg in six sets of fifteen lifts each. He began in late June, lifting eighteen pounds. By August it was thirty-six. "He was really dedicated," recalls Carson. "He never missed a day."

The dedication was a product of fear. The knee was getting stronger, but to Connie it didn't seem strong enough. "What Dr. Kerlan said relieved me," Hawk recalls, "but I was still worried. Would it be strong enough to make my kind of moves? I kept waitin for it to feel real good, but it didn't."

He was used to playing ball every day during the summer. But the knee was too sore. On three occasions, when he joined pickup games at the Y, Hawk found his shot off, his stamina low, and his reflexes shaky. When he tried to cut or sprint, there were sharp pains in the knee.

"There was a lot of pressure on me," he recalls, "especially with my friends going around boastin and sayin how I was gonna burn up the NBA."

His friends weren't alone. Testimonials poured in from NBA stars who had already seen Hawk play. "He's the only guy in the world, besides me, who can completely palm the ball," said Wilt Chamberlain. "Hawkins is one of the three best players I ever saw."

Kareem Jabbar went further: "I never saw *anybody* better. I've seen him play against NBA players in pickup games and embarrass them."

Seattle general manager Dick Vertlieb called Connie "Elgin Baylor plus three inches." Bill Russell, the retiring star of the Celtics, was even more expansive: "Hawkins is the only man I know in basketball who can play all three positions on a pro level. People say he's going to be a great forward in this league and they're right. . . . You won't see it, because he's too valuable up front, but Hawkins also could play guard. . . . I think Phoenix might make the playoffs."

That's what the people in Phoenix were thinking. The Suns had lost money in their first expansion season. The team was the worst in the NBA. There had been extreme depression throughout the organization when they lost the coin flip for Jabbar. But Connie gave the Suns a chance to turn everything around. The club had to draw 5,500 per game to break even (they'd averaged just 3,538 the previous year) and general manager Colangelo was extolling Connie in the local press to drum up season-ticket sales and interest in the team. "With Hawkins," he said, "we could do better than break even. He could change us from a last-place team to a contender overnight—and that would draw fans. If Connie's as good as he's supposed to be, we can make the playoffs."

Hawk had waited a lifetime to hear such praise. But now it did nothing but increase the pressure. "Everybody was expectin I'd be like I was before," he recalls. "But I knew I wouldn't. I worried about how people would react if I couldn't do what they expected, and I worried even more how *I'd* react. I was workin so hard on the therapy. That's why it was so discouragin. My mental thing got lower and lower. Then I got sick."

Two weeks before he was to leave for camp, his nose became clogged, his eyes teared, and the doctor told him he had the flu. Many of the Suns' players were already in Arizona for informal workouts, but for fourteen days, Connie lay on his back and worried. He was too weak for therapy. "All I did was think, 'This is a hell of a time to get sick,' " he recalls. "It started to hit me that I was gonna be going into my first NBA training camp—and I wasn't ready."

His weight dropped from 205 to below 190. Packing to leave for Arizona, he was still shaky. But the time had come. On the morning of September 12, Nancy borrowed a car, and she and the children drove him to the airport.

At the terminal, people milled around them, staring at the giant in the flashy, double-breasted brown suit ("I wanted to make a good impression on everybody out there," he confesses). The plane was called for boarding, and Nancy began to tell him not to worry, that everything would be all right. Connie could see Keenan's face sagging. His little fists pounded on Hawk's leg, angry that his father was leaving. "Nancy, I'm gettin all emotional," Connie said, quickly kissing the children. "I better get on the plane."

He took a window seat and looked out at his family. "Keenan was pokin his lips out all mad and flustrated," Connie says. "Nancy and Shawna were wavin. It was so hard to leave. I got all choked up and started to cry. All the people in first class were starin at me."

"Are you all right?" a stewardess asked.

"Yes," he snapped, then hid his face in his hands.

After several minutes, he looked out once more. They were still waving. He turned his eyes away, not wanting to cry again. "I tried to think about what I was facing," Hawk says. "I was excited. But I was depressed. I had to prove I was as good as people said—as good as I knew I was. But my leg kept worryin me. It was even uncomfortable sittin on the plane."

Then he felt the plane rising. He was in the air, heading for Phoenix and the NBA.

"Stewardess," he said, "I think you better get me a Scotch."

22

MARCH OF DIMES POSTER

*"John, please—after the money we've invested in Hawkins,
if you find out he isn't great, lie to me about it."
—Dick Bloch to John Kerr before training camp, 1969*

Despite Hawkins's private uncertainty, his life had begun to assume an almost fairy-tale quality. He was a rags-to-riches story, a Sleeping Beauty awakened. He was really there, in the NBA.

There were constant reminders that he had reached the big time. That summer, Phoenix owner Dick Bloch—a casual, unpretentious man with whom Hawkins was immediately able to joke and feel comfortable—hosted Connie and Nancy in Los Angeles for several days of shows and sightseeing. Bill Erickson's grandest gesture had been a free meal.

At training camp, Hawk learned that NBA players got a sixteen dollars (now nineteen dollars) per diem meal allotment on the road. In the ABA the per diem was eight dollars—when you could find Alex Medich. "Sixteen bucks!" Connie exclaimed. "For that kind of dust I can eat in my room. I may never leave—not even for games."

At Madison Square Garden, Hawkins looked up from the court and saw 19,500 people. In Minnesota, there had been 14,000 empty seats.

Later that season, the strong, unified NBA Players Association forced the owners to raise the minimum salary to $17,500. Once, its members trembled when Detroit owner Fred Zollner shrieked at meetings or men like ex-Laker boss Bob Short threatened to fire players who struck at the All-Star game. Now, however, the Association's leadership was composed of bright, educated athletes (including some militant, politically aware blacks) and, Hawkins discovered, it was often the owners who trembled. The ABA Players Association was then a rubber stamp for management, which partially explained why the NBA players' *average* salary of $35,000 per year was more than Hawk's highest ABA wage.

The media had dubbed pro basketball "The Sport of the 70's." The National Basketball Association was the overwhelmingly dominant factor in that sport. The league's attendance had increased 100 percent over five years. A new three-year, $17.3-million TV contract had been signed with ABC.

The NBA, however, was not to be confused with Valhalla. As its Silver Anniversary approached, the league hadn't outgrown many of the characteristics that had marked its infant, barnstorming years in such outposts as Oshkosh, Sheboygan, and Fort Wayne. Finances were more stable than in the ABA, and living conditions for the players were superior, but the NBA wasn't exactly wallowing in success.

Hawk was to discover that not every arena offered the opulence of Madison Square Garden. Chicago Stadium, home of the Bulls, was a virtual igloo. Players blamed low-scoring games on frostbite: "You weren't warmed up till the third quarter," Hawkins notes.

But Chicago wasn't the league's only ice palace. In Buffalo (where the NBA expanded in 1970–71), the visitors' locker-room was so frigid, the Suns once refused to return there at halftime. "We stayed on the bench tryin to keep warm," Connie explains. "We were afraid, if we went to the locker room all sweaty, we'd catch a cold."

At Boston Garden, the front row of seats was a short spit from the team benches. Spectators could—and occasionally did—lean forward to whisper advice in a coach's ear, ask for autographs while the game was in progress, or participate in the huddle. There were no lockers—just pegs on the wall —in the cramped, shabby visitors' "locker" room. The training table was a thin plywood slab, encased haphazardly in dirty brown wrapping paper. It sagged under the weight of anything heavier than a roll of tape.

Neither was officiating among the NBA's strong points. The ABA had wooed away four of the league's best referees (with the daring ploy of offering them a living wage). By midseason, when I asked Phoenix general manager Jerry Colangelo to name the NBA's five best officials, he replied, "I can't, because there aren't five good ones in the whole damn league." Commissioner Kennedy—never renowned for his bold decisions—was actually forced to overrule an official and order part of one game replayed. It seems the official had voided a game-tying basket and declared the contest over—because *he* heard the final buzzer. Unfortunately, the other 9,100 people in the building hadn't heard any buzzers and one second still showed on the clock.

For all the stratospheric player contracts and TV deals, the NBA pinched pennies almost as aggressively as it did in the days when clubs traveled by car between isolated midwestern villages. The league's New York office was understaffed and notorious for its miniscule salaries. When a young referee made two long-distance calls from the West Coast to check a controversial rule interpretation, Commissioner Kennedy himself admonished him for wastefulness.

The NBA still has no fulltime security force, despite the heavy betting on NBA games (and the pious statements during Connie's lawsuit). Pro football has been riding herd on the gambling scene for years, but the NBA didn't hire a single man to handle security until 1970.

Individual teams also cut corners. Atlanta supposedly shelled out almost two million dollars for Pete Maravich—so the locals could have a white face to cheer for—but played its games in an antiquated college fieldhouse. The lighting was too dim for color television cameras to function. The court, laid over concrete, was so hard that players complained of knee damage. Some Hawks, like guard Walt Hazzard, asked to be traded before their limbs gave out. Earl Monroe of Baltimore confessed on national television that he never gave a full effort during a first half at Atlanta, for fear of aggravating his weak knees.

Some of the corner-cutting was probably well-advised, however. Three expansion franchises paid $3.7 million each to join the league in 1970, giving the NBA 9 new clubs in a decade. Then the economy sagged. Loose money was scarce. The war with the ABA made pro basketball a less rosy investment. Prospects for further NBA expansion diminished, and a number of clubs suddenly found themselves in deep trouble.

Tickets moved well in New York, Los Angeles, Seattle, Chicago, Phoenix, and Milwaukee (with the arrival of Hawkins and Jabbar). But the prosperity was hardly universal. There was a sharp division between the "haves" and the "have-nots." In 1969–70, for instance, the gross gate-receipts (after taxes) of three teams—New York, Milwaukee, and Los Angeles—accounted for nearly half the NBA's total. The Knicks, Bucks, and Lakers took in $7,250,400.89. The other eleven franchises totaled $7,690,606.18.

San Francisco reportedly operated $900,000 in the red during 1969–70. The Warriors had just 119,067 paying customers, after an even-more-miniscule 93,233 the previous season. They eventually moved to Oakland. San Diego's owners had trouble paying back rent on the local arena, talked of moving to Omaha, then sold the franchise to Houston. The once powerful Boston Celtics considered a shift to Long Island. In Cincinnati, turnstiles clicked infrequently (just 192,521 in 1969–70). And the town's sagging basketball interest wasn't increased the night some promotional genius in the Royals' front office gave every paying customer a free hockey puck.

Hawkins couldn't have cared less about hockey pucks. He recognized the bush-league blemishes, but it was still the NBA: the league with the national TV contract; the league where everyone traveled first class; the league of Willis Reed, Kareem Jabbar, Oscar Robertson, and Jerry West. Now it was Connie Hawkins's league. For some time, that was very important.

Hawk had to prove he belonged. And he proved it. Connie might never be as great as before the knee injury; his legend (actually the reality of his obscure past) might always exceed his performance; but, by the end of his first NBA season, his greatness was without question. He turned the Phoenix franchise around. The year before, the last-place Suns won just 16 games and drew only 132,923 paying customers. In Hawk's first season they won 39, finished in a tie for third place in the Western Division, and almost upset the Lakers in the playoffs. Attendance more than doubled.

Connie averaged 24.6 points per game (sixth in the league), grabbed 846 rebounds, and passed for 391 assists. He drew more fouls, had more assists, and blocked more shots than any forward in the NBA. He started for the West in the All-Star game, finished fifth when his fellow players voted for the league's MVP, and was named to the NBA's first All-Star team. He was a bona-fide superstar—the most visually exciting and entertaining player in the league which had kept him in exile.

But it didn't happen overnight. The season, in fact, was Hawk's most crucial test as a player and as a man.

Connie limped into Phoenix, in September, to find himself the focal point of a tense and confused situation. General Manager Colangelo was in the second year of his two-year contract and under heavy pressure to improve the team's performance and gate receipts. Coach Kerr was an inept tactician and floundering leader. The players did not respect him. There was potential dissension and racial uneasiness on the squad. And the white scoring star, Gail Goodrich, wasn't inclined to relinquish his role to Hawkins.

Connie had been widely advertised as the answer to the Suns' problems. But, during his first few months in the NBA, Hawk didn't even have the answers to his own.

Before boarding the bus that would take them to the Suns' training base at the swank Pinewood Country Club, outside Flagstaff, Arizona, the veterans introduced themselves to Hawkins. But Connie sat alone. He wanted it that way. He was too old to mingle with the rookies, who sang and giggled in the back. Except for Paul Silas, whom he'd met several times, Hawk knew none of the veterans. "I had enough on my mind without worrying about gettin friendly," he says.

The black veterans sat in pairs, talking quietly. The whites were in the front of the bus, kibitzing with Kerr and Colangelo. Hawk stared out the window at the desert and the craggy mountain peaks, listened to the laughter and shouting around him, and finally fell asleep.

"He seemed uncomfortable," recalls Silas. "I guess he didn't know what to expect. Even up at camp, Connie kept to himself."

There were no radios, TVs, or telephones in the players' cabins at the country club. "We're going to get in shape," Colangelo told them. "There'll be no bullshit." They rose each morning at seven, had their ankles taped, ate at private tables in the club's dining room, then bused eighteen miles to the gym at Coconino High School in Flagstaff. In the afternoon they went back to the club, returning for another workout in the evening. No one had to push the players to make the midnight curfew. Flagstaff is the forboding place where Jim Ryun did his pre-Olympic altitude training. After a day of gasping for air, the Suns were too tired for anything but sleep.

The first day, the lanky, chain-smoking Colangelo addressed the team. "We had the second poorest record in the history of the NBA," the twenty-nine-year-old general manager said sternly. "We have done all we could possibly do to make this team a winner this year. Now it's up to you. We have the material to be a winner—a big winner. Last year, in the second half of the season, the team looked like losers. It won't happen again."

As they walked from the meeting, Stan McKenzie, a black guard who had been one of the Suns' top substitutes the previous season, whispered to Hawkins: "We didn't feel like losers. We just didn't have a big man—and we didn't have a coach."

Connie raised his eyebrows, but said nothing.

Hawk's roommate was Neil Johnson, a husky, white 6′ 7″ forward whom Connie remembered from their days in the New York schoolyards. Johnson had played with the Knicks before coming to Phoenix in the expansion draft.

While they were unpacking, Neil fixed Hawkins with a peculiar look and asked, "Have you got my shirt?"

"What are you talking about?"

"My shirt. When we played together on the Gems in the city about ten years ago, I loaned you a shirt at a tournament in Elmhurst. You never returned it."

"Oh, *that* shirt," laughed Connie, catching on. "Gee man, I'm sorry, I forgot it."

"Think nothing of it," said Johnson, waving his hand. "Consider yourself forgiven."

Johnson was the NBA's premier flake. By early ABA standards—where rosters seemed to have been mustered from state prisons and psychiatric wards—Neil wasn't much of a weirdo. But he had his moments. "Neil isn't playing with a full deck," Colangelo often noted.

Johnson did wind-sprints during rest periods at practice, "because it's good for the constitution," and invariably argued with stewardesses on team flights, because "they all have it in for me." The following season, when he was playing in the ABA, Neil told the press that he had injured his ankle "tripping over the foul line."

In Phoenix he once penciled "260" beside his name on the team's weight chart. "You're only 240," cried trainer Joe Proski, standing next to the scale. "Coach is gonna be mad as hell if he thinks you're 260."

"I'd rather be yelled at than ignored," Johnson explained.

No one was sure if Neil acted strange because he *was* strange or because he *liked* to act strange—and if it was the latter, no one was sure *why* he liked to act strange. "Sometimes he'd talk in this real serious voice, like he was lecturin in school," Connie recalls. "But if you paid close attention, you realized that what he was sayin didn't make no sense at all."

When George Kiseda of the Philadelphia *Bulletin* awarded him the Art Heyman Memorial Trophy, Johnson proclaimed, "My wife is overwhelmed. My baby will grow up to know that her father narrowly beat out Jim Barnett for Flake of the Year. I want to thank all the people who voted for me. I'm sure next year, with a little more playing time, I will be able to win more impressively."

Playing time was the rub with Johnson. He got very little of it. At New York, and later in Phoenix, he was the darling of the crowd because he sat on the bench so much they viewed him as one of their own.

Despite his demeanor, Johnson was usually serious about basketball. When Hawk asked him about the Suns, he became solemn: "We weren't as bad as our record. We had a chance to win a lot of games last year. But we had no bench and a lot of things got messed up. Gail [Goodrich] scored a lot, but he dribbled too much and he took too many shots.

"They say," Johnson added, "that Gail's gonna be switched into a playmaker now that you're here. I wonder about that. I don't think he'll like it if he isn't the star."

The chunky, twenty-six-year-old, boyishly handsome Goodrich had signed with the Lakers as a much-publicized All-American guard, the leading scorer on two national-championship teams at UCLA. With Los Angeles, however, Gail performed in the shadow of Jerry West. He never became a regular. After three seasons, his luster dimmed, Goodrich went to the Suns in the expansion draft. Gail's career and reputation were reborn in Phoenix. He was the hub of the Suns' attack.

Although never noted for his defense or passing, the 6′ 1″ Goodrich moves well without the ball, is expert at penetrating toward the basket, and has a good jump-shot. In Phoenix's first, floundering season, he led the team in scoring with a 23.8 average—fifth best in the NBA. Along with teammate Dick Van Arsdale, Gail played in the All-Star game.

But Goodrich took 1,746 shots (256 more than Connie had ever taken in a season) and hit only 41 percent. Now that the Suns had Hawkins—an offensive threat in the forecourt—Kerr and Colangelo planned to convert Gail into a playmaker.

On paper, the transition was to appear smooth and successful. Goodrich led Phoenix in assists, raised his shooting percentage, and still averaged 20 points per game. But on the court—and in the locker room—was a different story. Connie and other black teammates became increasingly suspicious that Goodrich's primary interest was his own point total. Gail had been a hero in high school and college. He had become accustomed to the role. After relative obscurity with the Lakers, he was a star once more. Now he seemed unwilling to step aside for Hawkins. "There were times," Connie says, "when I was sure Goody was freezin me out on purpose."

The raw edges might have been smoothed, had not Goodrich—through no fault of his own—typified the kind of white athlete many blacks (sometimes subconsciously) tend to resent. They sensed life had been easy for him. Gail came from a middle-class home. His college heroics had guaranteed a large initial salary. He was a Beverly Hills stockbroker in the off-season. His playing style had none of the flourishes which mark the ghetto game. His clothes were preppy. In the locker room, he seemed uncomfortable around the blacks. Though never unfriendly, Gail rarely conversed with them. When he did try to joke with Hawkins or Silas after a victory, his words appeared forced and stilted.

Worse, Goodrich gave the impression of being too close with the Phoenix front office. He was the Suns' captain—by appointment of general manager Colangelo. "The captain is supposed to be the players' man, not the owner's man," Connie notes. "We thought they just wanted a white captain."

Says Paul Silas, "Goodrich gave no leadership; he didn't take charge on the court. He just had the title. And he was a little bit more chummy with management than anybody else on the club."

The blacks had no such doubts about the other starting guard, Dick Van Arsdale. The blond, 6' 4" former Indiana All-American was a tenacious hustler who excelled on defense and usually guarded the opposition's top scorer. Sometimes Van lost his temper and became overaggressive or took wild shots. More often, his fiery play kept the Suns' offense in constant and productive motion. Connie nicknamed him "Mad Dog."

The previous season, playing forward, Dick had averaged 21 points per game. Now he was being asked to make the tough transition to the back-court, and had spent long hours that summer developing a respectable out-side shot. Van Arsdale's forte, and the primary reason he was to maintain his average, was his powerful, reckless driving. He didn't pass well—espe-cially off the drive, where he seemed to lack split-second peripheral vision —but Van plowed fearlessly into the lions' den around the hoop.

Away from the court, the twenty-seven-year-old Van Arsdale was quiet, mature (though hardly a prude), and popular. The former Knick had been the Suns' first choice in the expansion draft and was the Phoenix player-representative.

"Everybody liked Dick," Hawkins says. "You had to admire him, he put his whole self into his game. We didn't have much in common—like he didn't know a thing about soul music, just Glen Campbell—but, more than any white guy, he worked at relating to the blacks. I felt there was respect between me and him."

Behind the starting backcourt was 6′ 5″ Dick Snyder—a good shooter who was traded to Seattle early in the season for speedy defensive-special-ist Arthur Harris—and 6′ 5″ Stan McKenzie.

McKenzie was rough and combative, particularly on defense, where he had several strong games against Jerry West. But Stan was an uncertain ballhandler, still adjusting to the backcourt after playing center at NYU and forward with the Baltimore Bullets.

A flashy dresser, with a preference for green suits and wide-brimmed hats, the bright, volatile twenty-five-year-old McKenzie spoke fluent Ital-ian and was a serious student of basketball. But his personality was felt more in the locker room than on the court. Stan was black—and touchy about race.

When Goodrich innocently remarked, "Don't you think those clothes are a little loud, Stan?" McKenzie flared, "You're the one that ought to get hip! Why don't you get your ass out of those bullshit Buster Brown outfits!"

Goodrich never mentioned clothes again.

Connie admired Stan's aggressiveness but felt McKenzie sometimes un-settled the team by venting rage over personal disappointments (his playing time decreased after midseason) at moments when the players were trying to pull together.

The previous season, the Suns had been abused by teams with strong centers, and the situation was not substantially improved. The incumbent, lean Jim Fox, was a curly-haired, easy-going South Carolinian, who once declined an invitation to an NBA training camp because he preferred playing in Europe. Fox had a delicate touch around the circle—useful for drawing opposing centers away from the hoop—and was to run up many high-scoring games. But Fox's accuracy declined under pressure, and his rebounding suffered from a distaste for body contact. He was a gentle soul who looked forward to summer, when he could bum around the continent on a motorcycle. Once, faced with the prospect of aggravating an ankle injury by taking part in a crucial playoff game, the twenty-six-year-old scuba-diving enthusiast was heard to mumble, "I really wonder if it's worth it."

Behind Fox was 6′ 10″, 250-pound bonus-baby Neal Walk. The Suns picked the Florida All-American in the first round after losing the coin flip for Kareen Jabbar. Though strong and a willing mixer, he lacked experience and was far from agile. Walk worked hard and eventually made a real contribution. But he was no Jabbar. "All the tough black centers in this country," a black player grumbled, "and we got us *two* white dudes that can't get off the floor."

The NBA-ABA bidding war had left the twenty-one-year-old Walk one of the Suns' highest-paid players. His salary, his youth, and the fact that he was Jewish, made him the butt of the limited hazing that existed on the team. The veterans nicknamed him "Superhebe."

Neal was so earnest and gullible that even Connie, who liked the youngster, couldn't resist putting him on. "He believed whatever you said," Hawkins recalls. "And he was always askin questions, afraid he wouldn't know what was goin on."

When Silas called Lamar Green, a gangling, swaybacked rookie, "Physique," Walk rushed to Hawkins and inquired, "When Paul says, 'Physique,' is he talking about the way Lamar is built?"

"Yeah man," laughed Hawk. "You been to college. Why you askin *me?* You ought to know what 'physique' means."

Paul Silas, a 235-pound bear of a man, started opposite Hawkins at forward. The NBA's official guide listed him as 6′ 7″. Actually, he stood a shade under 6′ 6″. Yet Paul was a ferocious rebounder who played every moment in a swirl of dripping sweat and crashing bodies. He possessed excellent timing and an uncanny sense of how the ball would bounce off the rim, but the primary reason Silas out-rebounded taller men was that he wanted the ball more.

His addition to the Phoenix roster was almost as important as Connie's. Silas didn't shoot well, but he was devastating on defense, cleared the ball quickly to start the fastbreak, and gave the Suns a cool, experienced head on the court.

Paul had played five years with the Atlanta (St. Louis) Hawks. Occasionally he was a starter, more often a top substitute. Colangelo obtained him in a trade for Gary Gregor, a forward of limited potential. Why did Atlanta make this curious deal? Because Gregor was white. The Hawks' management—convinced it had too many blacks—wanted to "lighten up" the roster. Colangelo took advantage of that to steal Silas.

Strong-willed and independent, Silas became a leader in Phoenix—a black (and more outspoken) counterpart to Van Arsdale. He finished the season as the Suns' top rebounder. Gregor lasted just one year in Atlanta.

"Right away, in trainin camp, all the players, even the white guys, saw Paul was somebody to respect," Hawkins recalls. "He was always the first one to make suggestions and criticisms if Kerr said something wrong."

The twenty-six-year-old Silas had come out of the Oakland ghetto to star at Creighton University. He learned little more than basketball in college. By his own admission, "My life was pretty shallow in Atlanta." But now he was growing intellectually—even more rapidly than Hawkins—his horizons expanding and his outlook increasingly molded by racial awareness. "That season," Silas recalls, "I read a lot: *Betrayal of the Negro, Soul on Ice,* some African literature. I got more serious about things—my wife, my family, my future, my people. My dignity became a real important thing to me. I won't let anyone mess with my manhood."

Silas spoke of opening a business and pondered front-office work in pro basketball. But, when Colangelo offered him a summer job with the Suns, Paul declined. "Players and management shouldn't get too tight," he explained. "That's how people get bought."

Although overly sensitive to criticism, especially from whites, Paul was straightforward and blunt. "If he told me I was screwin up something," says Connie, "I'd listen to him."

Silas and Hawkins eventually became close friends. On the road, as the season wore on, they often talked long into the night.

"The black cat must learn he doesn't have to be nice," Paul would stress. "White people are all right. No sense hatin 'em. But they don't *respect* niceness. They respect strength."

Connie was impressed by Silas, but hardly awed. When Paul's black-machismo trip got excessive, or Silas exaggerated or became longwinded, Hawkins was quick to put him down: "I'd start laughin, and say, 'Paul, sometimes you're dealin in bullshit!' He'd stop and see I was right. Then he'd say, 'Right on!' and he'd laugh too."

The other forwards were Neil Johnson, 6′ 5″ Jerry Chambers, and 6′ 7″ Lamar Green. Chambers, a Utah All-American, had played one season with the Lakers, then spent two years in the Army. He had a picturesque jump-shot. But he rarely produced in tight situations. "Jerome needed a heart transplant," Hawkins says coldly.

Green was the surprise of the training camp. A sensational leaper, he had been acquired via a fourth-round draft-choice from a trade which also brought Fox from Detroit. The black rookie from Morehead State hadn't played basketball until his junior year in high school and was frightfully inexperienced. But he oozed uninhibited enthusiasm and improved rapidly.

"Lamar was a country-type dude," Connie says. "He came from Birmingham, Alabama, and we'd tease him about how he'd get lynched if he tried to drive his new Cadillac back home. At first, he was so nervous in games that he'd jump up a mile, hang in the air, get the rebound—then pass it to the other team. But he finally relaxed, and he helped us a lot."

Not that Lamar was always sure what he was doing. Total commotion usually followed his entrance into the game. He might block three straight shots, then knock the loose ball out of his own teammates' hands. No one, including Lamar, really knew what was happening as he bounded about the court. But, more often than not, his bumbling effervescence benefited Phoenix.

On paper—with the addition of Hawkins—the Suns were a more-than-respectable second-year expansion team. Credit for their improved roster belonged primarily to the youthful, ambitious Colangelo. By the close of that season, Jerry would be regarded as one of the most effective general managers in the NBA. The Suns' finances would be in the black, and their gross receipts would rank in the top half of the league. Colangelo's trades —which brought Silas, Chambers, Green, and Fox to Phoenix for nondescripts McCoy McLemore, George Wilson, and Gary Gregor—would be viewed as virtual larceny. And people would wonder, exactly who was Jerry Colangelo anyway?

Jerry grew up on the streets of a tough Italian neighborhood in Chicago. At Bloom Township High, where he starred in basketball, the 6' 4" guard was renowned for his angry outbursts when coaches pulled him from a game. Colangelo had a great outside shot—he can still outshoot every Sun —and went on to captain the University of Illinois team in 1961–62.

But after graduation, with the exception of some semipro ball, Jerry drifted away from the sport. He went into the tuxedo sales-and-rental business with a friend. Then there was a falling-out, and Colangelo went looking for a job. He found one in merchandising, working for a man named Dick Klein. Six months later, in 1966, Klein became part-owner and general manager of the Chicago Bulls, a new expansion club. As an afterthought, Klein brought along Colangelo as sales promotion director.

Jerry's eye for appraising basketball talent soon became evident. The role of chief scout was added to his duties. When the Phoenix franchise was organized in the winter of 1967–68, Colangelo applied for the general manager's post. He was twenty-seven years old. But he somehow talked his way into the job.

When Jerry arrived in Phoenix, the club didn't even have office space. He ordered stationery, ran a contest to name the team, and hired his old friend and fellow Illinois alumnus John Kerr as coach. Eventually he put together an efficient operation.

Even the Suns' horrendous first-season record couldn't stifle Colangelo's boundless regard for his own abilities. The first time I visited Phoenix, the general manager, without hesitation, handed me three clippings—each a glowing tribute to Jerry Colangelo.

Jerry's Machiavellian instincts and appetite for hard work, in fact, made him almost as good as he thought he was. A hustling, sometimes ruthless ("cross me and I'll cut off your balls," he warns) wheeler-dealer, Colangelo was totally engrossed in his job. The day after the season ended, he was phoning players, already anxious to talk about next season.

Colangelo will do anything to win. He considers the rulebook an obstacle course. Whether it's offering his players a little bonus money for winning a crucial game (forbidden by NBA regulations) or "suggesting" to the Suns' booster club that fans "remind" the officials whenever Wilt Chamberlain plays an illegal zone defense, Jerry is always searching for an edge. When Phoenix was battling Chicago for a playoff spot, Colangelo learned that the Bulls had lost in the Midwest. The Suns' game was still in progress. So Jerry ordered the Phoenix public-address announcer to tell the crowd— and the Suns—that Chicago had actually won. "I didn't want my guys to let down," he explained later.

Except when negotiating contracts, Colangelo went out of his way to keep the players contented. He did everything from finding postseason jobs to covering for them while they cheated on their wives. "You couldn't always trust him," said Hawkins, after a year with Colangelo. "But you had to kind of like him and admire him. He worked. He got things done."

At the start of the 1969–70 season, however, Jerry was hardly established, respected, or secure. Another bad season and he might have been back selling tuxedos. His trades seemed to have given Phoenix a team capable of challenging for the playoffs. Apparently Jerry had promised the owners as much. Now the Suns had to deliver—and that meant Hawkins had to come through.

From the first workout, Connie could feel his teammates eyeing him, waiting for a sign that he was indeed a superstar. But nothing went right. In honor of the NBA's coming to Coconino High, an overzealous janitor had given the court a vigorous oiling. Hawkins slipped during the first wind-sprints and pulled a muscle in his hip. Favoring the hip, he put added pressure on his knee and fluid developed. There was pain when he cut sharply. The knee was sore and swollen after the workout.

"I didn't feel quick at all," he says. "I couldn't make the first move to get away from my man. The leg felt like it didn't belong to me."

Fortunately, the Suns had an expert trainer—the first Hawkins ever encountered. Joe Proski was a short, dark-haired thirty-year-old with a merry disposition. He chewed tobacco, puffed thick cigars from the corner of his mouth, threw parties for the players, wore outlandish fur coats on Eastern road trips, and annoyed management by buzzing around on a motorcycle and driving a Cadillac on his modest trainer's salary.

"We all dug Proski," said Hawk. "But he wasn't just happy-go-lucky. He really knew what he was doin. Proski was the first trainer I ever trusted to tape my ankles."

Each morning, before the workouts, Proski drove Connie to the gym and supervised a series of exercises in which Hawk lifted weights to strengthen the leg. After practice, when everyone else returned to the country club, Proski remained to watch Connie push himself through the exercises again.

The trainer gave him constant attention. He soaked Hawk's knee in ice before and after each practice to reduce the fluid. He even carried a bucket of ice onto the gym floor and chilled the knee whenever Connie rested.

Yet Hawkins was still neither comfortable nor confident. His disposition wasn't improved when—after four days in camp—Kerr showed the players videotapes of their workouts. Hawk saw a zombielike creature, which looked distressingly similar to himself, limping cautiously across the screen.

Kerr, a 6′ 9″ redhead whose sense of humor was rated above his coaching ability even by admirers, cried, "Hawkins, see how you favor that leg. You aren't moving at all. You look like a March of Dimes poster!"

The players chuckled. Hawk's face remained impassive, but his gut tightened. "I was shocked," he says. "I knew I wasn't *speedin,* but I didn't know I was *walkin.* I was draggin the leg like a cripple. It frightened me. I couldn't get my body to do what my mind wanted."

Proski and Colangelo called Dr. Kerlan in Los Angeles. The specialist informed them that the water on the knee was a "normal reaction." Said Colangelo, "Connie may have to have the knee tapped from time to time. It's something he'll have to live with."

But the knee was to be a major problem until midseason. How much of the discomfort was in Hawkins's mind? Some, definitely. Hawk had always been a bit of a hypochondriac. He was also using the injury as a psychological crutch. The self-doubts Connie carried with him to Arizona were very real. For all his protestations, he is too sensitive not to have wondered whether he was really good enough to be an NBA star. Like most players in similar circumstances, Hawkins sought the most convenient excuse for imperfection.

Nevertheless, the pain and immobility were hardly figments of Connie's imagination. The healing may have been progressing normally, but the knee was not normal. "It was," says Proski, "about 75 percent."

Hawk lived with constant pain. He couldn't cut sharply, and he bore justifiable fear of reinjury. In addition, such damage and aching had a greater effect on Connie's delicate, twisting game, than it might have had on a player who relied on brute force or outside shooting rather than quickness and finesse.

As Hawk continued to gimp about—tiring easily because he was still underweight—Colangelo started to worry. At first, he tried to hide his concern behind a smile. "Connie," he would joke, "we're paying you a million bucks and I don't think you can make the team."

When three of the owners—Dick Bloch, Don Diamond, and Don Pitt—visited a workout and Connie was again less than scintillating, Jerry's edginess surfaced. While the owners and athletes mingled at the country club, he cornered Hawkins. "How's the knee?"

"It's gonna take time," Hawk said.

"The exhibition games are starting soon."

Hawkins felt himself getting annoyed. "I don't know if I'll be completely ready, man. It's comin along, but it's gonna take time."

"You're convincing yourself it isn't all right, Connie," the general manager said, his tone midway between pleading and anger. "Just say to yourself, 'The knee is fine, the operation is a success.' "

"Man," Connie snapped, "I know it's a success! But it isn't *respondin.* This isn't in my head. It just isn't workin right." Hawk whirled and walked away.

Recalls Paul Silas, "Jerry was getting pretty panicky. Every couple of days he'd say to me, 'What's wrong with that guy? He's just not doing it.' Jerry didn't understand all the pressure on Hawk, all the adjustments. He didn't realize how a bad injury can mess up a man's head. But Jerry wasn't the only one. I guess Connie got off on the wrong foot with everybody."

Hawk certainly hadn't impressed his new teammates. They had expected him to march in wearing seven-league boots. When he turned out to be mortal, they were disillusioned.

Silas, who'd been around, had tried to cushion the shock when some players held pre-training camp workouts in Phoenix, before Connie's arrival. "The cat is gonna be a rookie," he warned. "Give him time, don't make no rash judgments. He doesn't know our league."

"I knew there'd be trouble," Paul remembers. "Most of the players had expected Hawk to be a center. I'd been thinkin 'Wow, we got us a bad dude to block shots and clear the boards, so we can run.' But I met Connie in Phoenix in June, right after he signed, and the cat wasn't much taller than me. I knew he couldn't play center—not in the NBA, not skinny as he was. But people weren't peepin this, and the front office didn't help with all the bullshit buildup they gave him.

"At camp everybody was waitin for him to do something superduper. But he was just finding his way. Guys started sayin, 'Hey, this isn't what we expected. *This* guy is getting a million dollars?' "

Connie had never overextended himself during training. Now he was especially cautious, slowly working into shape. "Some guys thought he wasn't puttin out," says Silas.

Immersed in his own difficulties, Connie was unaware of his teammates' feelings. In the second week of camp, however, he gained some weight and felt a bit more secure on the knee. "I was still far off my game," he says. "But I started gettin out of my shell and I had my first real talks with Paul."

Their initial discussions concerned the coach. Kerr gave the Suns plenty of running and scrimmaging, but little work on one-on-one or team defense. Eventually, he installed a fullcourt press, but the coach did almost no teaching or instructing. "Kerr had the worst defensive team in the league last year," Paul would say, "and he's gonna have it again."

Connie was woefully deficient in defensive fundamentals. Like many of his youthful teammates, he would have profited from serious instruction. But none was forthcoming. Kerr was a product of the old school of NBA coaches, who believed that when a player became a pro there was little he could be taught. Says one Sun, "John was simply lazy. Plenty of coaches in this league think all you have to do at practice is roll out the balls. Well, Kerr didn't even bother to do that."

For a dozen years, Kerr had been a star center in the NBA. Although never a prolific scorer, he had excelled at rebounding and ballhandling with the Syracuse Nationals, whose patterned offense revolved around his deft passes, picks, and screens.

An affable, handsome man with flaming red hair, Kerr had a talent for funny quips that made him popular with sportswriters. Big John was always good copy. "I may not lead the league in scoring," he used to say, "but when I retire I'm gonna write a book called *Twelve Years in the Pivot Without the Ball.*"

Because he was known as a "heady" player and a public-relations asset, Kerr was long considered coaching material. Upon his retirement, the ex-Illinois All-American was appointed the first coach of the expansion Chicago Bulls. A fast start—the result of good conditioning—carried Chicago into the playoffs. The Bulls were quickly eliminated, but Kerr was voted Coach of the Year.

The following season, Chicago once more reached the playoffs. But the team was much less impressive and won just twenty-nine games. When they were again immediately bounced from postseason play, Kerr lost his job. But Jerry Colangelo hired him to coach the Suns.

Kerr and Colangelo had become close friends while working for the Bulls. Both were from Chicago and had captained the Illinois basketball team. But Kerr had not been Colangelo's first choice. Jerry signed him only after Press Maravich of LSU; K. C. Jones, the former Celtic; and Larry Costello, now at Milwaukee, turned down the job.

Kerr's leadership style was more reminiscent of Gomer Pyle than General Patton. "I never had to be motivated by a coach," he explained. "I didn't need any 'Win this one for the Gipper' locker-room speech. And I doubt, in big business, if executives say to themselves every day, 'Well, I'd better talk to my guys today and get them up for a sale.'"

Despite Kerr's charm and easy-going manner, Connie sensed the coach didn't control the club. Even during early workouts, he noticed that several white players could badger Kerr into adjusting the practice routine to suit their whims. "Somebody would holler, 'Hey John, let's scrimmage awhile,'" Hawkins recalls, "and Kerr'd just shrug his shoulders and say 'O.K.'

"Didn't nobody respect him," Hawk adds. "When he tried to make a tough speech, he didn't seem real. He'd always say, 'Tonight let's scratch their eyes out.' Pretty soon, guys were imitating him behind his back."

Kerr fraternized too closely with the white players—drinking beer with many of them after games on the road—and was unable to relate to the blacks. "Most NBA coaches don't know how to approach black ball players," says Silas. "But John didn't have any idea."

Modern black athletes are practically attuned to artificial "soul-brothering" (an updated version of "Some of my best friends are colored"). Yet this was Kerr's approach—when he approached his black players at all. "Johnny would try and use expressions like we use," Hawkins says. "But, comin out of his mouth, they weren't natural. He'd tell me that he used to room with Gus Johnson, how Gus liked him. I guess he thought, because

Gus is black, that would show me I should like him too. But his thing was forced. You could see right through it."

The coach's socializing would eventually contribute to suspicions of favoritism and aggravate the racial difficulties on the squad. Long before that, however, Hawkins was disappointed: "John didn't give us much strategy. Mostly, he was good at tellin funny jokes and drinkin beer with the white guys."

Kerr praised Hawkins freely in training camp: "He's the best passer of any big man I've ever seen, and he handles the ball well enough to be a guard. I won't tailor a team to one man, but I will tailor some plays for him. Whenever we can isolate him one-on-one with a defender under the bucket, he'll be devastating."

But, much to Hawk's surprise, Kerr did not build the Suns' offense around him. Despite the summer rhetoric, the focus remained on the guards (Van Arsdale and Goodrich), who were to cut off screens and picks set by the forwards, and seemed destined to do most of the shooting.

The coach did install several plays specifically for Connie. When Hawk got the ball in the corner, for instance, the center was to move to the high post, opening the middle for Hawkins to work one-on-one. "But that never seemed to happen in games," Connie recalls. "Mostly the offense turned into everybody freelancin and the guards havin the ball a lot."

Hawkins's reaction was mixed. It upset him that he would not be the kingpin, "but I guess I was relieved a little too." Since Kerr had not thrust responsibility upon him, Hawk didn't seek it. The coach's plans gave Connie an opportunity to avoid excessive testing of the knee and to slide away from some of the pressure.

But the pressure was always there. He was the center of attention for the Phoenix journalists, Joe Gilmartin and Dave Hicks, and visiting magazine writers. He handled the interviews gracefully. "I want to prove myself," he told Bill Libby of *Sport*. "Not to the NBA. Not to the press. Not to anyone but me. I got to prove me to *me*."

Was he still bitter over his treatment by the NBA? In reply to this, the most persistent question, Hawk was tactful. "It's not in my nature to be bitter," he would repeat. "No one's perfect. I take things as they come."

But each time he discovered how little he knew about big-league defense, each time he forced his leg to do things which once came naturally, Connie was reminded of the wasted years. He was a twenty-seven-year-old rookie. For that he would always be bitter—no matter what he said.

The atmosphere in camp was relaxed during the first week, but as the time for trimming the roster approached, play became frantic and tempers shortened. There were several fights. Van Arsdale and Snyder collided under the boards and came up swinging. Neil Johnson began mumbling to Hawk that he thought he'd be cut. Dave Lattin, a veteran black forward, dove for loose balls, threw elbows, and dunked at every opportunity.

"Last year they played white dudes all the time," said McKenzie, who feared the ax. "The black guys didn't play shit. They're prejudiced on this team."

The previous season, the Suns were the only NBA club with five white starters. But there was no evidence of racism. The oldtime quota system is virtually dead. There are so many talented black players that self-interest obviates against any team imposing a strict limit.

Almost all blacks, however, take for granted that if a white and a black player are of almost equal ability, the white man will get whatever job they are competing for. "They *prefer* whites, to balance it for the fans," Silas said. "They'll pay more to get white guys, too. But it's stronger on some teams than others. Baltimore keeps a lot of black dudes. San Francisco don't. Atlanta's got all black starters, so they try to get whites for the bench."

McKenzie was not cut. Instead, three rookie guards were released. But Neil Johnson was chosen over the hulking, 240-pound Dave Lattin for the last forward position and the blacks didn't like it. The night Lattin was released, Chambers, Silas, McKenzie, and Hawkins talked in hushed, bitter tones for half an hour. "He could have helped us more than Johnson," said Paul. "We could have used his muscle. This Kerr is a strange dude. Makes you wonder about him bein prejudiced, doesn't it."

Hawkins had his own problems. The days in training camp were evaporating all too quickly. "My game was still awful," he recalls. "I was afraid of bein embarrassed." He received several injections of cortisone in his knee.

The Phoenix veterans, however, were impatient with the training grind, tired of playing against each other and fighting among themselves. "It's time to get into the season," Silas said in the locker room. "We can't stay in camp practicing forever."

"Why not?" said Hawkins, forcing a laugh as Proski bound his knee in adhesive bandages. "I'm in no hurry. I'd just as soon stay here awhile."

In the early exhibition games, Hawk played gingerly, taking few shots. The Suns weren't looking for him on offense. Several times he was open but didn't get the ball. But Connie kept quiet. He was feeling his way, in the first phase of acclimating himself to new teammates and a new league.

"I was dealin with the intimidation thing too," Hawkins says. "That summer, when I saw Wilt Chamberlain in New York, he told me to be ready. He said the first time around the league, all the forwards would beat up on me real bad, to see if I could take it. He said, 'They'll try you. Stand up to 'em and they won't mess with you no more.'"

The initial assault came from 6' 8" Jerry Lucas, then with the Cincinnati Royals. As Hawk was jockeying for position near the hoop, Lucas slammed his knee into Connie's rear and rapped him across the neck with his forearm. Hawkins whipped his elbow into Lucas's chest. They shoved each other again and squared off. "Next time you swing an elbow at me, I'll kick your ass," Lucas warned, as an official pushed between them.

"Keep talkin," Hawk replied. "Is that all you do? Don't you do nothin but talk?"

"You throw that fuckin elbow," shouted Lucas, "you'll see."

On the next play, Hawk planted his elbow in Lucas's gut, then spun past him to score a layup. "He kept on bein rough, but he didn't try to punch me any more," Hawkins says. "After a while, he laid off the intimidation. Anyway, he wasn't that great a player."

Around the NBA, many blacks believe that Lucas has been overrated by coaches and the press because he is white. They claim that referees help him on defense by ignoring his obvious roughing. They think some official scorers pad his rebound totals to justify his image as a star—a white star.

As the start of the regular schedule neared, Hawkins showed occasional flashes of brilliance. "Then, just before the season began, I had a bunch of great games," Connie recalls. "I couldn't do anything wrong. But it was strange: I really wasn't playin that much better. My defense was real bad. The leg was still slowin me. I just had a lot of luck all at once. I'd get passes at just the exact right spot. Rebounds bounced to me. My shots all rolled in. I wasn't making great moves, but every time I'd look up, there was an open lane to the basket. So everybody got carried away again. They thought I was ready to go."

Against the Rockets, Hawk scored 28 points and had 15 rebounds. Against the Warriors, he had 35 points, 14 rebounds, and 7 blocked shots. Fans, teammates, and writers assumed this was the Hawkins they'd heard about. "It's really something to have a man you can turn the game over to in the fourth quarter," raved Kerr. "Now I know what it's like having an Oscar on your side."

The enthusiasm raged on. The day before the opening game—against San Diego in Phoenix—the Suns' management posed Hawkins for photographers before a huge billboard which proclaimed, "You've Got A Winner, Phoenix."

There was even talk of the Suns' finishing first in the Western Division. The players bubbled with optimism. The team had an abundance of scoring power, an effective fast break, strong rebounding, and a potentially balanced attack. But there were many obvious weaknesses—particularly on defense.

Hawkins was a poor defender. Neither of the centers could contain the league's better big-men. Both starting guards tended to penetrate toward the offensive basket, leaving Phoenix vulnerable to the fastbreak. The bench was mediocre, there wasn't a competent playmaker on the squad, and Kerr wasn't going to steal any games with his coaching.

Connie shared his teammates' excitement. But he sensed prospects weren't as rosy as they seemed. "It worried me that people were expectin so much," he recalls. "In the papers, they were talkin about me scorin fifty points in the first game."

Joe Gilmartin of the Phoenix *Gazette*, a droll wit and one of the most astute writers covering the NBA, sensed this also. "If you don't get fifty tomorrow night," he told Hawkins, "a lot of people will be disappointed. They don't just expect you to be a superstar; they expect you to be superhuman."

SLOW START

"Everybody says 'the kid will get better,'
but they forget for the moment that the kid is 27,
and that a big chunk has gone out of his life."
—*Dick Young, New York* Daily News, *October 23, 1969*

As Hawkins anticipated, he was far from superhuman. Surprisingly, however, Connie still captivated the Phoenix fans. Arizona is not basketball country. The local folk knew little of the game's refinements. But the Suns were the state's only big-league franchise, and the fans made up in volume and intensity what they lacked in understanding.

They berated referees for even the most obvious calls, blared horns and whistles which sounded distractingly official, harassed opponents (one threatened to shoot Archie Clark, others prowled the corridors in search of Walt Hazzard), and occasionally showered the court with garbage. Among visiting teams, Phoenix was known as the snake pit of the league.

But the fans loved Hawkins, the town's first pro superstar. His flashy Globetrotter gyrations turned them on. Even on his bad nights, Hawk could always conjure up a few spectacular dunks or passes.

On paper, Connie's NBA debut was an immediate success. During the first half of the season, he ranked among the league's leading scorers and was voted a starting spot in the All-Star game.

Still, knowledgeable observers were reserved. Hawk's performance was enigmatically uneven. The early days in Phoenix often seemed like an instant replay of his sluggish start in the ABA—but this time the pressures were greater and the volume of criticism was louder. Once more, Connie adjusted slowly to a new situation. He did not become the driving force in the Suns' offense. He did not take charge as a superstar is expected to do.

Some nights Hawkins was sensational, winning several games single-handed and five times scoring more than 35 points. Other nights he was lackluster. He seemed to go in spurts, unable to generate a sustained level of intensity. He still appeared cautious in heavy traffic, and he wasn't shooting enough. In 11 of the first 38 games, Connie took less than 14 shots.

There were prolonged scoring droughts, when Hawk seemed to drift away from the action. Once he went over 23 minutes without a point. Some complained that he slowed the Suns' attack by holding the ball (waving it over his head in one-handed Globetrotter fashion) too long before making his move to the basket.

"He had style and grace and eye-popping moves from the first day of camp," wrote Joe Gilmartin in the Phoenix *Gazette*. "But somehow he seems a hollow shell of his reputation. He's out of shape from a summer of flu, and he is unsure of his surgery-scarred knee and unsure of his role with his new team. Worse yet, his competitive edge has to be rehoned after a decade on stage and in the bushes."

Hawkins had never experienced the consistently tight, bruising defense which predominates in the NBA. The "book" on Hawk is to oppose him with a forward, who can stay with Connie's quick initial move, bump him off stride to prevent his setting up near the hoop, keep him away from the ball by overplaying him to the inside, and confine his shooting to medium-range jumpers. Night after night, Hawkins found men like Dave DeBusschere, Gus Johnson, and Tom Sanders, muscling him out of position and dogging his every step. Behind them, under the basket, were massive, agile giants like Jabbar, Reed, and Chamberlain.

Against this level of competition, Connie needed all his physical tools. But before the opening game, he weighed only 201 pounds (every Phoenix player except the 6′ 1″ Goodrich outweighed him). His weight never climbed over 204 and often dipped as low as 195. Forwards like Bill Bridges, Jerry Lucas, Johnson, and DeBusschere are listed at 235 pounds.

Hawk also became convinced that his body exerted a magnetic attraction on every germ known to man. "I was always gettin the flu," he recalls. "I think it was the change in climates. Each time we made an eastern trip, I'd catch a cold." Connie's medical woes also included an abscessed tooth which had to be pulled and a case of tonsillitis which caused him to sit out a game in San Diego.

Despite periodic cortisone injections, Hawkins's knee continued to affect him. Joe Proski had to soak the swelling in ice even after workouts. The degree of pain varied, but for months Hawk was convinced the knee wasn't sound. He still favored the leg, and his movements often lacked decisiveness.

"The man is great and he'll do well in this league," said Atlanta coach

Richie Guerin after his first regular-season look at Connie. "But this is not physically the same Hawkins who played in the ABA. He obviously hasn't come all the way back yet from surgery."

In addition, Hawkins also had to familiarize himself with NBA officiating. It was superior to ABA whistle-tooting, but still surprisingly low-grade. During Connie's first season, a district attorney in one league city was actually moved to investigate certain officials. "Their calls were so crazy we thought they might be shaving points," says a detective. "But it turned out they were just rotten referees."

Whatever their capabilities, NBA officials allow considerably more body contact than those in the ABA. The league's philosophy is "No harm, no foul." Few infractions are whistled if the contact does not prevent a shot or if it occurs away from the ball and has no bearing on the course of play. The players call it "No blood, no foul."

But more than the permissiveness, it was the officials' inconsistency that most disturbed Hawkins. Few could be counted upon to call a play the same way twice in a row.

"The NBA gets on kicks," said Detroit coach Butch van Breda Kolff. "They'll send out memos concerning the new loose-ball foul or bumping. . . . They'll call 'em tight for a few weeks and then slack off."

"Our Jerry Sloan got good position on Dick Van Arsdale," claimed coach Dick Motta of Chicago, "and Van Arsdale ran into him. Manny Sokol called Sloan for blocking. I asked Manny, 'Where is Jerry supposed to go?' You know what he told me? He said, 'Next time I'll call it for you.' "

Throughout the NBA, players take for granted that officials favor home teams, that the Knicks are especially pampered in Madison Square Garden, and that referees actively protect most of the superstars. Says Motta, "There are certain players you can't touch, like Dave Bing, Oscar Robertson, and Jerry West. Elgin Baylor traveled continually and it wasn't called."

Some stars may curse the officials with impunity. Robertson can loose a gamelong monologue of profanity. Others, however, get technical fouls for a loud "Goddamn."

Pushing a referee is supposed to result in an automatic technical. But in San Francisco, Hawk saw Jerry Lucas get away with it. The Warriors' star forward (he'd been traded from Cincinnati and is now with New York) was caught holding Connie. When the official turned his back, Hawkins jabbed Lucas with a sneak elbow. Lucas shouted angrily and moved toward Hawk. The referee stepped between them. "Get the fuck outta here," raged Lucas, shoving the official backward with both hands.

"Ain't that a technical?" Connie asked, when Lucas had been restrained. The referee shrugged and walked away.

There were even inconsistencies in the official rulebook. Make that official rule*books*. In 1969–70, the NBA had two—an appendix to the official NBA Guide and a separate twenty-six-page booklet—each with its own definition of the regulation prohibiting zone defenses. "Now," wrote George Kiseda in the Philadelphia *Bulletin,* "the winning coach can quote from one rulebook and the losing coach can quote from the other. That way there's an interpretation for everybody."

Hawkins occasionally wondered if there weren't some special interpretations for him. Several referees told Jerry Colangelo they bent over backwards to ignore the fact that Connie pushed off illegally with his free arm while driving. Some black players, however, tell a different story:

"When Hawk came into the league he wasn't accepted, definitely not by the refs," says a black superstar. "They saw him as a bad-seed dude, an outsider. They didn't call a lot of the shit people did to him—but they were always watching for *him* to do something."

Convinced he was saddled with picayune fouls, Connie became even more cautious on defense. "I'd get pissed and sulk," he says, "and it would screw up my whole game."

One night Connie asked captain Goodrich to inform an official that Hawk was being held constantly as he tried to maintain a position. "He says you have to keep moving," Gail reported back. "If you move without the ball, he'll call the foul. If you stand still and the guy holds you, he won't call it."

"That ain't a *rule,*" said Hawk. "It's not in the book. What are they talking about?" Goodrich shrugged. Connie took the matter to Kerr. The coach questioned the referee. He returned shaking his head.

"I don't know what he means," said Kerr. "I never heard of any rule like that, but he says they won't call a foul unless you move around."

Recalls Paul Silas, "In Philly one day, Connie got so frustrated he had to tell the coach to take him out of the game. He was ready to explode. He'd fake his man, the guy would fall on him, but nobody blew a whistle. Sure, Hawk was at the line a lot—but not nearly as much as he should have been."

During the exhibition season, Mendy Rudolph, the NBA's senior referee and chief of staff, gathered the Rockets, Lakers, Warriors, and Suns in a suite at the Vacation Village Motel in San Diego. He distributed rulebooks and explained new regulations. Then he told the players, "Our officials don't hold personal grudges. Even if you met one of our men in a restaurant and had an argument with him, he wouldn't hold it against you if he handled your game the next night."

A deep, rumbling laugh came from the corner of the room occupied by Wilton Norman Chamberlain.

"Mendy," said The Dipper, "you know that's a lotta bullshit."

Rudolph's face reddened as an undercurrent of laughter rippled about him. "No" he said firmly. "There isn't a man in this league who'd hold a grudge."

"Bullshit," repeated Chamberlain.

Hawkins soon got a hint that Wilt wasn't being facetious. Whistled for a charging foul, Connie turned questioningly to the official who made the call.

"This isn't the ABA, Hawkins," the referee sneered under his breath. "You can't pull shit like that in this league. We'll teach you—quick."

"The next time I saw Mendy I told him what that referee said," Connie recalls. "He said he'd look into it and get back to me. But he never talked to me about it again."

In fact, the dapper, gray-haired dean of NBA officials wasn't himself kindly disposed toward Hawkins. Rudolph is the best referee in the league, but he isn't always above pettiness. Connie's Globetrotter antics and outlaw-league background seemed to offend him. The Phoenix players felt he was unusually quick to hit Hawk with fouls and technicals. On several occasions, when Connie grabbed a defensive rebound one-handed and waved it over his head under the basket, Rudolph snipped, "Come on, come on, play ball. None of that crap. Play ball." Hawkins was doing nothing illegal. He just wasn't conducting himself the way Mendy thought a true NBA player should.

For some time, Connie's own teammates didn't think he was conducting himself like an NBA player either. In varying degrees, the disillusionment felt in training camp persisted until midseason. "Our club wasn't the best place for a guy like Hawk to break in," says Stan McKenzie. "He had enough trouble straightening out his own thing, but every time we didn't play up to expectations, he got the blame."

The Suns were a mediocre team, a .500 ball club. Consistent winners and hopeless losers establish fixed patterns of existence. A team like Phoenix, however, oscillates between emotional highs and lows. They are good enough to dream of great achievements, but not good enough to achieve them. When the players win a few games, they love, trust, and understand each other. When they lose, they hate, suspect, and look for scapegoats. Personal grievances are magnified. There are countless meetings, soul-searchings, and reconciliations. With every short winning or losing streak there are "turning points"—soon replaced by new "turning points."

Phoenix staggered from the gate, but early injuries to the Lakers' Wilt

Chamberlain and the Warriors' Nate Thurmond kept the seven-team Western Division packed so close, the Suns were always within hailing distance of fourth place—the final playoff spot. Every night seemed crucial and defeats were hard to accept.

Connie's periodic scoring explosions caused Kerr to dub him "Captain Marvel" and, says McKenzie, "made the guys feel Hawk could always score if he *really* tried." But this just compounded their frustration when Hawkins didn't carry Phoenix to victory.

The players suspected he pampered himself physically. "In San Diego, after the first Eastern trip, the team physician (Dr. Paul Steingard) told me that I had tonsillitis," says Connie. "Before the game I felt real sick and dizzy. I told Jerry and Dick Bloch I couldn't play, that I'd hurt the team. I could see they were mad. And I could see, the way guys stared at me, the players were pissed."

When Hawkins informed the press that "I'm going to have my tonsils removed this week," Colangelo angrily vetoed any operation. "He's going to play," the general manager retorted. "His tonsils will come out when *we* think they should come out!"

Connie didn't always go full throttle. He often seemed to save himself for the second half. To make matters worse, his teammates, like the people in Pittsburgh, initially mistook Hawk's facile movements and blank expression for laziness or disinterest. Wrote the Philadelphia *Bulletin*'s George Kiseda, "Connie Hawkins plays basketball the way . . . Joe DiMaggio used to cover center field, the way Mary Martin used to fly through the air in Peter Pan . . . with the greatest of ease. With cool grace. With perfect control. . . . Last night [he made] the game of basketball look so easy you had to wonder if he wasn't holding something back. . . ."

For a while, there was also disenchantment with Hawkins on a personal level. When Connie is playing well—when the "game," that is so much a part of his being, is in gear—he exudes an almost regal dignity, a commanding self-assurance. But, at first, Hawk's "game" wasn't right. The Phoenix players, unaware of the adjustment he was going through, saw only the superficial, external aspects of his character—his appearance, his speech, his lateness, and his Globetrotter style. These were at odds with the expected demeanor of an NBA superstar. "So," says Silas, "people felt Connie was the 'lazy nigger.' "

Hawk still got along well with Paul. He spent a lot of time with Arthur Harris, the twenty-three-year-old black guard acquired from Seattle. An intelligent, racially hip Stanford grad, Arthur shared Hawkins's nocturnal inclinations and had an apartment in the Camelback Towers where Connie lived in Phoenix.

But Hawkins turned off many teammates. He still had little awareness of time and managed to be late for planes, buses, and practices. "It annoyed people," notes Silas. "Everybody was just *waiting* to see when he'd miss his first plane."

They didn't have to wait long. During the Suns' first trip to Philadelphia, Connie was five minutes late for the bus to the Spectrum ("The players resented it," says Silas). The following morning, Nancy, who was staying at the hotel with Hawk, forgot to awaken him. He missed the flight to Phoenix, then arrived too late for a practice.

"There was a lot of complaining," Silas recalls. "Hawk was always late. Kerr had a system of fines. But he rarely enforced it. Hawk was only fined a couple of times. Guys felt if being late was good enough for Connie, it was good enough for them."

Some believed Hawkins was a prima donna, flaunting his star-status and testing Kerr to see how much he could get away with. Actually, Connie was just blundering along as he always had, oblivious to the clock. "I wasn't trying to show up nobody," he says. "I didn't do it on purpose. But I can't see what difference a few minutes made." They really made little difference. A team with a strong leader could have been more flexible. But, under John Kerr, the line between order and chaos was paper-thin. Spoiled by his kid-glove treatment in the ABA and absorbed with his own problems, Hawkins didn't realize that he had to establish himself—and earn his teammates' respect—before making his own rules.

Because Connie's sleep habits are upside down—he's a night person— he often arrived at morning workouts droopy-eyed, his natural uncombed and straggly. Hawkins had an expensive wardrobe, but unless scheduled for a public appearance, he wasn't preoccupied with his clothes. Hawk wore old bellbottoms and dashikis day after day.

It took a rookie to say what most players were thinking. "Why do you dress like that?" asked Lamar Green, whose bonus money had gone for a Cadillac. "You got bread now, man."

"*That's why,*" Connie tried to explain. "When I was poor, I couldn't afford to change my clothes, and it embarrassed me. Now I've got plenty of nice stuff. I can change all I want. So I don't *have to.*"

"That's crazy," said Lamar.

Even among most militant blacks in the NBA, there is an often subconscious attempt to "fit in" by white standards—to maintain racial identity, but also to exude the sophistication and affluence whites will respect. "Watch the white boys when we travel," Silas would say. "They're talkin about business deals or they're readin books or the financial page. Too many black cats are playin cards or talkin about broads. That shouldn't be.

You have to cope with this white boy on his terms. To beat him at his own thing, you have to conform to some of *his* things."

Connie, however, wasn't anxious to conform. Unlike other NBA blacks, Hawkins hadn't been sifted through four years of college and seasons in the big-league limelight. He was pleased that he could function with greater ease and effectiveness in public, integrated situations. But his interests, tastes, and style were still ghettoized—"I wouldn't want a white-collar job"—and Hawk was comfortable that way.

Eventually, his black teammates would recognize this. "It took me awhile to tune him in," says Silas. "He came from so far off the stereotype NBA bullshit. I guess, after five years in the league, I'd become kinda stereotyped.

"Finally, I peeped where Connie was at, how strong the dude is inside, the pride he has, what his 'game' means to him. He still has a lot of growing up to do. The lateness wasn't cool. But that got better, and he got smoother, too. Even the white boys came to respect him. But Hawk never stopped being himself."

No one in Phoenix knew how unsettling the first half of the season was for Connie. Like most black athletes, he has learned to mask his fears behind a cool, detached presence. In a nightclub crowd, Hawkins could appear confident, relaxed, thoroughly content with himself. After a game, he might needle a rookie in the locker room, exchange raucous reminiscences with friends waiting outside, but then slip back to his hotel room and spill out his doubts and disappointments to Nancy over the phone. His long-distance bill in Phoenix averaged almost five hundred dollars a month.

"Maybe," Jerry Colangelo was to concede, "John and I put too much pressure on Connie. He thought people expected him to walk on water."

Ignored for years, Hawk now lived under intense scrutiny. "If you're a real basketball fan," advised the Philadelphia *Daily News,* "come out to the Spectrum and judge for yourself. He wears No. 42. He's 'The Man.' " Hawkins had to put up or shut up, not only for the public, but for himself. He had to fulfill his own expectations, validate the self-image he had lived with since his late teens.

Playing in New York—the memories, the symbolism of the Garden, his friends and family in the stands—was more than he could handle. "It psyched me out," he admits. "Everybody I wanted to be impressive for was there. I was never so nervous." David Litman met him at the airport before his first game in the city. As they drove to the hotel, Connie opened the *Times,* saw his name in a headline, and burst into tears.

The Suns made three appearances at the Garden that season and were

routed each time. Hawk never played badly—he scored 27, 19, and 26—
but he never played *his* game. The Knicks, on their way to the championship, overmatched Phoenix at center and in the backcourt. Connie, aggressively guarded by Dave DeBusschere and harassed by New York's swarm-
ing defense, got little help from his teammates. He was always pressing,
trying too hard to please—yet sometimes retreating from the spotlight for
fear of failure.

Hawk's troubles would have been eased if he had seen the ball more regularly, but, there was no preoccupation with feeding him. Connie was
partly to blame. He wasn't always open. At times, he didn't move well
without the ball. "When he isn't moving," said Philadelphia's Jim Washington, "it isn't hard to keep it from him."

"However," Washington added, "they don't look for him much. A guy
with that potential, you'd think he'd get the ball more than he does."

But Kerr's offense wasn't programmed around Connie. The coach, although supposedly elated at gaining a superstar, didn't integrate Hawk's
special skills into the flow of the Phoenix attack.

Both backcourt starters overlooked Hawkins, but Connie felt Goodrich
was the primary culprit. "He dribbled too much," says Hawk. "Somebody'd get open, but Goody'd be so busy setting up his one-on-one moves,
he wouldn't notice till it was too late. I think he was tryin too hard to compete with me—to be the star. He'd take bad shots, force passes, try to do
things by himself. He made too many turnovers."

Goodrich also overdribbled on the fastbreak—missing numerous opportunities to feed Connie for swooping drives. Hawk was soon convinced
that Gail ignored him by design. "For a while, I wasn't sure," Hawkins
says. "I thought, 'Maybe he doesn't have peripheral vision.' Guys like Fox
and Walk missed me when I was open. But I wasn't mad, cause they just
couldn't see me. Gail was different. I watched what he threw to other people. If he didn't see me, it was cause he didn't want to."

When Hawkins first complained to Silas and Harris, their response was
evasive. "They didn't have confidence in me," he recalls. "Later, they
wanted me to have the ball. They'd check to see why I didn't. And they'd
see Gail lookin at everybody but me."

"You're right," Silas told Hawk in December. "That little dude's really
passin you up."

Even Connie's opponents sympathized. "It's nothing new," said Atlanta's Walt Hazzard, who played with Gail at UCLA. "He pulled that shit in
college."

"Goodrich is a loser," said one of the Celtics. "He hurts you the way Jo

Jo White hurts us. They're talented, but they want their twenty points first—then they'll see if you're open. It makes everybody go for himself."

Advised Milwaukee veteran Guy Rodgers, "You ought to punch Gail in the mouth."

Yet Goodrich seemed immune to criticism. "Kerr let him bounce it, or kick it, or spin it off his head," Connie claims. "Nobody knocked Goody."

Phoenix opened the season by edging San Diego, then promptly lost five of six. Fox was scoring well from medium range, the Suns dominated the backboards, but their defense was porous and their ballhandling horrendous. Turnovers led to every defeat.

Nervous and unsure of his knee, Hawkins still played respectably. But his passes were catching teammates unawares. "That made my game more hesitant," Connie says, "and I wasn't seein the ball much."

In Philadelphia, Hawk spoke out. He had scored 12 points in the first 16 minutes—then was ignored by the guards. He went scoreless the next 23 minutes and Phoenix lost by 3. "I definitely should be gettin the ball more," he told reporters without rancor, after the game. "I could contribute more if they were lookin for me. I think a team should go to its strength."

John Kerr hedged: "Connie should have the ball more—but it's a 50-50 thing. We aren't looking for him enough and he's not looking for the ball enough."

Said Goodrich: "I honestly wasn't aware it was a problem."

But the 76ers' All-Star forward, Billy Cunningham, thought the Suns were spiting themselves by not emphasizing Hawk. "He'll give them the ball every time," he said. "Once you get it to Hawkins, then you move. He'll get it back to you."

A week later the Suns discovered what Cunningham meant. Hawkins blocked a Cincinnati shot, retrieved the ball, and started a fastbreak. At midcourt in full stride, he faked left, then flipped a blindside pass to Chambers on his right.

Chambers returned the ball. Hawk dribbled behind his back, pulled up fifteen feet from the hoop, faked a jumper—and whipped a pass between his scissored legs to Silas, alone under the basket. Paul blew the layup. But Connie darted inside, ripped a one-handed rebound from 6′ 10″ Connie Dierking and, in the same movement, tossed the ball over his shoulder to Goodrich. Gail canned a five-foot shot.

With 16 seconds remaining, and the score 104-104, Goodrich inbounded to Hawkins at midcourt. Connie spun past a defender, slithered down the lane, and rose toward the hoop. Two Royals leapt with him—and Hawk dumped a soft pass to the unguarded Neal Walk. The rookie scored the winning basket.

"He's a tremendous threat," said Cincinnati coach Bob Cousy, once king of the playmakers. "Hawkins has floormanship—and a team can't win without it."

Connie's confidence grew. The Knicks slaughtered the Suns in Phoenix, but Hawk, moving with less pain, scored 39 points. Neither DeBusschere nor Dave Stallworth, who fouled out, could contain him. In Los Angeles, he hit for 21 as McKenzie scored on a last-second rebound and Phoenix won, 122-120.

Back at the Coliseum, Hawkins personally demolished the Detroit Pistons. He went to the hoop with force and unfurled for 35 points. Phoenix won, 140-129. The Suns had taken three of four. They were just one game under .500.

"I felt great in the locker room," Hawk recalls. "I was showin what I could do. The guys were lookin at me different—with respect. And I hadn't felt real pain in my knee all night. I hadn't moved so good since I got hurt."

In the shower, Silas playfully bounced a soap bar off Connie's shoulder. "You were doin it out there, Hawk," he shouted. "You were beautiful!"

"I didn't feel no pain, man," Connie said, unable to stifle a smile. "My leg is ready. *I'm* ready."

The euphoria lasted four days.

Before the Suns met Philadelphia at home, Kerr diagrammed a 3-1-1 zone press. "This should surprise them," he announced.

"Their guards handle the ball too good," Silas told Hawkins, as they walked to the court. "We don't have the speed to press 'em."

The press not only surprised, but also delighted, the 76ers. Hal Greer, Wally Jones, and Archie Clark zoomed through Kerr's brainstorm for a torrent of unmolested layups.

Playing in the front line of the press, Connie found himself chasing smaller guards. He had little success. On offense, he was even less successful. Philadelphia assigned Matt Guokas, a wiry, 6' 5" benchwarmer, to set up in front of him in the corner and low post. The 76ers' center and weakside forward dropped off to help when the Suns tried to lob passes over Guokas. Hawk rarely saw the ball.

When Connie made several quick moves to dodge the clinging Guokas, he felt the ache return to his knee. When few passes reached him, he got disgusted and stopped moving. He scored only one field goal in the first half. The 76ers exploited the press to roll up a 72-58 lead.

"John, you got to take off the press," Silas implored at halftime. "They're passing too quick. They're gettin too many layups."

"You guys just aren't doing it right," Kerr persisted. "Stay with it. It can work."

They stayed with it—and it didn't work.

But Connie brought the Suns back in the second half. Pushing himself, ignoring the pain, he eluded Guokas to score 13 points in 16 minutes. Phoenix drew within 2.

In the fourth quarter, however, Philadelphia replaced Guokas with taller, stronger Jim Washington. By then, Hawkins was tired. The pain had increased. The guards suddenly looked elsewhere, and Connie didn't score in the last eight minutes of the game.

"Our stupid press had wore me down. Then Washington overpowered me," he remembers. "I tried a couple of shots, but I missed bad. I didn't feel agile. I couldn't do *anything*. I got this heavy feeling of flustration and my mind just drifted out of the game."

Philadelphia won, 124-110. The Suns' locker room was silent. Hawk slumped on a bench and stared at the floor. Beside him, Silas grumbled, "We could have won, if that dumb coach didn't fuck us up."

Kerr entered the room, his face crimson. "Shit," he cried, thrusting his arms over his head. "You tell me! What's wrong out there? We came back, we were close, we could have won. I want to know! What's wrong?"

The coach's gaze moved among the tight-lipped players. There was no response. Kerr turned and walked out. "He knows he blew it," said Silas.

But Connie wasn't thinking of John Kerr. "Paul," he said, "my leg's hurtin again. It ain't healed like I thought."

"Easy Hawk. You're gonna be all right."

"I don' know, man," Hawkins sighed, "I don' feel like it's ever gonna come back."

Late that night, alone in his apartment, Connie phoned his wife. "I'm messin up," he told her. "I'm just not playin good. These guys ain't into my passes. Everybody expected more than this."

For over an hour, Nancy tried to console him. But Hawk couldn't shake his depression. "I was crushed," he says. "I'd built myself up after those good games. I'd felt I was all right—cause I wanted so bad to believe it. Now I felt I'd *never* be right."

He opened a bottle of Cold Duck and drank himself to sleep.

Phoenix lost to the Lakers the following evening, and Hawk played badly again. The Suns then rebounded to beat Los Angeles and Atlanta. Connie shot well—scoring 23 and 29—but he remained dispirited. "Most guys were talkin it up," he recalls. "But our offense still wasn't together. I knew I wasn't movin good. I wasn't gonna let myself get too high."

Hawkins's skepticism proved well-founded. The team traveled to the East coast and collapsed, plunging into a seven-game losing streak.

Against Boston, the Suns blew a five-point lead in 72 seconds. The following night, Hawkins was humiliated by Baltimore's Gus Johnson. It was the worst game of his professional career. He couldn't shake Johnson's tight defense. When he got the ball, he forced bad shots. Johnson jostled him around like a rag doll, whipped him constantly on the boards, and drove through him for easy layups. Then, Gus added insult to injury, turning on the crowd with some Hawkins-style Globetrotter tricks.

Frustrated and embarrassed, Connie became lethargic. Early in the second half Kerr benched him. Hawk finished with just 7 points and 4 rebounds. Johnson scored 21 and had 18 rebounds as Baltimore coasted, 133-118.

For several minutes no one spoke to Hawkins in the locker room. Then Silas approached him. "You played a fucked-up game, man," he said, visibly angry. "You were bad."

"I know," Connie snapped. "I couldn't get involved. There wasn't nothing I could do." Silas shook his head and walked away.

"I was mad at Paul," says Hawkins, "cause I knew he was right. I was ashamed of myself."

Recalls Silas, "After that game, some guys felt that Connie just didn't have it for the NBA, that if somebody stuck his chest against him, Connie couldn't do his thing. Everyone was disgusted with him."

"When they get around to filming The Connie Hawkins Story," wrote Joe Gilmartin, "they should sign Gus Johnson to play the lead."

Two nights later, Hawk geared himself for a rematch with Johnson, drove aggressively on Gus, forced him into early foul trouble, and outscored him 20-10. But his teammates played badly and were routed again.

The Suns' tailspin continued at Madison Square Garden, where the Knicks won with ease. Connie reverted to his listless play. He took just 11 shots, and seemed to be moving in slow motion.

"Why isn't he shooting more?" I asked Kerr that night.

"You can't reach him," the coach said bitterly.

When the dressing room had emptied, I told Connie, "You're playing the whole game as though you've got five personals. You're still protecting the knee. You aren't playing like the guy I saw last year."

"I know," he said, looking away. "I just don' want to talk about it now."

Hawk's performance improved in the next few games. But the team kept losing. Fox's shooting touch had deserted him. Walk's play was erratic. The backcourt continued to throw the ball away. Silas's rebounding fell off.

Goodrich took even more bad shots and, wrote Joe Gilmartin, was "looking good in the box score and bad on the court." The bench contributed little. Only Van Arsdale was consistently effective, and even Van committed too many turnovers.

"The Suns," noted Dave Hicks in the *Arizona Republic,* were "threatening Seattle for last place."

The atmosphere on the club became tense. "When you're losin," says Hawkins, "guys tend to get on each others' nerves. We had a lot of bitchin and gripin. Guys complained about Kerr and Goodrich and—I guess, when I wasn't around—about me."

While the team was winning, Hawkins, Silas, Chambers, and Harris usually ate together on the road. Now they were eating alone—often in their rooms. The once-noisy locker-room was quiet. Players changed quickly and left by themselves.

"Everyone was edgy," notes Connie. "People would get bugged by little things that didn't bother them when we won."

One night, when Goodrich tried to advise Walk on his defensive play, the rookie flared, "You haven't been so hot on defense yourself."

When Silas thought Van Arsdale had told Gilmartin that Paul was dribbling too much, he telephoned captain Goodrich at home and warned, "Tell Dick he better not talk to reporters about me again!"

"Neil Johnson used to sit in front of his locker like he was in a trance," Connie recalls. "One time, Fox and Walk came up behind him and hollered, 'Boo!' Johnson jumped a mile. They were just kiddin. But Neil got real mad. He kicked 'em in the ass."

The veterans' resentment of Walk's huge bonus also surfaced. Walk told Connie he felt none of the white players liked him. In the locker room, Johnson cracked, "You're some bonus baby. You got all that money—and you aren't worth it!"

Hawk's relationship with Goodrich continued to deteriorate. Gail was averaging more shots per game than Connie. Several times, Hawk told Colangelo that the little guard was intentionally freezing him out. But Jerry refused to believe it. "I don't think Gail is selfish," Colangelo told the press. "But being the competitor that he is, he has a tendency to try and bring the club back by himself when it's down on the scoreboard."

"In warmups, me and Gail were supposed to rebound for each other," Connie remembers. "Kerr had made us a pair. But Gail wasn't throwin my ball back to me. So I looked the other way when *he* shot."

Silas, McKenzie, and Harris were also complaining about Goodrich. In fact, a degree of racial tension had emerged on the team.

The Suns' troubles were neither momentous nor unique. Most NBA clubs have some black-white friction. The racial climate of the larger society—and the differing backgrounds, philosophies, and interests of black and white players—almost guarantees some suspicions, misunderstandings, and dislikes.

Because black superstars dominate the game, however, there is less discrimination in pro basketball than in any other major-league sport. But the black players—sometimes as an excuse for their own failures, sometimes with justification—still maintain they are not always accorded equal treatment with the whites. "The teams, and the NBA itself, want to build up whites as drawing cards," asserts a black player. "Even the referees aren't color-blind. They'll call the little things faster on us. It's a superstar's league, but they protect the white stars—like Havlicek, Lucas, and West— more than the black."

"Dave DeBusschere is allowed to be a little more physical on defense than a black guy could," claims another black. "People like Jerry Sloan can draw charging fouls by falling down. We can't. Jeff Mullins is protected. But the refs don't like Billy Cunningham. He's white, but he plays like a black man—schoolyard—so they don't dig him."

In Phoenix, the complaints were typical. Paul and Connie believed the team went out of its way to praise and publicize Van Arsdale and Goodrich. They resented Gail being named captain. "Coaches and front-office people are more sensitive about white players' feelings," says Hawk. "It figures. They used to be white players themselves, so they identify more. Like John Kerr: he'd yell at a black guy faster than he'd yell at a white guy. Gail would make a stupid play and wouldn't nothing be said. Van had all these chargin fouls, sometimes in bad situations, but Kerr didn't criticize him. But if *I* made a stupid foul, he'd jump ten feet off the bench, attract attention to me, and yell, 'What are you doing, Hawkins?' Same with Paul and Arthur and Lamar."

The black players also thought Kerr and Colangelo were less sympathetic to their injuries. "We're supposed to be supermen," Silas complains. "If a white boy is hurt, they don't doubt him. Fox didn't play because of a cold. Nobody said a thing. But they think unless we're in the hospital, we should just forget the pain.

"Later in the season, I was told by a doctor that I had a bone spur in my elbow," Paul adds. "The pain was killin me, but I played that night. Jerry thought I was *too cautious*, that I was protectin the elbow too much. After the game, he said, 'I shouldn't have let the doctor tell you about the bone spur.' That was too much! It was like the only reason I thought I was in pain was because the doctor said so."

In the Suns' locker room, two tape recorders played simultaneously. One blasted Otis Redding, the other Credence Clearwater. On planes and buses, the blacks sat close together, usually in the back. Neil Johnson was the only white player who regularly joined their card games.

There was little interracial socializing when the team traveled. "At night, we were never with the white guys," Connie recalls. "They don't eat soul food. They don't dance. We don't drink beer. There was nothing in common."

Black NBA players tend to have more active sex lives on the road, partially because the white athlete's profession and income does not command comparable status and notoriety among his own people. Black players also have a greater sense of community. Opponents are more likely to get together after games. Reciprocal introductions are commonplace. In addition, the female camp-followers display more interest in the blacks. On some clubs, black players believe this makes their white teammates jealous or resentful.

For instance, the already shaky rapport between the black star and white star of a certain NBA team wasn't improved when a white girl, who regularly slept with the black man, told him that his white teammate had said, "Why does a girl like you screw Negroes? The only thing they do well is play basketball. They don't have IQ's like us. And the ones that do—those are the Negroes that have some white blood in them."

"On our team," says Silas, "there wasn't any deep racial trouble. A lot of it was misunderstanding because of the coach. We weren't close to the white boys. When we found out Kerr was drinking buddies with some of them, it made us feel he favored them."

The coach often drank with Van Arsdale and Johnson. Sometimes, Goodrich and other white players joined them. "We felt that's why Johnny didn't criticize them more," notes Hawkins. "And we felt he would have played Stan and Arthur more if they weren't black. Kerr didn't seem to want them in the game at the same time."

The newspapers called the coach "Red" Kerr. Some black Suns began calling him "Redneck" Kerr.

Although most white players liked Kerr personally, it developed that many shared the blacks' low opinion of his coaching talents. The rookies were concerned about the absence of advice and instruction. The veterans thought Kerr substituted badly and made poor use of the bench. He wasn't giving Hawkins enough rest. Connie was wearing down toward the end of many games.

McKenzie and Harris didn't hide their bitterness. "We give him good defense every time," Stan griped. "But Redneck always wants *his* boys, Van and Gail, in the game."

Kerr still hadn't gotten around to giving the Suns any in-bounds plays or set-patterns for the final seconds of a game. "In a home-court victory over Cincinnati," wrote the perceptive Gilmartin, "they had to call time-out twice to complete one pass. In Los Angeles, they got off a terrible shot but had the miss bounce right to them [McKenzie] for a winning basket."

They weren't always so fortunate. Against Boston, the Suns had seventeen seconds to set up a shot with the score tied in regulation time. "Kerr did his mumbling thing in the huddle," Hawkins recalls. "We had nothing arranged." Goodrich wound up missing a desperation heave, and Phoenix lost in overtime.

On several occasions, Kerr became confused over the number of team fouls Phoenix had—and took one more than he should have. This gave their opponents extra foul-shots and eventually cost the Suns a game.

The coach was unable—or unwilling—to enforce discipline. Connie wasn't the only player coming late to practices. "But Kerr wouldn't fine people," Silas emphasizes. "He was weak. Our morale broke down."

Kerr threatened to fine Jerry Chambers two hundred dollars unless he lost ten pounds in a week. Chambers made no effort. Seven days later his weight was unchanged. But the coach didn't fine him.

Johnson showed up for a road game with his white home uniform, explaining "my wife packed the wrong one." This was supposed to be an automatic $150 fine. Kerr did nothing.

"We had no curfew," recalls McKenzie. "A couple of times Johnny said, 'Be in by midnight.' But he didn't check our rooms. He was probably out drinking."

As the losses multiplied, Kerr became morose. There were no more jokes in the locker room. "But," says Connie, "he never got his coachin thing together."

When Kerr privately implored Hawkins to take more shots, Connie responded, "I've got to have the ball."

"I'll take care of that," said the coach.

"You got to name names," Hawkins stressed. "Tell Gail and Van to pass it to me."

"I will," Kerr promised.

But he didn't. "He'd say things like, 'Let's pass it to the man who's hot,' " says Connie. "But he wouldn't say *who*."

When Kerr spoke in the huddle, the players' attention wandered. They gazed into the stands or stared at their feet. Once, Hawkins became so annoyed with the coach's inane instructions, he sat by himself at the far end of the bench. "Come here," Kerr said. "You won't be able to hear me."

Hawk ambled back to the huddle and slouched, arms folded, while the coach rattled on.

"It looks bad for the fans," Colangelo admonished in the dressing room.

"I'm tryin to get my head into the game," Hawk replied. "But his talk just gets me flustrated. The other guys feel the same as me."

"But they don't *show* it," said Jerry. "You can't be so obvious."

Several times, however, Connie moved two or three seats away from the huddle—and Kerr left him alone.

By mid-November, the Suns' owners were urging Colangelo to find a new coach. Rumors swirled that the position had been offered to Alex Hannum and that Kerr planned to resign.

"The worst thing," Colangelo said later, "was that there was no sign of improvement."

Nevertheless, Colangelo tried desperately to save his fraternity brother's job. "Jerry was around the team a lot more," remembers Hawkins. "He seemed real tense. He kept buggin me and Paul to become leaders, to pull the players together. But we knew the white guys would resent it. Anyway, it was Jerry that made Goodrich captain!"

Phoenix blew an 18-point lead—and its seventh straight game—when Chambers, trying to run out the clock, lost his dribble to Seattle's Tom Meschery. As the Suns watched helplessly, Meschery sank an unmolested layup to give the Sonics a 130-129 victory.

On the bus to the airport, Colangelo interrupted the players' grumbling. "I want to introduce you to Scotty McDonald," he said, nodding toward a small, well-dressed, fiftyish man who stood beside him. "Scotty has a great basketball background. He'll be helping John from now on."

"Ain't that some shit," Silas said to Hawkins. "If I wasn't doin *my* job, you think they'd bring in some dude to help me? I'd be gone!"

"They gonna keep Kerr no matter what," nodded Connie. "This new guy ain't gonna help us."

Hawk was wrong. Edwin A. "Scotty" McDonald would help the Suns considerably. The prime beneficiary would be Connie Hawkins.

In esoteric basketball circles, the fifty-three-year-old McDonald was considered one of the game's most astute—if unconventional—minds. He was an attorney by profession: assistant general counsel of the U.S. Borax Corporation. But basketball was his passion.

McDonald had coached Loyola University of Los Angeles and numerous AAU teams. He was an assistant coach with the Los Angeles Jets in the old

ABL. For fifteen years he scouted for the NBA Hawks. He also did scouting for more than a dozen colleges and was on the board of directors of the National Association of Basketball Coaches.

Although his courtside manner was often eccentric—as the Suns would soon discover—Scotty was known as a genius in defensive tactics and a superb teacher. Many top coaches called and wrote him for advice. As a "consultant" to the Suns, he would commute regularly from Los Angeles, attend many Phoenix home games and practices, and counsel Kerr.

Hiring McDonald was an obvious commentary on Kerr. But Colangelo could no longer worry about ruffled sensibilities. Scotty was there, in his own words, "for one purpose only: to help save John Kerr's job."

McDonald made an immediate contribution. Before the Suns met Seattle the following evening in Phoenix, he convinced Kerr to use Van Arsdale against Lennie Wilkens. The Sonics' player-coach had run rings around Goodrich. But Van kept him from penetrating the Suns' defense. This slowed Seattle's attack and helped Phoenix snap its losing streak, 116-108.

Hawkins, however, was the deciding factor. Late in the game, with Phoenix ahead 99-98, he quickly hit two free throws, grabbed a defensive rebound, then scored a twisting baseline drive to give his teammates some breathing room. He finished with 15 points in the fourth quarter and a total of 26.

"I was startin to feel confidence in him again," says Silas.

Before the next game, against Chicago in Salt Lake City, Goodrich ordered the locker room cleared for a players-only meeting. "We've got to talk things out," the captain said.

The Suns exchanged frank, constructive criticism for over an hour. "We went through every phase of our game," Van Arsdale said later. "There were no fights, but we pointed out each others' mistakes and suggested everyone of us could put out a little more than he had been."

Paul was urged to dribble less and station himself closer to the basket. Arthur was reminded to cut down foolish fouls, Van to be more aware of charging violations, and Fox to get tougher on the boards.

Although the atmosphere was tense, no voices were raised. Most criticisms were cautious, delicately phrased. When Gail knocked Harris, he was quick to add, "I know I'm not playing the best defense in the league, either."

But when Goodrich turned toward Hawkins, Connie sensed a different tone. "Hawk, I don't know what makes you tick! I just don't know," Gail lashed, emotion building suddenly in his voice. "Sometimes you play like you're worth a million dollars. Sometimes, you don't try at all. I don't know what's wrong with you. What makes you tick?"

A chilly silence fell over the room. Players shifted uneasily. "Gail had gone too far," Silas recalls. "Some of what he said was right. But he wasn't justified in the way he said it. Connie can take criticism about his playing. But Gail was puttin him down as a *man*. You don't do that to a black man, not in front of the other ballplayers. Who the hell is Goodrich to tell Connie he doesn't know what makes him tick? He's *nobody!*"

Struggling to keep his composure, Hawk stared coldly at Goodrich. When he finally spoke, his words were flat, dispassionate. "I know I got to hustle more," Connie said. "I'm workin on it. But I think I could help the club more if you guys looked for me a little sooner."

Hawkins remembers, "Inside, I was mad. I wanted to hit him, right there. No white motherfucker talks to me like that. Not bad as he was playin. But I didn't want to bust up the meeting."

The session continued. Hawk even provoked some laughter. Moments after Silas admonished the rookies for never speaking up, Walk asked a silly question about his own assignment in an obscure play. "If that's all you got to say," Connie cracked, "I see why you haven't been participatin."

But when the meeting ended, Hawkins was still seething. He waited until most of the players had left to warm up. Then he approached Goodrich, who was lacing his sneakers by a row of lockers.

"I want to talk to you."

"What's up, Hawk?" Gail said innocently, rising to his feet.

Hawkins stepped closer. Their bodies were inches apart. Goodrich's mouth opened slightly as he looked up into Connie's narrowed eyes.

Hawk sensed that Gail knew how close they were to a fight.

"Hey, you little motherfucker," Connie said in a whispered growl, "don't you worry about what makes me tick. It's not for *you* to know what makes me tick. Next time Goody, next time you talk to me like that, I'm gonna punch you in your motherfuckin mouth!"

Gail lowered his eyes, seemed about to speak, then pivoted away from Hawkins and hurried from the room.

The Suns crushed Chicago that night. Van Arsdale hit for 38 points. Hawkins, his elbows flashing around the boards, scored 19 and took 15 rebounds. Gail found him with several snappy passes. Every Phoenix player performed well. As suddenly as their slump had begun, it was over.

During the next two weeks, the Suns were the hottest team in the NBA. They won seven of nine and plowed back into playoff contention.

Spirits rose with the victory total. Laughter returned to the locker room, friendships were revived and the black players forgot about Kerr's drinking companions. The coach recaptured his sense of humor. For good luck, he wore the same sport coat and slacks four games in a row. "The outfit," Kerr joked, "smells better with each win."

Emotional momentum fed on itself. The Suns' play became fiery, aggressive, and confident. Their togetherness extended to the court. They looked for the open man and helped each other on defense.

Most startling was the transformation of Gail Goodrich. Suddenly, Gail was the playmaker everyone hoped he would become. He directed the offense with authority, reduced his turnovers, kept scoring, but rarely forced a bad shot. "Goody was settin guys up fantastic," Hawkins remembers. "He was even passin to *me.*"

One night in the locker room, after Gail had played exceptionally well, Silas said to Connie, "The dude's been different. He should know we see it."

Goodrich and Hawkins had exchanged a few words since their confrontation in Salt Lake City. Apprehension crossed Gail's face when he saw Paul and Connie standing above him. "You were great, Goody," Hawkins said, smiling and reaching to shake his hand. "Man, you're the quarterback now."

"Yeah Goody," Silas added, "you're really impressive. We can dig what you're doin."

Goodrich seemed relieved. He grinned and slapped Connie's hip. "Thanks," he said. "Thanks a lot. Really. I think I can do this every night. This club is going somewhere now."

"Right on," said Hawk.

Hawkins's performances, meanwhile, were so exciting, so filled with flash and dash, only those who had watched him before the injury knew he still wasn't at his peak. During the nine-game stretch, he averaged over 23 points and shot 60 percent from the field. More important, Hawk took charge in crucial situations.

For the first time, Kerr was allowing him an adequate breather, usually in the second quarter. Playing about forty minutes a game, Connie no longer sagged in the stretch. "I had the ball more," Hawkins says. "My knee was better, too. There was still pain—Proski had to give me pills— but it hurt less. And my mind was better. I didn't think as much about reinjuring it. There were things I couldn't do like before, but I wouldn't let it bother me as much.

"Part of the reason was Scotty," Hawk adds. "He'd given the whole team a winnin feeling."

Scotty McDonald had brought to the Suns a fascinating combination of basketball theory, sixth-grade rah-rahism, and uninhibited guerrilla theater. He introduced the young, inexperienced club to the basics of "team" defense, explaining how, while still playing man-to-man, they could cover for each other and place extra pressure on the ball. The Knicks already employed such tactics with great success, but it was something new in Phoenix.

"Scotty showed us how the strongside forward can overplay his man, if he knows the weakside forward has sloughed off in the center to protect him against a 'backdoor' play," Hawkins says. "He gave us basketball awareness and helped a lot of guys with special advice. He helped our whole defense."

McDonald also prepared detailed scouting reports—the first the Suns received that season. "When Loughery is guarded by a tough man on his dribble," Scotty would note, "he will start left, then turn back and come toward the middle with right-handed dribble to quickly take jumper—remember—he will come toward middle!"

Not all Scotty's printed offerings were as mundane. McDonald was, by his own proud admission, "old-fashioned." He saw athletic events as majestic confrontations, athletes as holy warriors, and victory as the only worthy goal. Thus, along with the scouting reports, he inundated the Suns with such mimeographed wisdom as "The 13 Principles of Bench Behavior" and "The 30 Commandments of Defense." One of the Bench Principles stated:

I—I no longer exists as "I," because I became part of "we" and we are part of "us." Us is the name of our ball club—and our ball club consists of two groups (five guys on the court) and you (the guys on the bench), but both groups are US.

As a successful, full-time attorney, Scotty may have been dabbling in basketball "for the giggles," but he approached his consultant responsibilities with messianic fervor. When the Suns were on the road, he called players long-distance and wrote them letters almost every day.

Lacking an official coaching title, McDonald was prohibited by league rules from sitting on the bench. Undaunted, he rushed about the arena, charging along the courtside, screaming instructions to the athletes, as he played musical chairs with any seat he could find. Patrons often returned from the concession stand to find their place occupied by a wild-eyed bespectacled stranger, yelling: "Be aggressive Neal! Out further Connie! Ferocious! We must be ferocious!"

When Scotty felt his message wasn't getting through, he dispatched incredulous ushers to the huddle with handwritten notes like, "Will someone please tell Mr. Hawkins that Mr. Cunningham is left-handed!"

McDonald's teaching methods were also a bit unorthodox. He thought nothing of removing his shirt and rolling about on the floor as he lectured. All instructions were delivered with magnificent overstatement and melo-drama.

"This team," Scotty told the Suns at his first practice with them, "has no offense, no defense, and no continuity. However, every once in a while, as I watched you lose to Seattle, I had a glimpse of something grand. You have great individual talent. But you must become cohesive. A unit. You must learn to trust and feel and share with each other. You must build a faith, an *undying faith,* in your teammates and your team."

No dramatization was too graphic, if it helped McDonald make a point. At the St. Mary's High School gym, where the Suns practiced, he seated the players in the bleachers and instructed Silas and Green to join him on the court.

"Now," Scotty announced, "Paul, you will be Lamar's 'husband.' You stand way over there, under the basket. Lamar, lie down."

The rookie from Birmingham hesitated, then stretched out uncertainly on the floor.

"Paul, I'm your wife's lover," Scotty explained. "I'm in her boudoir. I'll proceed to whisper sweet nothings in her ear."

As the players began to chuckle, McDonald seated himself on the court, beside the prone Lamar, and removed his shoes and socks. Green, wearing only a sweatshirt and shorts, giggled and eyed him apprehensively.

"Now remember," Scotty continued, unbuttoning his shirt. "I'm whis-pering sweet nothings in your wife's ear."

"I don' think I wanna be no wife," said Lamar, attempting to sit up.

"You *are* the wife," repeated Scotty, pushing Green down and holding a forearm across his chest. "You are very beautiful, Lamar." Laughter echoed through the gym. Connie felt tears on his cheeks.

Still discussing "sweet nothings," Scotty unzipped his slacks and low-ered them to his knees. Then, as Lamar's eyes widened, McDonald knelt beside him. "O.K. Paul," he cried, moving as though to mount the 6' 7" Green, "you can come into the room now."

Silas walked toward them, but Scotty suddenly bounced to his feet, licked his lips, and cried: "It's too late! Too late! I've already been *in there!*"

Paul threw his hands over his face and roared. The other Suns were laughing so hard the bleachers shook. Lamar jumped up and sprinted away. He didn't look back at Scotty until he was five rows up in the stands.

"You see," cried McDonald, above the noise, his slacks still bunched at his ankles, "that proves what I'm trying to show you. On defense, if you concede your man his normal area of operations, it's too late. If a man like

Jerry West can murder you from a certain spot, you've got to anticipate it—and beat him to that spot. If he arrives ahead of you, it's *too late*. He'll do what he wants. See?"

The Suns remained a weak defensive team, but even in a few practices Scotty improved them considerably. "He got us thinkin about each other, workin together," says Hawkins. "He also helped our confidence. He made us feel we could be winners. And, I think, some of his emotionalism got to us too."

While all the Suns respected his knowledge, McDonald had a better rapport with the blacks. Some white players found Scotty's passionate pregame exhortations ludicrous and juvenile. After Kerr's bland, generalized criticism, they were also annoyed by McDonald's blunt, often disparaging critiques. Scotty made no effort, for example, to hide his dislike for Goodrich. "Gail still plays like the spoiled brat he was as a kid," he told Hawkins.

Under most circumstances, McDonald's coaching philosophy would have endeared him even less to the blacks. Scotty saw the players as "boys" and "kids" and, as he once wrote to a coach, "I never believe in letting kids do things—I like to make them do it; it is the only way." Happy to lecture and advise, he had no patience with disagreement.

Nevertheless, the black players gravitated to him. Unlike Kerr and Colangelo, Scotty made them feel appreciated. He was most vocal and expansive about Hawkins and Silas, but he had kind words for every black player. "We all thought the world of him, especially in the beginning," says Paul. "Scotty paid most of his attention to us. We felt—and I think the white guys did too—that Scotty liked us better."

McDonald's overbearing manner occasionally angered Silas. They quarreled over defensive tactics. But Paul sensed that Scotty—in his own way—felt real affection for him. "Big Paul, my fat forward," McDonald would say, "you should be the captain of this team."

It was Hawkins, however, who felt most strongly about Scotty. "I liked his style," says Hawk. "He was outspoken. He had a don't-give-a-damn attitude. And he cared so much about the game. I never met anyone who could explain things like him. He'd talk basketball with you twenty-four hours a day. He was a beautiful man."

The feeling was mutual. McDonald saw Hawkins as an unpolished gem. "I am in love with him," Scotty wrote to a friend. "He is quite a human being, and a great basketball player—if I ever get a real chance to devote time and energy to it, he will be the best that ever played the game. That is bragging quite a bit—but truly not—because he's the one with the God-given talent."

McDonald showered Hawk with praise—something Connie had received little of in Phoenix—at a time when his confidence was shaky. "He made me feel a lot better about myself," says Hawkins.

Scotty also worked to improve Connie's defense. "Right now," McDonald told him in front of the entire team, "you are known as the worst defensive player in the NBA. But it needn't be. You have the talent, the reflexes—all you need is the training."

"You aren't physical enough," Scotty would stress. "You give your man too much room. You make foolish errors, you turn your head looking for the ball, and you lose your man. Study him, know his moves. Learn what he does best, then overplay him to take that away."

In truth, however, the bad habits were too deeply ingrained. Hawkins would never become an accomplished defender. After years of playing center on defense—or no defense at all—Connie would always have trouble staying with shifty forwards away from the boards. But he did improve. With Scotty's help, he made fewer glaring errors. He blocked more shots and made more steals.

"But the biggest thing Scotty did for me was just bein there," Hawkins says. "He was somebody I could go to for advice—somebody who respected me. We'd sit and talk in the locker room after every game. Maybe I let him talk down to me too much. But I felt he really liked me. It was so long since I'd had a coach who could teach, I just went overboard sayin, 'Tell me more.' "

There was no apparent friction between McDonald and Kerr. Big John was just happy the Suns were winning. "Overall, I think Scotty's helped us quite a bit," Kerr noted. "But I told him I won't be a puppet."

December 12, the Suns belted Seattle, 130-116. The victory raised their record to 13 wins and 17 losses and moved them into a fourth-place tie with Los Angeles. Once more, Hawkins was the driving force. With the score tied, 87-87, he blocked a shot by 6' 9" center Bob Rule, ignited a fastbreak, and hit Chambers with a behind-the-back pass for an easy layup. Seattle missed its next shot. Hawkins grabbed the rebound, dribbled over midcourt, and swished a long jumper. He finished with 37 points and 9 assists.

Said Sonic captain Tom Meschery, "Hawkins is everything they say. He can really shoot, but I think he honestly looks for the pass first. It's an admirable quality."

The next evening, Phoenix routed Cincinnati. Hawk scored 22. Joe Proski, a fanatical Packer rooter whose father is head groundskeeper in Green Bay, emerged from his training room to bestow the ultimate compliment. "You guys," he said, "are playin like the *official* Green Bay Packers. I can see paydirt comin!"

The players cheered.

"Fourth place," Silas marveled later that night. "Hawk, I ain't jivin, this club could go all the way!"

Phoenix lost six of its next seven games.

The skid began with a coaching error. Kerr once more bungled the "bonus" foul rule. In regulation play, each foul after the fourth carries a bonus shot. But, in overtime, it's each foul after the *third*. With the Suns leading Cincinnati by 5 and eighty-six seconds remaining in overtime, Kerr ordered Goodrich to foul deliberately. John thought he had one to "waste." He didn't. Phoenix already had three fouls in the overtime. The Royals hit the bonus shot, went on to tie the game, and won in the second overtime. A 37-point night by Hawkins was wasted.

Kerr stormed into the locker room shouting, "It was my fault! All right, all right, it was my fault! But the guy at the scorers' table said we only had *two* fouls."

"I guess the players believed him," Connie shrugs.

Two nights later, Philadelphia routed Phoenix by 22. The Suns' teamwork and harmony disappeared. The defense, despite Scotty's lung-bursting pleas from the sidelines, was awful. When the officials accused the 76ers of playing an illegal zone defense, Gilmartin wrote, "It was a charge to which the Suns would have been delighted to plead guilty. Indeed, the Suns would have been gratified to have been accused of playing any kind of defense."

"All of a sudden, everything went back to bad," Hawkins recalls. "We made awful mistakes. Guys were arguin. Goody stopped playmakin. He tried to save the team all by himself and he started holdin out on me again."

Kerr was soon panicky and irascible. He made little use of his bench. Hawk's playing time increased. Although Connie still scored well, he was again tired and ineffective in the final minutes.

The complaints about Hawkins's tardiness resumed. When he entered a meeting ten minutes late, Kerr screamed, "We're losing because of *you*, because you won't come on time!"

The local papers pictured the Suns as battling to save Kerr's job. Actually, the substitutes were bitching, Hawk was nagging Kerr for the ball, and Silas was telling Colangelo to "find us a new coach."

Several days before Christmas, Goodrich called a meeting and announced, "Last year, everyone chipped in some money to get the coach and the trainer a present. I'll start at twenty dollars."

Johnson and Van Arsdale nodded passively. The black players were mum. "Well," Gail asked, "what do you guys think?"

Silas shook his head: "Man, I'm not gonna give twenty dollars to *that* coach."

"Why not?" Goodrich stammered. "We did it last year."

"Fuck last year," shouted McKenzie. "I'm not givin that dude twenty dollars!"

"If I have to give twenty dollars," said Harris, "I want to give five dollars to Kerr and fifteen dollars to Proski. Joe does more for me than him."

They finally agreed on ten dollar donations—divided equally between the trainer and the coach. "Damn," Gail said to Harris after the meeting, "I didn't know *you* guys felt that way about him!"

"We always thought the whites liked Kerr as a coach," Connie laughs sadly. "But it turned out most of them felt the same as us. But they'd thought *we* liked him."

Hawkins scored 31 and 37 in the final games before New Year's, 1970. But a bickering, disorganized Phoenix team was routed by New York and Seattle. The Sonics forced 28 turnovers.

The Suns' record had slipped to 15 wins and 23 losses. They were in fifth place, $9\frac{1}{2}$ games out of first, 2 out of fourth, and skidding rapidly.

After a practice New Year's Day, Gail informed them of a meeting at 11:00 A.M. the following morning. The players arrived grumbling. They were to play San Diego that night—and meetings had ceased to be popular.

"More bullshit," said Silas.

Then Jerry Colangelo, his narrow features pinched and tired, opened the locker-room door. For a moment, he seemed to hesitate in the doorway, staring at the players. "Good morning," he said stiffly. "Everybody take a seat."

The Suns knew this was not to be an ordinary meeting.

"I'm going to lay my cards right on the table," said the general manager. "I hope you guys do the same. I'm going to get very personal."

Colangelo lit a second cigarette and turned to Neil Johnson. "Right now, tell me, are you putting out one hundred percent all the time?"

"When I play," Johnson answered glumly.

Jerry's gaze moved about the room. Each player was asked, "Are you giving one hundred percent?" Each answer was affirmative—until Hawkins's.

"No," said Connie.

"What?"

"No."

"Why?" Colangelo shot back. "At least you're being honest, but *why* aren't you putting out?"

"I put out," Connie said, annoyance building in his voice. "But maybe not always one hundred percent. I try. But I get confused by these idiotic situations. I get flustrated when I'm passin the ball and hittin somebody in the back of the head. And the coach, man, he don't ever get you up."

"But some games you hardly shot," replied Colangelo. "Personal pride should make you shoot more than eight or nine times."

Hawkins's mouth opened—then shut. He considered mentioning Gail and the absence of the ball, but changed his mind. He still isn't sure why.

Colangelo moved into a harsh, but accurate, analysis of each man's performance. "For a guy who never played pro," Connie recalls, "I was impressed by his knowledge." When Colangelo finished, the players seemed drained. They bowed their heads or picked nervously at splinters in the wooden benches. "Next," said Jerry, his Roman chin thrust forward, "do you think your losing record is the coach's fault?"

"Yes, definitely, yes."

The voice belonged to Kerr's drinking companion, Neil Johnson.

Surprised, Colangelo's head snapped slightly to the side. The cigarette quivered in his hand. Quickly, he pointed at Hawkins.

"Fifty-fifty," said Connie, measuring his words. "The players have lost games with stupid plays. But the coach lost a lot with dumb coachin. Too much dumb coachin."

Now voices tumbled on top of each other as players rushed to chime in. "He never helped me," said Neal Walk. "I was excited when I came here. I knew he'd been an NBA center for twelve years. I thought he'd help me learn. But this was a farce."

"I got to go to Hawkins for help," added Green. "I'm not saying a coach should take a lot of time with rookies. But *some*. We need the help."

"No plays, nothing for in-bounds," said McKenzie. "We were never prepared."

Colangelo tried once more: "How can you complain about his strategy? There were times when some guys didn't even go to the huddle. You'd sit at the end of the bench during time-outs."

"Yeah," Hawkins flared, "it was me. And you know how come! The first ten time-outs, I listened to his shit. We'd sit for fifty-eight seconds, he isn't sayin a damn thing. The whistle blows. Then, he says, 'Try a Red' [a play]. Well shit, I can go up in the stands and sell popcorn and use my time better. I got enough trouble psychin myself, without him gettin me down in the time-outs."

Colangelo, chain-smoking, dragged hard on his cigarette. "You guys are partly at fault, you know," he shot back. "None of you assumed any responsibility."

Hawkins's head jerked up again. "Look, we got an obligation to be ballplayers," he said, "not coaches. You been puttin some of us under a lot of pressure—you want us to do Johnny's job."

"You brought in guys to *save* his job," Silas added. "You got to know there's something wrong with him."

Blood rushed to Colangelo's cheeks. "Do you think he can change?"

"How's he gonna change?" asked Harris scornfully. "He knew his job was in jeopardy, the last few weeks. He still wouldn't get tough and say, 'Gail, pass it to Hawkins,' or 'Connie, I'm fining you for being late.'"

"Jerry," Hawkins interrupted, "can I say something?"

"Go ahead."

"I know ballplayers always blame coaches when they fuck up. I guess we're doin it now. But you and me have talked a lot of times. You know the game, otherwise you wouldn't have told us what you did today. But these were things *Kerr* should have told us two months ago! *Now* you got to do something."

"All right," Colangelo said, breathing deeply, "then it comes down to this: Do you respect him? Can you play for him any more?"

One by one the players shook their heads.

"Van?"

"John's the kind of guy you love to laugh and drink with," Van Arsdale struggled softly. "I like him. All this isn't his fault. It really isn't. But he's just not the kind of man who'll earn a ballplayer's respect."

"What about you, Gail?" Jerry asked.

"Not as a coach," said Goodrich. "I can't respect him as a coach."

Eleven players. None had spoken for John Kerr.

Colangelo lowered his head. It crossed Connie's mind that, just then, the cocky general manager looked very young. "O.K." Jerry sighed. "Here's a lesson for you. Never mix business with friends. It never works. If I hadn't been John's friend, maybe we wouldn't have reached this point. Now we're stuck. No college coach with any ethics will leave in the middle of the season. No *good* pros are available. What are we going to do?"

"Don't ask us," Hawkins said. "You *tell* us. You're the general manager."

That afternoon, Hawkins heard on the radio that John Kerr had resigned.

Connie reached the locker room half an hour early. He was the last player to arrive. "Who's the coach?" he asked Proski.

"GM."

The general manager was making a gutsy move. He had recently signed a new "multiple-year" contract. The owners apparently were not holding him responsible for the team's poor showing. Now, however, Colangelo had placed himself on the hot seat. He had forced his close friend to re-sign—actually fired him—and he was taking Kerr's job. He had never played professionally and had no previous coaching experience. "I'm an in-terim coach," he stressed. "I have absolutely no ambition to become a coach. If the team wins every game, I still won't coach next year." But if the Suns continued to stumble, there would be no one to blame but Colan-gelo.

Jerry entered the room with Scotty McDonald. "We're going to forget what's happened in the past," he told the players. "I'm going to coach. Scotty will assist me, when he's available. It's a whole new ball game."

Hawk felt strangely unaffected. "I'd had lots of 'interim' coaches in Min-nesota," he notes.

Before the players left to warm up, Colangelo beckoned Hawkins to a corner of the locker room. "How's the knee?" he asked aggressively.

Hawk grinned. "It's all right."

"I'm glad," said Colangelo, his head bobbing to emphasize each word, "because this is it. You'll see the ball. I'm staking my job on you. You're going to have to do it for us, Hawk. There's no one else. The destiny of this team depends on you. The Phoenix Suns will go only as far as *you* take them."

Recalls Connie, "I was glad. I still felt pain, but in my mind I was ready not to worry about it. I knew the pressure—the pressure Jerry was puttin on me—had to come. Now it was there. I thought, 'I'm gonna go hard and if something happens to the leg—well, it happens.' "

That night, with thirteen seconds remaining, Phoenix trailed by 3 points. In the huddle, Colangelo pointed at Hawkins.

Connie, who had already scored 20, took a pass at midcourt and drove, curling his body toward the hoop, trying for a 3-point play. San Diego's Toby Kimball hit his arm just as Hawk released the shot. The ball rolled around the rim—and dropped out. Connie's shoulders sagged. Fans moved toward the exits. Hawkins hit two foul shots, cutting the margin to 120-119. But the situation seemed hopeless.

Phoenix pressed the Rockets. Elvin Hayes, San Diego's star center, took the ball under his basket and searched for a free man. Fox waved both hands in his face. Hayes became flustered and heaved a pass toward the sideline. It went out of bounds, untouched. The Suns would take posses-sion at the sidecourt.

Colangelo, who had been booed all evening by pro-Kerr fans, signaled for time out. Hawk knew what he would say. "We're going to get the ball to Hawkins," Jerry told the Suns. "Does everybody agree?" Heads nodded solemnly.

Colangelo looked at Connie. "O.K. We start tonight. It's up to you."

Hawkins said nothing. The warning buzzer sounded, and he pushed off the bench and walked slowly onto the court. There was a slight tingling in his palms and fingers.

Connie faked to the baseline, then dashed back toward the ball. With John Trapp a step behind, he took Van Arsdale's pass, dribbled twice, and lofted a sixteen-foot jump-shot.

Hawk held his breath. The ball hung above the hoop, then slid over the front rim into the net. The crowd exploded. Phoenix had won, 122-121.

His teammates embraced him at the bench. Colangelo gripped his hand. "It's a whole new ball game," Jerry shouted. "Hawk, I told you, it's a whole new ball game!"

24

SUPERSTAR

"As of today, our offense is built
completely around Connie Hawkins."
—*Jerry Colangelo, January 7, 1970*

The Suns continued to play in streaks—good and bad—during the final three months of the season. The emotional roller-coaster of internal disharmony still rumbled periodically through the locker room. But the personal frictions, especially the racial tensions, were far less severe and divisive. Jerry Colangelo, though he would never be mistaken for a tactical genius, brought a semblance of cohesiveness to the team. For the first time in the history of the franchise, the Suns were winning more games than they lost.

Phoenix won 24 and lost 20 under Colangelo and finished with a 39-43 record. For a second-year expansion club—defeated 66 times the previous season—it was a staggering accomplishment.

"Thousands of words have been written by way of explaining this phenomenal progress," Joe Gilmartin would note, "but, in truth, only two are necessary: Connie Hawkins!"

Colangelo reconstructed the offense to accentuate Connie. He shifted Hawk from the corner to the high (and sometimes low) post, where he was more accessible to passes and had more room to operate. With Scotty McDonald's help, the novice coach also fashioned several plays specifically for Hawkins and announced publicly that "everything will be built around him."

The responsibility seemed to ignite Hawkins. He still had lapses of concentration and took short vacations from pressure, but when the Suns needed him, Connie was there—again and again.

Of the 44 games Colangelo coached, 16 were decided by five points or less. These were the heart-stoppers, the furnace in which a successful season is molded or melted. Under John Kerr, the Suns rarely won close games. With Colangelo, however, Phoenix took 10 of 16, including 6 of the

333

last 8. In seven of the Suns' ten hair-breadth victories, Connie scored the winning points.

Part of his pre-injury repertoire was still missing. But Hawkins moved with complete confidence on the damaged knee. He was alive again. His "game" was once more his clearest expression of self.

"Right now," said Boston's Don Nelson in late February, 1970, "Connie is the best forward in the NBA. A few months ago, he was either lazy or hurt. Maybe he just wasn't adjusted. But now, he's a different player. He's moving. How can you stop him? Nobody can do more things with the ball."

"Hawk took charge," recalls Paul Silas. "He was the Man of the Hour. He knew it and we knew it."

With his improved play, Connie was also more assertive off the court. He carried himself with assurance and his personality became an important force in the locker room. The players treated him with respect, even deference. When he spoke, the Suns listened.

Though still essentially a loner, Hawkins spent more time talking with his teammates. On planes, for instance, he often sat with Neal Walk, advising the rookie on pivot play. "He was a nice kid," Connie explains. "He had guts. But he needed help, and there wasn't nobody to help him."

Hawkins's sense of humor, submerged for months, now surfaced regularly. At the Atlanta airport, as the Suns deplaned, Connie ambled over to white broadcaster Hot Rod Hundley and said, "Let me show you something they never seen in Georgia."

"What?" asked Hundley.

"This," Hawkins exclaimed—and slapped Hot Rod across the face.

Connie was now a hero as well as a celebrity in Phoenix. Wearing striped bellbottoms, open-necked body shirts, black flat-brimmed hats, and shades, he was the most recognizable figure in town. At the Pancake House, where he and Arthur Harris ate their postnoon breakfasts, or at Bill's Record Shop, where he invested fifty dollars a week in his passion for soul and jazz, Hawkins was the center of attention. Children and "parents" besieged him for autographs. Men shook his hand and asked inane questions. Women stared at the towering black man and sought excuses to touch him.

Hawkins was polite, smiling, but reserved. "I'd worried that Phoenix was gonna be a bad place to be black," he says. "But, maybe because I was a ballplayer, I didn't have no trouble. Still, I kept pretty much to myself or hung out with Arthur."

With children, however, the reserve disappeared. Connie stood outside the locker room after every game signing autographs. His car was usually the last to leave the parking lot. When a group of high school boys and girls trailed him home from the airport, Hawk invited them in for Cokes and sat talking for over an hour. The next day, they returned with two huge cakes.

Connie was still ultrasensitive to any mention of gambling. When Carl Scheer, then Kennedy's assistant, gave the Suns their annual lecture on the dangers of involvement with shady characters, Hawkins was offended. He mistakenly thought the warning was specifically for him.

Hawk had braced himself for catcalls and ugly reminders about scandal. But, to his surprise, he was cheered by the fans in every NBA city. "I never heard one person yell about Molinas or fixin games," he says. "If they had, *I* would have heard it."

The afternoon of a home game against the Lakers, Connie and Arthur entered the Food Bazaar, a self-service restaurant. A middle-aged, cigar-smoking counterman greeted them effusively. He was a fan and they often bantered with him about the Suns.

"You guys got to win tonight," he said. "This is a big one."

"We will," Hawk replied.

"I hope so," said the man, flashing a yellow-toothed smile, "cause you guys got to win by more than three."

Connie froze. He glared at the man's grinning face. "*What* you say?"

"I need you guys to win by . . ." The words trailed off. The smile vanished.

"Hey, I don't want to hear no shit like that," Hawkins said angrily.

The counterman's forehead wrinkled, then his eyes pressed shut. "Oh," he cried, "I didn't think Hawk. I forgot. Oh, I'm sorry."

"Yah," Connie snapped. "You *are* sorry!"

With Arthur several steps behind, Hawkins strode quickly toward the door. "We went back to that restaurant a lot of times," Connie says. "But I never spoke to that man again. I wouldn't even say Hello."

Connie now felt more comfortable, less like an outsider, in NBA surroundings. Actually, however, from the beginning, many opponents—aware of his tortured past and recalling his great performances against them in the summer schoolyards—had gone out of their way to help ease the transition.

Rather than knock Hawk's early efforts, they had been quick to praise him. After Gus Johnson held Connie to seven points in November, he heatedly rejected a writer's inference that Hawkins was overrated. "I wouldn't say Connie *ever* looks bad," Gus said. "He's probably the best forward in the country. It just happens things were going good for me tonight and bad for him."

"I think he's smart the way he's handling himself," said Dave DeBusschere, a few days later. "He's been through a lot. You'd think he'd come in here trying to prove things and hog the ball. But he's not."

"So many guys were friendly," Connie recalls. "Like in Philly, Billy Cunningham—a beautiful dude—would rap with me about when we were kids in Brooklyn. Earl Monroe and Nate Thurmond and Walt Hazzard invited me out on the road. After we played the Bucks, I'd get together with Kareem."

In Milwaukee, at Jabbar's apartment, they would eat dinner Islamic-style—on the floor, without utensils—then stretch out to listen to Kareem's huge collection of jazz and West Indian music.

Jabbar appears cold and unapproachable, even to some NBA blacks. Hawkins, however, found him fascinating to be with. "He's a very serious, mysterious-type guy," Connie says. "He doesn't kid around much. But I really like him. First of all, I like the way he plays basketball. Then, I like him because he's straightforward, tells it like it is. I respected him for writing those articles in *Sports Illustrated*.

"Being from New York," Hawk adds, "he has a certain amount of arrogance about him. He's not stuck-up, but he lets people know he won't be trifled with. And he's intelligent. We didn't have a lot of heavy raps, but I enjoyed it when we talked."

Somewhat in awe of Kareem's formal education and the range of his reading, Hawk senses he could learn much—particularly about racial issues—from Jabbar. He wants to know him better. "The only time I don't like to see him," says Hawkins, "is when he walks out on the court against us."

Jabbar's feelings for Hawkins were similarly warm. Connie never felt Kareem talked down to him. One even sensed that, because of Jabbar's acute social and racial awareness, he was especially eager that someone with Hawkins's background succeed. Kareem never missed an opportunity to laud Connie's skills. Jerry Colangelo even maintained that, when the Bucks held safe leads late in the game, Jabbar allowed Hawk to score inside, rather than block his shot.

Not everyone, however, welcomed Hawkins with open arms. Bill Bridges, Atlanta's husky forward, was quick to denigrate him in the press. "We didn't like each other way back in the ABL," Connie notes. "It's always rough when we play. The thing started at a party he gave in Kansas

City about ten years ago. I left with this white girl. It turned out she was his."

Hawkins discovered that Bridges is not among the NBA's most popular players. When Lennie Wilkens feuded with Atlanta's management and coach Richie Guerin, Bridges had sided with the bosses. "A lot of guys don't like him," Silas told Connie. "He's too tight with the front office."

After a midseason game in Chicago, Hawkins was visited in the locker room by The Reverend Jesse Jackson. A serious basketball fan, the head of Operation Breadbasket is close to many NBA players. Connie was nevertheless flattered that a major civil-rights leader was interested in him. "He really knew the game," Hawk recalls. "He told me how he dug my moves. Then he said, did I know Bridges."

"You know he's not ready, don't you?" Jackson asked.

"How do you mean?"

"As a Brother, he's not ready. I was talking about you with Walt Hazzard. Walt said how great you are. But Bridges starts with, 'You must understand that this isn't the ABA, that Hawkins can't take it if you bump him.' "

"He said that?"

"If you know Bridges"—Jackson nodded—"you *know* he said it. He thinks along with the owners, not the Brothers. He still looks down on you as something out of the street. Remember that, the next time you play Atlanta."

Connie remembered. He ripped the Hawks for 30 points, and Phoenix won easily.

The harshest criticism of Hawkins came from San Diego's high-scoring center Elvin Hayes. Even during the exhibition season, Elvin declared, "There are no clowns in this league. If people want to see clowns they can go watch the Globetrotters. In the NBA, there are only two things to do with the ball—go to the hoop or pass it to a teammate."

Elvin appeared miscast in the role of critic. The previous season he had led the NBA in scoring, but his unwillingness to share the ball with teammates created dissension that made the Phoenix locker-room seem like a love-in by comparison. Hayes averaged all of 1.38 assists per game. One night he shot 28 of the 29 times he handled the ball.

The Rockets' other scoring star, Don Kojis, disliked Hayes so intensely, he eventually forced the owners to trade him by threatening to quit. Later, coach Alex Hannum tried to trade Hayes to Detroit. But management vetoed the move.

Hawkins was less than mortified by Elvin's put-down. "Opinions are like assholes," he told reporters. "Everybody's got one. I see Wilt Chamberlain holding the ball over his head with one hand and passing behind his back. I don't hear much criticism of him. Anyway, I've seen Hayes play and I don't think he'll lead the league in assists."

Although Hawkins saw the ball more often, under Colangelo, he still had his own troubles with people who weren't throwing enough passes. Once more, Hawk pointed an accusing finger at Goodrich. "Sometimes Goody played great, but many nights he still wanted to do it all himself," Connie says. "Scotty saw it. The black guys saw it."

Van Arsdale, Goodrich, and Hawkins had a three-on-two fastbreak against the Bucks. Connie, in the left lane, was open. Gail never looked left. Instead, he bulled through a defender, stumbled, and thrust up a weak underhanded shot.

The ball struck the bottom of the rim and dropped back into Gail's hands, directly beneath the hoop. Connie, still unguarded, was so close to Goodrich he could have reached out and taken the ball from him. But Gail attempted to muscle a backward pass between two Bucks to Van Arsdale. The pass was stolen.

As play whirled in the opposite direction, Hawkins threw his arms in the air, turned his back, and stomped off the court, cursing. He didn't step back in bounds until Phoenix had regained possession.

Even some white players were annoyed with Goodrich. Not all, however, felt Gail intentionally withheld the ball from Hawkins. "He just likes to shoot," maintained Neil Johnson. "It's nothing personal against Hawk."

"For several games, I specifically concentrated on watching Goodrich," said Joe Gilmartin. "And I'm still not sure."

Connie got no comfort from Colangelo. Gail and Jerry, he learned, were good friends. They ate together regularly on the road and often conferred in private after practices. "Jerry told us to get Hawk the ball," Silas noted. "But he didn't put much *specific* weight on Gail. He's the general manager too, and his thing goes deeper than the game. He has to think about the gate—and he wants a white boy for the fans."

Like Kerr, Colangelo rarely criticized Goodrich in front of the team. This infuriated Hawkins. "I don't mind you bawlin me out," he told Colangelo. "But don't go tellin me to carry the whole team when you never say anything to Goodrich!"

In Phoenix one evening, the Suns had a three-on-one fastbreak. Hawk burst toward the basket, open on the right. But Gail continued to dribble. Finally he passed to Van Arsdale. The defender deflected the ball off Van's leg, out of bounds. Jerry called time out.

At the bench, Colangelo ripped into several Suns. But he made no mention of Goodrich. The warning buzzer sounded. "O.K.," Jerry concluded, "keep running 'em."

"Wait a minute!" said Connie. "Aren't you gonna mention the pass?"

"What?"

"Jerry, the pass! There was a three-on-one and a man wouldn't give up the ball."

"Yeah, right," Colangelo said, hurriedly. "If a man is free, give up the ball."

After the game, Jerry motioned Hawkins outside the locker-room door. "Gail's been in a slump," he said. "I'm trying to help him play his way out. Thats why I didn't say anything."

"That's bullshit," replied Connie. "When *we* make a mistake, you bawl us out, you embarrass *us*. But you don't do it to *them*. You damn sure don't do it to Gail!"

The players were less than awed by Colangelo's technical expertise. In fact, they often laughed at him. "Did you see Jerry in the huddle," Silas smirked one night. "He didn't know what to say. He told me to tighten up the defense. So I said, 'Jerry, how should I do it?' All the dude could come up with was, 'Get out there and dig harder.' "

"Yeah," Connie laughed, "Scotty tells things to Jerry, then Jerry tries to make us think *he* thought them up himself."

It is in the nature of athletes, however, to deride coaches. Their psychological well-being almost demands it. Over a season, even great players have so many disappointing moments that, if they assumed total responsibility for all of them, their confidence in themselves or the team might be shattered. This is often avoided by shifting the blame to the coach.

Colangelo couldn't X and O them to victory. But, when pressed, most Suns admitted that Jerry deserved considerable credit for their improvement. "He wasn't as tough as he tried to act," says Hawkins, "but Jerry helped the discipline thing. We were organized better. When he had a curfew, he really checked the rooms."

Shortly after the coaching change, Colangelo took Hawkins to lunch. "You don't realize how your lateness pisses off the other guys," Jerry said. "If you continue to be late, it's going to reflect on me. I show you respect —I've gambled everything on you. Now, for me, show up on time."

Connie still set no standards for punctuality. He and Arthur Harris overslept and missed a flight to New York. But it was his only major foulup. Hawk took Colangelo's request seriously and was usually on time. "I can't afford to be late any more," he said one morning, roaring past red lights on his way to a workout. "At least not too many times."

Colangelo's aggressive personality also rubbed off on the team. The blacks may have resented his relationship with Goodrich, but they respected his combativeness and knew they were getting all he had to give.

Early in his tenure, after a thrashing by Chicago, Colangelo berated the Suns for thirty minutes, then fined each player three hundred dollars. "And I'll do it again," he warned, "every time you aren't mentally ready to play."

The following evening, Phoenix struggled valiantly before losing to the powerful Bucks. When Colangelo entered the locker room, the exhausted players expected another tirade. Instead he announced, "There's nothing to be ashamed of. This was a total effort. That's all I'm asking. I'm returning the three hundred dollars. Tonight you earned it."

Jerry once offered the players a one hundred dollar bonus for winning an important game. On another occasion, when they were hopelessly behind at the half, he ordered, "Get rough. I want you to hit people. We may lose, but let's remind them we were here." The Suns' play was so vicious, Colangelo received a reprimand from the league office.

"Even his coaching was an improvement over Kerr," Connie concedes. "Especially, while Jerry still got along with Scotty McDonald. We finally had some in-bounds plays and some stuff to use at the end of a game."

Colangelo established a slightly more controlled offense and, for a while, made good use of his bench. "Everybody got enough playing time to keep them happy," Hawkins notes. "And Jerry rested me enough so I didn't run down."

Colangelo went out of his way to force Hawk to shoulder responsibility and become more involved. When he unveiled a new play for use in the final seconds, Jerry said, "Connie, this is for you. When we absolutely must score, we've been trying to find you with a prayer. I stole this play from the Lakers and it should work. But *you've* got to get free."

"In case I don't," said Hawkins, inspecting the diagram, "in case they block me off, you better tell Van to fill the spot."

Colangelo grinned knowingly and shook his head. "No Connie," he said. "Not for the first few games. It's all up to you. Just you. By hook or by crook, you've got to get open. If you don't, we lose. There'll be no options."

The play was used twice. Each time, Hawkins shook free. Once he hit a jump shot. Once he fed Silas for a layup. Phoenix won both games.

The Suns won 9 of 19 during Colangelo's first month. Even in defeat they were no longer patsies. Lamar Green bounded off the bench to block four Gus Johnson shots one night. Hawkins pulled out several victories with blazing finishes. His 15-point fourth quarter buried Atlanta. He got 16 of the Suns' 20 points in a spurt that defeated Cincinnati. His eight straight in the closing minutes downed Baltimore.

With the division tightly packed and most clubs losing more than they won, Phoenix even pushed into fourth place for a few heady days. By February, however, the Suns had slipped back to fifth, and the Western Division standings read:

	W	L	*Games Behind*
Atlanta	31	26	—
Los Angeles	29	24	—
Chicago	25	32	6
San Francisco	23	30	6
Phoenix	24	33	7
Seattle	21	34	9
San Diego	19	33	9½

Then Hawkins erupted. In the next five games he poured in 144 points, grabbed 51 rebounds, and passed for 30 assists. "I never saw anything like Hawk during that streak," says Silas. "The cat just took over, and the rest of us related around him. It was beautiful." The Suns won five straight.

Hawkins drilled five consecutive fourth-quarter field-goals at San Diego and finished with 24 points as Phoenix won 105-103. At one point, Connie palmed the ball over his head, then flipped it behind his back to himself, dribbled past his stumbling defender, and banked a jump shot.

He was even better against the 76ers in Phoenix. Matt Guokas, once his nemesis, couldn't contain him. No one could. Connie had 28 points, 13 rebounds, and 9 assists. "He was hitting bombs from far out," wrote George Kiseda. "He was putting the ball on the floor and going to the basket, making moves with his 6' 8" frame that 6' 2" Archie Clark would be proud to make. He was going without the ball. . . . He was setting picks. He was even playing defense . . ."

In the final two minutes, with the 76ers closing in, Connie was a one-man attack. He burst through Philadelphia for 8 points, once rebounding his own miss of a driving layup, on which, Kiseda exclaimed, "he proved it is possible to walk on air." Phoenix won, 131-123. The victory moved the Suns into a third-place tie.

"Connie comes through when we need him," cried Colangelo. "In the last quarter he goes berserk. He's everything everybody said he was!"

Next, the Suns took sole possession of third place by beating San Francisco. Hawkins scored 20 and grabbed 10 rebounds. His floor game drew a standing ovation. "I played with Elgin," Jerry Chambers told him, "and I never saw him do things like that."

I had begun work on this book and was often in Phoenix, usually living at Connie's immaculate apartment. During the winning streak, I found Hawk more relieved than exuberant. "Man, I'm just glad it's happened," he sighed one evening as we sat in his living room. "It's like waking up from a bad dream."

Though still occasionally swollen and watery, the knee was no longer a factor. "I ignore it naturally now," Connie said. "The pain is gone. I guess it's been all right for a while. Now my mind is all right."

"Then why is it you still don't seem to go as hard—don't take over—till the second half?"

Hawkins frowned and toyed with the sapphire ABA All-Star ring he continues to wear on his left hand. "First of all," he said finally, "the guys still don't look for me till they're in trouble. I don't handle the ball as much in the first half. But, I guess, I'm also pacing myself to be strong at the finish. A lot of guys do that."

"Isn't there more?" I pressed. "Sometimes you don't look for the shot."

"I do find myself overpassin. Maybe, subconsciously, I'm tryin to prove I'm not selfish," Hawkins said. He thought for a moment, then added, "Maybe I'm searchin."

"For what?"

"That's a good question."

The periodic lethargy, which marked his childhood, remains a central facet of his character. Away from basketball, Hawk is often unable—no matter how good his intentions—to focus his energy on obvious responsibilities. At that time, for example, he still hadn't gotten around to paying the hospital bills for the delivery of his first two children. Shawna was six years old.

Hawk received a flood of fan mail in Phoenix. Most went unanswered. It wasn't that Connie didn't appreciate the letters and autograph requests. He did. Yet even after Ruth Dryjanski, a secretary in the Suns' office, addressed and stamped the envelopes and supplied him with one thousand glossy photos, Hawkins never got himself sufficiently together to sign more than two hundred.

Any coach disturbed by his lack of punctuality should try Connie in the off-season. An appointment with Hawkins is an exercise in wishful thinking. "He so fouled up our office schedule, we almost dropped his lawsuit the first year," says David Litman. "But it usually isn't selfishness. Connie will miss appointments that are solely for his benefit, even appointments he made."

"I don't know what happens," Connie said to me at the apartment in Phoenix. "There'll be things I want to do, I have to do, but I won't get them done. I'll think about it, it'll be on my mind, but I won't be *doin* anything. Like, when I was in school and I wanted to do my homework, but I never did. After a while, the whole thought drifts away. I forget about it, till somebody reminds me I've fucked up again."

"It happens on the court too," I said.

"Yeah. In regard to pressure."

The mythology of sports portrays the superior athlete as relishing pressure situations. In fact, relatively few are eager to perform in the clutch. "When one shot means a game," laughs Silas, "everybody in the huddle points at somebody else."

"I suppose," Connie said, "I feel better stayin away from too much pressure. That's why I admire Jerry West. He's known as 'Mr. Clutch.' He's always the one that has to pull his club out. I wouldn't want that for anything."

Whether in a Harlem schoolyard or an NBA arena, Hawkins plays to his audience. In some ways, his temperament—reinforced by years with the Trotters—is really better suited for entertaining than competing. But he is not an entertainer. He's a competitor.

Wherever Connie had played, he had to carry the team. As alien as the role might have been, as unpleasant as he found the responsibility, Hawk always forced himself to face the challenge—and met it with success. In Phoenix, the pressure was more intense than he had ever encountered. But now he was responding once more.

"You say you wouldn't want to be the one who always has to pull out the club," I noted, "but that's what you're doing right here."

"I know," Hawkins said. "I guess part of me doesn't want the responsibility. But the other part knows that's what I've got to do, if I'm gonna be what I want. Still, sometimes—the same as with things that don't pertain to basketball—I'll be out there, knowin I got to take charge, but floatin along and not doin it."

"But, eventually, you get it together. You've done that now."

"I have to," Connie answered slowly. "I mean, basketball—that's where I *can't* fuck up. That's me, what I am. So, somehow, I do it. This season is the hardest. But man, I went eight years being shitted on, not bein known. I couldn't come into this league and fail."

"Are you happy now, Hawk?"

"I have security," he said after a long pause. "My name is cleared. But, right now, I'm tense. I can't relax till everything comes together. I've been strugglin and strugglin and now I feel the momentum is finally goin my way. But we've got to make the playoffs. If we make the playoffs, I can say I'm happy. I will have accomplished something."

With the Suns in third place, basketball fever was sweeping Phoenix.

When the Lakers invaded the Coliseum, more than ten thousand bellow-ing fans turned out. They saw an incredible game. Elgin Baylor scored 42 points. Jerry West scored 33. Yet the Suns hung on. Harris, Silas, Walk, and Fox played with a ferocity that pleased even Scotty McDonald. But it was Hawkins who kept Phoenix alive.

With four seconds remaining, Hawkins had scored 30 points, but the Suns still trailed, 109-107.

"They'll double- or triple-team Connie," said Colangelo in the huddle. "We've got to go to Gail."

"I was so involved and fired-up, it didn't exactly register that I wouldn't get the shot," Hawkins remembers. "When I walked out on the court, I felt tense like I couldn't get enough air inside me."

The referee handed the ball to McKenzie near midcourt and began counting off the five seconds Phoenix had to put it in play. Players burst into motion. But as Stan peered into the swirl of bodies, his expression turned desperate. Goodrich had been unable to elude Jerry West.

Double-teamed in the low post by Baylor and Mel Counts, Connie in-stinctively darted toward McKenzie. Stan spotted Hawkins's waving hand and he released the ball a heartbeat before the official's arm came down for the fifth time.

Hawkins took the pass with his back to the basket. There was no time to drive. With one dribble he was in the right corner, near the baseline, twenty-one feet from the hoop. Fans gasped as he whirled and arched an off-balance jump-shot. The ball was in the air when the buzzer sounded. The shot was good.

Connie clutched his head with both hands and sank to his knees on the court. "I felt like my heart had stopped," he says. "I was dizzy, like all the adrenalin had washed out of me."

"Hawk, you all right?" Silas cried above the cheers.

Connie looked up, still holding his head. Players from both teams were staring at him, afraid he was hurt. "I'm O.K.," he said blankly.

"I guess I was still dazed in the huddle," Hawkins recalls. "I could feel people slappin me on the back. I heard Jerry talkin, but his words didn't come through. Next thing I knew, it was overtime and we'd fell three points behind."

But Neil Johnson hit a free throw. The Lakers lost possession, and Con-nie drove for a 3-point play. Phoenix widened its lead to 117-115. Then, with eight seconds left, Dick Garrett's jump shot tied the score.

One second later, Hawkins was fouled.

The crowd hushed as he stepped to the line. "I was scared," Hawk ad-mits. "All I could think was, 'If I don't make both shots, they'll come down and score and we'll lose.' "

His first shot was short. The ball hit the front rim, spun against the back-board—and bounced in. Connie threw his head back and sighed. "I was too nervous to shoot again," he says. "I saw a spot of blood on the ball, so I asked the referee for another."

The new ball, however, felt heavy in his hands. "Gimme back the first one," he told the official. The ball was returned. By then, Hawkins had calmed the throbbing inside him. His second shot went through cleanly. It was his 37th point. In a moment Phoenix had won again.

That night, Connie dreamed of the game. "I kept takin the jump shot from the corner," he says. "It went in every time."

Three nights later, in Boston, the Suns' winning streak reached five as Hawkins shook the Celtics with 35 points. His ball handling was so remark-able that, when Boston employed a last-ditch fullcourt press in the closing minutes, the Phoenix guards stepped aside and Connie dribbled the ball up by himself.

"He probably reached some kind of peak, even for him," Gilmartin noted, "when he waved the ball a couple of times and the entire right side of the Celtics' defense disappeared. He went in all alone for a stuffer."

The Suns were just four games behind the second-place Lakers. "No sec-onds for us," shouted Silas, who had muscled down 21 rebounds. "We're chasin Atlanta!" The standings read:

	W	L	Games Behind
Atlanta	35	28	—
Los Angeles	32	28	1½
Phoenix	29	33	5½
San Francisco	26	34	8
Chicago	27	36	8
Seattle	24	37	10
San Diego	19	37	12½

"In the locker room, I saw Bill Russell pushin through the crowd," Con-nie remembers. "We'd been introduced once, but I didn't really know him. I was excited just seein the man. I'd been in awe of him for so long."

The great center, in his first year of retirement, made his way to Hawkins. "You were fantastic," Russell said, smiling. "You do things with the ball I've never seen before."

Connie swelled inside, but fought back a grin. "Naw," he replied, "if you were out there, you'd have blocked half those shots."

Russell shook his head and cackled loudly. "I don't know, man. I don't think so. Hawkins, you're too much!"

Russell invited Connie to join him. But Hawk declined. Larry Friend, a part-owner of the Suns, was throwing a party for them in a suite at their hotel. "I was flattered just havin Russell talk to me," Connie says. "I wanted to go with him, but I felt too close to the team. Everybody'd been playin good. We all felt like a unit. I didn't want to break that feeling."

The feeling was soon broken, nonetheless.

The players, broadcasters, sportswriters, and team officials were joined at the party by about a half-dozen young white women. Connie thinks they were secretaries from Friend's Boston office. For a while, the mood in the suite was jovial. There was plenty of booze, and the players felt loose. "All the guys kidded with each other," Hawkins remembers. "We rapped about goin after first place."

When Connie arrived, the women had been talking with white players. But, as the evening wore on, and the decibel level of the party increased, they began gravitating toward the blacks. "I didn't think nothing of it," Hawk says, "till I looked up and saw that *all* the girls were talkin to black guys. The white guys were standing back, just lookin at 'em."

"At least ask her if she has a roommate for me," Hawk heard Fox say to Harris. Fox was smiling, but the smile seemed forced.

Silas jabbed Connie's shoulder and nodded toward the sullen knot of white players standing at the bar. "This is gettin a little heavy," he whispered. "We better split."

Connie slid over to Harris and edged him away from the women. "We're splittin," he said. "We gotta go now."

Arthur was about to protest. Then he noticed the bar. "I'm hip," he said.

During the next two weeks the Suns' dream of first place was reduced to a prayer that they even qualified for the playoffs. Phoenix lost seven of nine games. They stayed in contention only because Chicago, San Francisco, and Seattle were losing almost as regularly.

The entente among the club members began to dissolve once more. "Some closeness was gone after that party in Boston," Connie says. "But it was the losin that really messed up people's heads."

Some players were simply tired of being around each other since September. Lamar Green, for instance, was fed up with Chambers's and McKenzie's teasing him about being a hick from the deep South. Silas, deep into his black-machismo trip, decided that Arthur Harris was too frivolous. "The dude just deals in bullshit," Paul complained. McKenzie antagonized several teammates with constant gripes about playing time. "He doesn't deserve to play," the usually mild-mannered Van Arsdale said to Connie. "If Stan doesn't shut up, I may just shut him up."

Hawkins, meanwhile, was pricing coffins for Goodrich. His frustration with Gail had driven him past objectivity to the point where Hawk was ready to blame Goodrich for everything but natural disasters. "One night," Connie told Arthur, "that little white motherfucker's gonna freeze me out once too many, and I'm gonna kick his ass right on the court."

The squabbling extended even to the players' wives. Six were living in Phoenix and met regularly when their husbands were on the road. "I didn't want to know nothing about it," Connie says, "but, in the locker room, I'd hear players tellin how one wife would tell another one what her husband was sayin about guys on the team. I guess there was a lot of gossipin and a lot of little putdowns over whose husband made more money."

When Paul and Carolyn Silas bought a new home in nearby Tempe, the wives gave a housewarming party. The following day, Paul marched into the locker room and dumped half a dozen packages on the floor. "These are the housewarming gifts your wives brought my wife," he announced. "We don't need cheap shit like this. If that's all you think we're worth, you can have it back!"

The defeats resulted more from injuries than from dissension, however. Lamar Green overdid his jumping routine and broke his hand on the rim. Silas played the last month of the regular season with a painful chipped spur in his elbow. Goodrich hobbled on a jammed left foot. The pain was so acute, doctors marveled that he was able to play at all. "He's doing it on guts," said one physician.

The most consequential injury was Hawkins's. During the overtime game against Los Angeles, he had been kicked in the calf. "It didn't hurt too bad at Boston," Connie recalls, "but then we went to Milwaukee, and I got hit hard on the exact same spot."

The Suns played well. Connie scored 32 points against Jabbar. But their five-game winning streak was halted. The next afternoon, the calf was sore and swollen. Phoenix was to meet the Bulls that night, so Proski wrapped it in hot towels for several hours. The leg loosened, only to tighten once more when Hawkins tried to warm up.

Connie returned to the locker room. "I can play," he told the trainer, "but you got to massage it, get some stiffness out." Proski stretched Hawkins on the rubbing table and gently kneaded the calf.

When Connie limped through the door, Colangelo was standing at the urinal. Bitterly determined to beat his former employers in his old hometown, he was so pent up he had gone back to the locker room to be alone with his thoughts.

"Hey Colangelo," yelled a reporter, "Hawkins is hurt!"

"What!" Jerry cried, whirling around, his face ashen. "What's the matter with him? What is it?"

Hawkins looked up from the rubbing table, did a double-take, and began to laugh. "Don't worry about me, I'll be able to play," he said. "But Jerry, you got a problem yourself."

Only then did Colangelo realize that in his concern for Hawkins's condition, he had turned from the urinal too soon. His pants leg was drenched.

"Jerry smelled great in the huddle," Hawk recalls.

The laughter was short-lived. Despite Hawkins's 37 points, Chicago won on a shot at the buzzer. The following evening in Detroit, Hawk was in agony. "You've got a deep bruise, there's hemorrhaging," said Proski. "What you really need is rest." But there was no time to rest. The Suns played their fourth game in four nights—and were routed by the Pistons. Connie took only 11 shots and was held scoreless in the fourth quarter. "I couldn't make my moves," he recalls. "I stood around a lot. I got down on myself."

Two days later, in Philadelphia, he scored just 12 points and appeared almost apathetic. The Suns were slaughtered, 159-125. It was their fourth straight loss.

Colangelo pounced on Hawkins. He insinuated that Connie was coddling himself again, exaggerating the injury. Jerry also believed Hawk was sinking into another period of listlessness.

Hawkins was angry. He had played two bad games—after averaging 34 per game in the previous eight—and already the coach had turned on him. "Jerry's got a short memory," he said. "I'm not fakin any injury. I'm in pain—why can't he see that?"

Colangelo was wrong about Hawk's calf. The injury was real. But Jerry wasn't entirely incorrect about Connie's state of mind. Hawk was suffering from a common athletic malady, a case of "late-season blahs."

The NBA schedule is eighty-two games. The travel grind is exhausting. From October to April, sleep and eating habits are constantly disrupted. "You can't be up for every game," says Silas. "Some nights the whole team doesn't feel like playing. Toward the end of the season, everything gets run down for a while."

One way Hawkins combated the mental and physical fatigue was by raising his intake of pep pills.

The green and orange, heart-shaped, three-milligram diet pills (Dexamyl and Dexedrine) are used by many NBA players. These relatively mild amphetamines increase the pulse rate, making the athlete feel stronger and more alert. Sometimes they also provide a heightened sense of well-being.

Unlike numerous football and baseball players, few in pro basketball rely on amphetamines. Some find the pills make them hypertense and hurt their shooting touch. Nevertheless, especially on long road-trips, after heavy partying, or when an afternoon game follows a night contest, Gobies come in handy.

That season, Connie and I asked one of the Celtics to explain his team's poor performance during a game in Los Angeles. "Our Gobies were stolen," he laughed. "We played in Frisco the night before, and some hippies must have broken into the locker room. They didn't touch our money. All they took was pills—every Gobie we had. The next afternoon, it was cold turkey in LA."

Hawkins had used pep pills occasionally since his first ABA season. But he was careful to avoid a psychological dependence. He had seen several players, like Chico Vaughn, who believed they couldn't perform without pills and eventually, as their bodies developed a tolerance, had to increase the quantity of amphetamines they took for each game.

"In the NBA," Hawk says, "I still didn't use them too much. But I took more. On a six-game road trip, maybe I'd use a pill three times. If we had a day or two of rest, I wouldn't need one. But, at the end of the season, I started takin 'em for most of the important games."

Connie's mental state wasn't improved by the escalating feud between Jerry Colangelo and Scotty McDonald. At first, they had worked effectively together. Scotty arranged leaves from his legal work and made road trips with the team. But it was inevitable that he and Colangelo would clash. There wasn't space in the dressing room for two such sizable egos.

McDonald, a basketball theoretician all his life, couldn't help viewing Jerry as a young punk. "He is a good man . . . most receptive and quick," Scotty wrote to a longtime coaching friend, soon after Colangelo took over. "But he has never coached, and that is a big difference. You have to go through the mill and suffer a hell of a lot before you know how to coach— and maybe even then you realize you just don't have it."

As the Suns improved, Colangelo had gone on a Walter Mitty trip. He was beginning to imagine himself the second coming of Red Auerbach. Jerry publicly denied any thoughts of keeping the coaching job after that season. But those who knew him best, said he was thinking seriously of continuing his dual role.

"It's not too difficult to coach," Jerry would say. "If you've been involved in the game long enough and know the rules and have the respect of the team and you can control them, then you can coach."

Many players disagreed. When Phoenix started slipping again, they complained that Colangelo had run out of things to offer them. Part of their criticism was—as usual—unfair and exaggerated. But the feeling was too widely held to be ignored.

"He didn't have much new strategy," Connie recalls. "After a while, it seemed like all he did was yell at us and call us 'quitters.' People got mad."

One night, as a time-out ended, Van Arsdale whispered to Hawkins, "If he keeps saying we've got no guts, Jerry's gonna wind up with a punch in the face."

Many Suns found Colangelo's pregame talks soporific. "He reached us for a while," Silas says. "Then it became the same old soup warmed over."

Jerry was understandably jealous of the black players' respect for McDonald. He also seemed bent on ensuring that he—not Scotty—received credit if Phoenix made the playoffs. "Scotty really wanted to be a part," notes Silas, "but Jerry didn't want that. He said 'Wow, I got something going for me. This here is *mine!*'"

They often differed over strategy. Phoenix was repeatedly burned by fastbreaks because Van Arsdale and Goodrich were preoccupied with penetrating on offense. Scotty urged that either Harris or McKenzie get more playing time. "I think the whole league loves to see our guards come on the court," Scotty wrote in a memo to Colangelo. "They know that we will concede the fastbreak every time." Jerry rejected the advice.

There was also acrimony over Goodrich. Unlike Kerr and Colangelo, McDonald didn't hesitate to blast Gail during clubhouse meetings. "I'm sorry," Scotty would say, "but I must tell you that you don't know the first thing about the fastbreak. Gail, you dribble, dribble, dribble, and it hurts, hurts, hurts!" One night, Goodrich became so incensed, he stormed out of the locker room.

Colangelo gradually reduced McDonald's access to the players. Scotty got less time to speak in pregame meetings. Sometimes Jerry would interrupt with remarks like, "Is that all?" or, "Make this quick."

McDonald begged for more time to teach. "Jerry, this is *awfully serious* to me," he memoed. "If we could only get time to really practice hard and make the kids learn the patterns and the rules of defense and the basic fundamentals of the game, we would increase our performance by 30% to 40%. . . . I *know damn well* these kids do not understand basketball . . . [and] I would gamble a peso or two that not one boy on our team can successfully diagram all our offensive patterns." But McDonald got few opportunities to instruct at practice.

Scotty, of course, didn't help himself by openly badmouthing Colangelo in front of the players. At a Suns' Booster Club party he sat at a table with Silas, Chambers, McKenzie, and their wives, and proclaimed, "Jerry Colangelo just wrote a book about basketball coaching."

Everyone looked up in surprise. "Yes," McDonald said. "There's one page in it!" When the laughter subsided, he added, "And that page is blank!"

McDonald's final undoing occurred late in the season when he bumped into owner Dick Bloch on a flight back to Los Angeles after a Phoenix defeat. "Bloch asked me what was wrong with the team," Scotty maintains. "I told him he wouldn't want to hear, but he persisted. So I told him that Goodrich was a major factor, that someone had been wiping his ass since he was a little boy and Jerry was still doing it. I said, 'It's not just the coach's fault, it's the owner's fault too, because you all coddle him. Gail hogs the ball, he particularly hurts Hawkins. Some players are on the verge of rebellion over it.' Bloch was angry; he said, 'Rebellion? We'll see about that when it comes to talking contract!'

"Then I got angry. I said, 'I've heard that from every owner. You people are all the same. You think money is everything. Well, it isn't. This team should have made the playoffs easily, but it's struggling. It should do well in the playoffs, but it won't.' A few days later, I was informed by Jerry that it wasn't necessary for me to join the team in San Francisco."

McDonald still appeared occasionally in the locker room. But, during the last month of the season, his contact with the Suns was minimal.

When I asked Colangelo why Scotty was no longer around, Jerry answered, "He outlived his usefulness. He didn't seem to realize there can only be one boss—and that boss is the coach."

Connie was upset by Scotty's departure. "I missed having Scotty to talk to," Hawk says. "And I missed his speeches before the game. Maybe all his yellin was silly, but somehow—cause he cared so much—it fired me up."

In late February, the Suns were routed by Milwaukee and New York. Their position was becoming precarious. Eleven games remained. They were barely clinging to fourth place. The standings read:

	W	L	Games Behind
Atlanta	40	31	—
Los Angeles	37	33	2½
Chicago	32	38	7½
Phoenix	31	40	9
Seattle	29	41	10½
San Francisco	27	42	12
San Diego	23	43	14½

"The team is fallin apart," Silas said to Hawkins, on the plane to Detroit. "The guys are mad at Jerry, and the dude ain't givin us no direction."

"We keep playin like this," Connie agreed, "we ain't gonna make the playoffs."

"Then we got to do something, Hawk. You and me. I got to forget the pain in this elbow. You got to really take charge again. It sounds like silly-ass college bullshit, but that's it. We got to turn things around before it's too late."

"I know."

Hawkins scored 33 points and had 6 assists in Detroit. Silas, Van Arsdale, and Goodrich each scored over 20. Phoenix rallied to win.

In Boston, two nights later, Connie seemed drowsy in the first half. He scored just 9 points. Only the hustling Van Arsdale kept the Suns in the game. But early in the third quarter, with Boston leading by 5 and Hawkins saddled with four personal fouls, Connie suddenly awakened. He ignited the Phoenix fastbreak with a succession of long passes, off one-handed rebounds. He hit three twenty-foot jump-shots, a squirming drive, and a pair of free throws. He found Goodrich, Van Arsdale, and Fox inside for layups. The Suns entered the fourth quarter leading, 98-90.

With Colangelo kneeling in front of the bench, shouting "Gail, find Connie!" Hawk drove for ten more points. Boston's hulking "Bad News" Barnes finally became so frustrated by Connie's slippery moves that, when Hawk faked again toward the basket, Barnes wrapped him in a bear hug. "Least I know where you are," he grumbled.

Connie hit two foul shots and finished with 29 points. Phoenix won, 134-125. "You were beautiful, Connie," a grinning Colangelo exclaimed to him in the locker room. "You're doing it for us again. Now we're rolling!"

"After that game," Hawkins recalls, "I didn't have to psyche myself up any more. I was up and involved naturally. Every game meant so much. The depression was gone—Jerry, Goody, I wasn't gonna let anything fuck up my mind."

Phoenix climbed into third place when Connie scored 30 and took 17 rebounds in a victory over Atlanta. Then the Suns stumbled, losing to Chicago and San Francisco. Hawkins continued to excel, but his teammates were getting jittery.

"After we lost to the Warriors," Connie remembers, "everybody was way down. Guys were all mad at each other. It was an hour before anybody got dressed and left the locker room. Foxie said we should get together for some beers and talk things out. But nobody showed up. Everybody was tired of meetings."

Six games remained on the Phoenix schedule. The Suns were still third.

Phoenix	34	42
Chicago	33	41
Seattle	33	41

But Seattle had won five straight. The Sonics and Bulls were just percentage points behind Phoenix—and the Suns faced two consecutive games with division-leading Atlanta.

In the Coliseum locker room, Hawkins was so tense he only half-listened when the unusually grim-faced Colangelo addressed the team. "If we lose tonight," Jerry said, "we could fall to fifth place. We can't afford that. So let me make myself clear: Gail, you're bouncing the ball too much."

Hawkins, stretched on the rubbing table, was so startled he snapped into a sitting position. Colangelo continued, "Gail, you've got to make the offense run. *That's* your job. If you don't do it, this team is shit. Tonight, the game is going to be won down low. That's the way it will be for the rest of the season. Let's start making our big men happy. Get them the ball."

Connie's eyes met Silas's. They smiled.

The Suns rolled up 75 points in the first half and went on to crush Atlanta. Hawkins controlled the ball and the game. As the huge crowd screamed and chanted, Connie scored 22, passed for 9 baskets, and combined with Silas to dominate the boards.

The rematch in the Atlanta went badly. The Suns' shots were off-target, Hazzard dominated Goodrich and scored 36 points, and Phoenix fell far behind.

Then Hawkins led a rally and the Suns cut a 19-point margin to 9. Atlanta called time. "We've got 'em," Jerry said in the huddle. "The momentum's turning. Get the ball inside to Hawk!"

Goodrich promptly fired a twenty-five-foot jump shot. Atlanta took the rebound and scored on a fastbreak. Gail hurried into the forecourt. Hawk waved for the ball. Goodrich ignored him and tried to drive. He was called for charging. The Suns' momentum dissolved. They lost by 15 points.

There was fury in the dressing room. "We got to do something," Silas steamed. "Jerry, Jerry, me and Hawk want to talk to you, right now!"

But Colangelo begged off, saying, "I've got to see the writers." He avoided them on the plane to Phoenix. "Fuck him," said Paul.

However, after a workout, the next morning, Colangelo asked Goodrich, Van Arsdale, Hawkins, and Silas to meet in his office. The door was shut. Jerry cleared his throat nervously. No one spoke. "Well," he began. "Well, does anyone have anything to say?"

Paul and Connie shook their heads. But Van Arsdale turned to Goodrich and rasped, "You're playing like your head is in your asshole! Can't you stop going for yourself?"

Gail seemed hurt and bewildered by his friend's words. "Look, I know I'm playing badly," he said. "But my foot is still sore. I'm trying. I'm doing all I can."

"That's not the point . . ." Van Arsdale began, but Colangelo cut him off.

"It's too late in the season for dissension," Jerry said. "It's no good to argue now. We've just got to pull together. You guys are the leaders of this team. It's up to all of you."

Hawkins remained silent. But he was angry. "Van had the guts to say what was right," he explained later. "Jerry should have backed him up. But he just wouldn't be rough enough with Gail."

Later that afternoon at his apartment, Connie poured a huge glass of pink Ripple wine, placed a Temptations album on the stereo and lay back on the couch. "Jerry really disappointed me," he said.

"What do you do now?"

"Nothing. There ain't time to worry about Gail any more. We're a game and a half ahead of Seattle for fourth. We're two behind Chicago for third. We got four left—and we got to win every one."

"Is that realistic?"

"Now it is," he said. "My head is just right. I'm concentratin. I'm not thinkin about anything but winnin. Not points or fans—just winnin."

Hawkins proceeded to carry the Suns past San Francisco and Boston. His play approached perfection. At times, it seemed his size 14 sneakers never touched the ground, that he was gliding above the court, suspended by invisible strings.

Hawk dominated the action as though he had choreographed it. In a sense, he was doing just that. His teammates, even Goodrich, got him the ball. Connie dictated the tempo of play, parceled out open shots, and radiated a self-assurance which seemed to calm and bolster the other Suns.

"He's close to two thousand points for the season," marveled Harris, after the victory over Boston. "But Hawk doesn't care. He's passing up points to get *everybody* involved. I know he goes out of his way to set me up, to help my confidence."

In the locker room, players pressed around Hawkins, as though hearing his voice or shaking his hand would heighten the sense of collective worth which now enveloped the team. "We got to hold on to that feelin," rumbled Silas.

Entering the last weekend of the season—home and home games with San Diego—the Suns needed just one victory to eliminate Seattle and clinch a playoff spot. They trailed third-place Chicago by a single game.

Chicago	38	42
Phoenix	37	43
Seattle	35	45

Friday night, the Phoenix crowd was chanting even before the game began. Colangelo hunched on the bench, smoking nervously. "If we win this one," he said to himself, "We've done what I set out to do in January —make the playoffs."

Crisp and confident, the Suns rolled to an early lead. Jerry knelt in front of the bench, screaming, "Find Connie! Get it to Connie!" Hawkins was everywhere, bringing both benches to their feet with stuffs, off-balance drives, and twisting jumpers. By halftime, he had scored 19 points, and Phoenix led, 69-53.

The margin widened in the second half as Hawkins set up plays, blocked shots, and once more directed the game's flow—but he no longer looked for points. "Some night," said Joe Gilmartin, at the press table, "The Hawk's going to let go and score seventy-five. At least, he *could*—but I guess it's not his way."

The public-address announcer read the final score from Chicago. The building rocked. The Bulls had lost to Baltimore. A victory would not only clinch fourth place but lift the Suns into a tie for third.

Colangelo removed Connie midway through the fourth quarter. Hawk had scored 27 points. His passes had helped Harris, Goodrich, Silas, Van Arsdale, and Walk join him in double figures. The fans stood, screaming and applauding, for over a minute.

The final score was 127-104. The Suns were in the playoffs.

Champagne splashed in the locker room. Colangelo, puffing a thick "Red Auerbach" cigar, tried to act cool and unconcerned. He managed the pose for almost thirty seconds. Then Jerry's features softened and he sighed, "Fantastic. Amazing. Great!"

Van Arsdale and Hawkins embraced amid the turmoil. "You were beautiful," Dick said. "Hawk, what else can I say?"

"For a whitey," Connie laughed, as he tousled Van's hair, "you're beautiful too." Then Hawkins reached over Van Arsdale's shoulder and dumped champagne on Silas's head.

"I couldn't lose tonight," Paul trumpeted. "I had God on my side—Connie Hawkins!"

When well-wishers, reporters, and cameras had gone, the Suns became subdued. Still in uniform, they sat before their lockers, sipping champagne. A warm glow filled the room. In this unreal setting, the antagonisms of the long season were momentarily washed away. When Goodrich extended his hand, Hawkins gripped it hard.

"We love each other," Arthur Harris said seriously as he looked around at his teammates. "We've jelled. We've come together because of Hawk, and now we love each other."

Players drifted toward the showers. But Hawkins remained seated—the adrenalin gone from his limbs—slowly emptying a bottle of champagne.

"We did it," he murmured to himself. "The playoffs. This has got to prove something."

Finally, he showered, then slid into white bell-bottom levis. He pulled a white silk body-shirt—with a plunging neckline—over his pink undershirt. Around his neck was the peace medallion he wears even on the court.

"You look beautiful," Proski said. "You really do."

"Tonight," Hawk replied, "it ain't how I look. It's how I feel. And I feel beautiful."

Neal Walk, slightly tipsy, lumbered to Connie's locker. "It's been a pleasure playing with you," said the rookie, his voice choked, his arms suddenly around Hawkins's shoulders. "If I never played another game in my life, it would be all right. I've played with Connie Hawkins."

"Neal's gettin heavy," Arthur teased.

"Let him do it, man," Connie said. "What he's sayin sure don't bother me."

The locker room emptied. Connie and I were alone. He took a final gulp of champagne and began to cry. "I'm just so happy," he sobbed. "Oh man, I just feel so happy. There's things in my head I can't explain. But I'm happy. It's done. I done it."

The morning of the final day of the season, the NBA office announced that if the Bulls and Suns remained tied with identical records, both would be credited with finishing third and would receive the full $5,000 third-place money. A coin flip would decide their opponents in the playoffs.

That afternoon, Chicago defeated Milwaukee. The pressure was on Phoenix. In the locker room, Hawk could feel his teammates getting ready to choke up.

"Everybody was real quiet," he recalls. "They seemed scared to talk loud. Jerry made a speech about how important the game was—how we had to win it for the five thousand dollars and the pride of finishing third. Then we went out and really fucked up."

Phoenix had beaten San Diego six straight times. The Rockets were in last place. But San Diego had played winning ball at home, had nothing to lose, and was very loose. The Suns soon fell far behind. "We were tight," Connie says. "Each guy tried to put the burden on his own shoulders. There was no teamwork. We just fell apart."

Hawkins's frustration mounted with the San Diego lead. Late in the first half, he and Arthur had a two-on-one fastbreak. As the defender committed himself, Connie dropped a soft pass over his shoulder to the unguarded Harris. The ball bounced off his friend's palms and rolled out of bounds.

"Goddamn it!" Hawkins screamed.

"I'm sorry, man," Arthur said, moving back on defense.

"You motherfucker!"

"Hey Hawk, I *know* it was my fault. I'm sorry."

"Fuck it," Connie snapped, waving his hand angrily.

Hawkins explains, "Afterwards, I apologized to Arthur. I just felt so mad, so emotional. I wanted third place. I felt we'd built something we could be proud of—and we were throwin it away. Then, I got depressed and disgusted, and I stopped caring for a while."

While Connie pouted, the Suns continued to stumble and fumble. In the third quarter, with San Diego leading, 85-62, third place seemed out of the question.

Colangelo, hoping to add speed, inserted McKenzie and Harris. Van Arsdale moved to forward. Hawkins shifted into the pivot. He would go head-to-head against Elvin Hayes, the man who once called him a "clown."

Stan fed Connie, who swished a five-foot jump-shot, then drove for a three-point play. "All of a sudden," Hawkins recalls, "my adrenalin was flowing again."

Connie banked a rebound, hit a long jumper, and slammed a dunk directly over Hayes. Defenders came at him in waves. Hayes. John Trapp. John Block. Toby Kimball. Don Kojis. They double-teamed and triple-teamed him. But Hawkins kept scoring.

"The other guys were lookin for me—every time," Connie says. "Paul had a two-foot jump-shot, but he turned to look for me instead. I felt they really believed in me, that they thought I could pull out the game. That made me push harder."

Hawkins stuffed a driving layup with one second left in the third quarter. He had scored 17 points in less than eight minutes. But San Diego still led, 103-89. "You've got a chance now," Jerry hammered in the huddle. "Third place is out there to be taken. Five grand is out there!"

Connie continued to score, but Phoenix could not hold the Rockets. The margin climbed to 119-101 with 6:39 to go. "It didn't seem like there was time to come back," Hawk recalls. "But *I* felt so good, I was movin so light, I couldn't let myself focus on it."

Colangelo went to a line-up of Hawkins, McKenzie, Goodrich, Silas, and Green—and the Suns' press tightened. McKenzie's rough, slashing defense unnerved the Rockets' guards. San Diego's turnovers mounted. Hawkins smothered Hayes, twice blocking his shots.

Phoenix narrowed the lead. Connie's arms and hands were everywhere. That quarter, he would block 5 shots, grab 10 rebounds, and make 5 steals. Eyeball-to-eyeball with Hayes, Hawkins whirled for a pair of stuffs. With 2:53 left, the lead had dwindled to 126-119.

Colangelo rushed Van Arsdale and Harris into the game. Arthur's pass found Hawkins. Connie drove across the lane, jack-knifed his body, and threw in a 15-foot jump-shot as Stu Lantz hit his arm. Hawk swished the free throw. It was his 42nd point. "I was like, in a daze," he remembers. "I had no sense of time or pressure. Everything was just fallin into place naturally."

Block and Van Arsdale exchanged baskets. Only 2:11 remained, and Phoenix still trailed by four. "I decided to forget about guardin a man," Connie says. "I started floatin around, gamblin for steals."

The gamble paid off. Hawkins darted between two Rockets to intercept a pass. He swung the ball around his head, then whipped it to Van Arsdale, driving for a layup.

The Rockets' Bernie Williams in-bounded at the baseline—and Hawkins intercepted again. His pass hit Van Arsdale for another layup.

The score was tied, 128-128. Phoenix had erased an 18-point lead in less than seven minutes.

San Diego worked the ball to Hayes. Silas fouled him. Hayes would have three chances to make two shots.

As the league's leading scorer stepped to the line, Silas glared at him. Elvin is not among the most popular men in the NBA. Hayes took aim. Arthur Harris leaned forward and hissed, "You're gonna miss, big dummy."

Hayes missed.

"See," said Harris. "You'll miss again."

Hayes missed again.

His third shot, however, was good. San Diego led, 129-128.

The Suns stalled until the twenty-four-second clock had almost expired. There was no need for Colangelo to designate the shooter. The pass came to Hawkins.

Connie dribbled twice, pulled up, and fired a jump shot. It hit the back of the rim and bounded in the air. Five Suns crashed the boards. Silas had the rebound, shot and missed, rebounded and missed again. Green tore the ball from Hayes, but his hurried shot was too hard. It caromed off the backboard, glanced off several hands, and bounced toward the baseline. The clock had almost run out.

Hawkins lunged, grabbing the ball just before it went out of bounds. "Shoot, shoot," he heard Colangelo shriek.

Hawk didn't look at the basket. He dribbled once, then left his feet. His long, thin body leaned toward the hoop. Hands waved in his eyes. He flicked his wrist, arching a short, soft jumper.

The ball dropped through the net. Hawkins threw his arms above his head in exultation.

Six seconds remained. The Rockets again went to Hayes. But Lamar Green leapt over Elvin to intercept. Phoenix had won, 130-129. The Suns

—a last-place expansion-club the year before—had finished in a tie for third.

Hawkins had scored 44 points. He had 20 rebounds and 8 assists. Thirty-one of his points had come in the second half. "That," Colangelo shouted at reporters, "is one of the greatest . . . no, *the greatest* basketball performance I've ever seen!"

Teammates pummeled Hawk's back and reached for his hand as he slowly moved off the court. "I had so much energy," he remembers. "Then, the second the game ended, I felt weak. My legs trembled. But I didn't go straight into the locker room. First, I stood outside in the hall—by myself. I put my face up against the coolness of the wall and I closed my eyes.

"I thanked God for allowin me to feel so wonderful."

THE PLAYOFFS

"In the NBA, Connie, you'll find
that the playoffs are the *real* season."
—*Jerry West to Hawkins*
On West's TV show, before the first game

The physical and emotional strain on an athlete during the NBA playoffs is among the most intense in all sport. The regular season is just a prelude—champions are crowned in the playoffs. Six months of work and accomplishment can be undone in a few weeks. Successful seasons can be irreparably tarnished and mediocre ones completely redeemed. The playoffs are the NBA's big apple, the moment everyone gears for, the time when defenses are toughest and superstars play to their full capabilities.

In this crucible of pressure—when top money is on the line and concentration is total—a player's reputation is made or broken. Men find out about themselves.

For Hawkins, there was an additional challenge. The Suns were matched against the powerful Los Angeles Lakers, with veteran superstars Jerry West, Elgin Baylor—and Wilt Chamberlain.

Wilt had been Connie's idol since Hawk was a teenager at Boys High. This was their first real confrontation in the NBA. Chamberlain had suffered a bad knee-injury during the Lakers' initial match with Phoenix. He had undergone surgery and missed most of the season, returning only for the last four games. Wilt was not completely ready—but the Suns still didn't relish the thought of facing him.

Although Chamberlain has played on only one NBA championship team, the most prolific scorer in pro-basketball history is venerated throughout the league, especially by black players. No one calls him "Wilt the Stilt." Chamberlain prefers to be known as "The Dipper" or "The Big Dipper." Most players simply refer to him as "Dipper."

"He's admired because—more than anyone else—he's his own man," says Hawkins. "A lot of players would like to be able to say the things he says, to knock their coaches or call the NBA 'bush league.' But they're afraid. Dipper isn't—and he gets away with it.

"They also envy him because of his wealth and fame," Connie adds. "And there's his body; he's a giant even to *us*. Dipper is way over 7′ 2″, he's near 300 pounds—and he's still quick.

"Man, his name is all over the record book. You can't believe some of the things he's done. One hundred points in a game! Fifty-four a game for the whole season! And fifty-five rebounds in one night! You want to throw those numbers out of your mind—but you can't."

To many black athletes, Wilt seems the embodiment of their dreams and ambitions. He has reached almost all of the goals—and has almost all the possessions—considered important when one grows up poor.

Chamberlain exudes aggressive opulence, from his dazzling wardrobe and expensive cars to his huge diamond ring. ("You'll have to play in this league a long time before you can afford something like this," he told Connie.) Who else but The Dipper would design and build a million-dollar mansion with ceilings, doorways, furniture, and toilets scaled to a giant's dimensions?

Wilt is actually a wealthy capitalist—a landlord, businessman, and Nixon Republican (when he remembers to register). He isn't noted for his harmonious relationships with teammates. But The Dipper's interminable battles with owners, coaches, and league officials have caused many players to view him as a symbol of hard-nosed anti-Establishmentism.

Chamberlain-sized tales abound in the NBA. Everyone has a "Dipper" story. And Wilt has done nothing to discourage the colorful accounts of his enormous appetite, herculean sexual exploits, terrifying strength, and high-rolling casino excursions.

A significant part of the Chamberlain mystique is the conviction—held by most of his opponents—that Wilt rarely makes use of all his ability. Although he is older and slower, many still assume Dipper can do whatever he *really* wants on the court. They point to the record book, then remind each other not to antagonize him.

Chamberlain's legion of admirers pay scant attention to the curious contradiction in his approach to the game: while Wilt often seems disdainfully unwilling to make constant use of his skill and power, he clearly agonizes over his inability to lead teams to championships and angrily chafes under the "Loser" label the press has assigned him. Bill Russell was revered for winning—and for squeezing the utmost from his potential. The Dipper, on the other hand, attracts a strange admiration for refusing to make a total commitment during most games. That Chamberlain has become fabulously rich and famous, *without* giving completely of himself to teams, fans, or employers, has a cool ring of ripping off "Whitey."

Hawkins had grown up in awe of Chamberlain. He is still awed by him. They became friendly at schoolyard tournaments while Hawk was in his late teens. Connie was always welcome at Wilt's Harlem bar, Chamberlain took Hawk for spins in his newest autos, and Dipper even came to watch him play with the ABL, the ABA, and the Globetrotters.

But Chamberlain is often condescending toward Hawkins; either too busy to speak with him or quick to put him down. Wilt is the only person around whom Connie sometimes loses his poise. Hawk tries too hard to please. When Dipper tells a joke, Hawkins may clap his hands and laugh much too loudly.

"In an awful lot of ways," Connie says seriously, "Dipper comes close to bein perfect—on the court and in the kind of life he's got for himself."

But Chamberlain wasn't the Suns' only problem in the playoff. Even without Wilt, Los Angeles had finished a strong second in the Western Division. They were heavily favored to beat Phoenix. Baylor, West, and Chamberlain each had played in more playoff games than all the Suns combined.

Nevertheless Phoenix had several reasons for hope. First, the Lakers were torn by their usual dissension. The superstars didn't get along, and Chamberlain wasn't fond of coach Joe Mullaney.

Second, Wilt was far from his peak physically. He was expected to slow down the other Lakers. In fact, some Los Angeles players preferred that Dipper not return that season. They had played well without him—generating a solid running game with 6' 9" rookie Rick Roberson at center—and they wanted a shot at taking the title on their own.

Third, Phoenix had been winning recently—and the Suns had Hawkins.

The playoffs turned out to be a season in microcosm. All the fluctuating tensions and emotions of an eighty-two-game schedule were compressed into two frantic weeks of sustained pressure. Eventually, it was more than the youthful Suns could handle.

But, for Hawkins, the playoffs were added proof of his stature within the league. Connie played superbly—averaging 25 points, 14 rebounds, and 6 assists—and almost led Phoenix to an astonishing upset.

The flight to Los Angeles for the opening game was delayed twice, from 5:30 to 7:00 to 9:00 P.M. But, at 8:15, Hawk was still wandering about the apartment collecting his things. Arthur, wearing an Indian headband, was ready to leave. "Man, it's all right for Hawk to always be late," he worried, "but I haven't got his situation—and I can't afford the fines."

Nevertheless, by 8:25 we were leisurely driving toward the airport. For once, Hawk and Art would be early. Typically, however, Connie had forgotten something—his checkbook.

"I got mine," said Harris, "but it's empty."

When they reached the boarding gate, Connie noticed that Joe Gilmartin had yet to pick up his ticket. "I hear he's usually one of the last to board," Arthur noted.

"Oh yeah?" Hawk exclaimed. "I didn't know that."

"How *could* you know," chuckled Harris. "*You're* always *the* last one!"

A beautiful, long-haired blonde met Fox in the lobby of the Sheraton Airport Hotel, when the Suns arrived in Los Angeles. "Foxie is an idiot to let Jerry see his broad the night before a playoff game," said a player—on the way to meet his own date.

Hawkins appeared relaxed. But the tension had begun to build. "I think everybody's startin to feel it," he said, eating a midnight hamburger in the coffee shop. "You can't put your finger on it, but they're actin kind of different."

Chamberlain already dominated his thoughts: "They say he did everything the other night; twenty-one points, seventeen rebounds—I guess he's ready."

"How did you do against him?"

"He'd only played twenty-eight minutes when he hurt his knee," Connie said. "But I could tell how different he was from the schoolyards. Much tougher. You couldn't get inside, he blocked everything."

Proski and Neil Johnson were the only Suns at the hotel bar. "What are you doin tonight?" Neil asked Connie, grinning.

"Just watchin TV. Tomorrow is business, I ain't goin out."

"Great," said Johnson. "I like to see you taking good care of my money."

Colangelo's pregame exhortation was delivered in a less-than-inspiring monotone. "We have everything to gain," he told the players. "There's really nothing to lose. No one expected us to be here. But there's no doubt in my mind that we're going to win. We've got to get one of the first two here in LA. Then, three of the next four are in Phoenix—and you can call it quits, because it's all over. They haven't beaten us in Phoenix all year.

"We came this far, men, because everybody put it together. It took us a while, but we've done it. All right now, I think everybody is loosey-goosey and anxious. This is it. We're young, we're eager, and we're ready. Let's go!"

Colangelo's strategy was to draw Chamberlain away from the basket by having Fox shoot from outside. But Los Angeles was aware of Fox's touch and Wilt's immobility. Mullaney assigned Chamberlain to guard Silas—usually a weak long-range shooter—while Baylor took Fox. Wilt hung back, clogging the lane.

At first, the move backfired. The Lakers were sluggish and disorganized. Silas, left unguarded by Chamberlain, hit often from the perimeter. Connie fed him twice for layups and hit Fox with a behind-the-back pass. The Suns' fastbreak caught Los Angeles off-balance. Early in the second quarter, Phoenix led, 36-25.

Then veteran John Egan replaced rookie Dick Garrett in the Laker backcourt, and the game turned. Egan got the ball to Chamberlain, West, and Baylor. He forced Goodrich into numerous turnovers.

As the Lakers closed the gap, Phoenix got its first taste of playoff pressure—and responded badly. The togetherness of the previous weeks disintegrated. Silas (26), Hawkins (24), and Van Arsdale (20) shot well, when they had the ball. But they didn't have it often. The jittery Suns took bad shots and committed 23 turnovers. The substitutes seemed frozen by fear. Arthur Harris, moving in a virtual trance, twice passed directly to a startled Elgin Baylor. Chamberlain, though hardly agile, overpowered Phoenix for 29 points and had 19 rebounds.

The Suns were routed, 128-112.

"We've gone back to the same shit we did months ago," Hawk fumed after the game. "Everybody got tight and went for himself. Fuck, if this is the way we're gonna play, I wish we hadn't even made the playoffs! There's no way things could be more screwed up."

Hawk soon discovered that there was a way—and Neil Johnson had found it. "He punched some guy," explained a haggard Colangelo, in the hotel lobby.

A drunk had insulted Neal Walk outside the hotel. Then Johnson insulted the drunk—who went inside and returned with two more drunks. "Now what are you going to do?" he challenged.

"What do you want me to do," asked Johnson, "hit you?"

"Try it," said the drunk.

Johnson tried it. As the drunk sagged to the pavement, Neil tried it again. When the drunk's friends had scraped their buddy off the concrete, they called the police. It took Colangelo an hour to smooth things over.

"I spent the next four days in Phoenix takin things real easy," Connie remembers. "By the second game, I had my composure back."

This was fortunate, because Colangelo had a surprise for him. "Connie," he said in the huddle, with the score tied 17-17, "you guard Wilt."

"What?"

"Wilt. I want you to guard Wilt."

Recalls Hawkins, "I was scared. I was sure I couldn't stop him, that I'd foul out."

"How's the leg?" he asked, sliding behind Chamberlain in the Lakers' forecourt.

"All right," The Dipper answered coldly. Then he took a pass from Baylor, bulled past Hawkins, and dunked.

The matchup was visually ludicrous. Wilt dwarfed Connie, accentuating his frail physique. When Hawkins stood close behind Chamberlain, The Dipper's shoulders filled his horizon. But Connie soon realized that Wilt wasn't too offensively inclined. "He was like me after my operation—worried about the knee," Hawkins says. "He wasn't turnin to the basket as quick. That made me a little more confident."

Hawkins boxed Chamberlain off the boards and kept him from shooting at point-blank range. Once, Connie spun in front of The Dipper, batted away a pass, and started a fastbreak.

Positioned behind Chamberlain's inside hip, Hawk placed his hand on Wilt's side. The Dipper bitched to the officials that Connie was holding. Finally, he brought his hand down hard on Hawkins's forearm. "Now," said Chamberlain, "stay off me."

"I thought he'd broken my arm," remembers Connie. "The pain was brutal for a couple of seconds." The arm was discolored for a week.

Hawk continued to use his hands on Wilt—but much more gently. With help from Silas and Green, he guarded Chamberlain for 11 minutes during the first half and held him to four points.

Egan was slowed by a groin pull. Without him, the Lakers' offense was disjointed. Phoenix might have moved ahead, but Hawkins's shooting was off—"I was pressing"—and the bruising, sloppy first half ended, 47-47.

Hawk was the last to leave the Phoenix locker room. He looked up to see Scotty McDonald standing in the doorway. "Calm down," Scotty said, placing a hand on Hawkins's shoulder. "You're dribbling ten feet in the air. Just relax and play your game. One man can turn it around tonight—and that man is you!"

The second half belonged to Connie Hawkins. As 17,501 hostile fans gasped and groaned, he put together everything in his repertoire. On defense, Hawk continued to hold Chamberlain. He beat Wilt to rebounds under both boards, led the Phoenix running game, hit long arching jump-shots, and challenged The Dipper—driving at him to score a succession of acrobatic dunks and twisting layups.

Connie finished with 34 points, 20 rebounds, and 7 assists. He scored 15 in the final quarter, including 9 in a row. It was the most spectacular individual performance of the series.

As the Suns took control, Hawk darted from behind Wilt to block a layup by Keith Erickson, then sprinted to the other end of the court, caught a long pass, and dunked. Later, he took the ball deep in the right corner, bolted around Happy Hairston, and slid along the baseline. Chamberlain loomed in front of him. Hawk moved the dribble from his left to right hand, slipped past Wilt on the inside, and crossed under the basket. Just before he emerged on the far side of the loop, Hawk left the floor, shifted the ball back to his left hand, and extended his arm to the side—as though he was passing to someone cutting down the middle. Instead, still hanging in the air, he suddenly swept the ball over his head into the net. Behind him, Chamberlain waved futilely, staggered, and almost fell.

A momentary silence gripped the Forum. Then the building vibrated with noise. The Phoenix players leapt off the bench, waving their fists. "It was," Van Arsdale said later, "the most incredible shot I've ever seen."

Roused by Hawkins, the entire Phoenix team played with confidence. The snap was gone from the Lakers' attack, the veterans were tired, and the old antagonisms soon surfaced. Baylor glared at Chamberlain. Wilt yelled at the officials and barked at Egan. Happy Hairston lost his cool and swung at Silas, but Wilt dragged them apart. Even West cast annoyed looks at Garrett, when the rookie failed to get him the ball.

At the buzzer, the Suns skipped around Hawkins like excited teenagers. They had won, 114-101. "Now," shouted Silas in the noisy locker-room, "those motherfuckers got to come to us!"

Down the hall, the Lakers dressed in near-silence. "With their quickness and outside shooting, they have the type of club that can beat us," said a weary Jerry West. "And, right now, I'd have to say Hawkins is the best all-around forward in the NBA."

An hour later, Hawk sat at the bar in the Forum Club. He was still exhausted, but feeling no pain: "I'm on top of the world. I calmed down after Scotty talked to me. He made me relax. Then everything went smooth. All the guys played great. Elgin looks real tired now. They all do. I think we're gonna run 'em out of the gym."

Then the confidence melted from his expression. In a darkened corner of the room, sitting on the edge of a table, was Wilt Chamberlain. The Dipper had scored just 19 points—few during the twenty-five minutes Hawkins guarded him—but any reminder of his existence still unsettled Connie. "We got to hope *he* don't start comin on," Hawkins said. "Maybe I better say something to him."

Hawk approached Chamberlain, who was talking to a girl. "How you doin Dipper?"

"All right man." Wilt nodded. "You played a hell of a game."

"Thanks. You too."

Chamberlain smiled coldly. "How's your family?" he said.

"Pretty good. Nancy woulda come out for the playoffs, but she didn't want to leave the kids."

For a moment, neither man spoke. Finally Connie said, "See you in Phoenix, man."

"Yeah," said Chamberlain, "I'll be there."

As Hawk moved away, he heard the girl ask, "Wilt, what sign were you born under?"

"The dollar sign," answered Chamberlain. "The dollar sign."

The next day, several players sat in the locker room after practice, discussing their opponents. The Suns' tone was almost disdainful. "They've got all kinds of personality problems on that team. Elgin really hates Wilt," noted Goodrich, who had played for the Lakers. "He always has. And Wilt hates him. When Chamberlain sets up on the same side as Elgin, Baylor hasn't got any room to drive. It ruins his game and he's always mad about it. Wilt knows. That makes him mad."

"Dipper doesn't like West either—and the feeling is mutual," said Chambers, another ex-Laker. "They all pretty much dislike each other. But, the one nobody likes is Hairston."

"How come?" asked Connie. "The man plays good, but all you hear is that he's a bad dude."

"They say Happy talks behind people's backs," said Fox.

"I know this," Silas added. "West acts like he digs *everybody*, but he don't dig Hairston. After I had that fight with him the other night, West comes over to me and says, 'I wish you'd busted his ass!' "

Colangelo, working hard to orchestrate his team's emotions, invited the Suns' bachelors (Fox, Walk, Harris, and Green) and Connie and me to dinner at his home, the night before the third game.

With the exception of Hawkins—the superstar—the players were clearly uncomfortable in the boss's expensively furnished house. They talked in muffled voices and giggled nervously. When wine was served, they seemed preoccupied with not spilling it on the rug. There was much self-conscious teasing.

"Lamar, you sure you don't want fried chicken?"

"Hey Neal, I don't think this food is gonna be kosher."

After several bottles of red wine and a large Italian dinner, however, the mood turned mellow. Colangelo uncorked some Chianti. The players sat in soft chairs or sprawled on the rug in front of the fireplace in the dimly lighted den. Now the laughter was real.

"Did I tell you guys about my negotiations with Heyward Dotson, the Rhodes Scholar from Columbia?" Jerry asked.

Dotson, a high-strung backcourt man, was considered by some—himself included—to be a black Bill Bradley. This opinion was not shared by pro scouts. Dotson had been Phoenix's ninth draft-choice.

"His agent phoned me," Colangelo recalled. "The guy said, 'Heyward is going to England for the next two years, but before he goes—so he can better finance his education—we'd like to sign a three-year, no-cut contract for about three hundred thousand dollars.' I said, 'Oh, that's fine. Only the contract we're offering is for one year—without a no-cut clause— for fifteen thousand dollars. And Dotson doesn't get a penny till he comes back and plays for Phoenix!'

"The agent didn't even argue," Jerry continued. "He said, 'All right, but can we *announce* that Heyward got three hundred thousand? He is a very proud young man. His feelings would be hurt if people thought he didn't get a lot of money.'"

When the laughter subsided, Colangelo asked, "Hey Connie, how was your evening with Joe DePre?" Between the first and second playoff games, Jerry had given Hawkins fifty dollars to entertain DePre, the Suns' third draft-choice.

"He ate too much Mexican food," said Hawk, reclining on the rug. "He spent the whole night on the toilet."

"But how did you like him."

"Nice guy, bad bowels," Connie answered. Everyone cracked up.

There was a warmth in the room, a feeling of closeness that had not existed all season. Colangelo poured another glass of wine and looked at his players. "I feel something building here," said the young general manager. "I get the feeling something incredible could happen. This could be the impossible dream."

Phoenix had gone slightly daffy over the Suns. A huge crowd greeted their plane. As Connie and Arthur drove to the third game, people on the street yelled to wish them luck. A "Sold Out" sign was posted outside the Coliseum for the first time in the history of the franchise. Scalpers were getting forty dollars a ticket.

In the locker room, Colangelo announced that Connie would start at center. Hawk was worried. "It might set off Dipper," he said to Silas during the warmups. "He might get mad, go to the basket, and get me in foul trouble."

"The old lineup, with Fox, is better," Paul agreed. "No sense rufflin Dipper."

Three minutes before game time, Hawkins approached Colangelo at the bench. "He took our advice right away," Connie recalls. "He said, 'You guys are right.' That's what I liked most about Jerry. He was open-minded, not like Kerr. Especially after Scotty left, you could always talk to Colangelo."

The Suns drubbed Los Angeles, 112-98. They outscrambled the Lakers, battered them on the backboards (66-47), and eventually ran them down with a blistering fastbreak—sparked by Hawkins.

The usually placid Fox turned aggressive at center. He scored 17 points and no longer seemed terrified by Chamberlain. Silas, who had lost ten pounds late in the season and was leaping brilliantly, had 21 points and 16 rebounds. Goodrich scored 29, while Van Arsdale harassed West into another poor shooting night.

But, once more, the difference was Hawkins. Early in the fourth quarter, with Phoenix leading, 79-78, and the crowd on the verge of mass apoplexy, Connie swished a fifteen-foot jumper over Hairston, hit another jump shot from behind the circle, fed McKenzie for a layup, then stole a pass and threw a long strike to Goodrich. Gail blew the shot, but Lamar tipped it in.

Los Angeles became more physical with Hawkins. Hairston, 7' Mel Counts, and 6' 9" Rick Roberson bumped and elbowed him on every play. Connie left the floor two minutes early—with 19 points, 10 rebounds, and 9 assists—when Roberson's finger mysteriously appeared in his eye.

But the injury was minor, and the Lakers seemed near total collapse. Chamberlain—for reasons found only in the murky depths of his singular psyche—stationed himself almost exclusively at the high post. He took just 8 shots, rarely went to the boards, and had only 11 points and 12 rebounds.

Wilt had always objected to playing the high post. When Mullaney stationed him there for several minutes, Chamberlain apparently decided to spite the coach by remaining all evening. "I wanted him there to help run a few plays for West," said the befuddled Mullaney. "But we certainly didn't want him way out there all the time!"

The Lakers got progressively more quarrelsome. With twenty seconds left in the first quarter, they tried to set up West. But Garrett became confused and threw a sudden pass to Wilt at the foul line. The Dipper, less than a threat from that distance, pushed the hot potato to an unsuspecting Baylor. Elgin's off-balance shot didn't come close. Hairston and Baylor walked to the huddle shouting at Garrett.

Later, when Hawkins sprang in front of Chamberlain to steal a Hairston pass, Wilt put hands on hips and cursed Happy while everyone else ran in the other direction.

The thirty-five-year-old Baylor, unable to stay with the Suns on defense, was incensed at Mullaney's criticisms from the bench. At one point, he ran past the coach and yelled, "Shut the fuck up, I know what I'm doing!"

The Lakers' frayed unity wasn't improved when Chamberlain—instead of brooding over the defeat—examined the stat sheet and complained loudly that the official scorer had cheated him out of several rebounds.

There was glee in the Phoenix dressing quarters. "Those dudes just quit," shouted Lamar. "The superstars aren't so super!"

"We're gonna have to get out our cold-weather clothes again," Silas cried. "We're goin to New York or Milwaukee for the finals!"

Hawkins shared some of his teammates' giddy confidence, but remained apprehensive. "Nothing's safe, long as they got Dipper," he said, shaving flawlessly before the fourth game. "I feel good about myself. But Dipper is like a volcano. You never know when he's gonna explode."

Chamberlain exploded that night. He scored 29 points, had 19 rebounds, and shut off Silas's offense for the first time in the series. But Phoenix won nonetheless. The Suns jumped to a 19-2 lead, let most of it slip away, then saw Hawkins carry them to victory, 112-102.

Mullaney toughened his defense by benching Baylor and Hairston in favor of rookie Rick Roberson (6′ 9″, 230 pounds), and much-traveled John Tresvant (6′ 7″, 220 pounds). He used 6′ 5″ Keith Erickson for Garrett. This "Thug" unit—as the Los Angeles writers dubbed them—pounded the Suns physically and matched Phoenix under the boards. But Los Angeles's shooting was again off.

Chamberlain, however, kept the Lakers in contention. The huge Phoenix lead was cut to 56-53 at halftime. Tresvant's punishing defense had limited Hawkins to just five shots in the opening half. When Connie didn't score in the first nine minutes of the second half, the Suns appeared to be winding down.

Then Hawkins broke loose.

Hitting several long jump-shots over Tresvant, driving past Chamberlain for dunks and layups, Hawkins scored 16 points in the next nine and one half minutes. Twice he passed to Goodrich—who scored 34—for easy baskets.

"Hawk," yelled Harris, amid the pandemonium in the Phoenix locker room, "you are one bad motherfucker."

"Yeah," said Hawkins, smiling. "I guess I'm the baddest motherfucker in the whole wide world!"

Connie had scored 24 points and grabbed 13 rebounds, but for fifteen minutes he was too exhausted to strip off his uniform. "Tresvant and Roberson were beatin the hell out of us," he said to Silas. "Every bone in my body hurts."

"I'm dead too," Paul replied, his voice a hoarse whisper. "The Dipper was really on his thing. He's frightening."

"But we won, anyway. That should give 'em something to think about."

"We won," said Silas, "because this ballclub has grown up, grown together. Everybody was doin it. Even Dipper can't stop us."

"Just one more win," Connie said softly. "It's unbelievable."

Twenty-four hours later, the Suns were no longer swaggering and self-confident. The Factory nightclub had been reserved for a victory party and champagne bottles had peeked from buckets of ice in the locker room, but Chamberlain had scored 36, West had scored 36, and the Lakers had slaughtered Phoenix, 138-121.

Fox, who suffered a sprained ankle late in the fourth game, was unable to dress. Neal Walk, his replacement, scored 18 points, but slowed the Phoenix offense and had no outside shot to lure Chamberlain from the basket. When Los Angeles raced ahead, the Suns came unstrung. They committed 18 turnovers and shot badly.

Connie had 28 points and 19 rebounds, but couldn't control the tempo. Back-to-back games had drained him. The quick, strong Tresvant muscled Hawk far out of position. Connie no longer had the strength to resist. When Hawk did drive around Tresvant, Chamberlain emerged to block more than half a dozen of his shots.

But the Suns still might have won—if not for a coaching error by Colangelo.

With Los Angeles ahead, 83-67, in the third quarter, Connie mobilized a Phoenix charge. He took five straight rebounds and started fastbreaks, often dribbling into the forecourt himself. He fed Van Arsdale and Walk for layups and hit a pair of spinning rebounds. Phoenix outscored Los Angeles, 16-2.

Goodrich's jumper sliced the lead to 85-83, with four minutes remaining in the quarter. Counts hit from the baseline, but Goodrich quickly broke free and was fouled for two shots. The Suns appeared in control.

Colangelo signaled for a time-out.

The players exchanged puzzled glances as they walked to the bench. "We had momentum rolling for us," Connie says. "The Lakers were getting ready to blow. The time-out let them get reorganized. We lost our edge."

"Why did you call time?" Goodrich asked in the huddle.

"You guys looked a little tired," Jerry explained. "I thought you could use a rest."

But it was the Lakers who benefited. They gathered themselves, corrected strategic mistakes, and turned the game into a rout.

"I've never felt this beat-up," Connie said, eating dinner later that night.

"Everytime I moved, I got hit by Tresvant or Counts or Dipper. There's pain all over my body."

Hawk's emotions had made a complete turn. He was so fatigued the fork quivered in his hand as he pecked listlessly at the food. "I'm down," he said. "We played lousy and I'm just plain depressed."

The Suns still led, three games to two. But Colangelo—apparently convinced they had no chance if the series returned to Los Angeles—gambled everything on the sixth game in Phoenix.

In the locker room, Sunday, after losing the fifth game, Jerry had grimly told the players, "As you all know, we've got to get it Tuesday in Phoenix —period. There's no tomorrow. I don't want you down. Goddamn, we're still up. They got to beat us on our own floor Tuesday. I want you to be confident, cause that's what I am. Remember, Tuesday is it."

"I think Jerry's makin a mistake, puttin it all on tomorrow," Connie said at his apartment the following afternoon. "All we really need is one out of two. But he's making tomorrow life or death. That puts more pressure on everybody."

That night, Connie and I sat up late—talking about anything but the Lakers. He seemed more composed. Before turning in, Hawk grinned and said, "Like Jerry always tells us, 'Tomorrow is just another day.' "

"You've become a wit."

"A semiliterate wit."

The telephone awakened me at 1:30 Tuesday afternoon. "Let me speak to The Hawk," a voice demanded.

"Who is this?"

"Never mind who it is," said the voice, which clearly belonged to Colangelo. "Let me speak to him."

"You'll be happy to know he's still sleeping peacefully," I said, after checking Connie's room.

"What time did he go to sleep?"

"About three."

"How does he seem now?"

"Jerry, he's *asleep*. How can I know how he seems?"

"Oh, yeah. Well, ah, how do you think we'll do?" Colangelo groped, so uptight he was even willing to talk with a writer.

"I think you'll win. If you do, when is the first game in Atlanta?"

"The paper says Friday, but it's Thursday. No, wait a minute. I think the paper says Thursday but it's Friday. Hell, first we got to win tonight."

There was a silence. Then Jerry said, as matter-of-factly as possible, "I called because I thought maybe Hawk and I should go out and have some lunch and talk. Maybe he's nervous. It would help him relax."

"Maybe *who's* nervous? Coach, he's asleep!"

"Yeah," said Colangelo. "Well, tell him I called."

Hawkins woke up an hour later. We ate quietly at the Pancake House, then drove back to his apartment. In the parking lot, Connie shut off the motor, leaned back, and closed his eyes. For several minutes he was silent.

Before leaving for the Coliseum, Hawk shaved—and cut himself half a dozen times. "It's really hittin me now," he conceded, looking at his bleeding face in the mirror. "I can feel the pressure."

Los Angeles won, 104-93.

West was brilliant, scoring 35 points. He stole the ball 12 times. Garrett and Erickson combined for 34, while Baylor had 19. Chamberlain took only eleven shots, but made 26 rebounds and blocked a dozen shots.

The game was frantic, emotional, and close until the final moments. Play was rough and ragged; bodies crashed constantly to the floor. Errors were plentiful. Tresvant missed an unguarded dunk. Three overanxious Suns collided and knocked a Los Angeles shot back into the hoop. The noise from the screaming, sellout crowd was ear-splitting. The players disputed every call. Both benches berated the officials. Some fans even fought among themselves.

The Suns took a 22-9 lead in the first quarter. Then West and Garrett hit from outside, Phoenix's ballhandling got shaky, and the Lakers rallied. Hawk made several steals. His passes were crisp and accurate. But he was slammed and battered as he glided through the Lakers' defense. Connie no longer had the strength to go head-to-head with Chamberlain. His outside shot was off-target. When he drove, Dipper pounded the ball into his face. Soon, Hawkins was blowing layups, shooting off-balance to avoid Wilt. The Suns trailed at halftime, 46-43.

The Lakers' experience and maturity was increasingly evident. They made fewer foolish errors and their lead widened to 59-52, midway through the third quarter. Then Colangelo sent Harris and McKenzie into the backcourt and gambled on a press. Stan and Arthur tore at the Los Angeles guards, jostling West and stealing the ball from Garrett.

"Stanley and Arthur really had 'em shook up," Connie recalls. "West was even hollerin at the refs. They weren't getting clear shots no more. The fans were goin nuts. I was sure we'd win."

The third quarter ended, 73-73.

Colangelo returned Goodrich and Van Arsdale for Harris and McKenzie. "They'd done their job," Jerry explained later. "We had to go back to our offense."

"It was a mistake," says Hawkins. "We had the momentum. Stan and Art were givin it to us."

The Suns hustled feverishly in the final quarter. Hawk broke loose for 8 points and the game was tied five more times. With seven minutes remaining, Connie swished a sixteen-foot jump-shot, was fouled, and completed the 3-point play. Phoenix led, 85-83. Once more, Hawk raised his fist triumphantly.

The Suns were never ahead again.

With less defensive pressure against their backcourt, the Lakers scored 7 straight points. Phoenix panicked. As the crowd begged them to rally, the Suns heaved wild passes and forgot to cover against the fastbreak. Hawkins, almost doubled over by exhaustion, missed a pair of free throws. Los Angeles pulled far ahead and won by 11.

In the stunned quiet of the locker room, Connie—who had scored 24—paced back and forth, fists tight. "We let it get away," he mumbled, fighting back tears. "We let it get away."

An ashen-faced Colangelo addressed his downcast team. He tried to sound calm, confident—but his voice wavered and the conviction was gone from his words. "Practice here at one o'clock tomorrow. All right, we lost the game. It's a good thing we've got another one to look forward to. It could be the end of the fuckin series tonight, but it's not. We've got another shot at it. I *know* we can win."

But Colangelo had bet all his psychological chips on the sixth game. Now his fighting words rang hollow. A sense of imminent doom hung over the Suns.

"That night, he took us to a restaurant and bought everybody steaks," recalls Connie. "We got pretty loose and drunk. It was a good idea. At the table, I told Jerry that I thought he'd done a fantastic job for us—I criticize him a lot, but I still meant what I said—that we couldn't have come this far without him. He seemed really gratified."

As the players ate and drank, however, the talk was of the season past—not the game upcoming. It was as though the Suns knew their year had already ended.

"Jerry held a practice the next day," Silas remembers, "but all we did was shoot. We needed some new strategy—something to make us feel we could turn it around. But he just called a meeting in LA and asked for suggestions. We voted on plenty of ideas, but nobody could agree."

"Do you think you're going to win?" I asked Connie, the night before the seventh game.

"*I* think we're going to win," he said, frowning. "But, other than Paul—and maybe Stan and Arthur—I don't think the other guys really do."

"What does that mean?"

Hawk lowered his eyes and shook his head. "It means I got to try, somehow, to get things together myself."

The Suns were tense in the locker room. Van and Gail sat together, looking vacantly at the wall. McKenzie lay on the floor, eyes closed, fists clenched. "You could feel the fear," remembers Silas. "Connie was quiet, edgy—ready. But the team had no closeness. The other guys were so frightened, I knew it was over."

Colangelo entered the room with Scotty McDonald, their feud apparently forgotten in the magnitude of the moment. "We're not changing anything, men," Jerry told the Suns defiantly. "All the marbles are on the table. There's no tomorrow. That must be our approach tonight. Play one hundred and one percent and we'll come off as winners."

Voice quivering, Scotty followed with three minutes of rambling free-association, in which he appeared to compare the Suns to the 1955 University of San Francisco NCAA champions. "I didn't know what he was talkin about," says Hawk, "but it seemed real emotional."

"The theme for winning tonight is one word—*ferocity*. How ferocious can you be?" McDonald said, spitting out the sentences in short bursts. "Once, in Philadelphia, I said my prayer to you. I'm gonna say it again. Joe [Proski] is a Catholic. Joe will think about it. The rest of you can do anything you want.

"Our Lady of Victory, give us grace that by His assistance, first, that we win. Second, that each one plays and so conducts himself on the court as to earn the respect and the confidence of his fellow teammates. Third, may this be another step forward on the long road back."

While the players pondered what "long road back" he might be referring to, McDonald cried, "Now, one second, hold it—giggle. Now, go out there and *fuck* and be *ferocious!* All right, let's go!"

Thus inspired, the Suns burst onto the court and proceeded to collapse. Unable to generate an offense, they drove blindly at Chamberlain—who blocked shot after shot. West scored from outside and the Lakers' fast-break swept unopposed.

Only Hawkins kept his cool. "But I couldn't try and do it alone—like I did against San Diego," he says. "I couldn't get inside consistently, cause of Dipper. They double-teamed me, so I passed to the open man—but guys kept droppin the ball or throwin it away."

Phoenix trailed at half-time, 63-40.

"I couldn't believe it," says Silas. "I felt we could still come back. I waited for Jerry to get us reorganized. Like, he had to remind the guards to stay back against the break. We needed *specific* instructions. But, I guess he didn't know what to say."

Unable to control his anger, frustration, and disappointment, the young general manager instead lashed out at the players. "What I'm going to talk about is what we're going to do in the second half," Colangelo rasped. "I'll be a motherfucker, if you don't do it, you're gonna be sittin next to me on the bench or you'll go take a fuckin shower, cause *my* fuckin year is not gonna be ruined in the last game of the year—and yours either. I'll see to that.

"You better be hungry in the second half because you didn't do a fuckin thing in the first half. You forgot about *everything* we said! I don't want to see anybody shoot a layup over Chamberlain, except Hawkins and Silas. The first cocksucker who does is comin out! If you want to make a mockery out of it, I'll do it. And I'll do it with some fuckin class!

"I don't care if they outscore us ninety to zero in the second half," he added, "you're gonna do what I tell you to do—period."

Silas began to speak, but Colangelo cut him off.

"It's too late, too late," Jerry cried. "Men, we can still win it in the second half—if we put it all together. Now get loose, cause nothing more is going to be said in here. But I hope you got the message: we're going down together, or we're gonna win it together. If you put a hundred-percent effort into it, we've got a shot. Now, let's go!"

Heads bowed, they returned to the slaughter. Hawkins, Silas, and Van Arsdale stood at midcourt during warmups, trying desperately to concoct a new strategy. But there wasn't enough time.

Thrashing with the helpless frenzy of drowning men, the Suns were soon in total disarray. Chamberlain, West, and Baylor—temporarily at peace with one another—scored almost at will. The Dipper had 27 rebounds.

Alone, amid the débâcle, Hawkins continued to play his game. Expression unchanged, moves still smooth and precise, he seemed a lonely island of dignity. "I couldn't relate to what was happening," he says. "It hurt too much. I kept tellin myself we'd come back. I felt, if I could set up guys for some easy baskets, they'd get out of their defeatist thing and we'd start to move."

Hawk scored 25 points and took down 15 rebounds. But it was hopeless. "I blanked out the score from my mind," Connie recalls. "But, with three minutes left, I looked up and saw we were behind by thirty. Then, I knew it was over."

Los Angeles won, 129-94.

The realization of the defeat left Hawkins dazed. He doesn't remember walking from the court to the locker room. He has no recollection of sitting before his dressing stall, slapping his hands together.

The eerie, uneven cracks were the only sound in the room.

Colangelo locked the door and spoke haltingly. "It's been a hell of a year. I want you all to realize that you did a good job. It's been a great experience for me. I'm sorry it's over."

Jerry turned away and covered his eyes. "We'll be back," he said, choking on the words, "we'll be back."

"All of a sudden, I kind of snapped out of it," Connie recalls. "I saw Jerry standin there, and I just wanted to let him know I felt he'd done fine."

Connie rose and draped his arm over Colangelo's shoulder.

"It wasn't Jerry's fault," Silas said, when the door was unlocked. "He isn't a coach, so what could you expect? Man, we've got nothing to be ashamed of. We've come a long way."

Paul nodded toward the fatigued Hawkins, leaning against a wall, towering above a knot of reporters. "That dude, he's the biggest reason for everything we accomplished. What he did this year was amazing. Man, his whole life is amazing. When I try and imagine what he's gone through—a proud man like Hawk, bein an outcast, playin with the *Globetrotters!*—I feel I'm gonna break down and cry.

"I think back to when Connie and I played in that All-Star game in New Jersey, right after high school. I try and conceive what it would have been like for me, at that age, to have my college years taken away, to be scorned as a crook, to be forced to go out and face life. I couldn't have handled it. I don't know how Hawk kept his sanity. But he did—and now he's proved he's as great as they say. And this is just the beginning. Next season, Connie's gonna put everything together and show he's the greatest player in the world."

EPILOGUE

Hawkins entered his second NBA season confident that he was about to reach his peak as an athlete. His health was excellent, his weight was up around 210 pounds, and his position with the Suns was established and secure. It was to be the season in which Connie would finally fulfill all the promise of the years of exile.

But it didn't work out that way. Hawk remained a star of considerable magnitude. He averaged 20.9 points per game, was the Suns' MVP, and was again voted a starting spot in the All-Star game. But the loose ends were not tied. No exclamation point was added to his tale of vindication.

The season was a step backward. He suffered a badly sprained ankle and a broken nose. The healing process was disquietingly slow. Connie missed twelve games. He had few sensational performances in the second half of the schedule. Rugged young forwards, like Dave Cowens and Spencer Haywood, emerged to muscle his name from the headlines. Hawk's teammates still treated him with respect and deference, but they won nine of twelve in his absence and sometimes appeared more effective when he wasn't in the line-up.

"Probably far too much has been written and said about his spectacular plays and not nearly enough about his glaring deficiencies—not the least of which is his health," wrote Dave Hicks in the *Arizona Republic,* when the season ended. "In short, Connie Hawkins has not contributed like a superstar . . . [and] that is one reason why the Suns did not make the playoffs. And several reasons why he is now expendable."

There were stories that Hawk would be traded. "The club has already extracted full value out of Hawkins," Joe Gilmartin maintained.

378

Connie was still just twenty-eight years old. But 1970–71 was his tenth season as a professional. "He's played so many games," said trainer Joe Proski that winter, "they have to take a toll. He never had any twenty-five-game college seasons. He was playing 250 a year with the Globetrotters. All that pounding up and down on concrete in the playgrounds, all the traveling in the bushes with the lousy food and the injuries that never got treated right—Hawk is a very old twenty-eight."

For the first time, Connie was forced to consider the possibility that his greatest games might already be behind him—lost in the obscurity of glass-strewn Brooklyn schoolyards or empty Minnesota arenas.

Although none of Hawkins's personal expectations were realized, the Suns were still much improved. They finished with forty-eight wins and thirty-four losses, tied with Los Angeles for the fourth-best record in the NBA.

Colangelo ditched Goodrich, shipping him to the Lakers for 7′ Mel Counts. (Interestingly, teamed with acknowledged superstars like Chamberlain, West, and Baylor, Gail accepted a subordinate role and played well—even leading the scoring when West and Baylor were injured during the playoffs.) Goodrich's spot was filled by Clem Haskins, a black guard acquired from Chicago in a trade for Jim Fox. Haskins was reputed to be a playmaker. Unfortunately, he wasn't. Phoenix continued to suffer from an absence of ballhandling in the backcourt.

But Haskins shot well and didn't intentionally monopolize the ball. When Hawkins or Van Arsdale was hot, he *tried* to find them. And Van was almost always sizzling. He had a superb season, leading the team in scoring. Silas, after a slow start, also excelled. Counts added occasional scoring punch, while Neal Walk, Lamar Green, Arthur Harris, and rookie John Wetzel made substantial contributions. Only the misfortune of re-alignment kept the Suns from the playoffs.

With three expansion-franchises joining the league, the seventeen teams were split into four divisions (the first-place and second-place finishers entered the playoffs). Phoenix found itself in the Midwest along with Milwaukee (Kareem Jabbar and Oscar Robertson), Chicago, and Detroit. How did the usually crafty Colangelo wind up in the NBA's toughest grouping? "It's just a temporary setup," Jerry assured Hawkins that summer. "A merger is coming soon. The ABA clubs will be mixed with ours. I've been guaranteed that we won't be placed with Milwaukee. Our future is protected."

The future soon appeared a bit less secure. The NBA Players Association obtained a court order blocking the merger on anti-trust grounds, then mounted a tough lobbying campaign against Congressional legislation to legalize it. With the ABA-NBA marriage delayed for at least two seasons, the Suns were marooned with Milwaukee.

The most immediate consequence was a third-place finish—behind the Bucks and Bulls—in 1970–71. Phoenix's 48 victories would have been good enough for first place in the Pacific and Central Divisions or second place in the Atlantic. But Chicago won 51 games and left the Suns with the less-than-soothing knowledge that no team in the NBA's twenty-five-year history ever won more games, or achieved a better winning percentage, yet failed to qualify for the playoffs.

A major factor in the Suns' improvement was their new coach, Lowell "Cotton" Fitzsimmons. The short, flaxen-haired thirty-nine-year-old had been hired by Colangelo, when Jerry wisely returned to the front office. Fitzsimmons had a good record at Kansas State, but at first, Hawkins was hardly elated. "Connie called me," remembers Colangelo, "and he asked, 'Hey, what is this? I've been reading Eldridge Cleaver all summer and you go out and hire a coach named Cotton!' "

Hawk's concern was genuine. "I'd never play for another coach that I really believed was a racist," he says.

But his apprehension was soon eased. "If you think you were worried when you heard about me," Fitzsimmons told him, the first day of training camp, "how do you think *I* felt knowing I'd be coaching a famous black superstar like the Hawk?"

In fact, Fitzsimmons prided himself on his rapport with black athletes. Several years earlier, to learn more about them, Cotton had shared an apartment with a black coach in Houston's toughest ghetto. "I came away with a better understanding of how black people think," he says. "Now I know their habits, their slang. I know what black players are up to. They can't put anything over on me."

Even if there seemed to be an underlying element of condescension in this approach, Fitzsimmons was still a vast improvement over the Neil Johnstons, Jim Hardings, and John Kerrs. The black players were impressed. "Cotton understood how we relate to our music, how we talk," Hawkins notes. "He didn't know as much as he thought he did, but he was *tryin,* and that's important."

Fitzsimmons's unfamiliarity with the NBA led to some early-season strategic blunders. His frequent putdowns in the locker room ("Now that you've played well in a scrimmage, why don't you try it in a real game?") caused several young players to dislike him. He annoyed many veterans by fantasizing about opposing stars. "Jeff Mullins ain't on *this* team," Hawkins would grumble to Silas. "So why don't Cotton quit tellin us how much he'd like to have him?"

Nevertheless, Fitzsimmons had a good working relationship with the players. "We respected his knowledge," says Connie. "He could teach. Trainin camp was like a clinic. After a while, he really improved our defense. We were more physical and aggressive. Cotton had us doin more switchin and helpin each other out."

To compensate for the absence of a towering superstar at center, Fitzsimmons installed a scrambling, opportunistic offense, which relied on an unusual number of set plays. "With people like Silas, Walk, Counts, Van Arsdale, and Green, we're basically strong but slow," Cotton said. "We're not a flashy team. Sometimes we even look bad when we win."

"It was a good offense for our kind of ball club," says Connie. "Cotton took advantage of our good shootin and all the physical power we had to crash the boards.

"But I think the offense cut down my scorin a little," he adds. "I set up further from the basket, and the way it worked out, I didn't handle the ball as much. The plays went according to the defense the other team used— the ball usually moved away from its strength. Since most teams concentrated on me, the plays went in the other direction."

After a sluggish start, the Suns adjusted well to Fitzsimmons's methods and were among the most physically punishing teams in the league. By Christmas, despite a slump, they were 21-18 and close on the heels of Chicago and Detroit in the scramble for second place. Hawkins had been a shade less spectacular than the previous season, but had still produced some glittering moments.

Recalls Cleveland coach Bill Fitch, "We're down a point with a couple of minutes to go. I call time and I'm coaching my butt off, talking it up with the players. Then I look down at the other bench and they've got four guys sitting around drinking Gatorade while Fitzsimmons is talking to Hawkins. What happens? Hawkins goes out and scores the next six points. Their guy is playing one-on-five and they still win!"

As usual, there were evenings when Connie's mind seemed elsewhere and his shot-total barely hovered around a dozen. When he did open up, Hawk's accuracy occasionally deserted him (7 for 26 against Atlanta and 4 for 18 against New York). But Hawkins was still "The Man" in the clutch.

When Connie scored eight points in the last four minutes to push Phoenix past Detroit, Joe Gilmartin wrote in the Phoenix *Gazette,* "The Suns are still a last-place team. But they may be one of the stronger last-place teams in professional sports. In fact, Connie Hawkins is one of the strongest any-place teams in professional sports all by himself."

In December, Connie appeared to pick up momentum. Against the Warriors, he scored 22 points, grabbed 12 rebounds, and passed for 5 assists. He jumped center against Nate Thurmond, shut off Jerry Lucas's offense in the second half, brought up the ball against a fourth-quarter press and, wrote Phil Finch in the San Francisco *Examiner,* "put on a display of all-around basketball talent not to be seen anywhere this side of Oscar Robertson."

Hawk scored 25 in the Suns' first post-Jabbar win over Milwaukee. He saved a victory by somehow overtaking San Diego's jackrabbit, Calvin Murphy, and blocking his shot with a desperation leap. He had 29 points, 18 rebounds and, Gilmartin noted, "another routinely sensational night," as Phoenix beat Detroit in overtime.

Connie moved into tenth place among NBA scorers with a 23-point average. He felt he was playing well. "Everything was fallin into place," he reflects. "I didn't feel I'd lost any speed or quickness. Actually, I thought I was gonna have a big second half in the season."

Then he was injured.

It was a freak accident. The night after Christmas, Connie went up for a rebound against Portland. His right foot landed on top of Dale Schlueter's. "I could hear the bones in my ankle," Hawkins remembers. "It sounded like walnuts—crack, crack, crack."

Connie was in the hospital for three days. At first the doctors believed the ankle was broken. But X-rays disclosed it was only a bad sprain.

A sprained ankle: a seemingly minor injury, hardly cause for serious concern. But this was to be different. Hawkins would sit out almost an entire month.

"When they said it was just sprained, I was relieved," Connie recalls. "I'd had a lot of ankle sprains before. They'd never taken long to heal."

Hawk left the hospital on a Tuesday. "There's an outside chance he might be ready for Frisco on Saturday," said trainer Proski. "It looks as though he'll definitely be ready for our Eastern trip next week."

Hawkins was on crutches for several days. He took heat and whirlpool treatment. "I figured I'd be back fast," he says.

"But, after a week, it was still swollen and sore. The same after two weeks. All of a sudden, I realized my body wasn't respondin like it used to. It was definitely takin me longer to heal."

"It happens when you get older," Proski advised. "You just don't bounce back as fast."

For the athlete, this moment is akin to discovering a first gray hair. Hawk always knew his career might suddenly end through injury, but aging—especially for a man whose body is his primary instrument of self-expression—had been an almost foreign concept.

Hawkins's sense of athletic immortality was gone forever. "It shocks you to realize your body is changin," he says. "You think differently about your future. You're more concerned about the time you have left."

Connie soon felt the stares of incredulity. Stories about his malingering and hypochondria were revived. Colangelo, who had kept out of Fitzsimmons's way, couldn't resist pressing Hawkins. "Jerry felt I was exaggeratin the pain," Hawk remembers. "He thought it was impossible for a sprained ankle to take so long."

Even Joe Proski suspected that Connie—dejected by the implications of his slow recovery—might be magnifying the discomfort. But, the trainer conceded, "there's still some pain and swelling. It's a day-to-day thing."

Colangelo's annoyance grew when Connie refused to accompany the Suns on the Eastern road trip. "I couldn't even get my foot into a shoe," Hawk explains. "I was no good to anybody. I wanted to stay in Phoenix, where I could take whirlpool and heat. But, I guess, some people felt I didn't care about the team."

His troubles with management increased when Fitzsimmons phoned Connie's apartment from Philadelphia late one night—and Hawk didn't answer. "I was asleep," says Connie. "The phone stopped ringin before I picked up. Cotton thought I was out partyin."

In fact, Hawkins rarely left his apartment. "I was too depressed to mingle with people," he says. His roommate, Arthur Harris, had just married. Connie was living alone. He spent much of his time brooding.

"What bothered me most," Hawk says, "was the feelin that the team didn't need me no more."

The Suns were winning without him. Aware they could no longer depend on Connie to bail them out, the players seemed to be pushing themselves harder. Hawk's position was shared by Lamar Green and John Wetzel. Both were playing effectively. Wetzel, an unheralded 6′ 5″ rookie, had blossomed into a fine defender. Fitzsimmons was matching him against some of the NBA's best forwards, and the scrappy Wetzel was making so many steals his teammates nicknamed him "Al Monday," after the hero of TV's *To Catch a Thief.*

Phoenix won eight of eleven while Hawkins was on the sidelines. The Suns had a tight, aggressive defense and a balanced attack. Six or seven players often scored in double figures. The team was literally outrunning its physical limitations, beating more talented opponents with hustle and selfless play.

Connie's frame of mind didn't improve when he finally returned. "I was out of shape from not running for so long," he says. "I favored the ankle. Maybe I was afraid of contact. It still hurt, I couldn't get good leverage to go up for my jumper. I was takin shots off-balance. I couldn't start quick on my drive. So, I didn't help much on offense—and my defense was even worse."

Hawkins felt—and looked—out of place. His teammates appeared to be dancing to a different tune. "With me gone, they'd been all helter-skelter and scramblin," Hawk reflects. "When I came back, I slowed them down. My tryin to finesse on offense—my one-on-one stuff—cut their tempo. I wasn't clearin the ball quick enough for their fastbreak."

The Suns continued to win. But the wins came harder and with a bit less regularity. Hawkins's contribution was often minimal. (In 31 appearances following his return, he would average only 18 per game and score over 20 points just 11 times. On 12 occasions, he would score less than 15.) His rebounding lacked fire. He appeared to play defense on his heels.

"My body wasn't right," he remembers, "and neither was my mind. It wasn't just the ankle. Even after I stopped feelin pain, my reflexes still weren't sharp. I got tired easy. I knew I was hurting the team."

It was an emotion he had never experienced. Hawk was used to people relying on him. Now he was a weight around his teammates' neck. "Sometimes Van and Paul pushed me to play better defense, but none of the guys really criticized me. I felt I still had their respect," he says. "But I was lettin them down."

Connie remained outwardly cool. Inside, however, he ached with the realization that the season was slipping away. Increasingly, he kept to himself.

Finally, Hawkins approached Fitzsimmons and volunteered to leave the starting line-up.

"I'll be the sixth man," he said. "Maybe that way I wouldn't hurt the other guys as much."

The coach was shocked. "No Connie!" Cotton exclaimed. "I appreciate what you're trying to do, but that isn't the way. I've got to have you in there. You're still our key man."

But Hawk wasn't playing like the key man. One night, Royals coach Bob Cousy was overheard saying, "Phoenix is going so well, we're in for a rough time—unless they play Hawkins a lot."

"What's the matter with him?" Colangelo asked me testily in New York. "Connie isn't going to the boards. Since he came back, he's been a perimeter player."

In Boston, late one evening, Suns broadcaster Hot Rod Hundley, once a colorful player with the Lakers, pointed across the bar at Connie and said, "Hawk and Elgin Baylor are the two greatest forwards I've ever seen. The Hawk has more talent. But, in his prime, Elgin was better. He had killer-instinct. The Hawk is like I was—he plays like he knows the sun is still comin up the next morning, no matter what happens. He knows his opponents are just guys, not the enemy.

"The other day in Buffalo, Cornell Warner—a nobody—blocks The Hawk's shot, beats him to the ball and Connie fouls him," Hundley continued. "So what does The Hawk do? He pats Warner on the ass, because the man *had* made a hell of a play. But Elgin wouldn't have done that. Man, he'd cursed out the motherfucker and then beaten him bloody."

By mid-February, however, Connie's performance started to get better. His stamina and mobility improved. The offense still didn't revolve around him, but the Suns were turning to him again in crisis situations. Hawk scored 25 against the Knicks in the Garden. At Boston, he scored 17 in the fourth quarter—and finished with 27—to single-handedly beat the Celtics.

On February 26, when the Suns arrived in Philadelphia, they had won four of five. "I was beginnin to feel a little happier about myself," Connie recalls. "My confidence was comin back. Then, while I was sittin in the coffee shop with my wife and son, Jerry Colangelo walked over and handed me the paper."

A headline in the Philadelphia *Bulletin* read, "Sixers Oppose A Tarnished Legend."

The story, by Alan Richman, was the harshest slap at Hawkins since he had entered the NBA. Richman wrote, "It now appears that he [Hawkins] plays the game with a wooden heart."

The writer described Connie's record that season as "meager" (although Hawk was averaging 21.1 per game) and added, "He might still be the best basketball player in the United States, but only on rare occasions does he still turn it on.

"Unless Hawkins happens to be inspired tonight—perhaps by the Suns' drive for a playoff spot—you probably won't see the passes that had coaches calling him the best passer in the league last year," Richman concluded. "And unless he stops worrying about his legs (he chose to sit out nearly a month with a sprained ankle), you won't see those moves to the basket. The legend will be at the game, but he might play like a wooden shell."

Connie's eyes were on the page for a long time. Then he silently handed the article to Nancy. "I didn't want to show how angry I was," he says. "Later, when I was alone in my room, I kept thinkin about it. I felt I was bein called gutless. I thought it was a slander on my whole game—and that's a slander on me."

Hawk made a shambles of the 76ers that night. He scored 30 points, took down 17 rebounds, and passed for 11 assists. But the statistics only hinted at his dominance on the court. Connie controlled the ball, clawed rebounds under both boards, and drove hard and often. The rim vibrated as he whipped through stuff after stuff.

Hawkins had 13 points in the first quarter and led a 24-3 burst near half-time. Phoenix walked off with the lead, 55-44.

Late in the game, Philadelphia rallied. The Suns' margin dipped to 85-80. But Connie exploded again. He severed the 76ers' defense with a flurry of passes and whirled inside for a savage dunk. Phoenix scored 12 straight points and won, 108-94.

"Hawk, you were incredible," Fitzsimmons said in the locker-room. "I've never seen a man play a game like that. You picked up the whole team. I knew you were great—but I didn't know you were *that* great."

"I felt I'd proved a point," Connie says. "I'd proved I wasn't washed up."

Hawkins believed he was about to resume his role as the Suns' leader. He felt he could now be more assertive, yet still mesh with his teammates' style of play. The dejection and frustration that had knotted his insides and stifled his instincts on the court, were gone. "That night, on the plane to Detroit, everybody came over to shake my hand," he recalls. "It was like a welcome back. The feeling inside me was beautiful. I was real calm. I closed my eyes and thought about how I could still turn my season around, how I could help the team make the playoffs."

The following evening, his nose was broken.

Early in the opening quarter, Hawk moved to guard Bob Quick, a lanky forward. "I was on him real tight, crouched over," Connie remembers. "Quick had the ball in both hands. He put it over his head and swung it around. His elbow caught me smack on the nose. It could have been on purpose, I couldn't tell. My nose was pourin blood. I reached up to touch it—and it was pushed over on the side of my face."

Connie was rushed to a hospital. The nose was set immediately. Late that night, heavily sedated, he phoned me from his hotel room. "It's unbelievable," he said. "Just when everything was workin out. I'm lying here with a towel pressed on my face to soak up the blood. I got bandages all over, like a fuckin mummy. And it hurts like a bitch. All I can think is, 'Why me?'"

"Did the team win?"

"Yeah. I guess it really don't matter if I play or not."

The Pistons had slipped from contention, leaving the Bulls and Suns to battle for second place and the playoffs. Chicago was a game and a half ahead with 12 remaining—but there was confidence in Phoenix. "The Bulls" wrote Joe Gilmartin, "have nobody who is a match for the Connie

Hawkins who played at Philadelphia last week, or in the fourth period in Boston a couple of weeks before that."

The Bulls had won seven straight when they came into Phoenix four days after Hawk's nose was broken. Connie wanted desperately to play. A protective face-mask was fitted by Joe Proski. The day before the game, Hawkins worked out with the team.

"He really wants to be in there," said Fitzsimmons. "And we're going to go with him and see what happens. He'll look like the Masked Marvel, but he feels he can get the job done."

"I'm still in pain," Hawkins said over the phone that night, "but I got to play. This game is so big. After everything that's happened, I can't miss this one."

Connie awakened the next morning with a fever. The doctors told him it was "the flu." He was too sick to leave his apartment. Playing was out of the question. He listened to the game on the radio.

Once more, the Suns won without him.

As a sellout crowd rocked the Coliseum, they rolled over Chicago, 115-90. Lamar Green excelled as Hawkins's replacement. The 6' 7" jumping jack scored 11 points and had 12 rebounds, 6 blocked shots, and 3 steals. He and Paul Silas held the Bulls' star forwards, Bob Love and Chet Walker, to a combined 5-for-31 from the field and 14 points.

Chicago coach Dick Motta didn't hesitate to say what many people were thinking: "They (the Suns) are definitely stronger defensively without Hawkins, and there is more movement in their offense."

Connie returned for the next game—and the Suns started losing. Ironically, after two subpar performances, Hawkins had his most productive offensive burst of the season. During a crucial stretch, Hawk scored 49 in two games against Chicago, 55 in two against Milwaukee, and 35 in one against the Knicks. But his teammates' effectiveness declined. Phoenix lost four of five.

"Hawk, I don't know why it happens," Van Arsdale said during a team meeting in Chicago, "but, when you're out there, I find I don't always go as hard. I guess, subconsciously, I'm letting up a little because I count on you to do so much for us."

Recalls Hawkins, "Other guys said the same thing. It was so flustratin for me. What could I do? My defense wasn't great, but overall I wasn't playin bad. Cotton even put me at center and I scored a lot against Kareem. But we were losin, and it looked like it was my fault."

The Suns were eliminated from playoff contention by an overtime loss to the Knicks. Connie's play was exceptional—yet he blew a point-blank followup which would have won the game in regulation time.

Hawkins outleapt Willis Reed for a rebound with four seconds remaining and the score tied. Rather than risk a foul, Reed drew back as Connie went up. But Hawk still rushed his shot—and missed. "I was thinking of Reed coming at me," he admitted in the locker room.

"That was the final crusher," Hawkins reflects. "I felt lifeless after I missed that shot. Everything had gone wrong."

With the Suns' elimination came rumors of a trade. Soon the rumors were in print. "He may well be traded," wrote Dave Hicks. ". . . When Connie first came here he *was* the franchise. Now, the franchise is bigger than any one player—even a first-class guy like The Hawk."

In the midst of this depressing period, Hawkins received an astonishing offer to leave Phoenix and jump back to the American Basketball Association.

With the merger still tenuous, the ABA-NBA dollar war had escalated to holocaust proportions. Ethics, rules, and the sanctity of contracts, had disappeared in a tidal wave of dollar bills. Veterans were jumping leagues, collegians were signing secret agreements with the pros, and old-fashioned team loyalty had long since disappeared. The players took their cue from the owners. Even under benevolent management (as in Phoenix, where the owners took the entire team on postseason trips to Hawaii and Acapulco), the athlete had constant reminders of his mercenary status. Until the ABA was founded, he was forced to play with the franchise that drafted him. He could be uprooted—by trade or expansion-draft—at the owner's discretion. When management felt his skills had declined—or didn't like his personality or politics—the player was simply released. He had no say in the matter. Tenure or dedication to the team were of no consequence. Severance and pension benefits were acquired only after the athletes unionized.

The NBA-ABA war cemented the athletes' cynicism. They saw the owners ignoring their own rules—and agreements with the colleges—by holding early draft meetings, signing college players before their eligibility expired, and encouraging pros to break contracts and switch leagues.

The players caught on fast. They hired agents and lawyers and went looking for the highest bidder. Rick Barry, Zelmo Beaty, Joe Caldwell, Ray Scott, Spencer Haywood, and Haskins jumped leagues. Dave Bing, Billy Cunningham, and Luke Jackson signed with ABA clubs, then chose to stay in the NBA when they received huge salary increases. Dozens of others—like Walt Frazier of the Knicks—used negotiations with the rival league to force better contracts from their current employers.

Both leagues were plotting new raids as the 1970–71 season ended. Many approaches had already been made. For instance, only the timidity of the Phoenix management kept the Suns from stealing John Brisker, Pittsburgh's star forward.

The ABA, meanwhile, was tossing around the name of almost every top NBA player—including Hawkins.

Connie was in Phoenix, nursing his broken nose, when David Litman called to report that the ABA's Pittsburgh team—by then known as the Condors—was about to offer Hawk a huge package deal.

Since Hawkins's departure, much had happened to the Piper franchise —little of it good. In 1969–70, Gabe Rubin moved the team back to Pittsburgh. He wasn't exactly welcomed with open arms. The Pipers hadn't drawn when they were ABA champions. Without Connie, attendance was even more dismal, and they sagged to fifth place.

Rubin's notorious penny-pinching reached new dimensions. He eliminated his advertising budget and stopped serving hot dogs to the press at halftime. When Gabe was accused of running a "two-bit operation," a local writer noted, "The charge is valid, but the price is vastly inflated."

To pad the gate, Rubin allowed teenagers to sneak through a side door and pawned off cut-rate tickets to the sponsors of industrial-league teams that played preliminaries. But even the exaggerated attendance-figures barely averaged 1,000 per game.

After the season, Gabe finally folded his tattered tent and sold the franchise to Haven Industries, a large, prosperous, New York-based conglomerate. The new owners hired Marty Blake, Atlanta's general manager, to run the front office.

But fresh money didn't change the team's luck. Concluding that the Pipers needed a new image, Blake staged a contest to rename the club. "Pioneers" was selected. It turned out to be an unfortunate choice. The athletic teams at Point Park, a local college, were already nicknamed the Pioneers. The college threatened to sue.

Blake decided that he really preferred "Condors," anyway.

In 1970–71, the Pipers-Pioneers-Condors kept losing. Fan interest was non-existent. Blake couldn't even give away tickets. One night he opened the gates—announcing free admission for everyone—and still didn't get a full house. Haven Industries fired him at midseason.

Blake was replaced by Mark Binstein, a fast-talking young businessman, who had once captained the West Point basketball team. His early months with the Condors had been impressive. Several trades (Connie's old teammates were long gone) strengthened the team. Imaginative promotions increased attendance. But the franchise had been through seven coaches, three nicknames, and wholesale roster changes in four years—and still hadn't sold more than seventy-five season tickets in any one year. Binstein needed "name" players to solidify his future. He made loud noises about raiding. Baltimore's Gus Johnson and Earl Monroe were mentioned. But the player Binstein wanted most was Hawkins—the only man who had ever generated basketball interest in Pittsburgh.

The Litmans—still very close to Connie and handling all his affairs—pleaded with Binstein to leave Hawkins alone until the season ended. With Phoenix fighting for a playoff spot, Hawk had enough on his mind. But business was business, and Binstein had no intention of waiting.

Several days after Hawkins returned to the Suns' line-up, the phone rang in his room at the Pontchartrain Hotel in Detroit. It was 3:00 A.M. The caller was Mark Binstein. "I'd like to come up and talk to you informally," he said.

Any discussions in Connie's room would have been even more informal than Binstein intended. Hawk's roommate, rookie Joe Thomas, was sharing his bed with a female companion. Assessing the atmosphere as inappropriate to high-level contract-talk, Hawkins told Binstein he would join him in the lobby.

"When David first said Pittsburgh wanted me to jump back to the ABA, my reaction was negative," Connie recalls. "But I thought I should find out what they were offering."

The Condors' offer was staggering. Hawkins would get a two-year contract for $150,000 per season with a mutual option to renew for one additional year at the same price. Connie would thus become a free agent—able to negotiate with any team—after three seasons.

In addition, Hawk would receive a bonus of $100,000 worth of stock in Haven Industries, the Condors' parent conglomerate. If the over-the-counter price of the stock dipped under $100,000 during the term of Connie's contract, Haven Industries guaranteed to make up the difference. The Condors would also cover the mortgage payments on Hawkins's Pittsburgh home and supply him with a new Cadillac to use each season.

What about the June, 1969, settlement of Connie's lawsuit? Since Hawk's signing with Pittsburgh might void his NBA agreement, Haven Industries guaranteed to make up every penny that Hawkins and the Litmans would lose. In other words, Haven Industries would assume all of the NBA's remaining responsibilities under the settlement (still about $800,000) and make all payments coming to Connie and the Litmans, including the $30,000 Hawk was to receive annually from age forty-five to age sixty-nine.

If the NBA and Phoenix sued Hawkins for breach of contract, Haven Industries and the Condors would take care of Connie's legal expenses. They would also guarantee to indemnify Hawkins against any damages the league or the Suns might win against him in court.

Since the long-range financial security of the settlement would remain intact, Binstein's offer added up to this: if Hawkins signed with Pittsburgh, he would make at least $250,000 more than if he remained in Phoenix the next two seasons (the $100,000 in stock, the mortgage payments, the car, and a $125,000 increase in salary) *and* he would become a free agent after three years.

"The whole thing was hard to believe," Connie says. "But I felt, if it was bona-fide, I'd better look into it. I had to be tempted."

Binstein pressed Hawkins for a verbal commitment. Hawk shook his head. "The onliest commitment I can give is that I'm interested," he said.

Once a return to the ABA would have been inconceivable. Now there were many new considerations. Hawk's future with the Suns was uncertain. The trade rumors had escalated. Connie was tired of the insinuations that he was a malingerer. The injuries had heightened *his* awareness that his big-earning years might be numbered. Nancy was pregnant again. His mother was ill. The Condors were offering a standard of living he could never achieve under his contract with Phoenix.

The NBA was no longer the light at the end of the tunnel. "A lot of people in the league still treat me like a piece of shit," he said. "At the All-Star game in San Diego, Commissioner Kennedy was walkin around shakin hands with everybody. When he got near me, he turned his head, stuck up his nose, and wouldn't even say Hello. And the referees, man, they still have it in for me. I don't get equal treatment, and I'm sick and tired of it."

There were additional—private—pressures. His wife and children were in Pittsburgh. Connie's relationship with Nancy was much improved. They had been married for 9 years, but for long periods—while he traveled with the Trotters or played in Minnesota and Phoenix—they had been apart. Hawk loved her deeply, yet things had not always gone smoothly when he was at home. Since the settlement, however, they had grown toward each other. Connie found Nancy less clinging, more understanding of his need to often be alone. When the season had turned sour, when self-doubts weighed on him, she had been responsive, sympathetic, in a way he had not previously felt. "She'd always stood by me," he says. "She was always in my corner—I couldn't have gotten through those eight years without her—but now there's more. I honestly feel she understands what I'm going through. She wants to help me."

Connie, meanwhile, had become more sensitive to Nancy's problems, more aware of the strain she endured raising two children virtually alone. "Sometimes you love and you don't always show it," he explained. "Or you think you show it, but it doesn't come through. Now I want it to show through, so she sees the respect I have for the way she kept our family together, kept *me* together when I was ready to come undone.

"I know she doesn't want to live in Phoenix," Hawk added. "Pittsburgh is what Nancy knows. Now I want to be with her. I want to get home."

Hawkins had made no commitment to the Condors. He believed his meeting with Binstein had been confidential. But Binstein had other ideas. The Pittsburgh executive immediately announced that an offer had been made to Connie—and that Hawk was interested. Binstein then sent wires to the media, proclaiming an imminent news conference at which he would make an announcement that would completely change the "value" of the Condor franchise.

When news of the Detroit meeting hit the papers, Colangelo demanded an explanation. "I saw the guy," Connie said.

"And?"

"He made an offer."

"Are you considering it?" Jerry asked angrily.

"I'd be a fool not to," Hawkins replied.

"You have a contract with us. What about that?"

"Jerry, I don't know anything about it, but I got to find out."

"We'll never let you break the contract," warned Colangelo—who was, at the same time, busily trying to convince several ABA players to break *their* contracts.

The response of the Phoenix basketball writers—both of whom Hawkins respected—was affectionate, but less than flattering. Dave Hicks concluded that Connie was "expendable." Joe Gilmartin wrote, "The Hawk turned pro basketball around in this town and established it once and for all as a major-league market. He is enormously entertaining and lovable, [but] he falls short of superstar status, and it is hard to believe anybody wants to pay him more than the Suns. As far as local operations are concerned, tomorrow will be Thursday no matter what The Hawk does."

Several days before the season ended, Binstein leaked a story to the Associated Press that Connie had made a "verbal agreement with the Pittsburgh Condors to sign a contract." This was a lie. But it increased the pressure on Hawkins.

Colangelo demanded, at least half a dozen times, that Connie publicly announce his intention to remain in Phoenix. "It's hurting our season-ticket sales," Jerry said. "You've got to make a statement." But Hawk held his ground.

His teammates supported him. "Go where the money is," Silas said.

"The player can't worry about the team—cause the team ain't worryin about him."

"If they're offering a better deal," said Van Arsdale, "money is what it's all about. Everyone of us feels that way."

Connie was torn and confused. "If it's really like Binstein says, if I can really break the contract, I'd have to say I'm leaning toward Pittsburgh," he told me on the phone from Phoenix. "How can I turn down that kind of money? I could do so much more for my family and my mother and my brothers. Man, you know I still don't have no idea what I want to do when I can't play any more. This would make my future more flexible. I guess I'll have to bury my pride and go back to Pittsburgh.

"A year ago," he added, "when the NBA was all I dreamed about, I couldn't have considered it. But I've proved I can play in the NBA. At least, I've proved it to *myself*. Look, times change, people change."

Then Connie hedged. "When it's really in front of me," he sighed, "maybe I won't be able to go through with it. Back to the ABA! Money or pride, what do you do?"

The season went out with a whimper in San Diego. One year before, the final game had been crucial and Connie had carried Phoenix to victory. But this time it was meaningless—and the Suns played it accordingly. Hawkins scored just 11 points. San Diego won, 132-114.

That night, Fitzsimmons met privately with each player. "I'm looking forward to a great season from you, next year," he told Connie. "Look how close we came, even with your hurt. Next year, we'll be in the playoffs." There was no mention of a trade.

The following day, however, a national wire service story declared, "Cotton Fitzsimmons, coach of the Phoenix Suns, says that he has discussed trading Connie Hawkins to Cincinnati for Tom Van Arsdale."

The coach was quoted as saying, "He's the only ball player I'd trade Hawkins for. Every team needs a draw, and Connie is quite popular with the crowd. But having Tom and Dick together would be great."

What about Hawk's possible jump to the ABA? "Connie's got a five-year contract," the story quoted Fitzsimmons. "He'll do what we tell him."

The Phoenix management treated the team to a postseason week in Acapulco. But Connie didn't join them. Less than a day after the final game, he flew to Pittsburgh to meet with the Litmans.

Roz and David faced a serious dilemma. They had helped write the contract Hawk was being asked to break. Since the settlement, they had done some legal work for the NBA. They owned stock in the Phoenix team. For a time, they had even represented Mark Binstein. But their primary allegiance was to Connie.

For ethical reasons, they hoped he would not break the contract. They worried that he would also be accused of running away from NBA competition. But they knew he couldn't play forever. "I'm really upset," Roz conceded, as she waited for Hawk to phone from the airport. "I want him to do the honorable thing—call a press conference and say he's staying in Phoenix. But I can't *tell* him that. What if he's traded—after he turns down Pittsburgh's money—and winds up in Cleveland or Buffalo, where he'll take a physical beating every night and shorten his career?"

David received a call from Phoenix owner Dick Bloch, who was in New York for a business meeting. Litman asked Bloch to fly to Pittsburgh. The club president refused indignantly. "Connie is an ingrate," Bloch snapped. "He won't get any more money out of us."

"Connie is upset by the stories about a trade," David explained.

"He's not entitled to any special protections, no player has that right," said Bloch. "But Colangelo tells me he has no plans to trade him."

Soon Colangelo phoned. Jerry maintained that Fitzsimmons had been "misquoted" and that no trade with the Royals had been seriously considered. "We've been approached," he added. "A lot of people want him. But I can guarantee Connie isn't up for trade under any circumstances."

"Do you really mean that?" David pressed.

"If Alcindor was offered, of course we'd consider it," Jerry said. "But realistically, I can guarantee Connie won't be traded."

Hawkins arrived in Pittsburgh at 3:00 P.M. A local radio station was already reporting that an anonymous source (named Mark Binstein) had disclosed that Hawkins had signed with the Condors and would play with them if they made the playoffs.

Connie went directly to the Litmans' office. David's phone had been ringing all day. Many calls were from the press. But the most persistent caller was Mark Binstein. "I want to talk to Connie today," Binstein demanded. "I mean it, David. Is he back yet? I've got to see Hawkins."

Litman finally hung up on him.

David and Connie drove to the Litmans' home. They joined Roz and Howard in the living room where, six years before, Roz had put Hawkins through the first intensive questioning about the scandal. "I won't be a party to your breaking the contract," David told him. "But I'll give you any advice you ask for."

Before their discussion became serious, Connie spoke with me on the phone. "Other than being tired, hurt, pressured, and mixed up, how are you?" I asked.

"Oh, just fine, man. Other than those little things you mentioned."

"Do you know what you're going to do?"

"No," he sighed. "I'm still confused. You realize how easy it would be for me to make the wrong decision, to really screw things up?"

Yet Hawk wasn't panicking. "A couple of years ago," he said, "this would have blown my mind. Not now. It's a bitch, but we'll work it out."

"We spoke for three or four hours," David recalls. "I tried to act as a sounding board. I explained that—if the offer was valid—it was worth about an additional quarter of a million dollars. That was obviously important to Connie. He even said he could adjust if the Suns got an injunction and forced him to sit out a year.

"Roz was clearly against breaking the contract. She tried to be neutral, but the moral aspect was too important to her. I got the feeling Connie approved of what she said."

But nothing was decided. David drove Connie home. "We have to move fast," he said, as Hawk left the car. "Binstein may sense he's losing you and withdraw the offer. He could make you look bad by announcing he's signed another NBA player and doesn't want you any more."

"I talked with Nancy for a while," Hawk remembers. "She said she'd love to have me in Pittsburgh. But she wanted me to play where I was gonna be happy. Shawna and Keenan were up. I fooled around a little with them. Then I went into our bedroom and I shut off the light and lay there by myself.

"I thought about all the money, and about what people would think if I went back to the ABA. I thought about Phoenix, and the way the NBA treated me.

"Then," he says, "I thought about my pride."

The next morning, Hawkins walked into the Litmans' office and said, "I've decided to stay in Phoenix."

"Are you sure?" Roz said.

"Yeah," he answered, a tiny smile creasing his mouth, "it's just like me to throw away a quarter of a million dollars in a few minutes."

She hugged him.

David called a press conference. As television cameras rolled, Hawkins issued the following statement: "I have been happy in Phoenix, and the management has been very fair to me. Above all, the fans there have been the most considerate and devoted I have ever encountered. Their voting me Most Valuable Player in a season in which I was injured and unable to play much of the time is a cherished honor.

"Furthermore, I have no wish to nullify my years of work to prove myself in the National Basketball Association, nor to break a contract which both sides made in good faith.

"I therefore wish to announce that, though I am flattered by the Pittsburgh offer, I have chosen to remain in Phoenix to fulfill my contract and help bring a championship to the fans there next season."

Mark Binstein attempted to wipe the egg off his face by telling another lie. He claimed that Hawkins actually wanted to sign with Pittsburgh, but the Condors had withdrawn their offer because of rumors that the ABA and NBA were near a new agreement (soon after, in fact, the leagues did cease raiding each other's players). But Hawk denied Binstein's story—and the local press believed him.

That night, Sam Nover, a young Pittsburgh sports commentator, said over the air, "The whole thing boils down to one fact—Mark Binstein is an overzealous general manager who was excited about the prospect of pulling off the coup of the year. . . . Mark Binstein thought he had Connie Hawkins in his hip pocket and he convinced me beyond a shadow of a doubt. But Mark learned a very valuable lesson—that money doesn't always talk. Especially when you're dealing with someone like Connie Hawkins, who has a great deal of loyalty and integrity."

That summer, Connie made a tour for the federal Street Academy program, speaking to young dropouts in the ghettos of Chicago and Detroit. "I told them about me," he says, "about how things might have been a lot easier if I'd had a good education. I told them the world is too rough if you don't get that diploma."

Hawkins was also active in the Black Athletes Foundation, a non-profit group working to raise money for research and education in the field of sickle-cell anemia, a blood disease which affects black people almost exclusively. One in every forty blacks in America has sickle-cell anemia, and one in every ten blacks has sickle-cell traits. There is no known cure. But minimal research has been done. The Black Athletes Foundation, which David Litman helped form, raised funds—staging sports events and providing speakers—and sent athletes into black neighborhoods to encourage people to get blood tests and demand that hospitals be staffed by doctors trained to treat the disease. The athletes did more than lend their names. They were seriously involved. Muhammad Ali was the B.A.F. board chairman. Willie Stargell was the president. Hawkins was vice-president.

At Indianapolis, along with top stars from both leagues, Connie played in the nationally televised Martin Luther King, Jr., benefit game. He was named the Most Valuable Player.

Shortly after Hawk's decision to remain with the Suns, he visited me in

New York City. I learned that he had stopped eating pork and had begun to read the Koran. "The more I talk with people about Islam," he explained, "the more it sounds like a religion that's relevant to black people, to people like me. I want to find out about it." He had named his new son Dawúd Hakeem Hawkins.

When we walked on the street, during the day, there were always a few people who recognized Connie. New York—even the predominantly Jewish and Puerto Rican Upper West Side of Manhattan—was still Hawk's town.

After midnight, however, the response on the street was much different. Around Times Square—which the police were supposedly trying to clean up—it seemed that every third person stopped and called his name. "The Hawk! Hey man, that's Connie Hawkins. You playin up at the Ruckers this summer, Hawk?"

These were the night people, the street people—the pimps and hustlers and junkies and hookers and hangers-on—who grew up in the same urban rot as Connie Hawkins. Few knew which NBA team he played for. Some didn't even know he was in the NBA. But they remembered him from Boys High—and from the schoolyards. For them, his would always be a special name.

One evening, we borrowed a friend's car and drove to Bedford-Stuyvesant. The temperature was in the nineties. The sidewalks and stoops were crowded. Soul and gospel blared from open windows. Beneath the pale glow of the street lights men clustered, shooting craps. Down the block from Connie's old apartment on Lexington Avenue, two blond-wigged prostitutes, their legs toothpick-thin, leaned against a building. At a stop-light, Hawk stared at a heavy-set junkie who sat on a stoop, his head rolling unevenly from side to side. "That guy used to be one of the quick-est, toughest guards that ever played at Boys High," Connie sighed. "He was almost in a class with Eddie Simmons. Man, now he might as well be dead."

"What's happened to Eddie?" I asked.

"I saw him a couple of days ago," Hawkins said, frowning as he thought of the man who was once his mentor and closest friend. "Ed just got out of prison. He stole money at his job. But he says he's off junk now. He's in a methadone program, and he looks a little better, I don't know, it seems like he's just tradin one drug habit for another. But at least he's tryin."

"Are you still going to stay away from him?"

"No. As long as Ed's clean—off junk—I want to try and help him. Ed was there when *I* needed help."

A pimp named Ralph joined us for dinner at a nearby restaurant. "Me and Hawk was old buddies at the High," Ralph noted. A stream of people came by our table to shake Connie's hand.

"The neighborhood was bad when we were comin up," a husky numbers-writer named Plate told Hawkins, "but now it's cruel. Every time you leave the apartment, you got to wonder if some junkie's gonna break in and steal all your clothes."

As we stared at the menus, a gaunt figure in a faded sports-jacket hovered nearby. "Hey Connie," said Ralph, looking up, "you remember Charlie Donovan, don't you?"

Hawk caught himself in midgasp. "Yeah, sure," he said, eyes fixed sadly on the little man. "Sparky Donovan. How ya doin?"

"Sparky" Donovan—the name once rang loud in New York high school basketball. In 1961, Donovan had been a pint-sized Connie Hawkins. A shifty little guard, with a shaved head and an unforgettably cocky gait, he led Erasmus to the city championship at the Garden. The crowds loved his flashy ballhandling. The girls squealed at his every move. In the semifinals, Donovan had thrown in a push shot from midcourt as the first-half buzzer sounded—then ambled off with a blasé shrug of his shoulders. He duplicated the shot to end the third quarter, and swished another to give Erasmus a last-second victory. The Garden went crazy.

When Erasmus won the title, the adulation increased. Donovan was just a junior. He was a big man in the schoolyards and in the street. The following year, he played so well that a gambler tried to bribe him to throw a high school game. He reported the offer and received a commendation from the superintendent of schools.

Then Sparky returned to the Garden. A full house came to cheer him. The opening game of the city tournament ended with Erasmus trailing by one point. But Donovan had been fouled at the buzzer. The court was cleared, and the cocky little kid stepped to the line.

Donovan missed the foul shot. His high school basketball career was over. The cheering stopped. He never graduated from Erasmus. Soon, Connie recalls, he wasn't even playing in the schoolyards. Donovan was on drugs.

Now he stood beside the table, the skin tight over his bony face, the life gone from his eyes. "Charlie," said Ralph, "this is Connie Hawkins. You remember."

"Yeah, Hawkins." Donovan nodded, shifting uneasily. "You in the pros. You good."

"Thanks, Charlie."

The small man's mouth opened. He hesitated a moment, then said, "I don' mean to bother you. I'll be on my way. Hey Ralph, loan me a dollar?"

"Aw Charlie, a dollar!" Ralph groaned.

"Here," said Hawkins, quickly pulling a five from his pocket.

Donovan stared at the bill, then at Connie. Hawk nodded his head.

"Thanks," Sparky Donovan mumbled. Then he slowly walked away.

Back in the car, Hawkins was quiet, pensive. He looked out at the squalid streets and finally said, "Plate's right. It does get worse. Every time I come back. Man, so many guys I grew up with never made it out of here. Some people do. My sister Lena and my brother Randy are workin with the Black Coalition. Freddie's daughter, Pat, is national champ in the hurdles. But two of my brothers got no work. They're men, they've got pride. They want jobs, but they can't find anything.

"The drug thing is just swallowin people up," he continued. "Remember Earl Wright, that great forward for Lane? He played with us in the schoolyards. Me and him were in a picture in *TV Guide*, our senior year. Now he's dead. An overdose. The same with Theodous, the kid I used to pitch pennies with.

"Last year, before I played at the Garden, Hal Halliburton came up to my hotel room. Me and him used to be tight, playin hooky and listenin to records up his apartment. He was a strong ballplayer. Now I hardly recognized him. He's a junkie, all sickly and shriveled up. All he wanted was to borrow ten bucks."

Hawk stopped the car at the corner of Lafayette and Green. We walked into the schoolyard. Several boys, in their early teens, crowded around him, admiring his orange dashiki.

"Can I have your autograph?" asked a tall, thin youngster.

"Sure," Connie said, "you got something to write on?"

"Just this," said the boy, handing him a small brown paper envelope filled with marijuana.

"Well, if it ain't The Hawk!" said a flashily dressed man who had been standing nearby. "How you been?"

"I been O.K.," Connie said coolly.

"We never see you around here no more," the man continued. "Once you got yourself some bread, you split. You quit comin around to see all the people you useta know."

Connie handed the autographed envelope to the boy, then turned toward the man. "Look," he said, his voice suddenly angry. "I'll come back here to visit my family. I'll come back to help, if people want me to work with kids. But I ain't gonna hang out on no street-corner with a bunch of junkies, so somebody can come along and stick a needle in my arm!"

The man said something inaudible and moved off; the boys faded into the darkness. The schoolyard was empty. Connie sat down on a splintery wooden bench and leaned forward, his long fingers clasped beneath his chin.

"Have you given any more thought to what you'll do after basketball?" I asked, sitting beside him.

"Some."

"Come up with any serious ideas?"

"No," he said, "I still haven't come up with a thing."

"Then was it really worth giving up $250,000, just to keep playing in the NBA?"

For more than a minute, Hawkins was silent. He watched a police car roar down Lafayette Avenue, its red light whirling, its siren crying out in the night. When Connie spoke, the words came slowly, chosen with care: "It was worth it. The NBA was my lifelong dream. After all those years— all the work people did to clear my name—I couldn't run away. I know some people think I've slipped, that I'm not the Connie Hawkins they used to know. Well, next season, I'm gonna prove they're wrong."

Hawk paused again. His large, sleepy eyes stared out at the asphalt courts where he first learned to go one-on-one. "You know, in a way, it really don't matter," he said. "Whatever I've got, whatever's left of my game, I want to play it against the best."